The Return to Keynes

THE RETURN TO KEYNES

Edited by

BRADLEY W. BATEMAN

TOSHIAKI HIRAI

MARIA CRISTINA MARCUZZO

The Belknap Press of Harvard University Press

Cambridge, Massachusetts, and London, England   2010

This book is dedicated to
"the possibilities of civilization"

Library of Congress Cataloging-in-Publication Data

The return to Keynes / edited by Bradley W. Bateman, Toshiaki Hirai, and
Maria Cristina Marcuzzo.
   p. cm.
  Includes bibliographical references and index.
  ISBN 978-0-674-03538-6
  1. Keynesian economics. 2. Keynes, John Maynard, 1883–1946.
I. Bateman, Bradley W., 1956– II. Hirai, Toshiaki, 1947– III. Marcuzzo,
Maria Cristina, 1948–
  HB99.7.K476 2010
  330.15'6—dc22

                   2009031505

Contents

Acknowledgments

Compiling a volume that has editors on three continents requires both great patience and a remarkable amount of goodwill. In this, we have been very lucky to have formed an editorial team that was able to work easily together while still pressing to always make the volume better.

But in addition to good luck, it also required substantial resources to bring this volume to fruition. This volume had its genesis in a series of seminars held in Japan that received generous funding from the Japan Society for the Promotion of Science. Sophia University and Hitotsubashi University hosted the seminars and also provided substantial support. We thank all three institutions for their support. Without them, this volume would not exist. Denison University and the University of Rome (La Sapienza) have also provided support to us.

When the essays in this volume had been collected and the various introductions written, Iolanda Sanfilippo did the editorial work to ensure that they met the style requirements for Harvard University Press. She also compiled the bibliography for the volume. We owe her a debt of gratitude for her excellent work.

Finally, we wish to thank Mike Aronson for his enthusiasm and support from the first stages of our planning.

Introduction: The Return to Keynes

Bradley W. Bateman, Toshiaki Hirai,
and Maria Cristina Marcuzzo

Our original intent

When we undertook the work on this volume, we believed that it was time to point out a quiet revolution in economic policymaking that had gone largely unnoticed: the return of a more active use of economic policy for purposes of stabilizing the economy. Now, after collecting all the essays from those economists we invited to contribute to the volume, the world has shifted beneath our feet. This introduction was originally written in October and November of 2008, while the world was slipping into an economic crisis; the final revision was written in February 2009, as governments around the world wrestled with how best to fashion their fiscal and monetary responses to the crisis. Suddenly our argument has more force and more urgency than we could have imagined.

The story we originally set out to tell is no less important and remains the backbone of this volume. That story explains how a strong counterrevolution against Keynesian ideas of stabilizing the economy that had taken place during the last three decades of the twentieth century had itself been overturned. We intended to show that politicians and policymakers had found their way back to the idea that monetary and fiscal policy had a role to play in stabilizing the economy.

During the last three decades of the twentieth century, a dedicated and brilliant cadre of "free market" economists were successful in propagating an argument that the active use of economic policy was not only not helpful but actually hurt the economy. This anti-Keynesian counterrevolution involved many people and worked on many levels. Some of those involved denigrated Keynes and his character; others chose to ignore Keynes and simply built brilliant and sophisticated models demonstrating economic policy's detrimental nature.

By the 1990s, these economists defined a new mainstream in economic theory and exercised a strong influence over policymakers around the world. This movement influenced the climate of opinion not only about macroeconomic policy but about any government intervention in the economy; not only should governments resist the temptation to try to stabilize the economy, they should also resist the temptation to regulate individual markets. By the end of the century, there was even a spate of articles in the popular press asking whether Friedrich von Hayek or Joseph Schumpeter was the greatest economist of the twentieth century; the foil in these arguments was always John Maynard Keynes, whose ideas had held sway at midcentury but were now argued to have been eclipsed by the facts of history.

Yet despite the many assertions at the end of the twentieth century that Keynes was no longer relevant, as we entered the twenty-first century the broad sweep of Keynes's argument that stabilization was necessary began to overtake the new conventional wisdom of the "free marketers"; one of the most consistent facts about macroeconomic policymaking after 2000 was its focus on effective stabilization of the economy.

Following the collapse of the dot-com boom at the beginning of the decade, finance ministers and central bankers across the industrial democracies began to actively use government budgets and interest rates to attempt to steer their economies away from the shoals of trouble. And to a large extent, they were successful. Through 2007, the economies of North America, Western Europe, and Japan experienced extended growth with only moderate price increases.

The fall and rise of Keynes

This change to more active and explicit use of macroeconomic policy is the "revolution" that we originally set out to discuss in this volume. As we have noted, only a decade earlier this result would have seemed highly improbable, for during the 1990s the idea that macroeconomic policy was doomed to be ineffective had reached its apex. Perhaps it would be more correct to say that it seemed in the 1990s that a long battle had been fought over the usefulness of macroeconomic policy and that the advocates of "policy ineffectiveness" or "policy irrelevance" had finally won.

The stylized version of this story begins with the collapse of the Keynesian consensus in the early 1970s, when the combination of high unemployment and high inflation combined to discredit the tools of Keynesian economics. Keynesian economics was said to have been based on the idea that by using monetary and fiscal policy, the government could steer the economy away from the extremes of recession and inflation. However, the appearance of inflation and recession together (stagflation) in the 1970s marked a combination that not only was out of the reach of traditional Keynesian policies but was argued to actually be caused by Keynesian policies.

The response against Keynesian economics took many forms: monetarism, supply-side economics, rational expectations, and new classical macroeconomics. What all these responses had in common was that they explicitly took Keynesianism as their foil and made their mark by showing how to get past the "errors" of Keynesianism. Monetarists argued that Keynesians had erred by focusing on interest rates and federal budgets, rather than on the money supply; supply-siders argued that Keynesians had erred by focusing on the short-run stimulation to demand, rather than on the long-run incentives to growth; rational expectationists argued that Keynesians had erred by not understanding how the expectations of economic agents would undercut governments' efforts to stabilize the economy; new classical economists built on the rational expectations revolution to construct yet more sophisticated models proving the ineffectiveness of macroeconomic policy in the face of well-informed and forward-looking economic agents. By the 1990s, this anti-Keynesian counterrevolution seemed to have achieved complete victory with the award of several Nobel Memorial Prizes in economics to the movement's architects at the University of Chicago.

On the policy front, many had trumpeted the importance of the idea that traditional macroeconomic policy was more harmful than helpful. In 1979, Paul Volcker used the rhetoric of monetarism in initiating the monetary-tightening approach that he undertook to battle double-digit inflation in the United States; in the same year, Margaret Thatcher was elected prime minister after running on an explicit platform of monetarist ideas. In 1992, the European Union adopted the Maastricht treaty, which required budget discipline of its members, and by the end of that decade, President Bill Clinton had produced the first back-to-back budget surpluses in the United States in several decades.

But with the collapse of the dot-com boom in 2000 and the attacks of September 11, 2001, the nature of macroeconomic policy debate took a large, and largely unremarked upon, turn. The collapse of the dot-com boom was a severe blow to the arguments of the rational expectationists. In the world they so elegantly described, the stock market would never have formed a bubble, much less have collapsed. In a quick stroke, an idea that had only recently won a Nobel Prize was no longer an idea in good currency. In the corridors of power, no one seemed to take the time to wait for word that the policy ineffectiveness revolution had collapsed. Policymakers did what they are wont to do and looked for pragmatic solutions to their problems. Within the European Union, Germany, France, and Italy all spent the next several years violating the budget deficit limits written into the stability pact that had underpinned the formation of the common European currency, the euro; governments of both the right and left argued that they needed to run deficits larger than those allowed in the stability pact to keep their economies operating well. At the same time in the United States, George W. Bush undertook such mass spending that the resultant budget deficit would be the largest in American history. (As Yoshiyasu Ono explains in chapter 2, Japan was somewhat of an exception to this trend in fiscal policy in that the Murayama [1994–1996] and Obuchi [1998–2000] cabinets in the 1990s tried using fiscal stimulus, while the Koizumi cabinet [2001–2006] attempted to run a neoliberal course after 2000.) Across the world, central banks had already abandoned monetarism's goal of monetary aggregate targeting by the end of the millennium. In the new millennium, they became increasingly comfortable with the use of interest rate targets to ensure stable prices and employment.

Thus, in the first decade of the new millennium, macroeconomic policy shifted far back toward the open and unapologetic use of monetary and fiscal policy to stabilize the economy. This largely unnoted shift marked both the end of the influence of the "policy ineffectiveness" school and the return of a moderate form of Keynesian ideas. To be sure, no one was arguing for a simple return to the economic policymaking of the 1950s and 1960s; but in the battle between the advocates of macroeconomic management and policy ineffectiveness, the argument for active management has never seemed more persuasive than at the end of the first decade of the new millennium.

Keynes in spades

This change in the outlook of central bankers and ministers of finance is perhaps best illustrated by the initial responses to the global financial crisis that took place in autumn 2008. Beginning in September 2008, central banks pumped hundreds of billions of dollars of liquidity into the world's financial system to address the crises of confidence and illiquidity that had resulted from the subprime lending crisis, and the finance ministers of the G8 countries simultaneously agreed to take equity stakes in private sector banks to help recapitalize them and so avoid the crisis of insolvency. These interventions violate every tenet of the advocates of "policy ineffectiveness," and yet few serious voices rose to speak out at the time to say that these interventions were unnecessary or harmful. In fact, Alan Greenspan, who had been one of the most prominent and effective advocates of the free market philosophy as the chair of the Federal Reserve, admitted that "there was a flaw in my model."

It is no exaggeration to say that the world's economies were in crisis as this volume came to press. And while no one can have been happy with this state of affairs, it more than amply demonstrated the point that we originally set to note: economic stabilization had returned to the mainstream. Were this not true, it would not have been so easy to form the consensus that was necessary to address the crisis. The gradual, largely unnoted return to the Keynesian outlook had opened the door for making the kind of decisive moves that have been taken to address the crisis that began to unfold in 2008.

In fact, it is an important part of Keynes's legacy that governments were able to act relatively quickly in the face of the crisis. During the Great Depression, the ideology of free markets prevented effective policy responses for many years. Keynes often played the part of an unwanted Cassandra in offering his economic policy recommendations in response to the Great Depression. The same might have been true in 2008 and 2009, had we not been able to see in retrospect that those wasted years after 1929 had not been necessary. Of course, if the ideology of the 1990s had not already fallen out of favor, it might have taken longer to effect the necessary policy changes. Fortunately, the anti-Keynesian counterrevolution had already come to an end.

The structure of this book

The purpose of this collection is to take stock of this new moment in economic policymaking. We hope to illustrate the changing policy landscape of the last decade and to provide a short introduction to some recent scholarship on Keynes and Keynesian ideas. As seems fitting at a moment when the global nature of the economy is at the forefront of our thinking, we have invited contributors from around the world. We have included essays from economists in Asia, Europe, South America, and North America to help explain the return to Keynes.

The opening section of the book consists of three essays that focus on the reemergence of macroeconomic policy as a tool for stabilization in the United States, Japan, and Europe. Starting the volume with these essays establishes the recent return to stabilization polices and helps to delineate the quiet revolution that took place prior to 2008.

The three essays in the second section of the volume each address how contemporary economic theory deals with (or fails to deal with) themes in Keynes's own work. The purpose of this section is to turn the reader toward recent work in the field and to examine how the themes and methods of contemporary work address (or fail to address) themes that Keynes argued to be central to understanding how the economy works.

In the third section, five historians of economic thought consider the state of the art of scholarship on different aspects of Keynes's life and work. This section considers what we have learned in recent years about Keynes and the context from which his ideas emerged. During the last thirty years, the literature on Keynes has been very thin as the economics profession saw itself turning away from the idea that there is a role for effective stabilization policies. This section offers a chance to consider Keynes as a full historical figure and to appreciate the richness of his thought and his influences upon economic thinking.

The final section of the volume includes three essays that offer interpretations of Keynes's work relative to the current global crisis. These three essays focus on the international dimension of Keynes's thinking and how it relates to issues in international finance. In considering how Keynes viewed the nature of economic decision-making and how he addressed the global imbalances that would emerge in the postwar era, we see another area where his ideas continue to have contemporary relevance. Keynes explained very clearly the kind of panicked behavior that has characterized the recent crisis and thus was able to make policy recommendations that seem relevant again in the face of the failure of free market ideas to effectively steer the economy away from the shoals of disaster. As this volume went to press, many leaders were, for instance, calling for a return to a common, global framework for financial regulation, with the International Monetary Fund (IMF) returned to the role that Keynes had envisioned for it in the original Bretton Woods agreements.

A new age of Keynes

While making the final revisions to this introduction in February 2009, we were faced with an unusual demonstration of the extent to which macroeconomic stabilization policy has come to the fore. As we wrote, a second round of policy responses to the financial crisis was being formulated by governments around the world.

In the United States, President Barack Obama's plan for a massive fiscal stimulus of nearly $800 billion was being signed into law; likewise, his treasury secretary, Tim Geithner, had just announced the administration's plan for a new effort to deal with the toxic subprime assets that were crippling the banking system. In Japan, Prime Minister Taro Aso had announced plans for further fiscal stimulus, and the Bank of Japan was starting to implement new plans to increase liquidity. In the European Union, Germany, France, and Britain were each in the midst of rolling out new plans for fiscal stimulus, and the European Central Bank was examining new, supplemental measures for creating liquidity.

All of these responses served to further mark the degree to which the "policy ineffectiveness" arguments of the 1980s and 1990s have been replaced by the pragmatic demands of economic policymakers. In this sense, we undoubtedly live in a new Age of Keynes. Just as during the Great Depression, the reality of widespread unemployment is front and center in the minds of politicians and economists, who are looking for responses to mitigate the human suffering that comes with it.

Keynes himself was not dogmatic about the form that fiscal stimulus should take. Thus, it is not possible to find in his writings detailed treatment of the best way(s) to shape the response to a crisis such as we face. He did argue for large stimulus packages more than once during the interwar period, but the exact nature of his arguments was always shaped by the parameters of contemporary policy debate. While no one can know what Keynes would say about any particular policy on offer today, it is difficult to imagine him disagreeing with the need for a large fiscal stimulus under the conditions that prevail as we write this introduction.

However, during the Second World War, while Keynes worked within the Treasury, he developed nuanced versions of his ideas to help with postwar economic planning. Thus, at the same time that he was helping to develop the framework for Bretton Woods, he was also refining his ideas about fiscal policy. Much of what he wrote during this period was never incorporated into the body of ideas that became known as Keynesian after the war. For instance, it is impossible to find in his work during the Second World War any warrant for the kind of fiscal fine-tuning that was advocated in the postwar years by most mainstream Keynesians (Bateman 1996, 2006).

But our purpose here is not to pick and choose between the various policy proposals under consideration as we write this introduction and to give the imprimatur to those that are "most" Keynesian or "true" Keynesian. Our broad point, from a historical perspective, is that the need for macroeconomic management to stabilize the economy has been reestablished in the first decade of the twenty-first century after a hiatus of several decades, when many of the leading names in mainstream economics made the opposite argument. It is in this broad sense that the arguments for "policy ineffectiveness," laissez-faire, and neoliberalism have been displaced that we mean to claim that we are in a new Age of Keynes.

Nor are we interested in the kind of triumphalism that characterized the arguments of neoliberals immediately after the fall of the Berlin Wall. Just as they were wrong then to proclaim that it was the "end of history," it would be wrong now to believe that the kind of massive macroeconomic interventions we are experiencing in 2009 will be the norm in the future. Perhaps the best way to understand the current moment would be in Keynes's own terms. From early in his career, with the publication of *The Economic Consequences of the Peace*, Keynes began to consistently articulate a belief that capitalism was prone to instability. He did not, however, conclude that capitalism was always unstable—quite the contrary. What Keynes insisted on throughout all his work was that when the system got jammed, good macroeconomic policy was necessary to correct it. Keynes was not opposed to the market, only to the fetish that the market always functions well and always self-corrects when it experiences instability. Thus, while Keynes would almost certainly agree for the need for macroeconomic policy to help combat the growing unemployment we are experiencing in early 2009, there is no evidence that he would have seen such massive intervention as necessary into an infinite future. Once "animal spirits" return, he would not be surprised to see the government become less involved in managing the economy. What he would never cede, however, is the belief that the system could once again fall into a serious recession (or a raging inflation). And he would expect that when that happened, well-trained economists would step forward to explain the necessary interventions to mitigate unnecessary human suffering. Thus, if the future is truly Keynesian, it will be in this pragmatic sense that we will live with an understanding that despite the benefits of the market in good times, it also has the potential to cause great harm; and that we have the ability, and the responsibility, to mitigate that harm when it occurs.

PART ONE

Keynesian Economic Policy:
Past, Present, and Future

DURING THE 1980S AND 1990S, Keynes and Keynesian policies fell from favor. This demise was triggered by the stagflation of the 1970s, during which time Keynesian policies came to be seen as undesirable. Then, during the next two decades, increasingly sophisticated models were developed to support the argument that government intervention to stabilize the economy is not only unnecessary but harmful. By the end of the century, many governments and central banks had taken this advice to heart, and monetary and fiscal policy had been greatly curtailed.

Over the past decade, however, this consensus has begun to crumble in the face of the reality of increasing economic instability. The unraveling of the "policy ineffectiveness" consensus has followed different paths in different countries.

Bradley Bateman argues in his essay that in America the policy ineffectiveness consensus began to unravel at the turn of the century. In 2000, in the midst of President Clinton's successful efforts to balance the budget at the end of his second term, and the Federal Reserve's cautious interest rate targeting under Alan Greenspan, this outcome was not obvious. But the collapse of the dot-com bubble in 2000 marked the beginning of new economic instability that eventually elicited a more activist policy response. First, the Federal Reserve began to rapidly lower interest rates in response to falling output; then President Bush began what was at the time the largest fiscal stimulus in American history. Clearly, activist macroeconomic policy was no longer seen as ineffective or unnecessary.

In Japan, the history of macroeconomic policy in the last two decades is colored by the severe recession that started at the beginning of the

1990s. In 1990–1991, a sharp drop in real estate prices was triggered by the Treasury's "Souryo Kisei" policy (which limited the amount available for real estate loans); this was followed by a sharp decline in stock prices. The plunge in the stock market led to a collapse of the banking system in 1997, which prolonged and deepened the recession. Finally, in 1998, the Obuchi cabinet turned to the idea of active stabilization. As Yoshiyasu Ono explains in his essay, Japan has swung back and forth for the last two decades between large-scale fiscal stimulus and contractionary supply-side policies. Although Prime Minister Junichiro Koizumi was popular among the public, his efforts to effect structural reform rather than using fiscal policy were not successful in stimulating the economy. Ono argues that the limited success of expansionary policies in the last two decades are easily understood as a combination of Keynes's liquidity trap and excess household saving. He argues that while Koizumi's policies still have appeal to many in Japan despite their failure in bringing prosperity, a more finely focused Keynesian stimulus is the only effective counter to the current conditions of stagnation. In fact, in the face of the global crisis that began in the autumn of 2008, we know that the Aso cabinet has undertaken activist policies now that the supply-side measures, which had no theoretical backbone, turned out to have been incapable of addressing the worst problems of economic stagnation.

The story of the return of more active macroeconomic policymaking in Europe has also been unique. As Hans-Michael Trautwein argues in his essay, European economists were never as enamored of the policy ineffectiveness arguments as were American economists. The more sluggish performance of the European economies in the 1980s and 1990s made it difficult to have the same faith in the efficacy of the unfettered market. Nonetheless, within the European Union, the formation of the European Central Bank (ECB) and the adoption of the euro as the common currency within the eurozone led to the formalization of the Growth and Stability Pact that limited the ECB to focusing solely on keeping inflation in check, while the individual European nations within the zone were tightly limited in their ability to use fiscal policy to address instability. But as in America, the tightly limited policy has not done well in the new millennium. The rules against budget deficits were breached repeatedly in the largest eurozone economies following 2000, even as the ECB stuck to its inflation targeting strategy and refused to respond to high unemployment levels until after the financial crisis in autumn 2008. Trautwein explores the history of the European Monetary Union as a form of active stabilization policy and ends by suggesting that the evolving reality within the eurozone is broadly commensurate with Keynes's own ideas on stabilization.

Although the stories of the return of more active macroeconomic poli-cymaking differ in each case, the underlying story is broadly the same; policymakers around the world have begun to rethink whether active mac-roeconomic policymaking must always be either ineffective or harmful. Faced with increasing economic instability, they began in different ways and with different tools to once again use demand management to stabi-lize their economies.

The real proof of the changed landscape came in the autumn of 2008 when financial crisis swept the world's capital markets. If there had been any doubt before that moment that Keynes had returned, it dissipated instantly in the quick action of central banks and finance ministries who undertook the work of unfreezing the capital markets and recapitaliz-ing the banks and other financial institutions. Faced with true crisis and instability, leaders around the world turned to the ideas of the greatest economist of the twentieth century. Once again, Keynes was needed to save modern financial capitalism from itself.

CHAPTER ONE

Keynes Returns to America

Bradley W. Bateman

The rise and fall of Keynesian economics

When Richard Nixon proclaimed in 1971 that "We're all Keynesians now," he was accurately reporting the intellectual climate that prevailed in academic and policymaking circles in America at the time. In universities around the country, the basic Keynesian model that focused on aggregate expenditure as expressed in the IS/LM model was the centerpiece of macroeconomic analysis. When joined with the Phillips curve, which depicted a simple trade-off between inflation and unemployment, the Keynesian model provided the backbone of macroeconomic policymaking. Thus, regardless of what some of Nixon's supporters may have believed about Keynes and Keynesianism, it seems likely that he was reporting a basic truth that he must have encountered when looking at the advice that came to him through the various policymaking branches of the federal government. While there may have been differences of degree in the Keynesian suggestions that came to him, it is difficult to imagine that most of what came across his desk was not framed in Keynesian language and that it did not derive from a basically Keynesian outlook.

The truth of Nixon's remark in 1971, however, hides a long history of animosity to Keynes and Keynesian ideas in the United States. In fact, it also hides an essential truth about the origin of demand management in the United States.

If we look for the first intentional use of the federal budget to stimulate the U.S. economy, we would find ourselves in the spring of 1938 looking over the shoulders of the men who were crafting Franklin Roosevelt's budget for 1939. But as William J. Barber (1990) has shown, these men had gotten their ideas not from John Maynard Keynes's *General Theory of Employment, Interest and Money* (1936) but from work that had been done in 1937 in the U.S. Commerce Department. Trying to explain the rapid slide into recession that had occurred that spring, researchers at the Commerce Department had figured out that the joint effects in the previous year of imposing the first Social Security taxes and ending the First World War veterans' bonus had created a fiscal contraction that had tipped the economy into severe recession. Harry Hopkins, the commerce secretary, used these findings to convince Roosevelt in the spring of 1938 to deliberately undertake a deficit in order to provide a fiscal stimulus.[1]

Thus, nowhere in the story of America's first intentional federal fiscal stimulus does Keynes's name appear.[2] Keynes had tried twice to influence Roosevelt's fiscal policy during his first term in office, but Roosevelt was not having any of it. In fact, Roosevelt's campaigns in both 1932 and 1936 had contained firm promises of a balanced federal budget. In 1932 he had tarred Herbert Hoover as an irresponsible deficit spender, and in 1936 he took great care to argue that his own deficits had been no larger than the amount of the emergency relief expenditures that he had undertaken over the previous four years to ameliorate the problems of unemployment and destitution that he had inherited from Hoover.[3] When Roosevelt was finally converted to a vision of the need for a deliberate fiscal stimulus in 1938, it was on the basis of empirical results derived by researchers in his own government who had no direct acquaintance with Keynes's recently published ideas.

It did not take long, however, for Keynes's ideas to begin spreading in American universities, and by the early 1940s, Keynes's model had become the analytical framework for Roosevelt's macroeconomic policymakers.[4] This transformation to something that might more accurately be described as "Keynesian" policymaking also marks the onset of a long and determined fight in the United States to limit the power of the federal government to use fiscal policy to influence the economy. The battles during the 1940s about the creation of the Council of Economic Advisers and the various versions of "full employment" legislation that would have made it the legal responsibility of the federal government to ensure high employment were driven, on the one hand, by Keynesians who wanted more focus to be given to fiscal stimulus and full employment and, on the other hand, by conservatives who were determined not to allow the federal government any responsibility for the performance of the economy, especially not through tax and expenditure policies.

Throughout the 1950s, the basic Keynesian model spread in the academy, but policymaking remained relatively non-Keynesian. Although the Council of Economic Advisers had ultimately been created, there was no legal mandate for full employment.[5] Dwight Eisenhower was beholden to the anti-Keynesian wing of his party, and the predictable result was a turbulent decade of fluctuating employment and inflation. But the regular fluctuation between unemployment and inflation in the 1950s did at least seem to lend credence to the basic intuition that would animate the Phillips curve (first published in Britain in 1958) that there was a trade-off between these two problems: when one went up, the other went down.

Not until the election of John F. Kennedy in 1960 did Keynesian policymaking enter the federal government in a recognizable and pervasive way. Kennedy used some of the most brilliant Keynesians of his generation as economic advisers: Walter Heller, Kermit Gordon, and James Tobin. And for several years, they helped first Kennedy, then Lyndon Johnson, to stabilize the economy around an impressive growth path. Not until Johnson greatly increased spending on the war in Vietnam in 1968, while simultaneously trying to maintain high levels of domestic spending on his antipoverty programs, did the work of Johnson's Keynesian advisers come to grief.[6] The first six years of the Kennedy-Johnson administrations were at the time the longest period of uninterrupted growth since record-keeping had begun in the 1930s. Initially, the large deficits caused by Johnson's expenditure (and tax) policies continued this streak through 1967; but the excess fiscal pressure caused by the escalation of the war in Vietnam quickly led to rising inflation and an overheated economy by 1968.

By the time Nixon made his famous remark about everyone "now" being Keynesians, the framework for understanding and interpreting the relatively mild economic dysfunction were, indeed, still Keynesian. But it did not take long for the Keynesian consensus to come under intense attack.

Philosophical opposition to demand management had never completely disappeared in the United States, of course, particularly on the right wing of the political spectrum and in some business circles. In fact, there is little about the thrust of the anti-Keynesian rhetoric after 1973 that departs from the rhetoric used against demand management in the 1940s. What had changed was the analytical rigor and the sophistication of the anti-Keynesians. The most well-known academic counterattack during the twenty-five years after the Second World War was Milton Friedman's presidential address to the American Economic Association in 1967 (published in 1968). Friedman was already well known by this time for his work with Anna Schwartz in *A Monetary History of the United States* (1963), but his presidential address was a thoughtful and compelling argument for the importance of monetary policy and for attempting to control inflation rather than unemployment. Prominent Keynesian economists in the United States, such as James Tobin, had acknowledged the importance of monetary policy and had not ignored inflation as a potential problem, but these concerns had always been less prominent than the Keynesians' interest in the use of fiscal policy as a lever of demand management focused on unemployment.

But if Friedman's argument made a well-placed critique of the Keynesians' failure to place sufficient emphasis on monetary policy, there still was nothing like a consensus by 1970 that Friedman was right about how best to conduct monetary policy (targeting the growth of the money supply, rather than interest rates) or the relative unimportance of fiscal policy.

Only with the advent of stagflation in the 1970s would Friedman's ideas begin to gain a wider audience in academe and among policymakers. Keynesian demand management policy had always relied on the idea that there was scope for manipulating unemployment without worrying about inflation. Only if demand was pushed too far would inflation become a problem. In the 1960s, this idea was expressed in the Phillips curve, which showed a trade-off between inflation and unemployment that suggested real problems with inflation only at very low unemployment rates.[7] If the government stimulated aggregate demand, this would push down unemployment; but if pushed far enough, the stimulus would also lead to overheating and inflation. Conversely, a contraction in aggregate demand could be used to reduce inflationary pressure; but such a cooling off of the economy would inevitably lead to a rise in unemployment if pushed far enough.

The simultaneous existence of inflation and rising unemployment in the early 1970s led many economists and policymakers to conclude that Keynesian tools were no longer useful. If the growth of aggregate demand was dampened to help reduce inflation, the high levels of unemployment would only be made worse; if aggregate demand was stimulated to try to help alleviate unemployment, then inflation would only be exacerbated. Suddenly, the old Keynesian tools no longer seemed well suited to the situation at hand: they did not tell policymakers what needed to be done.

Into the wilderness

The fall of Keynesian ideas after the onset of stagflation in the 1970s was rapid and seemed nearly complete.[8] While it was true that all of the national income statistics (consumption, investment, government expenditures, net exports, and gross national product) were collected in categories that were congruent with Keynesian analysis, the number of people who interpreted the statistics from a Keynesian viewpoint and who made Keynesian policy recommendations shrank swiftly after the first oil embargo in 1973.

The first ideas to rush in to fill the vacuum created were the monetarist ideas of Milton Friedman. The timing of Friedman's presidential address could not have been better. Having staked out his ground as a strong critic of Keynesian policy in 1967, Friedman's was the most prominent voice of the anti-Keynesian opposition in the early and mid-1970s.

In its simplest form, monetarism is a doctrine about the relationship between the quantity of money in circulation and the level of nominal income: the larger the quantity of money, the larger the level of nominal income. With the right assumptions, this relationship must be true—it is a tautology.[9] However, since nominal income is the product of the price level and the level of real income, the monetarist assumption that the level of real income grows at a rate fixed by factors such as technological change and population growth means that any growth of the money supply beyond the growth rate of real output must be manifest in changes in the price level. Thus, beyond a small amount of growth in the money supply that is necessary to accommodate the growth in real income, increases in the money supply have one effect: to cause inflation.[10]

As described by Thomas Mayer (1978), however, monetarism in the United States was understood in the 1970s as an idea greater than this simple dictum about the relationship between the money supply and the rate of inflation.[11] Monetarism was also taken to be a doctrine that showed that fiscal policy was unimportant, that the business cycle was (normally) caused by pro-cyclical monetary policy, and that the only appropriate monetary policy was a simple rule dictating that the money supply should grow at a rate that would accommodate the prospective growth of real income (without causing inflation).

In Britain, Margaret Thatcher used the term even more broadly than it was used in the United States, including under the umbrella of monetarism not only Friedman's macroeconomic ideas about monetary policy and inflation but also his microeconomic ideas about the importance of unregulated markets. In the United States, however, monetarism remained an idea about how best to conduct macroeconomic policy. But the idea was not to be confined to the ivory tower for long, for Paul Volcker would invoke monetarism in the autumn of 1979, shortly after his appointment as the chair of the Federal Reserve, as the means to fight the double-digit inflation that plagued the American economy. With the same brevity and moral clarity as Friedman, Volcker argued that the only way to control inflation was to stop the rapid growth of the money supply. Following Friedman's prescription for how best to achieve the desired results, the Federal Reserve instituted growth targets for the money supply.[12]

This switch in policy at the Federal Reserve meant that the government would no longer try to target short-term interest rates, as it is impossible to target both short-term interest rates and the money supply. If the Federal Reserve keeps the money supply on target, it must allow interest rates to fluctuate with changes in the demand for money; if it targets interest rates, the Federal Reserve must be willing to adjust the supply of money to changing demand for it. Thus, the switch to targeting the monetary aggregates meant that it would have to let short-term interest rates rise while limiting the growth of the money supply. This tightening of credit, whether measured by rising interest rates or the reduction in the growth of loanable funds, triggered the worst recession since the Second World War and was very politically unpopular.[13]

Volcker would eventually become widely praised for his success at bringing down the rate of inflation, but his experiment would also involve a terrible irony for Friedman's legacy as an economist. For rather than confirming the preeminence of monetarism as the best tool for macroeconomic policy, the Fed's success at wringing inflation out of the economy would ultimately lead to monetarism's demise.

The reason for this demise lay in the failure of the assumptions that lie behind the theory to continue to hold after 1979. In particular, the velocity of money (measured as the average rate at which dollars turn over in a fixed period of time) failed to remain stable (or to grow at a stable rate) after 1979. The velocity of money is "invisible" and only becomes apparent in statistics that are released months later; nonetheless, there was soon evidence that velocity was dropping at unprecedented rates, and the Federal Reserve began to allow the money supply to grow at rates above its target levels without any inflationary effects. As early as 1981, the Federal Reserve was allowing the money supply to grow outside its target ranges. Faced with the reality that it was unable to rely on a stable velocity of money, the Federal Reserve risked driving the economy into deep depression as the decade wore on if it did not continue to allow the money supply to grow above its target levels. The Fed did not see the need to take the risk, however; by the middle of the decade, the growth rate of the money supply was in double digits, but inflation had not reignited.[14]

Initially, neither economists nor financial journalists were as quick to bury monetarism as they had been to bury Keynesianism. It was not until 1987 that the Federal Reserve first made an explicit acknowledgement of its systematic inability to adhere to its monetary targets, and it was not until more than ten years after first announcing their use, early in the 1990s under Alan Greenspan's rule, that the Fed was willing to formally abandon its regime of identifying targets for the money supply as its primary policy target because of the long-term instability of velocity.[15]

The failure of monetarism did not mark the quick return of Keynesianism, however. Far from it.

There are several reasons that Keynesianism did not return, not least that it was widely understood that while the Federal Reserve had not been able to hold to its monetary targeting, its attention to money supply growth had, nonetheless, played a role in eliminating the inflation of the late 1970s (even if the tightening had not faithfully followed Friedman's rules). American Keynesians in the postwar era had been adamant that fiscal policy was the most important and most effective tool of macroeconomic management; now, however, that view no longer seemed reasonable after the Federal Reserve's successful experiment. Likewise, Friedman's insistence that inflation was an important problem could no longer be challenged. In the three decades after the Second World War, American Keynesians had tended to argue that it was better to err on the side of some inflation in order to guarantee full-employment; they had never been forced to deal with the reality that high inflation could raise long-term interest rates high enough to cause unemployment by lowering investment and economic growth. Thus, many of Friedman's basic intuitions about the economy and macroeconomic policy had gained currency, even if monetarism itself had proven unworkable.

Another reason that Keynesianism did not make a comeback was that alongside the shift away from Keynesian economic policies, there had taken place a radical change in the theoretical framework used by professional economists, both in academia and central bank research departments. In the 1970s, Robert Lucas (a colleague of Friedman at the University of Chicago), Robert Barro, and others had laid the foundations of what came to be called the New Classical macroeconomics. Whereas Friedman's monetarism was a macroeconomic, empirically founded doctrine, the mantra of the New Classical macroeconomics was the rigorous application of theories of how rational economic agents would behave. For economists, even if they hesitated to accept the policy conclusions reached by Lucas and Barro, this approach was theoretically compelling. Even some Keynesians felt obliged to accept the New Classical rules of the game, creating models in which agents were completely rational, to attempt to defend Keynesian ideas.

One of the most powerful assumptions in this new approach to theorizing was the assumption of rational expectations—that agents could predict everything that could be predicted. This was fundamental to the New Classical claim that it was impossible (not just difficult) for demand-management policy to stabilize the economy. It was soon shown that it was hard to square Lucas's theory that the business cycle was caused by random shocks to aggregate demand, but it was a short step to Real Business Cycle theory, which explained the cycle by using much the same theory with random technology shocks.[16]

The significance of this for discussions of policy was that because the New Classical theory focused on the behavior of rational, well-informed agents, debates over macro policy shifted to focus on how agents would respond to government policy announcements. The effects of a policy regime would depend on whether it was credible.

The original attacks against Keynes and his ideas had not simply been against his macroeconomic ideas: for many on the right, Keynes stood for the idea that capitalism did not function well on any level, and so it became important to denigrate him and his work not just as part of an argument about what types of macroeconomic policy were desirable but as part of a larger and more pervasive argument about whether market economies needed any kind of intervention in order to work well. The most insidious attack on Keynes was probably James Buchanan and Richard Wagner's book, *Democracy in Deficit: The Political Legacy of Lord Keynes* (1977). Buchanan and Wagner explained Keynes's entire understanding of the economy as fallacious because it was based on a naive understanding of human nature. They used the phrase "the pre-suppositions of Harvey Road," a reference to the location of Keynes's childhood home, to argue that he had a simplistic and unrealistic understanding of the economy and human nature.[17]

Because New Classical theory assumed that markets worked perfectly and that agents were always as well informed as they could possibly be, the result was that these arguments all served to support the idea that the best way to insure economic growth and high employment was for the government to stay out of the way and to let markets work. At the same time, "public choice" theories, such as those of Buchanan, focused on problems with democracy, bureaucracy, and the political process that would make it hard for socially optimal policies to be implemented. Given this combination of a perfect private sector and an imperfect government sector, it was not surprising that Keynesian ideas on using government to improve economic performance lost their credence.

Can you please follow the rules?

A family trait of these anti-Keynesian ideas was the argument that to the extent that macroeconomic policy was to be used at all, it should take the form of "rules" that made the government's actions open and transparent and ensured that they were limited in scope. These arguments for rules depended on the assumption that economic agents, whether financiers, industrialists, or union leaders, had "rational expectations" of the economy and economic policy. According to this argument, economic agents would quickly see through any short-term efforts to adjust the economy through macroeconomic policy and would adjust their own behaviors in ways that would defeat the purpose of the policy. Thus, for instance, if the federal government tried to run a deficit to stimulate the economy, agents would know that this meant that taxes would eventually rise to pay for the deficits. This knowledge would cause them to respond in ways that would decrease aggregate demand at least as much as the government's efforts had stimulated it. From this point of view, it was best to work under the aegis of clearly defined rules for "good behavior" so that private agents could be left to make the best microeconomic choices for increasing investment and growth of the economy.

The appropriate rule for fiscal policy was obvious enough: keep the central government's budget in balance.[18] As regards monetary policy, when confidence in targeting the money supply evaporated, the focus switched to keeping inflation at a low and stable rate with open and transparent changes in interest rates geared to changes in inflation forecasts. A simple rule, paired with openness and transparency, was needed to ensure that the private sector did not get taken by surprise, with unpleasant consequences for output. Taken together, these rules embodied virtually all of Milton Friedman's concerns about macroeconomic policy: fiscal policy has no real role to play, macroeconomic policy should not be used to fight unemployment, and controlling inflation is the only legitimate goal of macroeconomic policy. These insights covered all of Friedman's most basic precepts except for his desire to depend on a strict rule for the growth of the money supply. Because of the instability of velocity, targeting the growth of the money supply was no longer feasible; interest rates were now the desired tool of monetary policy, but they were to be used to the same end of fighting inflation that Friedman had desired.

The power of these edicts about following rules was clear in both Europe and the United States during the 1990s. In Europe, the Maastricht treaty (1992) held the countries that would enter into the common currency zone to strict limits on their budget deficits, while the European Central Bank was created with the single policy mandate of limiting inflation. In the United States, the Federal Reserve switched to interest rate targeting, but it did so with a careful eye to not allowing inflation to get out of control again. And, of course, President Bill Clinton built a successful fiscal policy around the premise (articulated for him by Robert Rubin, his principle economic adviser and a former investment banker with intimate knowledge of bond markets) that balancing the federal budget would cause interest rates on bonds to fall and thus stimulate investment, increase economic growth, and lower unemployment. Thus, by the end of the millennium, it was difficult to find much dissent from the belief that with the government committed to the right macroeconomic policy rules, a capitalist economy would function well and create adequate jobs.

The return to Keynes

The rise of the idea that clearly articulated rules should limit macroeconomic policymaking was helped immensely by the fact that the economy had boomed so tremendously in the 1990s. Following a relatively mild recession at the beginning of the decade, the U.S. economy enjoyed high rates of growth through the rest of the decade as the technological changes wrought by new computing technology and the rise of the internet helped to raise investment and growth rates, lowered unemployment, caused the first significant drops in poverty in over twenty years, and helped propel the stock market to previously unimaginable levels.

Those who most advocated the use of rules to limit macroeconomic policymaking did so as a part of much larger belief that market economies worked well if they were left alone. The proof of the validity of this belief seemed not difficult to see: the economy was booming while macroeconomic policy was being held carefully in check.

For the first time in four decades, there were federal government surpluses in consecutive years (1998–2000) and the (Democratic) administration regularly reminded the public that such fiscal fortitude was an important element in the economic success they were experiencing; budget surpluses decreased the pressure in the credit markets (because the government was not competing for loanable funds) and the low long-term interest rates that followed from this reduced pressure kept interest rates on bonds low and helped to stimulate the investment that was driving the boom. Likewise, monetary policy seemed to be in safe hands. While the Federal Reserve was mandated by law to promote price stability, employment, and economic growth, it was choosing to accomplish these together by limiting inflation and inflationary expectations with clearly signaled messages about the direction of changes in short-term interest rates. If these signals about short-term interest rates were interpreted correctly, they would lead to low long-term interest rates, which would, in turn, promote investment, economic growth, and low unemployment. In the language of contemporary monetary theorists, the Federal Reserve had gained credibility through the open and transparent signaling of its intention to achieve economic growth and low unemployment by effectively fighting inflation with short-term interest rates.

In fact, in the language of contemporary macroeconomic theory, both the federal government (in the body of the Clinton administration) and the central bank (the Federal Reserve) had established their "credibility" by publicly stating their intention to adhere to rules and then demonstrating their resolve to stick to the rules. This theoretical construction of "credibility" depended deeply and thoroughly on the idea of rational expectations: since economic agents cannot be fooled about the future, the only way to conduct a successful macroeconomic policy was to tell the people openly and transparently that the government would adhere to the rules that left them free to make the economy grow.

When the dot-com bubble broke in the spring of 2000, however, it marked the beginning of the end for the complex range of ideas that underpinned anti-Keynesian macroeconomics. The most immediate problem, of course, was the collapse of the stock market. Millions of people lost wealth as the stock market lost more than 20 percent that spring and headed into bear territory; after years of claiming easy riches in the stock market, many people began to realize that their retirement savings were disappearing. This, in turn, had serious repercussions for the rest of the economy. Because of their stock market gains, many people had stopped saving from their regular income; likewise, as the value of their houses started to balloon at the turn of the millennium, the incentive to save from their income had diminished. This failure to save made clear sense: if your wealth can grow rapidly through the appreciation of the assets that you already own, why deny yourself the pleasure of spending your current income?

The unspoken problem in all this for the economics profession was that for anyone who had adhered to some form of rational expectations theory, there was no good way to explain all the poor investments that had been made by private agents during the dot-com boom. It was not just middle-income people who had put their retirement savings into high-tech stocks and had made poor judgments of the market's future value; it was also the savvy managers of many venture capital funds who had formed utterly irrational expectations of future market values.

The exuberance of the stock market created by the technological innovation in the computer industry had also led to many high-profile mergers and acquisitions that in retrospect had been based on ignorance, overoptimism, and self-deception. Take, for example, the purchase of Time Warner by AOL; AOL's inflated stock price made the purchase of a "content provider" like Time Warner look like a brilliant move that would allow the internet company to begin feeding high-quality news content and programming from Time Warner through its online portal. But, as we now know, AOL's stock price at the time of the purchase of Time Warner did not reflect anything like the true value of the company. Ignorant of AOL's true value, people kept buying the company's stock in the hope of realizing large gains. But not only uninformed fools and naive day traders mistook the value of AOL's stock; so did the professionals. Ultimately, the poor expectations of tens of thousands of market participants drove AOL's stock price to a level that allowed AOL to take over a much more valuable company by using the inflated value of its own shares. This type of error was rampant across the range of high-tech stocks.

By early 2001, the economy was headed into a recession, and the Federal Reserve stepped into action to begin trying to stimulate the economy. Well before the attacks of September 11, the economy was in trouble. Unfortunately for the proponents of the New Classical macroeconomics, the problem did not lie in any radical shifts in policy. The problem lay with the market agents who had been making bad decisions that were based on persistent errors in their expectations. These are precisely the agents who, in New Classical theory, are correctly predicting everything that they can possibly predict, and who are forced by perfectly competitive markets to allocate resources in the best possible way.

This was not the only bad news for those who had been arguing that the market always worked well if the government just kept out of the way. Another explicit dimension of the thinking of those who had argued for the ineffectiveness and possible destructiveness of macroeconomic policy was the idea that any microeconomic government regulation was anathema. Perhaps the best exemplar of this combination of microeconomic and macroeconomic laissez-faire was Milton Friedman himself, who in addition to being the intellectual progenitor of monetarism in its late twentieth-century guise also wrote widely about the ineffectiveness of government regulation at the microeconomic level. By the 1980s and 1990s, however, the nostrums of the advocates of laissez-faire went far beyond Friedman's arguments against rent controls and agricultural price supports; they were also expanded to include arguments against government oversight of financial markets. But here the new millennium would bring them yet more bad news, for several high profile business scandals (such as those involving Enron and Worldcom) showed that financial markets could be easily manipulated by unscrupulous profit seekers and con artists. When one of America's oldest and most respected accounting firms, Arthur Andersen, was forced into bankruptcy for its role in Enron's collapse, the argument that business needed no regulation other than the "self-regulation" seemed naive at best and disingenuous at worst.

While the intellectual underpinnings for the great laissez-faire arguments of the 1990s were coming undone on the nightly news and in the pages of the financial press, a funny thing happened to macroeconomic policy, both monetary and fiscal.

On the monetary policy side, the Federal Reserve undertook the most extensive monetary stimulation in a generation during the early years of the new millennium. In 2001, the Fed had already cut interest rates by three percentage points (from 6.50 percent to 3.50 percent) before the terrorist attacks on September 11; over the next two years, it would push them down to historically low levels of 1 percent and then hold them there for another year. Unworried by fears of inflation, the Fed now felt free to focus its attention on economic growth and unemployment.[19]

This intense focus on using interest rates to aggressively combat recession and unemployment could not have been more in line with the Keynesian consensus in American economics that prevailed in the postwar years. Although Keynesians in the twenty-five years after the Second World War preferred fiscal to monetary policy, to the extent that they did think about monetary policy they believed that it should be focused on using interest rates to promote economic growth and combat unemployment.

However, one cannot label the Federal Reserve's policies at the beginning of the decade as the most Keynesian aspect of American macroeconomic policy during that time. That title would have to go to the fiscal policies of President George W. Bush. Never in American history had the government run such large deficits and incurred so much debt. During his first presidential campaign in 2000, George W. Bush pushed hard to cut taxes for what he termed supply-side reasons: the belief that the cuts would provide incentives to investment that would, in turn, cause economic growth. But by the time he was in office and facing a rapidly accelerating recession, his rhetoric began to focus much more clearly on the immediate stimulus to aggregate demand that the tax cuts would foster. In fact, his first tax cut included tax rebate checks sent directly to households in hopes that they would spend the money on immediate consumption. The supply-side basis of his tax cuts remained a rhetorical sop for his supporters, but the actual intent of the cuts was old-fashioned Keynesian demand management. Faced with another serious recession in 2008, Bush returned to exactly the same strategy of sending tax rebate checks directly to households.[20]

Perhaps never in American history had macroeconomic policy been so solidly focused on using demand management to stimulate the economy as during the years from 2001 to 2008. Thus, even before the financial crisis of autumn 2008, American economic policy had returned to the use of demand management as the primary tool for stabilizing the economy. But while we have no other way to name these policies between 2001 and 2008 than to label them as Keynesian, we know now that unlike Keynes, their progenitors in the Bush administration failed to appreciate the potential for irrational speculation. Although Bush's economic policymakers had learned the usefulness of demand management, they did not see the likelihood that it would be needed on a much larger scale before the end of their time in office.

They were Keynesian in their use of policy, but they still clung to some of the most basic intuitions that had defined the anti-Keynesian ideology: that people have rational expectations of the future and that unregulated markets always work best.

Assessing the American return to Keynes

There are many ways to interpret the return to Keynesian macroeconomic policy in the United States. One obvious approach is to note the difference in the way that Keynesian ideas were deposed thirty years ago with the way that New Classical macroeconomic ideas have been displaced in the first decade of the new millennium. When Keynesian ideas were displaced thirty years ago, it was very much an intentional effort with support from right-wing think tanks, a much heralded "counterrevolution" that was widely discussed in the press.[21] On the contrary, the demise of the New Classical macroeconomic model was not the result of a coordinated, well-funded effort on the part of left-wing think tanks, and there has been nothing like the funereal press coverage for New Classical macroeconomics (or monetarism) that accompanied the demise of Keynesianism.

But it would be wrong to make too much of these differences. The demise of rational expectations and the New Classical macroeconomics did not require a concerted, well-funded effort: these ideas collapsed under their own weight. For instance, the severity of the economic problems brought on by the latest wave of dislocations (e.g., the subprime lending crisis, the first collapse of the American housing market in over sixty years, unstable commodity prices on world markets) has made it all too clear just how poorly the rational expectations hypothesis reflected reality. If economic agents really had rational expectations, then there would have been widespread predictions of the collapse of the internet stock bubble in 1999. Likewise, if people had rational expectations, then they would not have bought homes in the first part of the decade that would plummet in value after 2006. And who now wants to argue that the investment bankers who bought and sold the toxic assets backed by subprime mortgages had rational expectations?

As for the press, the context for market disruption in the United States is much different now than it was thirty years ago. Today's economic debate is much more complex than it was in the 1970s when the oil embargoes were layered over a domestic economy that was already stagnant; now, the press seems less sure of the causes of economic dislocation: Is it bad policy? Unscrupulous investment bankers? Poor regulation? Globalization? NAFTA? Financial crisis? But more to the point, many of these possible causes of economic dislocation have already combined in the public mind to cause a fundamental questioning of the efficacy of the free market to always provide optimum results.

But this questioning of the idea that the free market always produces optimum outcomes is seen now in a more nuanced way, not entirely attached to issues of macroeconomic policy. If poor regulation of the mortgage industry has caused problems, it is not clear that the answer lies solely in figuring out the right macroeconomic policy with which to respond. Even if the Federal Reserve can lower interest rates to help the mortgage market, not many people believe that monetary policy alone is the solution to that crisis. Until something is done that prevents abusive lending policies and until adequate regulation of the mortgage resale market is provided, the underlying problems will not go away. Unlike the counterrevolution thirty year ago, people today do not seem as prone to conflating macroeconomic and microeconomic policies into one grand ideological bundle. The differences between the demise of Keynesianism and anti-Keynesianism may be driven more by the different, more nuanced ways that the economy is understood than by differences in political tactics or external funding.

In addition, the realization that many of the planks upon which the New Classical macroeconomics was built are faulty has not caused people to throw out all the economic insights that have accrued since the collapse of American Keynesianism in the 1970s. No one today, on the right or left, would deny that expectations are important to take into consideration in crafting good macroeconomic policy. But rather than relying on brittle, unrealistic assumptions about perfect foresight and rational expectations, we are today forced, just as Keynes was in the 1920s and 1930s, to try to formulate policies that can deal with rapid shifts in confidence and expectations that are, in turn, formed on the basis of widespread ignorance of the underlying financial situation. Because of the widespread acceptance of the importance of expectations, it would not be easy today to find any proponent of the potential of macroeconomic economic policy who would argue that it was not possible to make mistakes with fiscal or monetary policy. A stimulus that was too large might trigger either inflation or inflationary expectations; either one could be counterproductive and create more problems for the economy. Likewise, a stimulus that was too small might fail to boost expectations sufficiently to insure recovery. Nor would it be easy today to find anyone who argued that only monetary or only fiscal policy is efficacious; both can be effective if used well, and both can make matters worse.

In this sense, perhaps, economic policy has the potential now to become more like what John Maynard Keynes envisioned than at any time since the Second World War. Keynes would have been the last person to want good economic management to become a partisan, ideologically loaded endeavor. While it is nearly impossible to imagine him not supporting the large fiscal stimulus package (nearly $800 billion) passed in February 2009, his satisfaction would likely come not from the prospect that fiscal fine-tuning might now become a staple of capitalist society but rather from his knowledge that economists had been able to recommend policies that could combat widespread unemployment and help stabilize the economy when their help was most needed.

Keynes always dreamed that good economic management would become like dentistry: a matter of technical competence and good will.

Perhaps now after the collapse of the ideological front that was arrayed against Keynesianism in the 1970s, we can more clearly see the importance of his dream and, likewise, the damage that can be done by simplistic economic ideas that were driven by political dictates. Laissez-faire does not always work well. Sometimes market economies need to be stabilized through macroeconomic policy. Not too late, Americans have returned to these basic Keynesian insights.

Notes

1. Perhaps the best account of this story is in Barber (1990). See also Stein (1969).
2. During the first half of the nineteenth century, there were often calls for individual states to stimulate the economy with public works projects such as canals or highways. These calls, however, were not based on any form of economic analysis.
3. For a good account of Roosevelt's deft use of fiscal deficits in his 1932 and 1936 campaigns, see Brinkley (1996).
4. See Hall (1989) for several essays on how demand management entered the political process in different nations.
5. From the inception of the Council, dating from the Employment Act of 1946, legislation in the United States has always forced federal macroeconomic policymaking to focus on the troika of employment, inflation, and economic growth.
6. This sad story, well documented by Bernstein (2001), revolved around Johnson's refusal to let even his Council of Economic Advisers know about his secret escalation of the war. By the time they learned of the escalation, inflation had already started to spiral higher. Of course, the episode demonstrates the principals of the New Economics that Heller, Gordon, and Tobin brought to Washington and which had been used to such great effect in shaping Kennedy's 1963 tax cut. But in the popular retelling of this story in the financial press and elsewhere, it was the New Economics that failed when, in fact, the story supports the New Economics theory about the results of an overstimulation of the economy.
7. The first application of Keynesian demand management principles in Britain was in 1941 to combat the potential inflation attendant to the economic overheating caused by the war effort. It was understood from the earliest days of demand management that the tool could be used in two directions, one to stimulate and one to dampen the economy.
8. There were, of course, still many Keynesians, but they tended to be older keepers of the Keynesian flame. The period after the oil embargoes also marked the rise of what came to be termed post-Keynesian economics. For a history of post-Keynesian economics, see King (2002).
9. The two basic monetarist assumptions are that velocity, the rate at which money turns over in the economy, is constant or grows at a constant rate and

that real output (real income) has a potential growth rate determined by such factors as technological change, population growth, and resource discovery.

10. Thus, another common summary of monetarism is the (formerly) well-known statement, "Inflation is always and everywhere a monetary phenomenon."

11. Technically, the relationship between the money supply and the rate of inflation expressed here is known as the quantity theory of money.

12. There are different measures of the money supply, and as the Federal Reserve began to face trouble with controlling the first measure it tried to target, it began to switch between different measures, looking for one with a predictable velocity that would give it the results it hoped for.

13. The unpopularity of Volcker's policies with the Reagan administration marked another important shift at the Federal Reserve under Volcker: the independence of the Federal Reserve from presidential power. As Wooley (1984) shows, before 1979 the chair of the Federal Reserve dependably undertook the monetary policy preferred by the president even when it was not the policy that the chair might have preferred.

14. DeLong (2000) discusses the success of many of the ideas embodied within monetarism against the background of its practical collapse as an effective policy guideline.

15. Milton Friedman would ultimately never address the failure of his ideas about monetary policy in an academic publication, only mentioning it in passing at age 91 in an interview in the *Financial Times* (June 3, 2003) that his ideas had not proven correct.

16. It is worth noting that in the 1980s, while unemployment fell rapidly from its 1982 peak in the United States, European unemployment remained stubbornly high for most of the decade. The result was that European macroeconomists became less enthusiastic about New Classical or Real Business Cycle theories. New Keynesian theories involving market imperfections were more common in Europe than in the United States.

17. The source of the term "the presuppositions of Harvey Road" is from Roy Harrod's (1951) biography of Keynes. Harrod used the term to refer to the entire set of Victorian ideas with which Keynes had been raised. It is a noteworthy feature of Buchanan and Wagner's book that they do not investigate any of the evidence regarding Keynes's own work as a policy analyst for the British government. Their entire portrait of Keynes is a straw man built on assumptions about his work and its effects.

18. The detailed implementation of this was, however, problematic. Should the budget balance every year or just balance over the cycle? There was also the problem of what should be included: just current spending or also investment?

19. With interest rates lower than the rate of inflation (1 percent versus 2 percent), the price of money was actually negative. Borrowing at these rates allowed the debtors to pay back their loans for less than they had borrowed.

20. It is tempting to compare Bush's fiscal policies to Lyndon Johnson's since they both increased the size and effect of their planned fiscal stimulus by

large war expenditures. However, there is also a wide chasm between them as represented by the fact that Johnson was already planning stimulus through large-scale expenditure on antipoverty programs when he layered major war expenditure on top of those plans, whereas the crux of Bush's fiscal policy before he layered on his war expenditures was on tax cuts for the wealthy.

21. Backhouse (2008) puts the foundation support for laissez-faire economics in America in context.

CHAPTER TWO

Japan's Long-Run Stagnation and Economic Policies

Yoshiyasu Ono

Introduction

Japan's economy has been facing serious stagnation since the stock market crashed in the early 1990s. Japanese governments have been moving back and forth between demand- and supply-side responses. They sometimes chose Keynesian expansionary policies (K. Miyazawa, 1991–1993; M. Hosokawa, 1993–1994; T. Murayama, 1994–1996; K. Obuchi, 1998–2000) and at other times promoted neoclassical contractionary policies (R. Hashimoto, 1996–1998; J. Koizumi, 2001–2006). The administrations that adopted Keynesian policies expected that they would stimulate business activity by creating new demand through the multiplier effect. However, the multiplier was found to be much smaller than expected. The Hashimoto and Koizumi administrations criticized this approach and strongly promoted supply-side policies, but Japan's economic performance was particularly bad under the latter.

This chapter gives an overview of Japan's stagnation in the 1990s and the present decade and proposes a theoretical framework of such long-run stagnation by combining the neoclassical time preference theory and Keynes's liquidity preference theory. In this framework, we analyze the effects of various neoclassical or Keynesian policies adopted in Japan and discuss why they did not produce the positive effects expected.

An overview of Japan's long-run stagnation

In the late 1980s, especially after 1987, Japan enjoyed a 6–8 percent annual growth of real gross domestic product (GDP) and an unemployment rate of less than 2 percent. The Nikkei Stock Average (Nikkei 225) grew at an annual rate of 20–30 percent and eventually reached its historical peak, 38,915, at the end of 1989. People had confidence in Japan's economy, and several books expressing that confidence—e.g., Vogel (1979) and Johnson (1982)—sold well. The Nikkei index never returned to the level it reached in 1989, however. Within only three years, it had declined by 60 percent and in 2003 reached 7,862, an 80 percent decline from its highest (see Figure 2.1). In February 2009, it was still around 7,900 yen. The real-estate market has followed the same pattern, but with a two-year lag.

The stock price decline in the Nikkei index was comparable to the 80 percent fall in the DJI index (Dow Jones Industrial Average) during the Great Depression, and the lead-up to the stock market crash was also quite similar. Until just before the crash of September 1929, Americans enjoyed rapid rises in stock prices and believed that they were in a new era without stagnation (see Allen 1931, 1939). Nevertheless, the crash came. The present U.S. economy and most of the rest of the world appear to be following a similar chain of events. If so, the DJI index will be less than 3,000 within several years.

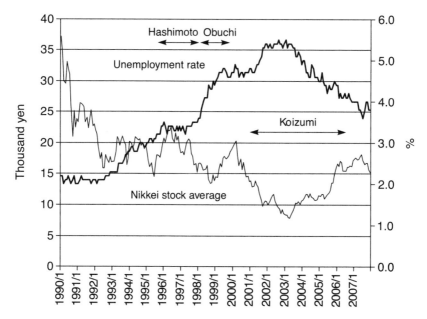

Figure 2.1 Unemployment rate and Nikkei stock average (Jan. 1990–Jan. 2008, monthly). Unemployment rate: The Ministry of Internal Affairs and Communications (www.stat.go.jp/data/roudou/longtime/03roudou.htm). Stock prices: The Nikkei Stock Average (www.nikkei.co.jp/nkave/index.html).

In accordance with the stock market crash in Japan, the real GDP growth rate sharply declined from 7 percent to less than 2 percent and sometimes even ran negative (see Figure 2.2). The average growth rate after the crash was much lower than rates in 1950–1990: 8.8 percent in 1950–1973, 3.8 percent in 1973–1990, and 1.3 percent in 1990–2000 (see Boltho and Corbett 2000). There were three time periods in which Japan's economic growth was negative: 1993–1994, under Hosokawa; 1997–1998, under Hashimoto; and 2001–2002, under Koizumi. During these periods, the unemployment rate substantially increased (see Figure 2.1), and financial crises occurred. Under the Hashimoto reform of 1997–1998, for example, the unemployment rate increased from 3.5 percent to 4.5 percent. Yamaichi Securities (one of four big securities companies), Hokkaido Takushoku Bank (the tenth largest commercial bank), Long-Term Credit Bank, and several others collapsed, producing serious social turmoil: the number of suicides per 100,000 people sharply rose from 26.0 to 36.5, for example.[1] For the age group of 55- to 59-year-olds, in particular, the suicide rate jumped from 47.0 to 70.2. Under the economic reform of 2001–2003 (by Koizumi), the unemployment rate increased from 4.7 percent to 5.4 percent, the worst rate since 1953, when the government first began keeping records of unemployment statistics. Resona Bank (the fifth largest bank) was in effect nationalized because of an excessively low capital–asset ratio, and several local banks collapsed.

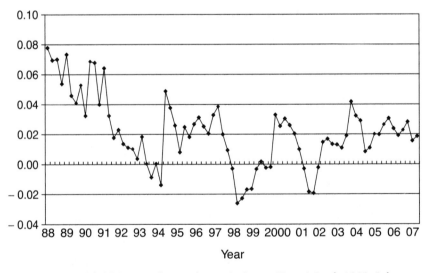

Figure 2.2   Real GDP annual growth rate in Japan (Jan.–March 1988–July–Sept. 2007, quarterly). Economic and Social Research Institute, Cabinet Office (www.esri.cao.go.jp/jp/sna/).

The rate of suicides per 100,000 people moved even higher: 38.0 for all ages and 71.1 for 55- to 59-year-olds in 2003.

The policies typical of the Hashimoto and Koizumi administrations were supply-side ones, which they called "structural reform." They insisted that Japan's stagnation was caused by various supply-side inefficiencies.[2] Such a view was just the other side of the same coin as the praise for the Japanese economy in the 1980s—i.e., that an efficiency improvement would boost economic activity. Therefore, these administrations urged firms to dismiss surplus employees and promoted the exit of inefficient firms. They also cut fiscal spending to reduce the government size since the public sector was supposed to be less efficient than the private sector. However, it is hard to believe that Japan's supply-side, which was once believed, in the late 1980s, to be the world's most efficient, suddenly became so inefficient within a few years that serious stagnation lasted more than fifteen years. Moreover, Japan's government size was, in fact, one of the smallest among Organisation for Economic Cooperation and Development (OECD) countries (see Figure 2.3).

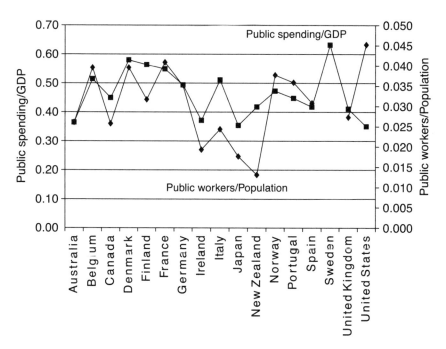

Figure 2.3   Government size: International comparison (1997). National Accounts of OECD Countries, Volume 11a, 11b, 1990–2001. OECD Data Bases, Social Expenditure (http://caliban.sourceoecd.org/vl=1251299/cl=63/ nw=1/rpsv/oecd_database.htm).

Although the two prime ministers reduced fiscal spending, they expanded government debt (1998 and 2002; see Figure 2.4). The financial crisis triggered by the Hashimoto reform forced him to step down in July 1998, at which time K. Obuchi took over the position. Obuchi expanded fiscal spending in order to stop the crisis and sharply increased government debt. Thereafter, the economy gradually recovered and the tax revenue expanded so that the deficit shrank quite a bit in 2000. Koizumi severely criticized fiscal expansion and declared that he intended to reduce the deficit by cutting fiscal spending, which was strongly supported by the Bush administration. However, it was Koizumi more than any other prime minister who increased government debt since his reform created negative growth, which caused tax revenue to decrease more than the reduction in fiscal spending.

In spite of those negative results, even after Koizumi structural reform was long believed to be the right policy, and Keynesian stimulative policies were mostly taken to be wasteful. This may have been because most governments that adopted Keynesian policies suddenly faced serious economic downturns and subsequently chose less effective pork-barreling policies as an emergency escape without closely examining other, better,

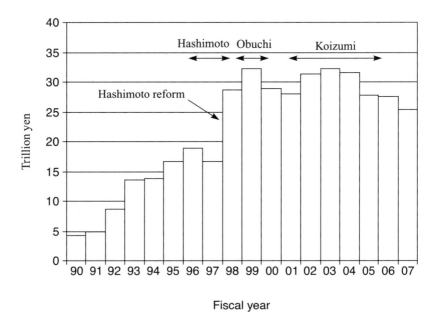

Figure 2.4   Fiscal deficit in Japan. Ministry of Finance (www.mof.go.jp/jouhou/syukei/zaiseitoukei/03.xls).

options for fiscal spending. The administration of Taro Aso, which came to power in 2008, seems to be making the same mistake. Since the U.S. subprime-loan problem triggered the worldwide economic crisis in 2008, Aso has significantly changed the government's approach from structural reform to Keynesian policies. However, one of his main policy proposals is a direct distribution of lump-sum benefits to every household, the form of Keynesian policy that has proven least effective in Japan.

The mechanism of long-run stagnation

This section proposes an analytical framework for understanding Japan's long-run stagnation.[3] Japan's stagnation is caused by a shortage of demand. People do not buy enough, which leads firms to face an excess in production capacity and a loss in profitable investment opportunities.

Figure 2.5 illustrates the mechanism of a consumption shortage. People earn income and allocate it to saving and consumption by comparing the benefits of the two. If they save, they increase assets and receive interest or liquidity. Assets consist of a noninterest-bearing asset, money, as well as interest-earning assets, such as stocks and bonds. Money holdings generate the utility of liquidity (such as convenience, security, and social status), which represents Keyenesian liquidity preference, whereas bonds and stocks generate interest or returns. The rate of return from bonds and stocks adjusts so that it covers the disadvantage of less liquidity.

The benefit of saving is measured by the relative utility of liquidity compared with consumption, namely, the liquidity premium. Keynes

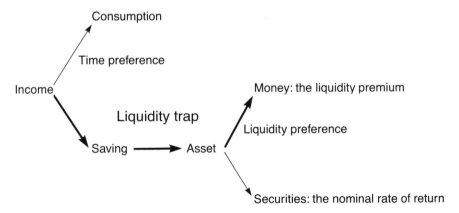

Figure 2.5 Portfolio choice and consumption-saving choice.

(1936, p. 226) defines this premium as "the amount (measured in terms of itself) which [people] are willing to pay for the potential convenience or security given by this power of disposal". The liquidity premium depends on the amount of consumption and money holding. If people consume little, they receive more utility from consumption than from increasing their money holding. If they consume enough, they want to accumulate money rather than to spend it on consumption. Thus, the liquidity premium increases as consumption increases. The ℓ curve in Figure 2.6 shows this relationship between consumption c and the liquidity premium. As people accumulate money, they want to allocate income to consumption rather than to money holding, implying that the liquidity premium decreases as real money holding increases.

Saving bears a cost of postponing consumption. Its magnitude depends on people's preference for their present consumption over their future

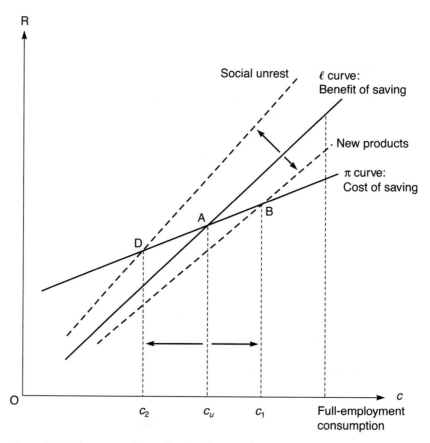

Figure 2.6   The cost and benefit of saving.

consumption, which represents a neoclassical time preference. Additionally, if commodity prices change over time, they bear an extra cost under inflation (or benefit from a cost reduction under deflation) when realizing the same volume of real consumption in the future. Since the inflation rate rises as aggregate demand increases, the cost of saving is positively related to consumption. This relationship is represented by the π curve in Figure 2.6. Note that the figure shows the case where under full-employment consumption, the ℓ curve is located above the π curve and hence the benefit of saving exceeds the cost of it, and a demand shortage occurs.

People compare the cost of saving (representing the time preference) with the benefit of saving measured by the liquidity premium (representing the liquidity preference) and decide the consumption-saving allocation so that they are equal. If the cost of saving (represented by the π curve) dominates the benefit of saving (represented by the ℓ curve), people increase consumption. If the opposite is true, they decrease consumption. Consequently, in Figure 2.6, consumption c is determined at the intersection point A of the π and ℓ curves, where c equals c_u. By exploring in the context of the Japanese economy what affects the two preferences and how, we will be able to understand the stagnation mechanism and the effects of various policies.

Using the above-mentioned mechanism, let us first consider the process of business recovery. In the presence of a demand shortage, unemployment occurs. This causes nominal wages and commodity prices to decline. There is, in fact, a clear negative relationship between the unemployment rate and the inflation rate (the Phillips curve) in Japan, as shown in Figure 2.7. Deflation has two mutually opposite effects. One is that it lowers the cost of saving and thereby reduces consumption (the deflation effect). The other is that it gradually increases real money balances and eventually lowers the liquidity premium, which stimulates consumption (the real-balance effect). Thus, it reduces consumption in the short run but gradually raises consumption as commodity prices decline. If the latter process continues, consumption should eventually be large enough to realize full employment.[4]

However, during Japan's long-run stagnation, deflation continued for a decade, and demand has still not yet sufficiently increased. This may be explained by the liquidity trap that works on consumption (see Figure 2.5).[5] If people maintain a strong preference for liquidity, the liquidity premium does not sufficiently decrease.[6] It gives a lower bound for the interest rate, namely, a liquidity trap. Even though deflation continues and real balances expand, people's preference for saving over consumption does not decline under the trap and hence consumption is not stimulated. Deflation reduces the cost of saving and thereby lowers consumption. The real-balance effect does not work; only the deflation effect does.

An economy with such a liquidity trap is the same as a monetary economy as defined by Keynes (1936, p. 239). He states: "Consider, for example, an economy in which there is no asset for which the liquidity-premium is always in excess of the carrying-costs; which is the best definition I can give of a so-called 'non-monetary' economy." Since the carrying cost of money is zero, a monetary economy should be an economy in which there is an asset for which the liquidity premium is always strictly positive. Such a situation may have, indeed, occurred in the Japanese economy.

In conventional neoclassical and Keynesian economics, a demand shortage and unemployment are mostly explained as being caused by some market imperfections, such as price–wage rigidities or false expectations of prices or interest rates. However, in Japan's stagnation, a demand shortage has lasted for about twenty years and the deflation rate has been considerably constant. It should not have been difficult for people to anticipate the price movement. Note that the above-mentioned mecha-

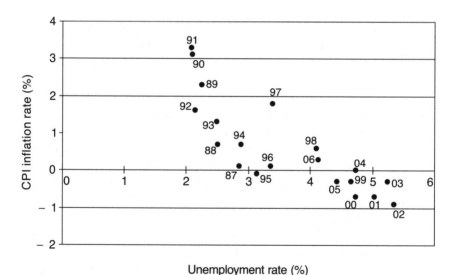

Figure 2.7 Phillips curve in Japan (1987–2006). Statistics Bureau, Ministry of Internal Affairs and Communications, Japan. Unemployment rate (www.stat .go.jp/data/roudou/longtime/03roudou.htm). CPI (www.stat.go.jp/data/cpi/ 200707/index.htm and www.stat.go.jp/data/cpi/longtime/index.htm).

nism of long-run stagnation obtains even if prices, wages, and interest rates are correctly anticipated.

Policy effects

Because people choose consumption by comparing the cost and benefit of saving, policies or structural changes that either increase the cost or decrease the benefit of saving will thus stimulate consumption. In this section, we examine the working of various policies or structural changes on the cost and the benefit and consider their effects on business activity. It will be found that supply-side policies mostly decrease the cost of saving or increase the benefit of saving and hence negatively work on consumption. This may explain why under the structural reform Japan's economic performance was particularly bad.

Furthermore, we find that some conventional Keynesian policies are ineffective, although others are useful under stagnation. This may have led structural reformers to regard Keynesian policies in general as wasteful.

The high-growth period and the long-run stagnation

Fluctuations in liquidity preference change the benefit of saving and thereby affect consumption. Such fluctuations are created, for example, by new product creation and social uncertainty. In Japan, these conditions led to high growth in the 1960s and to long-run stagnation in the 1990s and the present decade.

New product creation lowers the liquidity premium by making consumption more attractive than money holding, which decreases the benefit of saving. In the 1960s, various attractive products, such as refrigerators, vacuum cleaners, washing machines, color televisions, and cars, were introduced one after another. People scrambled to purchase them, and firms invested in new production facilities, both of which led to high-speed growth. Using the cost and benefit of saving mentioned above, Figure 2.6 illustrates the effect of new product creation on consumption. It shifts the ℓ curve (representing the benefit of saving) downward, with the π curve (representing the cost of saving) unchanged, and thus the equilibrium given by the intersection of the two curves moves from A to B. Consequently, consumption increases from c_u to c_1.

In contrast, social uncertainty raises the utility of money holding and hence increases the liquidity premium, urging people to reduce consumption and to save.[7] The stock market crash of the early 1990s created such uncertainty, and people lost confidence in the Japanese economy. They increased their liquidity preference and decreased consumption. The present economic crisis has had a similar effect on people's mindsets in many countries. This process is represented by an upward shift of the ℓ curve in Figure 2.6. The intersection point of the two curves moves from A to D, and hence consumption decreases from c_u to c_2.

Most neoclassical economists explain business fluctuations in quite a different way. They emphasize supply-side efficiency as a cause of business fluctuations since in their framework prices and wages adjust so that demand matches supply and aggregate demand equals full-employment output. A demand shortage should be a short-run phenomenon if it occurs. Liquidity preference affects only nominal prices without changing aggregate demand. Therefore, neoclassical economists appreciate firms' efforts to increase production efficiency and bureaucrats' support for firms during high-growth periods and blame business managers and bureaucrats for management failures and corruption during stagnation.

Productivity increase

Most neoclassical economists insist that firms have to improve production efficiency in order for Japan to recover from the present stagnation. Such a view is correct as long as full employment holds, since the increased production capacity is fully utilized under full employment. In reality, however, lots of people were unemployed and the GDP growth rate became negative especially under the administrations that promoted the structural reform.

In the standard Keynesian framework, an increase in the full-employment output does not affect aggregate demand. It only increases unemployment.

In the present framework, an increase in productivity leads to a typical fallacy of composition. Since less labor is required to produce the same amount, the deflationary gap widens, causing people to choose money holding rather than consumption and to reduce consumption. Decreases in prices expand real balances and reduce people's liquidity preference, which should naturally stimulate consumption. Under the liquidity trap explained above, however, this effect does not work; only the negative effect of deflation on consumption does. Consequently, aggregate demand and production decrease, resulting in lower efficiency of the economy as a whole.

This effect is illustrated in Figure 2.8. In the figure, the π curve and the ℓ curve are the same as those in Figure 2.6, and point A denotes the initial equilibrium. An increase in productivity shifts the π curve (the cost of saving) downward since it worsens deflation. Consequently, the intersection point moves from A to B and consumption decreases from c_u to c_u'.

In order to improve production efficiency, investment-promoting tax deductions were introduced in Japan. These are supported by both neo-classical economists and Keynesians. The former believe that new investment improves productivity and eventually increases aggregate production, whereas the latter hold that tax deductions increase investment demand. In the presence of a demand shortage, however, an improvement in productivity decreases labor demand and worsens unemployment. Therefore, the promotion of nonproductive investment, such as environmental investment, is desirable because such investment creates demand and benefits people without expanding production capacity. Especially after the Kyoto Protocol (1997) was adopted, the importance of environmental investment has been emphasized in Japan.

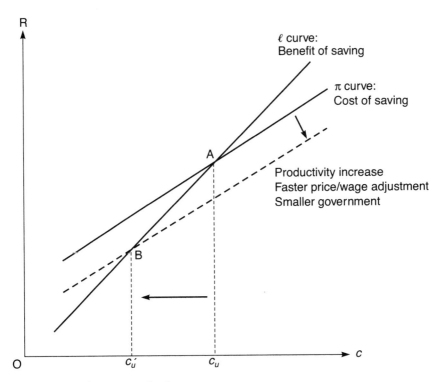

Figure 2.8 The structural reform.

Price–wage adjustment

During the stagnation in Japan, an improvement in price–wage adjustment has been strongly recommended as an important measure to help business activity to recover. For this purpose, the temporary personnel service industry has been widely deregulated and the use of irregular workers has sharply increased, as shown in Figure 2.9.

Most economists support a price–wage adjustment on the basis of the argument that a demand shortage occurs only while prices and wages are adjusting toward full-employment levels and because faster price–wage adjustment shortens the time period required to reach full employment.[8] However, Keynes (1936, chap. 19) states that a rise in the wage-adjustment speed decreases effective demand and hence worsens a demand shortage.

What occurred during Japan's stagnation was more in conformity with what Keynes had predicted. A demand shortage still exists although deflation continued for a decade. Such a state of the economy can be explained by the analysis of the π and ℓ curves. In the presence of a demand shortage, a rise in price–wage adjustment speed worsens deflation. Thus,

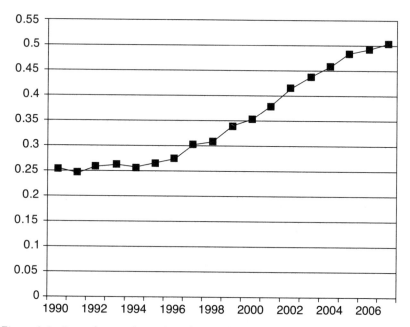

Figure 2.9   Irregular employees/regular employees. Statistics Bureau, Ministry of Internal Affairs and Communications, Japan (www.stat.go.jp/data/roudou/ longtime/zuhyou/lt51.xls).

it lowers the cost of saving and reduces consumption. Moreover, increases in the ratio of irregular employees over regular ones (see Figure 2.9) create employment insecurity, causing people to raise liquidity preference and to decrease consumption.

The effect of an improvement in price–wage adjustment is similar to that of an increase in productivity, as illustrated in Figure 2.8. An improvement in price-wage adjustment worsens deflation and thus shifts the π curve (the cost of saving) downward. Consequently, the equilibrium consumption given by the intersection point of the π and ℓ curves decreases from c_u to $c_u{}'$. Employment insecurity stimulates people's liquidity preference and increases the benefit of saving, which reduces consumption. This effect is illustrated by an upward shift of the ℓ curve in Figure 2.6.

Public works spending

Among various inefficiencies, Hashimoto and Koizumi particularly criticized the public sector as being very inefficient. They argued that the size of the Japanese government was too large despite the fact that it is actually one of the smallest among OECD countries (see Figure 2.3), and they reduced public works spending (see the data for FY 1996–1998 and 2001–2006 in Figure 2.10).

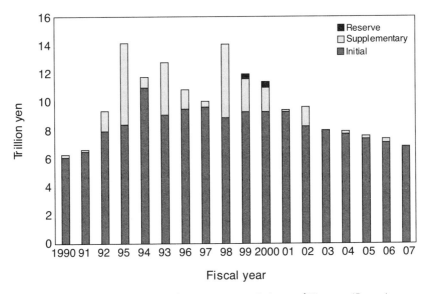

Figure 2.10 Public works spending in Japan. Ministry of Finance (Japan). (www.mof.go.jp/jouhou/syukei/zaiseitoukei/ichiran.htm).

Under full employment, a reduction in public works moves production factors from the public sector to the private sector, which is supposedly more efficient, and hence increases total production. In Japan, however, people were not fully employed, and the reductions in public works spending resulted in lower employment and negative economic growth, as shown in Figures 2.1 and 2.2. Such an outcome forced Hashimoto to step aside as prime minister and then forced the succeeding government (that of Obuchi) to compile a huge supplementary budget for public works in 1998 (see Figure 2.10) so as to prevent stagnation from getting worse.

In the present framework, a decrease in public works spending expands unemployment and escalates deflation, which lowers the cost of saving. It makes it more advantageous for people to save than to consume and worsens stagnation. This effect is illustrated by a downward shift of the π curve (representing the cost of saving) in Figure 2.8. It moves the stagnation equilibrium from A to B, decreasing consumption from c_u to c_u'. An increase in public works spending yields the reverse effect and increases consumption. Besides, public works produce direct benefits of facilities and services.

In the standard Keynesian framework, public works spending stimulates consumption through the multiplier effect. People who receive government payments expand consumption, which in turn increases employment and income. Thus, the magnitude of government expenditure and the propensity to consume are important. The effect of fiscal spending under a loan budget is considered to be larger than that under a balanced budget since the net payment is smaller under the latter. In the present framework, in contrast, the magnitude of employment directly created by fiscal spending matters, and hence the result does not differ under the two budget regimes.

In Japan's stagnation, the multiplier was found to be much smaller than would obtain in the Keynesian model although Japanese governments continued loan expenditure. This outcome is rather consistent with the present analysis. In order to produce a tangible effect on consumption, fiscal spending must create so much employment that the deflationary gap will significantly shrink. Warfare is an example of the kind of driver that will create such conditions. Since it is difficult to expand fiscal spending so significantly in ordinary times, the expansionary effect is limited. Rather, accumulation of government debt may create social and economic anxiety, which makes people prefer saving to consumption and reduces the expansionary effect of fiscal spending.

It is worth noting that in the present framework, direct transfers, such as tax rebates, lump-sum subsidies, and unemployment benefits, have no effect on aggregate demand, except through redistribution, since they do not create new employment.[9] In 1999, Obuchi adopted a lump-sum subsidy: he distributed merchandise coupons (about 700 billion yen), called Chiiki Shinko Ken. It hardly had any effect on aggregate demand. In 2008, Aso also proposed the distribution of lump-sum benefits to every household.

International context

By considering current-account balances, we can extend the present analysis to an international context.[10] A decrease in consumption due to a policy (or parameter) change lowers imports and improves the current account, causing the home currency to appreciate against the foreign currency. Therefore, the more a country stagnates, the more its currency appreciates. This is in sharp contrast to the implication of the neoclassical model. In the neoclassical model, an increase in supply-side productivity expands exports and improves the current account, which leads the home currency to appreciate against the foreign currency. It also increases income and hence raises consumption. Thus, the more a country booms, the more its currency appreciates.

Figure 2.11 looks more in conformity with the result of the present analysis. There is a positive relationship between the yen–dollar rate and the difference in Japan's and United States' growth rates of real consumption between 1988 and 2006—i.e., the Japanese yen appreciated against the U.S. dollar as Japan's economy stagnated more.

Conclusions

Japan suffered from serious stagnation for about twenty years, during which time neoclassical supply-side policies and Keynesian demand-side policies were implemented. The stagnation was particularly serious under supply-side policies, which included increased production efficiency, improved price–wage adjustments, and reductions in public works spending. If people were fully employed, they would increase national income. Higher efficiency expands full-employment production, faster price–wage adjustment shortens the time period required to reach full employment, and less fiscal spending reallocates production factors to the private sector, which is supposedly more efficient than the public sector. In Japan, however, serious unemployment existed and the above-mentioned mechanisms did not work. Rather, those policies reduced aggregate demand.

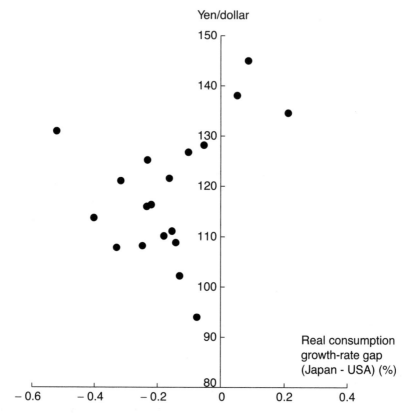

Figure 2.11 Japan-U.S. consumption growth-rate gap and yen-dollar rate (1988–2006). Exchange rate: Board of Governors of the Federal Reserve System (www.gpoaccess.gov/eop/2008/B110.xls). GDP: United Nations, "GDP and its breakdown at constant 1990 prices in national currency" (http://unstats.un.org/unsd/snaama/dnllist.asp).

The mechanism of Japan's long-run stagnation and the negative effects of the supply-side policies are explained in the framework I have proposed: because of some social unrest—e.g., a stock market crash—people lost confidence in their economy and preferred saving to consumption. This decreased consumption and worsened deflation, which made money holding more advantageous and further reduced consumption. Profitable investment opportunities also decreased due to such reductions in consumption. Under these circumstances, supply-side policies that improved production efficiency widened the deflationary gap and further reduced aggregate demand.

In this framework, it is also found that the effect of Keynesian fiscal expansion is much smaller than expected in the conventional Keynesian model, as was indeed the case in Japan. This is because fiscal spending increases aggregate demand not through the Keynesian multiplier effect but by reducing deflation and stimulating consumption only indirectly. Since the magnitude of employment creation plays a crucial role in easing deflationary pressures, direct transfers (e.g., tax deductions and the distribution of merchandise coupons), which do not create employment, hardly have any effect on aggregate demand.

Notes

Earlier versions of this research were presented at the OECD, the Delhi School of Economics, the University of Auckland, Sophia University, Rikkyo University, the University of Melbourne, and Australian National University. I am indebted to the seminar participants for many helpful comments. I also thank T. Mizutani and S. Takenaka for collecting data. Financial support from the Grants-in-Aid for Scientific Research, JSPS, Japan, is gratefully acknowledged.

1. Vital Statistics, Ministry of Health, Labor, and Welfare.
2. This view is one that most economists shared. Hayashi and Prescott (2002) argue that Japan suffered from stagnation because the government supported inefficient firms and industries. Prescott (2002) also declares that a reduction in productivity led Japan to stagnation. Morana (2004) mentions that technological slowdown and demographic changes lowered productivity growth and produced stagnation.
3. The subsequent properties are derived from a dynamic optimizing model. See Ono (1994, 2001) for its mathematical structure.
4. In the standard monetary growth model, this process is immediately achieved and full employment is always realized. See, e.g., Blanchard and Fischer (1989, pp. 188–191).
5. According to Keynesian economics, the trap occurs as a result of portfolio choice between bonds and liquidity. In the present analysis, the trap reflects consumption-saving choice, and its magnitude may not explicitly be observed in the market. The interest rate of bonds merely covers the difference in liquidity between money and bonds and hence is naturally very low.
6. See Ono, Ogawa, and Yoshida (2004) for empirical evidence in the Japanese economy of the existence of the lower bound of the liquidity premium that is derived from the consumption-saving choice.
7. Horii and Ono (2004) examine demand and liquidity-preference fluctuations caused by changes in people's beliefs about a random liquidity shock.
8. This property is valid also in the inflation-targeting model by Krugman (1998). Using a two-period monetary model with intertemporal substitution of consumption, Krugman shows both that a demand shortage arises only in the first period if prices are rigid during that period and that a monetary expansion in the future, namely, the inflation-targeting policy, makes people anticipate inflation and hence stimulates present demand. In this model, a demand shortage is a short-run phenomenon and immediately disappears if prices adjust in the first period.

9. Ono (2009) shows that even in the Keynesian framework, it is not the magnitude of government purchases but the value of social services produced by them that yields a substantial difference from transfers. Therefore, wasteful public works are equivalent to transfers, although the former are considered to be more effective than the latter in the conventional Keynesian economics for the reason that public works directly create new demand.

10. See Ono (2006) for the formal structure of the open-economy model.

CHAPTER THREE

European Macroeconomic Policy: A Return to Active Stabilization?

Hans-Michael Trautwein

Introduction

Few observers would describe the macropolicies that have been run in the core economies of the European Union (EU) since the late 1980s as strategies of active stabilization of real economic activity. Monetary and fiscal policies in the euro area (aka the eurozone or euroland) are generally interpreted as being more restrictive and single-minded than their American counterparts, as the former are bound by rules that set the focus on monetary stability and fiscal consolidation. The mainstream critique of active stabilization policies as inefficient strategies originated largely in America but seems to have been taken more seriously in Europe. The German Bundesbank and its successor, the European Central Bank (ECB), display most of the properties of rule-bound policy that the literature about dynamic inconsistency considers to be essential for avoiding the pitfalls of discretionary macropolicies. The Bundesbank and the ECB have used their relatively high degrees of independence to concentrate on fighting inflation and to criticize fiscal initiatives aimed at stimulating output and employment in the stagnation periods of the mid-1990s and the early 2000s. By contrast, and with some discretion, the Federal Reserve System allowed U.S. unemployment in the 1990s to fall below what had been believed to be the NAIRU (i.e., the non-accelerating inflation rate of unemployment); and when the dot-com bubble burst in 2000, the Fed mitigated the crisis by switching to monetary expansion. Only a few commentators have related the relatively poor growth and employment performance of Germany and other EU economies between

1992 and 2006 to their stance on a more restrictive macroeconomic policy. The majority of commentators have attributed the high unemployment and slow productivity growth of that period to rigidities in goods and labor markets. Keynesian macroeconomics, with its critical attitude toward restrictive monetary policies and its emphasis on the active role of fiscal policy in stabilizing output and employment, has long appeared to be an outdated minority position. The consensus among academic economists and opinion makers has settled on a rule-bound mix of supranational monetary policy with national fiscal consolidation, notwithstanding occasional criticism of the stability and growth pact (SGP) that defines the fiscal limits for stabilization policies in the euro area.

However, shortly after the creation of the European Monetary Union (EMU), half of the member countries, among them Germany, France, and Italy, violated the budget deficit rule (a maximum 3 percent of GDP)—in several cases, for more than three consecutive years. Out of the fifteen present EMU members, nine still failed in early 2008 to meet the government debt criterion of the SGP (a maximum 60 percent of GDP)—doing so at the end of a boom, when consolidation is easiest. Total government debt was, at that time, about 68 percent of eurozone GDP (ECB 2008).[1] Since the sanctions stipulated by the SGP were not enforceable against the big countries, the pact was reformed in 2005 to provide for greater flexibility in the application of the rules. Apart from procedural changes, the justifications for overshooting the 3 percent reference value were extended to include "growth rates below potential growth with considerable accumulated loss of output," "development of potential growth," "prevailing cyclical conditions," "public investment," and a host of other factors, including "structural reforms" (Deutsche Bundesbank 2005, p. 17). The reformed SGP gives more leeway to countercyclical fiscal policies, as it demands "less consolidation in 'bad times' " and "no sanctions if consolidation is not achieved" (ibid.).

Did the reform of the pact signal a return to active stabilization? The acts of breaching the deficit criteria prior to the SGP reform might be more appropriately described as passive stabilization, since they were presented as stopgap measures, taken to prevent the automatic stabilizers from collapsing. According to the European Commission and ECOFIN (the Economic and Financial Affairs Council of Ministers), the SGP reform provided no more and no less than the flexibility required to make the EMU system of rules sustainable (ECOFIN 2005). The hardliners in the central banks have nevertheless interpreted the reform as a first step on a slippery slope that leads back to a "looser fiscal regime" (Deutsche Bundesbank 2005, p. 21) and the temptations of discretionary policies (e.g., Morris, Ongena, and Schuknecht 2006). In academic circles, the views on the appropriate design of the pact are widely divergent. As Fischer, Jonung, and Larch (2006, p. 4) express it in their survey, there is a "veritable industry of SGP therapists." The reduction of government deficits and debt burdens, which took place in 2006 and 2007, can be given varying interpretations: in accordance with the old SGP rules, it could be described as fiscal consolidation; yet it might also be seen as countercyclical demand management. Likewise, the extraordinary rise of budget deficits, with which all EU members have reacted to the financial crisis in late 2008, may be interpreted as an appropriate application of the new SGP rules or as a scrapping of the pact altogether.

From a more fundamental perspective, it is misleading to speak of a return to active stabilization. On the one hand, the EMU was seen, by many of its proponents, as a project of active stabilization right from the outset. The supranationalization of monetary policy was considered a straightforward way to eliminate the negative output and employment effects of the interest and exchange rate fluctuations that characterized its predecessor, the European Monetary System (EMS), in which interest rates in Europe were anchored to movements in the German price level. On the other hand, it may be argued that the EMU is still far from a state in which the ECB and ECOFIN understand the need to develop a coherent strategy to stabilize both prices and output. Whether the EMU has the potential and appropriate design to achieve this aim is open to debate. Opinions are deeply divided, and the dividing lines run right through the established political and macrotheoretical camps.

Taking stock of the variety of opinions, this chapter examines both the perspectives on the EMU as a project of active stabilization and the shortcomings of the present policy mix. Section 2 recalls the dynamic instability of the EMS that gave birth to the EMU, and it provides a taxonomy of the opinions about the character and feasibility of the EMU prior to its start. Section 3 reviews the "policy ineffectiveness" literature, in which it is argued that active stabilization by discretionary policies suffers from a lack of credibility and that strictly rule-bound policies lower the costs of disinflation. With regard to the EMS experience, it is shown that the argument itself lacks credibility. Section 4 explains why launching the EMU as a stabilization project required some coordinating rhetorics for which the "policy ineffectiveness" literature came in handy, despite its lack of realism. The section concludes with the argument that the coordination of fiscal policies was necessary for establishing the EMU but that the present macropolicy regime is not well designed to safeguard economic stability. Paying tribute to the title of this book, Section 5 examines to what extent the EMU project could be considered Keynesian policy. There is textual evidence that Keynes might have favored the project. Yet, even though the present financial crisis has renewed the public interest in Keynes and his views on financial markets and economic policy, the present state of the EMU makes it obvious that modern concepts of active stabilization must evolve beyond what is traditionally considered as Keynesian policy.

As this article was written in spring 2008, it did not originally take into account the dramatic changes in European macroeconomic policies later that year, when the bankruptcy of Lehman Brothers turned the smoldering subprime crisis into panic and recession. Since the conclusions of the original article survive, the main body of the text (Sections 2–5) has not been changed. Nonetheless, an update (as of February 2009) is provided in the final section, where the changes and problems in European macroeconomic policies that have followed from the turmoil in the financial markets are outlined in the style of an epilogue.

The EMS and EMU

The instability of the EMS

When the EMS was established in 1979, the vision was to create a regime of fixed exchange rates with symmetric duties of intervention. The intra-EMS exchange rates were defined in terms of a parity grid related to a synthetic currency, the European Currency Unit (ECU), and exchange rates were to be stabilized within narrow bands by all of the involved central banks. However, market forces quickly replaced the ECU with the deutsche mark as the key currency. Not only was Germany the biggest economy in the EMS in terms of GDP and trade volumes; the country had also made its postwar fortune by transforming itself into an export nation with a chronically high trade surplus and large stocks of dollar reserves. A prerequisite for this position was a regime of restrictive monetary and fiscal policies that contributed to low inflation and hence, under the fixed exchange rates of the Bretton Woods system, to a persistent undervaluation of the deutsche mark. After the breakdown of the Bretton Woods system in 1973, the deutsche mark appreciated continuously and acquired the role of an international reserve currency. This made it a natural candidate for the role of the key currency in the EMS.[2]

The market-based selection of the key currency recreated, however, the *n-1* problem that had brought down the Bretton Woods system; but now it carried a reversed sign, i.e., a disinflation bias instead of an inflation bias. While all other central banks in the EMS attempted to preserve external stability through exchange-rate targeting, the Bundesbank gave priority to internal stability in terms of low inflation. This was to be achieved by targeting M3, a monetary aggregate. The German price level began to play the role of a nominal anchor for the EMS. Due to the liquidity premium on the deutsche mark (implicit in the higher interest rates of other currency areas), the Bundesbank set the levels of short-term interest rates for all EMS economies. Whenever those levels were not acceptable for other countries, the latter faced the problematic choice between devaluation by realignment and "competitive disinflation." Realignments led to a further softening of their currencies vis-à-vis the deutsche mark, with further increases in inflation and interest-rate differentials. "Competitive disinflation" had its costs in terms of output, real income, and/or employment; only rarely was it achieved by a boost in productivity growth. At the level of politics, both options became increasingly unsustainable.

In the late 1980s, the EMS was nevertheless believed to be self-stabilizing, since it provided incentives for all member countries to "import stability" by bringing their inflation rates in line with those of Germany. However, the EMS was dynamically unstable, as the key currency was based on success in export competition. Low rates of interest at low inflation gave German industries a cost advantage that led to persistent trade deficits in other member economies, which had to be compensated with interest premiums in order to attract (or retain) capital. Whenever German inflation was on the rise and the Bundesbank reacted by raising interest rates, other countries ran overproportional risks of recession. The Bundesbank raised interest rates strongly when the reunification boom after 1990 got Germany out of step with the cyclical downturn in the rest of the world. The dynamic instability of the EMS thus became particularly obvious in a system crisis in 1992–1993—at a time when the Maastricht treaty had already set the EU on the track to the EMU.

The pros and cons of the EMU

Stability issues played an important role in the Maastricht negotiations of 1991, during which Germany gave up deutsche-mark hegemony in order to achieve the union's full acceptance of German reunification. In those days of uncertainty about cyclical and structural changes within the European Union, the initiatives to set up a monetary union definitely looked like a project of active stabilization. A broader participation in the setting of interest rates, which would not be confined to German interests in competitive disinflation, was seen—by advocates and critics of the EMU alike—as a shift of emphasis toward stabilization of output and employment in Europe.

With due reference to the "single market" agenda of the 1980s, the general argument in favor of the EMU, propagated by the EU commission, was actually more structural than macroeconomic. The position may be characterized as a "single market line" argument, which stressed that a common currency had essentially four advantages. It would

1. eliminate costs of currency management;
2. reduce exchange-rate uncertainty and risk premiums;
3. increase price transparency and competition; and
4. induce asset demand for the common currency by creating a single financial market that is larger, deeper, and hence more liquid than the set of national markets in the EMS.

The single market line had some macroeconomic aspects, as points 1–3 would reduce costs and therefore tend to decrease the rate of inflation, and the positive network externalities implicit in point 4 would contribute to both greater stability and growth.

There were other, more directly macroeconomic lines of argument in favor of the EMU, interpreting supranational monetary policy as a strategy of active stabilization. One line, largely followed by the governments and trade unions of those countries whose currencies had "softened" in the EMS era, welcomed the EMU as a project that would give more breathing space for growth- and employment-friendly policies. The constraints of the EMS, as set by the pace of German inflation and export growth, would be replaced by broader European participation in the decision-making on interest rates. This "soft pro line" coexisted with a "hard pro line" maintained by politicians, economists, and other opinion makers in the "hard currency" countries of those days (mainly, Germany, Netherlands, and the United Kingdom). The hard pro line was based on the belief that the EMU would produce monetary stability because only those countries that could afford to give up the option of devaluation would enter the club.

At the same time, a lot of arguments were made against the EMU, and these were diametrically opposed to the soft and hard pro lines as well as to the single market line. Among academic economists in Germany (and elsewhere) a "hard con line" of argument gained popularity. It was taken for granted that the euro would become a soft currency, since it was believed that the ECB would be less determined to fight inflation than the Bundesbank and that fiscal free-riding in some member countries would produce endemic inflation.

When it became obvious that EMU membership would require compliance with the Maastricht criteria of convergence, which set restrictions on inflation, interest rates, exchange rate volatility, and deficit spending, a "soft con line" of argument developed. Trade union representatives in France, Spain, and elsewhere expressed concerns that the euro would become too hard a currency, because the ECB was not subject to democratic control and could not be held accountable for any losses of output and jobs that its policy might cause.

In addition to these lines of argument, a structural objection to the EMU was raised along the "OCA line," i.e., in terms of the time-honored Optimum Currency Area theory (Mundell 1961; Kenen 1969). It was argued that Europe was not ready to abandon exchange-rate adjustments, since there was neither enough flexibility in the labor markets nor a system of fiscal transfers that would help to overcome the shocks that hit the EU members in an asymmetric fashion. Even though economists made much of the OCA criticism, it did not really bite. The realignment era of the EMS (between 1979 and 1987) had proved that exchange-rate adjustments were not much of an option to lose. Furthermore, it was countered that the transition to a common currency would increase trade within the monetary union and, in particular, the share of intrasectoral trade. This would reduce the risks of asymmetric shocks. It was thus argued that the EMU would endogenously evolve into an OCA (Frankel and Rose 1998).

Credibility and the costs of disinflation

Rules versus discretion

As plans were made to replace the EMS with a more sustainable monetary regime, in which exchange rates would be irreversibly fixed, supranational monetary policy was the only solution acceptable to all sides. However, for those who propagated the EMU as a project of active stabilization, the transition from deutsche-mark hegemony to a common monetary policy posed a dilemma. The ECB, too, would have to set interest rates for all member countries, so it was essential to agree upon the aims, rules, and regulations on which this "one size fits all" policy would operate. Yet, at the time when the institutional design of the EMU experiment was discussed, the discourse on monetary policy was strongly dominated by the "rules versus discretion" literature that made a case against active stabilization. Any monetary and fiscal "fine-tuning" was equated with discretionary polices that, according to the consensus model of the time, lacked credibility even if and when the measures are aimed strictly at low inflation. The "rules versus discretion" literature made an impact on the public debates about the EMU, even though—to give the story a further twist—the underlying argument was not compatible with empirical evidence from the EMS. This paradox is discussed briefly below.

In the 1970s and 1980s, the "New Classical revolution" in macroeconomics amounted to the practice of putting any model of output fluctuations and unemployment under the categorical imperative of "rigorous" microeconomic foundations. The stochastic-dynamic versions of Walrasian general equilibrium theory that came to dominate the mainstream were generally based on the assumptions of rational expectations, flexible prices, and continuous market clearing. Prior to the 1970s, cyclical fluctuations of output had been treated as deviations from equilibrium, defined as potential output along the growth trend; they were essentially considered as disequilibria of aggregate demand and supply. In contrast with this view, New Classical models set the focus on the derivation of "natural rates" of unemployment and output and on the understanding of short-term output fluctuations as equilibria. Deviations of current GDP growth rates and unemployment rates from their "natural" levels were essentially explained as optimizing private-sector reactions to inefficient economic policies.

In this tradition, Kydland and Prescott (1977) and Barro and Gordon (1983) argued in their well-known papers about "time inconsistency" that discretionary policies would not be credible, even if they were explicitly aimed at monetary stability. Whenever the inflation target would be achieved, policymakers would have an incentive to promote growth and employment by way of low interest rates and a rise in public spending, in order to increase their tax revenues and chances of reelection. Since the private sector understands the incentives for such "surprise inflation" once it has happened, the expansionary effects of such measures vanish quickly. With rational expectations, market agents will adjust their plans to the extent that higher inflation rates result, but there is no gain in real growth. Announcing a policy of price-level stabilization is thus interpreted as a game between the government and the private sector, in which the government's position is dynamically inconsistent and, hence, not credible. Even if the government does not have "surprise inflation" in mind, an inflation bias arises. If the monetary authorities try to break inflationary expectations by means of high interest rates, disinflation will be achieved only at a substantial cost in terms of losses of output and employment.

The vast literature that followed Barro and Gordon (1983) led to the conclusion that stabilization policy is credible only if policymakers give up their discretionary flexibility of action and commit themselves to combating inflation by setting a clear rule for monetary policy.[3] Contrary to Milton Friedman's famous dictum, it was argued that the transition from active "fine-tuning" to rule-bound policy would provide a "free lunch." Strict adherence to a rule would facilitate the direct transition from an inflation-bias equilibrium to a low-inflation equilibrium at the same "natural rate of output" (the vertical long-run Phillips curve). Hence, it would significantly reduce the costs of disinflation in terms of output gaps and unemployment.

Despite the great popularity of time-inconsistency models, they are not very plausible. Given the well-known lags of monetary (and fiscal) policies, it is highly improbable that a central bank would be capable of "shocking" the markets out of their "natural rates" by surprise inflation, especially if rational expectations are assumed (Goodhart 1994). Moreover, the time-inconsistency models are at odds with the evidence from the EMS era, during which Germany experienced comparatively high costs of disinflation. This contrast between theory and evidence merits a closer look.

Contrary evidence

Germany was a model case of rule-bound monetary policy and credible disinflation in the 1980s and 1990s. After the breakdown of the Bretton Woods system, the Bundesbank was the first central bank that switched to rule-bound policy, when it defined a monetary target (in terms of base money, or M0) for the year 1975. In repeated games with trade unions, it was successful in breaking inflationary expectations by stepping up short-term interest rates until they would take effect in the goods and labor markets. Since the Bundesbank enjoyed a high degree of operational independence, followed a clear rule with the aim of keeping inflation low, and set the price for the key currency in the EMS, it was regarded as one of the most credible monetary authorities in the 1980s and 1990s. According to the logic of the "time inconsistency" (or "active policy ineffectiveness") argument, Germany's costs of disinflation should have been comparatively low in the EMS period. Likewise, other countries that made strong commitments to keeping their exchange rates fixed to the deutsche mark should have benefited in terms of low costs of disinflation.

The evidence presented in Figure 3.1 falsifies these hypotheses. To put it mildly, adhering strictly to monetary policy rules does not seem to have produced the predicted cost advantages, at least not in the 1980s and 1990s. The figure shows the disinflation costs for a representative choice of countries, incurred during the disinflation rallies of these two decades. Disinflation costs are measured in terms of sacrifice ratios, which relate the cumulative changes in the rates of unemployment to the difference of inflation rates achieved in the course of the disinflation process.[4]

Using sacrifice ratios alone may produce an "inflation bias." Given identical changes in unemployment and the same relative change in inflation, the costs of disinflation would appear to be higher in economies that start at low levels of inflation and unemployment. In Figure 3.1, the sacrifice ratios were therefore adjusted with the OECD misery index values, i.e., the sums of unemployment and inflation levels. The selection of countries corresponds to the G7 of the time—with the exception of Canada, which was replaced by Portugal and Sweden. The latter two are suitable examples of strict commitment (in the case of Sweden) and not-so-strict commitment (in the case of Portugal) to deutsche-mark exchange-rate targets in the early 1990s.

Ranking the countries by their disinflation costs in the 1980s, it is obvious that the level-adjusted sacrifice ratios for Germany were far above the average, despite low levels of inflation. Even in the 1990s, the German performance was poor, beaten only by Italy, which tried hard to meet the Maastricht criteria by cutting deficit spending, and by France and Sweden, which—in vain attempts to "preserve credibility"—stuck to exchange-rate targets at the cost of extremely high interest rates and

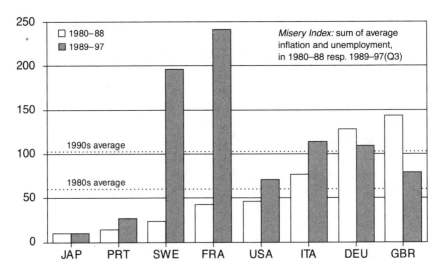

Figure 3.1   Level adjusted disinflation costs in the 1980s and 1990s. Sacrifice Ratios × Misery Indices. Sources: OECD, Bundesbank, own calculations.

strong recessions.[5] In the course of the EMS crisis in 1992–1993, all three countries had to give up their original targets as they became the targets of speculative attacks.[6]

Figure 3.1 is a simple piece of snapshot empiricism, but its key results are supported by more sophisticated studies that include estimations of output gaps and other concepts of disinflation costs (e.g., Fischer 1996; Gärtner 1997; Ball 1999). Moreover, by the 1990s, it was commonplace to see a connection between the disinflation rallies of the Bundesbank and the strong increases of unemployment in Germany and other countries that had pegged their currencies to the deutsche mark (such as France and Sweden). Even if the blame for the rises in unemployment was frequently placed on (alleged or observed) rigidities in the labor markets, the core argument of the "rules versus discretion" literature should have come under doubt: why would such rigidities survive in a world of rational agents? Asserting the superiority of passive stabilization in terms of disinflation costs was clearly at odds with empirical observations at all levels. Why were the credibility arguments of that literature credible enough to be used for backing the discussions about the institutional setup of the EMU?

EMU coordination problems

Coordinating rhetorics

It should not be forgotten that the EMU was the result of a political bargain, in which Germany gave up its exclusive advantage of setting interest rates and controlling inflation. It may have been hoped in some quarters—especially those that took the initiative to create the EMU—that a common monetary policy would give greater leeway for growth-supporting policies, just as argued along the soft pro line. Given the experiences with "softening" currencies in Italy, France, and elsewhere after 1973, it was nevertheless widely accepted that growth and employment could not be fostered by inflationary accommodation of fiscal spending. It was recognized that the Bundesbank had frequently been able to exploit its credibility in the financial markets to keep interest rates lower than required by the monetary targets. It had missed its targets on the expansionary side more than half the time (1975–1998), without losing credibility or generating expectations of higher inflation. This gave the hard pro line some advantage in the discussions about the design of the EMU.

In the 1970s and 1980s, the Bundesbank had used monetarist rhetorics to explain its strategy—for example, by formulating its targets in terms of a dynamic version of the Fisherian exchange equation. When the ECB (then the European Monetary Institute) was preparing to take over in the 1990s, continuity in communication was considered of utmost importance for establishing the common currency in the financial markets. The "rules versus discretion" literature provided such continuity plus more fashionable (Lucasian) foundations for a Bundesbank-like policy of inflation control. The literature's implausibility in terms of disinflation costs was not terribly important for acceptance in the world of finance. On the contrary, the credibility of monetary policy in financial markets may differ crucially from credibility in the political arena or in a welfare-maximizing general equilibrium model. For financial investors, hard-nosed policies that succeed with disinflation in spite of high social costs tend to be more credible than strategies of minimizing sacrifice ratios—as long as they are perceived to be politically viable.[7] To establish the euro as a prime asset in the financial markets was of primary concern not only from the points of view of the hard pro line or the single-market line. If the ECB succeeded in gaining credibility, other countries in the eurozone could hope to see their interest rates converge "downward" to those of Germany. In this roundabout way, the policy conclusion of the Barro-Gordon argument became plausible: rule-bound policies would lower inflationary expectations and nominal interest rates in some of the countries. However, if this helped to increase output and employment in a systematic fashion, the neutrality postulate inherent in the "natural rates" economics of the Barro-Gordon argument would not easily survive. The expansionary effects of interest-rate convergence were one of the reasons why the EMU could be interpreted as a project of active stabilization along the soft pro line of argument.

Similarly, the limits on deficit spending in the Maastricht criteria and the SGP were not particularly well grounded in theory but considered necessary to achieve fiscal consolidation to the extent that interest-rate convergence would become credible. There was no clear-cut economic argument for limiting deficit spending to 3 percent of GDP (and gross debt to 60 percent)—not even in terms of "Ricardian equivalence" in the tradition of Barro (1974). As the *Economist* reported during the Maastricht negotiations, the limits were chosen by an alliance of German, Dutch, British, and other officials with the intention of "keeping the PIGS out." "PIGS" alluded to Portugal, Italy, Greece, and Spain, which were deemed to be prone to fiscal profligacy and inflation. In the end, all four candidates qualified into the EMU, along with Germany, which had no small difficulties of meeting the deficit criterion. As a consequence of interest-rate convergence after the start of the EMU, Spain rapidly achieved a surplus position in its government budgets.

The EMU record

So far (as of summer 2008), the EMU has been a success story—at least, if the record is related to its prime objective of monetary stability. As Figure 3.2 shows, eurozone inflation has stayed close to the 2 percent target; on average, it was lower than German inflation during the 1990s. Some of the inflationary impulses can be considered endogenous to the EMU, as they resulted from tax increases in the course of SGP-related consolidation; the major impulses came from price rises in the world markets for fuel, food, and raw materials. From a European perspective, these developments can largely be considered external supply shocks, to which—even according to the logic of the "rules versus discretion" literature—monetary policy should not act in the same restrictive fashion as to internal demand shocks.

Furthermore, the effective exchange rate of the euro (its external value in indirect terms, both nominal and real) is currently 15 percent higher than at the start of the EMU in 1999 (ECB 2008). The changes in the dollar-euro exchange rate do not entirely reflect a depreciation of the U.S. dollar; they also signal an appreciation of the euro, which has begun to take over the role of an international reserve currency.

The growth and employment record of the EMU is less clear-cut. Compared with other world regions, the eurozone was considered stagnant, with weak growth and high unemployment, in the years after the burst of

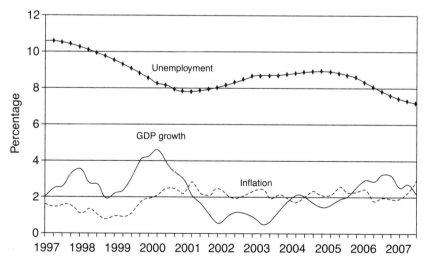

Figure 3.2   Macroeconomic indicators for the euro area, 1997–2007.
Source: ECB/Eurostat.

the dot-com bubble (i.e., 2001–2005). Yet it is far from clear that this can be ascribed to the ECB's struggle to achieve a hard-nosed reputation. Most of the comparative Taylor rule estimations suggest that the interest-rate policy of the ECB in its first years was not more restrictive than the Bundesbank's policy would have been under the same circumstances (for a survey, see Sauer and Sturm 2007, pp. 379–382). Such counterfactual exercises are, however, very sensitive to assumptions about expectations formation and long-run real interest rates. The ECB policy at the earliest stage looks more restrictive, if the estimations and simulations are based on forward-looking expectations and the generally lower level of real interest rates that prevailed in the markets after the bursting of the dot-com bubble (Hayo and Hoffmann 2006; Sauer and Sturm 2007). When the years after 2003 will be included in future studies, the picture might change again.

In a structural assessment of the monetary policy effects on different economies in the euro area, the picture is even more varied. Obviously, the "one size fits all" policy of setting identical nominal interest rates throughout the euro area generates different real interest rates, depending on local inflation and growth conditions. In this context, "active stabilization" can imply different things, namely, (a) boosting growth in peripheral member economies and achieving real convergence and (b) synchronizing and mitigating business cycles. Both meanings can be related to current discussions about "monetary stress" or "the stress of having a single monetary policy in Europe" (Sturm and Wollmershäuser 2008), where structural and cyclical stress is defined "as the difference between the ECB main refinancing rate and the policy interest rate" in a particular member country of the EMU "that would prevail if that country would have been able to follow a for that country 'optimal' monetary policy" (Sturm and Wollmershäuser 2008, p. 32).[8] It is generally concluded that the ECB rates were clearly lower than the (counterfactual) instrument rates that central banks in Ireland, Portugal, Spain, Greece, and Finland would have had to set if they had stayed outside the EMU. Germany is the only case of "positive stress," in which the ECB rates were slightly higher than independent German interest rates would have been. The other countries (France, Italy, the Netherlands, Belgium, and Austria) do not appear to have suffered much stress from the single monetary policy.

Ireland, Portugal (temporarily), Spain, Greece, and Finland have enjoyed relatively high growth rates since the time when it was expected that they would join the EMU. It might be argued that the euro has helped these countries at the periphery to catch up with the EMU core and that they thereby could overcome their structural disadvantages of EMS membership. The EMU could thus be interpreted as a success in terms of active stabilization—especially as it does not seem to have created much stress for the other member countries. However, it is less clear whether the single monetary policy has helped to synchronize and mitigate business cycles. At this point, the two interpretations of active stabilization may get in the way of each other. The drawback of rapid growth in the periphery is higher inflation vis-à-vis the EMU core. This implies an appreciation of the real exchange rates and reduces the price competitiveness of producers in the EMU periphery. This may produce asynchronous cycles and give rise to a dynamic instability of the EMU that is not well addressed by the current system of macropolicy coordination in the union.

The potential instability of the EMU

By articles 105–109 of the Maastricht treaty, the ECB was given a high degree of independence to pursue the single objective of safeguarding price-level stability. Ever since the inception of the ECB, its officials have emphasized that the bank is responsible only for inflation control. From an organizational point of view this is understandable, since this single-mindedness has made it easier to establish and stabilize the euro. The EMU shares, however, one basic problem with the EMS: the central bank that sets the interest rates for the system must work by the principle "one size *has to fit* all." The nominal anchor may have shifted from the German price level to a eurozone average, but the mission seems to preclude the use of interest-rate policies, not only for the stabilization of average output but also for minimizing structural and cyclical differences in growth and inflation between member economies.

This task has thus been left to national fiscal policies. Yet, under the auspices of the SGP, individual governments' room to maneuver had been limited. Even if governments resorted only to passive stabilization (in the sense of not tinkering with the automatic stabilizers), they found it generally difficult to stay within the framework of the pact. What the SGP reform of 2005 is worth in terms of coordinated active stabilization remains to be seen in the next recession.

Much of the burden of stabilization policies has thus been left to wage-setting institutions in the member countries, an arena where trans-European coordination is extremely difficult. In the years after the start of the EMU (in particular 2001–2006), wage moderation led to a "split business cycle" in the core of euroland: by keeping inflation extremely low, wage restraint in Germany contributed to an export boom but also to relatively high real interest rates and stagnation in the domestic economy. In other countries, such as Spain and Ireland, declining nominal interest rates encouraged investment and increased GDP growth at inflation rates above the eurozone average, which in turn spurned wage growth. The corresponding rise in the real exchange rates was compensated for by a fall in real interest rates, at least for a while. Sooner or later, however, the instability problem of the EMS might return through the back door: the surplus in the German trade balance vis-à-vis "appreciating" EMU members will put disinflationary pressures on those countries, either through reduced demand for their products or through a differentiation of nominal interest rates that is required to attract compensating capital flows. In the long run, such pressures might be even more detrimental for real investment and employment than they were in the EMS. Under the single monetary policy, wage moderation tends to strangle the German economy, while the countries with trade deficits can no longer resort to nominal devaluation.

At present, the EMU suffers from a lack of macropolicy coordination, since it is not clear which institution(s) would take the responsibility for stabilizing output at the European level. Nor is it evident how this coordination problem, if and when it manifests itself in a crisis, could be overcome by institutional reform. In order to assess the potential for active stabilization, it might be useful to step back and take a look at the similarities and differences between older concepts of active stabilization and the institutional setup of the EMU.

EMU and Keynesian policies

What would Keynes have thought of the EMU?

The question might appear a bit silly, given that Keynes—following his own prediction—has now been "dead in the long run" and that he changed his opinions quite a few times while he was alive, not to speak of the many different interpretations of his writings ever after. Yet, in a book that carries the title "The Return to Keynes" there is some temptation to relate Keynes's ideas about stabilization to the EMU project. Most obviously, the development of Keynes's proposals for an international clearing union, which eventually resulted in the Keynes Plan discussed at the Bretton Woods conference in 1944, provides some material for such discussion. At first sight, both the parallel and difference vis-à-vis the EMU may seem larger than they really are once the historical contexts of Bretton Woods and Maastricht are taken into account. There is actually a direct line of pedigree from the Keynes Plan of 1944 to the EMS and the EMU project of 1991–1998.

Already the first memoranda about "post-war currency policy" and "proposals for an international currency union" (CWK 25, pp. 21–40), both written in September 1941, contained notions that look surprisingly much like anticipations of the EMU debate. Keynes considered the currency union as "an ideal scheme which would preserve the advantages of an international means of payment universally acceptable, whilst avoiding the features of the old system which did the damage" (CWK 25, p. 32). He admitted that the proposal is open to the objection "not that it is impracticable, but that it assumes a higher degree of understanding, of the spirit of bold innovation, and of international co-operation and trust than it is safe or reasonable to assume" (CWK 25, p. 33). Five years later, when it had become clear that the new economic world order followed the White Plan (of the United States) far more than the Keynes Plan (of the United Kingdom), Keynes (CWK 26, p. 232) noted that "the Fund can scarcely be, at any rate in the early years, the nucleus of a super-central bank, such as we hoped." The fund in question was what came to be known as the International Monetary Fund.

Yet it would be rash to conclude from these citations that a full-scale monetary union with a supranational central bank, a single monetary policy, and a single financial market is what Keynes had in mind in the early 1940s. As various versions of the proposals document, he envisaged a clearing union between different currency areas, in which the "Bancor," the "international bank money" (CWK 25, p. 111), would function as a unit of account and exclusive reserve currency but not as a common currency in the sense of legal tender. Coordinated realignments of exchange rates would be allowed or even enforced whenever trade imbalances exceeded predefined levels. And the "super-central bank" would essentially be a trade-facilitating clearing agency, not an inflation-controlling interest-rate setter. Moreover, Keynes (CWK 25, pp. 52–54) pleaded for "central control of capital movements, both inward and outward" as a permanent feature of the system.

The core idea of the Keynes Plan was to avoid the contractionary pressures of the "old system," i.e., the gold standard, with its asymmetry of adjustment burdens in the case of trade imbalances and "debtor positions on the international balance of payments" (CWK 25, pp. 27–31). The plan aimed "at the substitution of an expansionist, in place of a contractionist, pressure on world trade" (CWK 25, p. 112). The clearing union was to work with overdraft facilities and a reserve fund fed by fees from debtors and creditors. The burdens of adjustments to trade imbalances would be shared symmetrically. Maximum debit balances were to be determined by reference to the foreign trade of the deficit countries, and surplus countries were obliged to discuss with the governing board of the clearing union "what measures would be appropriate to restore the equilibrium of its international balances"—including domestic credit expansion, appreciation, wage increases, reductions of tariffs and other trade barriers, and "international loans for the development of backward countries" (CWK 25, p. 120).

While the Keynes Plan failed to gain acceptance in 1944, many of its elements were incorporated in the construction of the EMS as envisaged by the European Council in December 1978. In a system of symmetric burden sharing, the ECU was supposed to play the same role as the Bancor, the exchange-rate mechanism (ERM) was aimed at multilateral stabilization within the ECU-related parity grid, and the setup of a European Monetary Cooperation Fund was planned in order to mitigate imbalances in the system. It should also be noted that exchange controls were still in place in many of the EMS countries at the time of the system's inception. However, as explained earlier, the EMS never worked symmetrically. The surplus countries (in particular, Germany) had no incentives to cooperate because it was unclear what would stop deficit countries from running into further debts and devaluations.

Given that in reality the EMS developed contractionary pressures, it is likely that Keynes would have welcomed the EMU as a leap forward into a more symmetric and expansionary regime. In a full-scale currency union, member economies with trade deficits do not encounter—or do so only with some delay—the liquidity restrictions that countries with "adverse" balances of payments face in other regimes. Even though the nascent "single financial market" of Europe is open to global in- and outflows of capital, the degree of autonomy in interest-rate setting enjoyed by the ECB is certainly higher than that of most EMS member banks when they had exchange controls in operation. Moreover, Keynes might have accepted the strong commitment to rules that has characterized the introduction of the EMU. In the second version of his proposal, written in November 1941, Keynes (CWK 25, p. 45) argued that an "international bank" differs from a national central bank in the sense that "much more must be settled by rules and by general principles agreed beforehand and much less by day-to-day discretion. To give confidence in, and understanding of, what is afoot, it is necessary to prescribe beforehand certain definite principles of policy, particularly in regard to the maximum limits of permitted overdraft and the provisions proposed to keep the scale of individual credits and debits within a reasonable amount, so that the system is in stable equilibrium with proper and sufficient measures taken in good time to reverse excessive movements of individual balances in either direction."

It is clear, however, that some of Keynes's rules—such as those for reducing net credit positions by way of credit expansion, wage increases, and development aid—would be considered rather unorthodox in the present EMU setting.

Keynesian standards

Even by the standards of postwar mainstream Keynesianism, the EMU can be judged as a project of active stabilization—at least in principle. As Padoa-Schioppa has argued since the early 1980s (based on Mundell's open economy trilemma), the EMS suffered from the problem of an inconsistent quartet—free trade, capital mobility, fixed exchange rates, and independence of national monetary policies (Padoa-Schioppa 2004, pp. 11–15). With the introduction of the EMU, the last element had to go. This could be put in more positive terms: ineffective national policies were transformed into a supranational monetary policy that is more autonomous and more effective. Apart from Germany, EMU members have a greater influence on interest rates than they did before.

This accords with the conclusions one can derive from that old Keynesian workhorse of international macroeconomics, the Mundell-Fleming model. Whatever one may think of its IS/LM foundations, some of the policy conclusions are pretty robust and plausible (Krugman 1995). The first conclusion is that a bigger currency area is more autonomous in terms of monetary and fiscal policies. The second conclusion is that, at low inflation, flexible exchange rates vis-à-vis the rest of the world (as is now largely the case with the EMU) make monetary policy more effective than fiscal policy in stabilizing output. However, within the union (where exchange rates are irreversibly fixed), fiscal policies are more powerful. This simple argument could give some guidance as to how the potential instability of the EMU could be prevented from materializing: the ECB should accept greater responsibility for mitigating cyclical fluctuations of eurozone output, whereas national governments should use their fiscal policies to synchronize the cycles (in order to make the "one size monetary policy fit all") and to reduce structural output risks.

Epilogue

The need to develop new instruments and strategies of European macroeconomic policy became particularly clear when the world began to talk about the return of Keynes and the urgent need for fiscal stimulus. This was the case in late 2008, when the collapse of Lehman Brothers first led to panic in financial markets and then to a global downturn in real economic activity. The ECB did not cut interest rates as quickly and strongly as the Fed or the Bank of England, nor did it openly take to "quantitative easing"; it even increased interest rates in reaction to rising inflation as late as July 2008. But right after the first fallout from the U.S. subprime crisis in European banks in the summer of 2007, the ECB had already begun to use a lot of discretionary leeway to pump extra liquidity into the system by accepting "subprime" assets in repo transactions with commercial banks. It also acted visibly as a lender of last resort in the panic after the Lehman bankruptcy, and it cut its repo rate by more than half, from 4.25 to 2 percent between October 2008 and mid-January 2009. It is noteworthy that Jean-Claude Trichet, the ECB president, defended the decision not to go further (to near zero interest, as the Fed had done) by referring to the risk of a liquidity trap—acknowledging that the argument is "Keynesian if you wish" (ECB press conference, January 15, 2009). At the same time, governments in EMU member states had started to prepare and spend fiscal packages to stimulate and stabilize aggregate demand in their economies.

The crisis mix of EMU monetary and fiscal policies provides clear evidence of intentions of active stabilization, but it has also exposed various flaws in the current design of EMU macroeconomic policy. In the sphere of monetary policy, the functioning of the ECB as lender of last resort was hampered by the national fragmentation of banking supervision and fiscal policies. The bailout of private banks with public money (or guarantees) was essentially considered a national affair, to be handled by the finance ministries, despite the transnational character of the underlying banking business and its failures. While the governments had to act as borrowers of last resort to restore confidence in their domestic financial systems and to provide an outlet for savers, the ECB did not act as the matching lender of last resort, because it was loath (if not restricted by the Maastricht treaty) to monetize public debt; it instead took the risks of acquiring more dubious private debt. Moreover, the fiscal stimuli were not well coordinated among the governments in the euro area, and debates about beggar-thy-neighbor policies and protectionist tendencies aroused fears of disintegration and exits from the EMU, which were further fueled by a considerable rise in the spread of government bonds of the PIGS countries (plus Ireland) over their German counterparts. As of February 2009, such fears appeared to be greatly exaggerated. Even those economies that have suffered most from the crisis would probably have fared much worse outside the monetary union. Given the global nature of the crisis, exchange-rate autonomy would hardly have helped.

There is nonetheless great potential for improving the coordination of EMU monetary and fiscal policies in times of crisis. In particular, the current lack of fiscal coordination must be overcome, as it forces national policymakers to assuage taxpayers' fears of free-riding and moral hazard by using protectionist rhetoric, thereby putting the single market and the agenda for further integration at risk. Moreover, there is the need to develop a strategy for "cleaning up" after the present crisis and for redefining the scope of the rules in "normal times."

The most likely way out of the present dilemma of rhetorical self-restriction and insufficient coordination is a "muddling through," so typical for progress in the European Union. By a more pragmatic approach, the ECB might (unofficially) accept lower degrees of wage moderation in the surplus countries, while national governments (re)discover some of the advantages of countercyclical deficit spending. In order to preserve the demand management option for times of crisis, fiscal consolidation would be enforced in the upswing—just as in some "old Keynesian" manuals for social engineers.

Such a scenario would accord with Keynes's own change of perspectives on rules and discretion. As Keynes (CWK 25, p. 117) noted in the third version of his plan in January 1942,

> If rule prevails, the scheme can be made more water-tight theoretically. But if discretion prevails, it may work better in practice. All this is the typical problem of any super-national authority. An earlier draft of this proposal was criticised for leaning too much to the side of rule. In the provisions below the bias is in the other direction. For it may be better not to attempt to settle too much beforehand and to provide that the plan shall be reconsidered after an initial experimental period of (say) five years. Only by collective wisdom and discussion can the right compromise be reached between law and licence.

Notes

1. Since the writing of this article in spring 2008, the debt situation has changed dramatically. On this more below.
2. Historical accounts and stability analyses of the EMS are provided, e.g., by Eichengreen (1998, chap. 5), Spahn (2001, chap. 7), and De Grauwe (2003, chap. 6).
3. Other ways to signal commitment and self-restriction, such as by installing a hard-nosed central banker, were also discussed but need not be considered here.

4. The sacrifice ratio is thus expressed as the sum of the deviations of unemployment from the quarterly rate in the initial period of disinflation (defined as the period when official short-term interest rates peak) over the difference between the initial and the final inflation rates. In formal terms: $CD = \Sigma(u_t - u_0) / (p_0 - p_T)$, where u denotes unemployment; p, inflation; and T, the final period of disinflation, after which inflation begins to rise again.

5. In the case of Sweden, the central bank charged the commercial banks up to 500 percent in overnight rates in order to reduce speculative outflows of capital in September 1992.

6. In the set of Figure 3.1, the European Union's top performer in terms of disinflation cost minimization was actually Portugal, a country not known for strict adherence to any rules for macroeconomic policies.

7. This was not the case in France, where the referendum on the Maastricht treaty in September 1992, in the middle of a recession, cast doubts on the viability of disinflation. The lack of credibility of the Barro-Gordon argument fed back to the financial markets and started speculative attacks on the French franc, even though France had, at the time, lower inflation rates than Germany.

8. "Optimality" is derived from a Taylor rule that minimizes deviations of inflation and output growth from their target rates, where output growth is defined as the expected change in the output gap. Obviously, a critical issue is the determination of potential output; see Trautwein (2009).

PART TWO

Interpreting Keynesian Theory
and Keynesianism

ART II IS COMPOSED OF THREE ESSAYS that are focused on evaluating some of the most important changes in macroeconomic thinking during the last four decades.

At the end of the 1960s, the dominant school of thought in macroeconomics was the Neoclassical Synthesis, which used the traditional neoclassical model of individual behavior to provide an underpinning for some of Keynes's aggregate models. This model neglected some of Keynes's most important insights, such as the centrality of expectations to capitalist economies, but it was a serviceable and easily tractable system that could be matched easily to the aggregate statistics collected for national income analysis.

The "old" Neoclassical Synthesis largely collapsed in the 1970s. The main cause for this collapse was (a) the model's inability to offer an adequate policy response to stagflation and (b) its arrival at a kind of "saturation point" in which further elaboration of a theory had been exhausted and nothing new could be hoped for within this well-established framework.

The next four decades might be conveniently divided into two phases—the dissolution within the Neoclassical School in the wider sense and the emergence of several anti-Neoclassical schools. Our treatment here is confined to the former.

Criticism of the "income-expenditure approach" was initiated by adherents of monetarism, with Milton Friedman as leader. The basic terrain for the dispute between these two schools was over the Phillips curve and the "natural rate of unemployment" hypothesis.

The Keynesian school was criticized even more harshly by the New Classical school of macroeconomics. The New Classical school maintains that economics is a science that should be deductively built from the following: (a) the "representative household," (b) rational expectations, (c) cardinal utility theory, and (d) dynamic stochastic general equilibrium (DSGE).

The New Classical school puts absolute trust in the working of the price mechanism (the equilibrating function) in the market economy. It severely criticizes discrete policymaking and forecasting based on Keynesian econometrics. The models of the New Classical school were not built just for the sake of abstract theory but were put forward as an alternative to Keynesian theory to explain and diagnose the actual economy, using the methodologies of "as if" modeling and "calibration."

In a sense, this approach might be said to have created a synthesis that incorporated only one point of view, traditional microeconomic modeling of individual behavior, while completely failing to include any serious treatment of many macroeconomic phenomena.

Within the mainstream of the economics profession, it was the New Keynesian school that first stood up against the New Classical school, emphasizing the imperfection in the working of the price mechanism in the market economy and searching for the causes for various kinds of price rigidities. Because they regard these price rigidities as the most essential elements in Keynesian economics, they call themselves the New Keynesians. However, the New Keynesian school shares in common the above-mentioned elements (a–d) with the New Classical school. Thus, it is not surprising that adherents of the New Keynesian school have come to be labeled the advocates of the "New" Neoclassical Synthesis.

The purpose of Chapter 4, by Richard Arena, is to compare the "old" and the "new" "Keynesian-Neoclassical Syntheses" (OKNS and NKNS, respectively). Arena discusses the extent to which the transition from the OKNS to the NKNS can be interpreted as a return to Keynes after the interim New Classical episode. In exploring this transition, the distinction between instrumental rationality and cognitive rationality is emphasized. Arena argues that the NKNS appears not to differ all that much from the OKNS. This similarity, according to him, underlines the long distance "Keynesianism" has, by now, traveled from Keynes's initial research program. Thus, while these two schools of thought have views that are split on whether the price mechanism of the market has the ability to adjust instantaneously or whether it possesses some kind of rigidity, the difference between the OKNS and NKNS has little to do with anything that Keynes was concerned with. The two approaches actually demonstrate an internal dissolution within the Neoclassical school.

Chapter 5, by Robert Dimand, is concerned with James Tobin as an innovator within the "old" Neoclassical Synthesis. In this chapter, Dimand examines what being an Old Keynesian meant to Tobin. Staking a distinctive claim to Keynes's heritage, Tobin criticized Post-Keynesians for "throwing away the insights of neoclassical economics," New Classical economists for sidestepping the central macroeconomic problems of coordination and stability, and the mainstream American Keynesians of his own generation for insufficient attention to asset markets and monetary policy. Tobin argued that the economy is self-adjusting for small shocks but not for very large ones.

In recent years, however, there has emerged another mainstream approach to macroeconomics, which pays more attention to Knut Wicksell's theory as argued in his *Interest and Prices* (1898). Michael Woodford is the representative of this movement, and his *Interest and Prices* (2003) melds the Wicksellian way of thinking with the New Keynesian model.

Chapter 6, by Mauro Boianovsky and Hans-Michael Trautwein, aims at evaluating the main parallels and differences between Michael Woodford's *Interest and Prices* (2003) and the issues raised by Wicksell and his followers, including Keynes. They explore the grounds where the Wicksellian connections of Keynes and Woodford diverge and argue that the New Neoclassical Synthesis cannot deal with some of the issues that were at the heart of the original Wicksellian and Keynesian approaches.

CHAPTER FOUR

From the "Old" to the "New" Keynesian-Neoclassical Synthesis: An Interpretation

Richard Arena

T HE PURPOSE of this contribution is to compare the two so-called Keynesian-Neoclassical Syntheses (KNSs), emerging in 1936 (with John Hicks) and in 1997 (with Marvin Goodfriend and Robert King), respectively, in terms of their origins, development, and theoretical contents. At first sight, this comparison between the "old" and the "new" KNSs (OKNS and NKNS, respectively) might come as a surprise: after all, more than sixty years separate the two "syntheses," during which our societies and economies, the state of economic thought, and the intellectual context of social sciences all have undergone such radical changes that such an exercise might appear to be of little interest. However, in this contribution, I argue that a careful comparison of both syntheses is actually useful if we wish to understand the overall evolution of the "Neoclassical" and "Keynesian" conceptual traditions as they always have and still prevail in the realm of macroeconomic theory. Moreover, I will also discuss the extent to which the transition from the OKNS to the NKNS can be interpreted as a return to Keynes after the interim New Classical episode.

This chapter consists of four parts. The first part stresses the historical and intellectual contexts of both syntheses, focusing on their emergence and on their respective interpretations of Keynes's research program. The second part is devoted to the notion of instrumental rationality. It shows that, far from being the reserve of the new synthesis, a systematic process of application of rational economic choice to consumption, investment, and monetary behaviors had already begun—if in a somewhat different manner—in 1936 and after. The third part considers the cognitive aspect of economic rationality and, in particular, the treatment of uncertainty and of the process of the formation of expectations, provided by the OKNS and the NKNS, respectively. Following on this discussion of microeconomic foundation, the fourth part focuses on the IS/LM model and dynamic general stochastic equilibria, the former being generally associated with the OKNS and the latter with the NKNS. I also analyze the rigidities that tend to prevail on the different macromarkets, generating short-run economic fluctuations. Surprisingly enough, at the end of the day, the NKNS appears not to differ all that much from the OKNS. In my view, this similarity underlines the long distance contemporary "Keynesianism" has, by now, traveled from Keynes's initial research program.

The emergence and formation of the OKNS and the NKNS

In many textbooks, the OKNS is presented as a comprehensive set of models and tools (including the IS/LM diagram, Modigliani's labor market, or the Phillips curve, for instance) as if these models and tools had been built simultaneously and formed a general and consistent view of Keynesian macroeconomics. In reality, these tools and models were developed gradually between the 1950s and the 1970s and progressively transformed the initial Hicksian version of the IS/LM model into a mature macroeconomic theory based on various famous successive contributions from Modigliani to Tobin. In this progressive development, four contributions played a major role, however. The first is obviously Hicks's famous 1937 paper in which Keynes's *General Theory* was summed up in the form of four interacting macroeconomic markets—the monetary, the financial, the consumer goods, and the saving/investment markets—culminating in two curves determining an equilibrium rate of interest and an equilibrium level of national income. During the decades to come, this IS/LM diagram gained canonical status and general acceptance as the rational foundation of the OKNS. The second essential contribution is Franco Modigliani's PhD dissertation published in revised form in a 1944 paper in which he suggested adding the missing labor market and production function equations to Hicks's model and abandoning flexible wages to restore Keynesian results. In this specific context, Keynes's "liquidity preference theory is not necessary to explain underemployment equilibrium; it is sufficient only in a limiting case, the 'Keynesian case.' In the general case it is neither necessary nor sufficient; it can explain this phenomenon only with the additional assumption of rigid money wages" (Modigliani 1944, pp. 75–76).

This conclusion is essential since Modigliani's contribution explicitly integrated a labor market into Keynesian macrotheory and attributed the origin of unemployment to exclusive wage rigidities. Klein's *Keynesian Revolution* (1947) also played its part, not because it produced new substantial analytical results but because it showed how the OKNS could be used as a set of theoretical principles capable of providing the rational foundations of an efficient macroeconomic policy. It actually generated a boost of new econometric model-building techniques and optimal policy design criteria, which helped governments to design and estimate the impact of various fiscal and monetary policies on unemployment and, later, on inflation. The last contribution to mention is certainly Samuelson's and Solow's 1960 paper. The authors were not the first to point out the empirical existence of Phillips curves, but they also stressed the difficulties arising for explanations of the relation between the rate of change of nominal wages and the level of unemployment. Their contribution paved the way to a more thorough study of the causes of inflation in a Keynesian framework that connected the labor and monetary markets in a way that differed from Modigliani's perspective.

Now, the emergence and foundation of the NKNS clearly displays a number of analogies with that of the OKNS. Like the OKNS, the NKNS is based on a canonical model. Inherited from Real Business Cycles theory, the dynamic general stochastic equilibrium (DGSE) model is not entirely different from the IS/LM model. To start with, the DGSE is an aggregate equilibrium model based on a series of interacting macromarkets, and it, too, includes only a limited number of (at least two) representative agents. Furthermore, the DGSE also provides a kind of benchmark model that facilitates the analysis of different scenarios, just as in the case of the various possible forms of the IS and LM curves, even if in the former case the differences between the various scenarios do not only derive from the nature of the relationships of saving, investment, and money demand, on the one hand, with the rate of interest and the national income, on the other. Rather, the different scenarios are also generated by rigidities or imperfections regarded as deviations from the market clearing and perfect competition of the DGSE model. By contrast with the IS/LM model, however, this model also considers the long-run path of the economy and therefore requires and makes use of specific dynamic methods and tools, such as dynamic optimization. This form of optimization involves a representative producer as well as a representative consumer who maximizes profit and utility within an intertemporal framework, a feature that obviously was totally absent from the IS/LM framework. In line with the OKNS, the NKNS also assumes market rigidities, even if their microfoundations are more sophisticated (namely, related to a sticky-information Phillips curve along the lines of Mankiw and Reis [2002] and monopolistic competition among firms along the lines of Calvo [1983]). Modigliani's assumption of wage rigidities is therefore developed further and generalized to the goods as well as to labor markets. Similarly, the NKNS is also closely concerned with the requirements of economic policy design. Most of the contributors to this new synthesis are also economic policy analysts, and the elaboration of an efficient macroeconomic policy is usually their main objective (see, for instance, Clarida, Galì, and Gertler's "The Science of Monetary Policy," published in 1999 in the *Journal of Economic Literature*). Thus, Goodfriend recently (2002) wrote what he called a "primer" of economic policy, defining it as "an introduction to the benchmark NNS [namely, NKNS in my terminology] macromodel and its recommendations for monetary policy" (Goodfriend 2002, p. 165). This remark shows that Goodfriend is just as involved in policymaking today as Klein was in the 1950s. Finally, one should note that, like the OKNS, the NKNS contributed to the construction of a Phillips curve. This New Keynesian Phillips curve provided microeconomic foundations by combining nominal rigidities with the optimizing behavior of representative firms. The resulting curve differs from the traditional Phillips curve mainly in that it is generally forward-looking whereas the OKNS Phillips curve is backward-looking. This difference entails, however, substantial consequences for the definition of an optimal monetary policy.

These analogies find further support when one considers the reduced version of the NKNS represented by a set of three equations sometimes called the "new IS/LM model." This model consists of a "forward-looking" IS curve, describing the demand for goods as depending on the current real interest rate and expected future income; the inflation-adjustment IA curve, adopting a Calvo-style assumption of price stickiness to characterize the forward-looking pricing behavior of firms; and the monetary policy MP curve that fixes the interest rate policy of the monetary authority (see, e.g., Clarida, Galì, and Gertler 1999; Goodfriend 2002; Walsh 2003; Woodford 2003; Ireland 2004; De Vroey and Malgrange 2006).

This said, these fairly substantial similarities between both syntheses should not distract attention away from the differences between them. The analysis of these differences does, however, require us to enter into a more detailed discussion of the respective analytical foundations of both syntheses. We start with a consideration of instrumental and cognitive forms of rationality.

Instrumental rationality

The conceptualization of expectations and uncertainty that today prevails in the NKNS is entirely different from the understanding of the concepts that Keynes tried to promote in his time (Arena 2004). Keynes never really rejected the instrumental side of economic rationality, namely, the capacity of agents to carry out calculations and to search for the best possible solution, given a set of pieces of information. From this perspective, his only criticism of the notion of economic instrumental rationality relates to his objection to the "second postulate of the classical theory" on labor markets in chapter 2 of the *General Theory*: the workings of goods and labor market implied that "there may be *no* method available to labor as a whole whereby it can bring the wage-goods equivalent of the general level of money-wages into conformity with the marginal disutility of the current volume of employment" (CWK 7, p. 13). In other words, wage earners could not minimize their labor disutility with respect to the real wage, but the reasons for this impossibility were to be found in the institutional mechanisms of a market economy rather than in the behavior of individual workers themselves.

By contrast, Keynes was strongly skeptical as regards the cognitive side of economic rationality, namely, the capacity of agents to gather the complete or a part of the complete information: for him, information was very often incomplete and imperfect, and subjective probabilities were not a satisfactory tool of decision-making (Arena 2004). Put differently, "Keynes drew a sharp distinction between calculable risks and the uncertainty which arises from lack of reliable information. Since the future is essentially uncertain, strictly rational behavior is impossible; a great part of economic life is conducted on the basis of accepted conventions" (Robinson 1975, pp. 125–126).

Let us now first consider how the OKNS and the NKNS, respectively, take account of the notion of instrumental rationality. Amongst the defenders of the old synthesis, Modigliani remarked that "[one of the] basic themes that has dominated my scientific concern [has been to integrate] the main buildings blocks of the *General Theory* with the most established methodology of economics, which rests on the basic postulate of rational maximizing behavior on the part of economic agents" (Modigliani 1980, p. 11, quoted by Blanchard 2008, p. 1).

This standpoint allowed the construction of a necessary "bridge" for those interested in a conciliation of Keynesian macroeconomics with traditional microeconomics. The problem was not to reconcile Keynes's macroeconomics and microeconomics since the latter was never fully developed. Rather, it consisted in reconciling Keynesian macroeconomics with neo-Walrasian microeconomics in order to avoid the "no-bridge" situation stressed by Samuelson. The "bridge" was consolidated by Klein, who dedicated a substantial part of his *Keynesian Revolution* to "the Keynesian system and rational behavior" (Klein 1947, pp. 56–74). Klein set out by stressing that "community consumption depends upon the rate of interest and the level of real community income" directly derived from the aggregation of neoclassical individual demand functions (Klein 1947, pp. 57–58). He then proceeded to argue that "the basic Keynesian theory of the demand for capital goods is based on the most classically accepted doctrine of profit maximization," adding that "again it seems best to develop a treatment from the behavior of an individual unit following an optimal principle, and then to derive the aggregative relationship for the economy as the whole" (Klein 1947, p. 62).

Finally, Klein also noted that "in order to derive the investment function from the theory of profit maximization, we had to introduce the production function which expressed the technological relationship between the total output and the input of the factors of production, labor and capital. The process of profit maximization with respect to variations of capital subject to the above technological relation enabled us to derive the investment function. Profits should also be maximized with respect to labor input which leads to the proposition that the average real wage rate equals the marginal product of labor, i.e., the contribution to output of the last man-hour" (Klein 1947, p. 74).

Klein's and Modigliani's contributions are perfectly convergent. Modigliani (1944) also began to build production function equations. He introduced a labor supply curve as a function of the real wage. He also derived a labor demand function from the production function, assuming labor market clearing in the "neoclassical" case (obtaining "classical" results from a "Keynesian-like" set of equations) and rigid money wages in the "Keynesian" case (obtaining "Keynesian" results without any help from the theory of liquidity preference).

As pointed out earlier, Keynes never denied this instrumental side of economic rationality. However, the emphasis put by Klein and Modigliani on the necessity of conciliating Keynesian macroeconomics with neoclassical microfoundations paved the way for the extension of the validity of a strong rationality assumption to the field of information search and, therefore, to the cognitive side of economic rationality. Second, the implicit introduction of microeconomic foundations to Keynesian macroeconomic theory facilitated the consideration, for both authors, of problems of wage and price imperfections. Moreover, the acceptance of the neoclassical concept of economic coordination as an analytical benchmark derived from the case of pure competition and the assumption of market-clearing implied an automatic focus on relevant causes of coordination failure.

The NKNS went much further down the road paved by the OKNS as regards instrumental rationality. As Blanchard noted,

> like the old synthesis, the new synthesis is derived from micro-foundations, utility maximization by consumers, and profit maximization by firms. But, while models in the old synthesis used theory as a loose guide to empirical specifications and allowed the data to determine the ultimate specification, models in the new synthesis remain much closer to their micro-foundations. Dynamics are derived from the model itself, and the implied behavioral equations, rather than being estimated, are typically derived from assumptions about underlying technological and utility parameters. These more explicit micro-foundations allow for a more careful welfare analysis of the implications of policy than was possible with the old models. (Blanchard 2008, p. 5)

Blanchard clearly refers to DGSE models in which agents are endowed with both instrumental and cognitive forms of strong rationality. Instrumental rationality means that agent decisions should respect the usual axioms of individual behavior required by the general economic equilibrium theory framework. There is here a continuity with the transformation, promoted by the OKNS, of Keynes's initial macroeconomic relations into optimizing "micro-founded" macrofunctions. This as well as the cognitive form of rationality does not apply to individual agents but to a representative agent. By contrast with the OKNS, the NKNS focuses on agents whose microeconomic behavior is explicitly representative of the behavior of all aggregated agents of the economy. This assumption is not negligible since it requires some form of homogeneity within the agent set: either agents are identical or else they are sufficiently numerous to form a continuum. This kind of reasoning has strongly be called into question by contributors to both the OKNS and the NKNS. Thus, Tobin (2001, p. 129) noted:

> I think it's important for the behavioral equations of a macroeconomic model not to contradict choice-theoretic considerations, to be in principle consistent with them. But I think the stronger version of "micro foundations" is a methodological mistake, one that has produced a tremendous

amount of mischief. I refer to the now orthodox requirement of postulating representative agents whose optimizations generate "macroeconomic" behavioral equations. That is a considerable sacrifice of the essence of much of macroeconomics. Suppose you have a lot of different types of agents, who are all maximizing. Then it's their aggregation into a behavioral equation that you want for a macro model. That aggregation won't necessarily be the solution for any single agent. To insist that it must be seems to me very wrong-headed. It has put us on the wrong track in macroeconomics, or what passes for macroeconomics.

The representative agent assumption was also severely criticized for its inability to reflect the "stylized facts" of the real world. Solow, for instance, considers that the relevance for the real world of the core of a DGSE model is very low since it is based on a single representative consumer able to optimize over an infinite time horizon with rational expectations. This is why, like some New Keynesians (e.g., Greenwald and Stiglitz 1993), he noted the following:

> What is needed for a better macroeconomics? My crude caricature of the Ramsey-based model suggests some of the gross implausibilities that need to be eliminated. The clearest candidate is the representative agent. Heterogeneity is the essence of a modern economy. In real life we worry about the relations between managers and shareowners, between banks and their borrowers, between workers and employers, between venture capitalists and entrepreneurs, you name it. We worry about those interfaces because they can and do go wrong, with likely macroeconomic consequences. We know for a fact that heterogeneous agents have different and sometimes conflicting goals, different information, different capacities to process it, different expectations, different beliefs about how the economy works. Representative-agents models exclude all this landscape, through the needs to be abstracted and included in macro-models. (Solow 2003, p. 1)

Cognitive rationality

Keynes considered the problem of cognitive rationality in relation to three different situations. The first situation corresponds to "rational beliefs" (not rational expectations). These beliefs are not really proved or demonstrated to be true, but there are possible grounds on which to consider them probable. According to Keynes (CWK 8, p. 5), probability relations express only "the degree of our rational belief in the conclusion." These rational beliefs cannot properly be characterized as knowledge since knowledge is not defined as a probable rational belief but as a certain one (CWK 8, pp. 10–11). This is why, for Keynes, knowledge is associated only with "the highest degree of rational belief" (CWK 8, p. 10). This corresponds to the second situation. In the third situation, the "weight" of any possible probability judgment tends toward zero. In this case, the "basis" of a "strictly mathematical forecasting . . . does not exist" (CWK 7, p. 59). Men behave according to what they think to be the best possible solution, but, obviously, most of the time rational arguments are replaced by "whim, feeling or luck" (ibid.). Other motives appear, which contribute to the substitution of rationality by "habit, instinct, preference, desire, will, etc." (CWK 29, p. 294). One of the most frequent motives is related to the necessity of creating a *convention,* understood as a common basis for the shared processes of forming varying individual expectations.

To some extent, the case of *short-term expectations* can be interpreted as a situation in which rational beliefs are valid. In this context, the influence of the past, that is, of a knowledge basis that can easily be acquired by everyone, provides the main explanation for individual decisions (see CWK 7). Therefore, producers tend to favor adaptive or extrapolative behavior since the reiteration of the past is the most likely possibility. This is the reason why "effective demand always reflects the current expectations of the real demand" (CWK 13, p. 603). By contrast, the context of *long-term expectations* does not allow the use of knowledge, strictly speaking, or even of rational beliefs. The main reason for this impossibility is the absence of an individual knowledge base that would allow entrepreneurs to make decisions. In these situations, the weight of probability tends toward zero, and sometimes probabilities even cease to be measurable. It is obvious that, for Keynes, long-term decisions are associated with incomplete information. Therefore, they exclude the use of the probability calculus. This is why in his 1937 *Quarterly Journal of Economics* article Keynes noted that what he meant by "uncertain" knowledge did not refer to the distinction between certainty and probability: there was simply no scientific basis on which to build any probability calculus. In such situations, agents adopt techniques of forecasting that are based on common sense or on the "practical observation of markets and of business psychology" (CWK 14, p. 161; see also Arena 2004).

Contrary to Keynes's threefold distinction (knowledge, rational beliefs, and conventional beliefs), the OKNS focused on the first two cases and considered that the use of the probability calculus is always possible, even if probabilities are subjective (Keynes did not accept the use of subjective probabilities; see Arena 2003). Thus, once Friedman introduced his "permanent income hypothesis" (Friedman 1957) and Modigliani and Brumberg their "life cycle hypothesis" (Modigliani and Brumberg 1954), Keynes's initial link between national consumption and income vanished. Little by little, the consumption function became an *intertemporal utility* *function*. The element that actually rendered the Modigliani and Brumberg multiperiod life-cycle analysis tractable under subjective certainty was the specification of a homothetic lifetime utility function. This made it possible for planned consumption for each future period to be written as a function of expected wealth as seen at the planning date. Therefore, the life cycle hypothesis changed not only the theoretical role attributed to the consumption function but also its contents. Wealth entered the consumption function as a new variable, and since intertemporal choices implied the consideration of discounted real wealth, the rate of interest also became an explanatory variable, which, after all, it had already been in the initial version of the IS/LM model. Some defenders of the OKNS also introduced an *investment function*. As noted, according to Klein, it was perfectly possible to derive the investment function from the theory of profit maximization. This task was accomplished by Eisner and Strotz (1963) and Jorgenson (1963). Hirshleifer (1958, 1965) had argued that investment ought to be conceived in the context of the maximization of the present value of the firm. Subsequently, Jorgenson (1963) provided a microtheoretic neoclassical theory of investment based on this notion. Effectively, Jorgenson's solution is to recast the optimal capital stock decision in an intertemporal form. Firms attempt to choose for their capital stock an intertemporal path that maximizes the present value of the firm. In this context, investment is defined as the instantaneous change in the optimal stock of capital. Thus, in principle, there is no investment unless there is some reason to change the optimal stock of capital or, alternatively, investment is derived from the adjustment path toward the optimal capital stock, K^*. Therefore, investment is seen as the adjustment from a given level of capital to the optimal level of capital stock, and thus Jorgensen's connection with Keynes is more than tenuous. In fact, for Keynes, "capital formation depends on long run appraisals of profits expectations and risks and on business attitudes toward bearing the risks. There are not simple predictable functions of current and recent economic events. Variations of the marginal efficiency of capital contain, for all practical purposes, important elements of autonomy and exogeneity" (Tobin 1977, p. 460).

However, here again and at least in the case of the investment function, the OKNS (or some of its advocates) opened the door to a theory in which the level of investment could be determined by solving an intertemporal optimization program. The OKNS also paid some attention to the role played by money demand and the demand for other financial assets. Markowitz (1952, 1959) was the first to argue that the element of risk needed be taken into account when decision-makers form expectations. In order to cope with risk, Markowitz made use of the newly developed expected utility theory and came up with the notion of optimal portfolio selection in the context of trade-offs between risk and return, focusing on the idea of portfolio diversification as a method of reducing risk. The idea of an optimal portfolio allocation was not alien to Keynes, which is why, in line with Baumol's 1952 theory of the money demand function, Tobin (1958) added money to Markowitz's analysis: Tobin argued that agents would diversify their savings between a risk-free asset (money) and a single portfolio of risky assets (which would be the same for everyone).

Here again, the NKNS retained but at the same time went beyond the concept of cognitive rationality that had tended to prevail within the OKNS. Cognitive rationality was presented as no more than a mere extension of the principle of rationality to the realm of expectations. In clear contrast to Keynes's views, agents behave "rationally," that is, as if they could permanently form mathematical conditional expectations of all the relevant variables revealed to them through available information, allowing them to avoid systematic errors. The hypothesis of rational expectations has repeatedly been contested by some defenders of the OKNS as well as of the NKNS (e.g., James Tobin), but it was not always obvious whether these criticisms were directed at the assumption itself or rather at the way in which it has been employed by New Classical theorists (see, e.g., Modigliani's critique). Be this as it may, this assumption has today come to be accepted by all the adherents of the NKNS. As S. Fischer (2001, p. 38) wrote, "the hypothesis, narrowly put, is simply that people form expectations using all available information and process it optimally. That seems to me a very nice methodological assumption."

The importance given to expectations and cognitive rationality within the NKNS is evident in the "New IS/LM model." This model incorporates expectations in ways that the traditional IS/LM model did not. Expectations affect both aggregate demand and aggregate supply. The theory provides precise indications of the particular way in which expectations should enter the analysis. The IS curve is derived (within the underlying microfoundations frameworks) from the utility function of a representative household with consumption and real money balances as endogenous variables and an intertemporal budget constraint, which introduces a forward-looking behavior on the demand side of the economy, since economic subjects face the choice between consumption and saving in every period. The IA curve refers to a form of price setting based on the assumption of firms acting under monopolistic competition and maximizing the present value of future profits. This maximization therefore incorporates forward-looking behavior into the supply-side of the economy. The LM curve results from the Fischer equation (based on an expected rate of inflation), the money demand function, and the money supply function. The Phillips curve is also expectational, being also related to the future rate of inflation by a forward-looking behavior.

Concerning information and economic policy, there is a clear contrast between both syntheses. The OKNS was supposed to provide the micro-foundations for the "fine-tuning" of economic policymaking (based on its Phillips curve, for instance). Within the NKNS, unpredictable recognition, implementation, and behavioral lags prevent the use of this policy design technique. By contrast, rough-tuning based on simple rules is of some use and may get the economy close to the optimum.

Macroeconomic market equilibria and price rigidities

As already mentioned, the IS/LM model came to occupy the place of a canonical model for the OKNS. However, the IS/LM macroequilibrium also served the purpose of a benchmark conceptualization. Based on a market-clearing labor market, this equilibrium is clearly Walrasian, and therefore, unemployment in the OKNS is measured as a deviation from this Walrasian benchmark. In order to generate "unemployment equilibria" as solutions to the IS/LM equations, the advocates of the OKNS appealed to rigid money wages, interest-inelastic investment demand, income-inelastic money demand, or some other imperfections of this system. Markets could no longer be seen as competitive. However, no explicit bridge was built between these new views of markets and the emerging theories of imperfect competition of the 1930s and subsequent decades. Market adjustments were supposed to take time, but no explicit and precise explanation was provided. Yet, an essential distinction had to be made. If, in the short run, markets worked imperfectly, ceased to be competitive, and gave some space to economic policy, in the long run they were assumed to continue to work perfectly: for the first time, we enter a theoretical world where the short run was "Keynesian" and the long run "neoclassical," in clear contrast with what we noted earlier on Keynes's views of uncertainty in the short and the long periods. This dichotomy explains why the theory of economic growth could be developed independently from that of business cycles as well as from the analysis of short-term adjustments. As Samuelson noted, "solving the vital problems of monetary and fiscal policy by the tools of income analysis will validate and bring back into relevance the classical verities" (Samuelson 1955, p. 360).

How then was it possible, however, to justify the stickiness of prices and wages within this framework? Since theories of imperfect competition had been left to one side notwithstanding Phillips's seminal paper (Phillips 1958), it was a matter of awaiting Samuelson and Solow's 1960 paper to obtain an explicit treatment of the link between inflation and unemployment: when inflation was high, unemployment was low, and vice versa. In the Phillips curve analysis, when the unemployment rate was low, the labor market was tight and employers had to offer higher wages to attract scarce labor. At higher rates of unemployment, there was less pressure to increase wages. The Phillips curve represented the average relationship between unemployment and wage behavior over the business cycle. It showed the rate of wage inflation that would result if a particular level of unemployment persisted for some time. Significantly, however, the relationship between wages and unemployment changed over the course of the business cycle. When the economy was expanding, firms would raise wages faster than "normal" for a given level of unemployment; when the economy was contracting, they would raise wages more slowly than normal. These differences in the speed of adjustments contrast with the usual economic assumption of instantaneous price and wage flexibility. Their rationale is that "in modern capitalist societies, prices and wages respond slowly to excess demand or supply, especially slowly to excess supply. Over a long short run, ups and downs of demand register in output: they are far from completely absorbed in prices" (Tobin 1977, p. 459).

Finally, the proclaimed independence between short-run and long-run theories within the OKNS also permitted the introduction of a long-run theory of economic growth that did not have to face the imperfections of the short period. In the *General Theory*, Keynes focused only on the short-run aspects of investment, assuming, throughout the bulk of his analysis, that the marginal efficiency of capital had to be considered as given. Joan Robinson thought that Keynes's considerations on the long-run were not altogether convincing:

Keynes conceived of accumulation in the long run raising capital per head of the population and reducing the usefulness of further accumulation until no more investment would be needed for any important purpose. He took for granted that the rate of profit on capital would fall *pari passu* with the rate of return to society from investment. There is no suggestion that they are not necessarily the same thing or that what a business finds most profitable is not necessarily the best use of resources for the rest of the population. . . . His vision of long-run growth appears today to have been unrealistic rather than pernicious. At the time when *The General Theory* was being written, Keynes, projecting the situation of the slump into the future, threw out the suggestion that the need for accumulation could be overcome in thirty years of investment at the full-employment level, provided that wars were avoided and population ceased to grow. (Robinson 1975, p. 130)

This weakness of the vision of the long-run process of accumulation may well have made it easier for advocates of the NKNS to stick to their belief that Keynesian results were strictly "short-run," thus not really venturing into the realm of growth and business cycle theory, *strictu passu,* and to borrow, instead and entirely, from neoclassical theory to build their own growth models. However, one could argue that Harrod's model of growth is consistent with Keynes's general framework. First, Harrod perfectly stressed the dangers of a long-run fall of the rate of profit on capital (Harrod 1949, p. 32). Second, in line with Keynes's views on the inherent tendency of capitalist economies toward instability, Harrod showed that this tendency was fairly probable, emphasizing the unlikelihood of stable-equilibrium economic growth. However, as we know, in 1956, one of the main builders of the OKNS, Robert Solow, turned the Harrod growth model into a neoclassical model by adding a neoclassical (Cobb-Douglass) production function, based on an income distribution theory derived from the marginal productivity theory of capital and assuming constant returns to scale. He argued essentially that some kind of market mechanism reflecting the mobility of factors of production would bring the economy back to equilibrium and to the warranted growth rate whenever it deviated from the "golden rule." A large part of the NKNS school agreed with the Solowian version of growth theory, arguing that it describes the long-run aspect of their synthesis, in which neoclassical elements seem to prevail. Therefore, one of the OKNS builders prepared the way for the emergence of the views of adherents of the NKNS, in which the long-run trend, driven by the supply-side of the economy, converges toward a DGSE. As noted, DGSE models are the canonical models of the NKNS. They are "simple" general equilibrium models to the extent that they include only a limited number of representative agents. A DGSE model is not only a tool, however. Just like an IS/LM equilibrium, a DGSE is a benchmark notion since it provides the basis for the long-run path of the economy, allowing rigidities or imperfections to be considered mere deviations from this path. Being General Economic Equilibrium models, DGSE models do indeed assume a priori market clearing and perfect competition. Taking "Keynesian" features into account, however, requires the introduction of an imperfectly competitive DGSE model. A neat example of this is the reduced form of the NKNS, referred to earlier, which includes a forward-looking IS curve, an inflation-adjustment (IA) curve, and a monetary policy (MP) curve. Price rigidities first appear in the IA curve based on a Calvo-type model. Firms are divided into two groups. In each period, a fixed percentage of randomly chosen firms are able to adjust their prices, operating in a monopolistic competition context. They fix their prices through a process of maximization of the present value of future profits and therefore adopt a forward-looking behavior in the determination of their aggregate supply. Another group of firms, not randomly chosen, keeps its prices unchanged at least until the next period. The MP curve reinforces these price rigidities since, as noted, the New Keynesian Phillips curve is forward-looking, not backward-looking like its traditional predecessor. Now, we know that in a forward-looking environment the private sector will respond to the anticipated effects of monetary policy, so that small changes in monetary policy can have larger effects and sometimes create disequilibria amplified by firms when they fix new prices.

The NKNS also modified the contents of the distinction between short and long periods already considered within Keynes's theory as well as the OKNS. Its centrality to the NKNS is, for instance, confirmed by the room it occupies in the American Economic Association Symposium published in the May 1997 *Papers and Proceedings of the American Economic Review.* The general theme of this symposium was "Is there a core of practical macroeconomics that we should all believe?" Contributors included R. Solow, J. B. Taylor, M. Eichenbaum, A. Blinder, and O. Blanchard. The contents of the debate confirm that among macroeconomists who accepted the NKNS, there already was a wide-ranging consensus ten years ago on what is going on in the short run as well as in the long run. Briefly, short-run analysis is dedicated to the study of business cycles predominantly driven by aggregate demand impulses, and this is certainly a "Keynesian" (not Keynes's) legacy. By contrast, long-run analysis focuses on the study of the trend driven by the supply-side of the economy. J. B. Taylor has labeled this long-term supply-side "the most basic and the least controversial principle." This autonomy of long-run analysis is obviously based on the systematic use of DGSE models in the analysis of economic growth. In the long run, labor productivity increases are generally assumed to depend on the growth of capital per hour of work and on the growth of technology or, to be precise, on movements along as well as shifts of a production function. The production function provides the constraint that applies to the program of intertemporal utility maximization operated by a representative consumer. This use of a production function is obviously combined with the optimization process of an intertemporal utility function. This increasing use of DGSE models, perceived to have canonical status, does not mean that Keynesian theorists actually welcomed the general assumption of price and wage flexibility in the same way as Real Business Cycle analysts had done. Instead, they simply used the opportunity to specify, measure, and test the dynamic effects of nominal and real price and wage rigidities in a DGSE framework. Concerning the short run, the NKNS abandoned the Real Business Cycle view that short-term fluctuations were just optimal supply-side adjustments to unforeseeable shocks to tastes and technology. Today, there exists a consensus that implies that, in the short term (and only in the short run for many NKNS macroeconomists), there is a trade-off between inflation and unemployment. The debate on the causes of this trade-off does, however, continue. The prevailing explanation is the sticky price/staggered wage theory, already mentioned in this chapter. That is, the relation between price rigidity and imperfect competition has today been adopted by most of the NKNS macroeconomists, in contrast to the OKNS. Furthermore, consensus also prevails as regards the assumption that fluctuations of aggregate demand usually dominate short-run variations in real output. This also derives from the assumption that at least some wages and prices are not flexible enough to clear the corresponding markets more or less continuously. The prevailing situation in the NKNS is, therefore, that while Real Business Cycle theorists have stuck to their DGSE long-run approach, "neo-Keynesians" brought in their short-term views based on new Phillips curves, on imperfect competition, and on staggered price setting and/or labor contracts. Again, but with a somewhat different meaning, long-run analysis is neoclassical, and short-term analysis is neo-Keynesian.

Concluding remarks

This characterization of the similarities and differences between the OKNS and the NKNS highlights a strong continuity, in the latter instance, between both syntheses. It also allows us to add a few concluding words concerning the compatibility of Keynesian and neoclassical approaches. The NKNS certainly copes with various Keynesian themes or preoccupations, especially concerning the role of aggregate demand, the nature of unemployment, or the contents of economic policy. It hardly includes, however, the analytical foundations of Keynes's original contribution. Ultimately, this conclusion reflects on the fundamental incompatibility between neo-Walrasian and Keynesian theories and intellectual messages. From this point of view, it is worthwhile pointing out that, being as it is based on a DGSE model, the NKNS implies a conception of economic rationality and coordination that clearly is in contradiction with what Keynes tried to promote. Keynes's conception clearly stressed the importance of the impact of ignorance and what, today, we could call incomplete information on individual cognitive rationality (see Arena 1989 and 2004). It also highlighted the crucial role played by conventions, coordination failures, and fallacies of composition in the process of interindividual economic coordination. Now, outside the NKNS, authors as different as Minsky, Clower, Leijonhufvud, Stiglitz, Cooper, and Howitt have tried to provide a different rational reconstruction of various aspects of Keynes's theoretical contribution, including elements of his views on rationality and coordination that contrast with the neo-Walrasian approach. Their diverse and somewhat heterogeneous contributions do not, as yet, amount to a consistent alternative interpretation of Keynes's message. While the purpose of this chapter has not been to enter into the requirements of such a systematic and modern reconstruction, it should be here noted that their important contributions are nevertheless at least sufficient to keep alive the hope of those who, in the present context of severe economic instability, remain outside the NKNS and continue to believe in the fecundity and originality of Keynes's message.

Acknowledgments

I would like to thank T. Asada, R. E. Backhouse, B. W. Bateman, M. De Cecco, H. Hagemann, T. Hirai, M. C. Marcuzzo, T. Nishizawa, H.-M. Trautwein, and all the participants of the Keynes Conference (held at Sophia University, Tokyo, March 2007) for their useful comments, suggestions, and criticisms without implication of responsibility.

CHAPTER FIVE

Tobin's Keynesianism

Robert W. Dimand

Introduction

In September 1936, when James Tobin was an eighteen-year-old sopho-more taking principles of economics (Ec A) at Harvard, his tutor, Spencer Pollard (a graduate student who was also the instructor of Tobin's Ec A section), "decided that for tutorial he and I, mainly I, should read 'this new book from England. They say it may be important.' So I plunged in, being too young and ignorant to know that I was too young and igno-rant" to begin the study of economics by reading Keynes's *General The-ory of Employment, Interest and Money* (Tobin 1988, p. 662). Pollard was right: the book did turn out to be important, not least for its lasting role in shaping Tobin's intellectual development. Tobin (1992, 1993) re-mained proud to call himself an "Old Keynesian" rather than a New Keynesian, New Classical, or Post-Keynesian, and when Harcourt and Riach (1997) edited *A "Second Edition" of the General Theory,* it was fitting that they invited Tobin (1997) to contribute the overview chapter, with the first part of the chapter written "as J. M. Keynes."[1] Although Sir John Hicks (1935a, 1937, 1939) and Irving Fisher also influenced Tobin,[2] his approach to economics was always most deeply shaped by Keynes and by the experience of growing up in the Great Depression of the 1930s.

Throughout his career, Tobin was concerned with developing macro-economic theory that would be relevant for stabilization policy, to pre-vent another depression and to improve people's lives by promoting growth and stability, rather than with analytical problem-solving for its own sake. The Great Depression was associated with the breakdown of the U.S. banking system and with Keynes's argument that depression due to inadequate effective demand was a distinctive problem of a monetary economy as opposed to a barter economy. More than any of the other leading American Keynesians of his generation—Paul Samuelson, Robert Solow, or Franco Modigliani—James Tobin concerned himself with the functioning and malfunctioning of the monetary system, telling David Colander (1999, p. 121), "I differed from that group [of American Keynesians in the 1950s] in that I taught that monetary policy was a possible tool of macroeconomic policy and that to neglect it was a mistake." Tobin set himself apart from Keynes's disciples at Cambridge University (such as Joan Robinson, Richard Kahn, and Nicholas Kaldor) and their Post-Keynesian allies in the United States because he objected to "throwing away the insights of neoclassical economics" (see Colander 1999, p. 121). Even his late-career mellowing toward the British side of the Cambridge capital controversies was subtitled "A Neoclassical Kaldor-Robinson Exercise" (Tobin 1989b). But he also stood apart from the New Keynesians: "If it means people like Greg Mankiw, I don't regard them as Keynesians. I don't think they have involuntary unemployment or absence of market clearing" (Tobin, quoted in Colander 1999, p. 124). Tobin thus staked a distinctive claim to Keynes's contested heritage. He reiterated this claim, using Keynes's term "liquidity preference" in the title of his article on demand for money as an asset (Tobin 1958), linking the proposed Tobin tax to restrain international currency speculation to Keynes's proposed turnover tax to curb stock market speculation (Keynes 1936; Tobin 1984), and building his theory of investment around Tobin's q (Brainard and Tobin 1968; Tobin and Brainard 1977), a concept closely related to the Q of Keynes's *Treatise on Money* (1930),[3] a notation that Keynes had chosen because of Alfred Marshall's quasi-rents.

The central propositions of the *General Theory* according to Tobin

In "How Dead Is Keynes?" Tobin (1977) summarized the central message of Keynes's *General Theory* in four propositions and argued that reports of the death of Keynes, like those of the demise of Mark Twain, were much exaggerated: "none of the four central Keynesian propositions is inconsistent with the contemporary economic scene here or in other advanced democratic capitalist countries. At least the first three fit the facts extremely well. Indeed the middle 70s follow the Keynesian script better than any post-war period except the early 60s. It hardly seems the time for a funeral" (1977, p. 460).

Tobin's first central Keynesian proposition was that "In modern industrial capitalist societies, wages respond slowly to excess demand or supply, especially slowly to excess supply" so that over "a long short run" fluctuations in aggregate demand affect real output, not just prices. A corollary of this was the second proposition, "the vulnerability of economies like ours to lengthy bouts of involuntary unemployment." The only distinctively Keynesian aspect of Tobin's first two central Keynesian propositions was the insistence on the phenomenon of involuntary unemployment, an excess supply of labor in a nonclearing labor market. Replace "involuntary unemployment" with "high unemployment" in the second proposition, and the two propositions would be acceptable to David Hume in 1752, Henry Thornton in 1802, Alfred Marshall in 1887, or Milton Friedman in 1968. Tobin (1977, pp. 459–460) pointed to the high unemployment since 1974 as supporting evidence, insisting that the increased unemployment was indeed involuntary: "People willing to work at or below prevailing real wages cannot find jobs. They have no effective way to signal their availability." In contrast, in Friedman (1968), with adaptive expectations and the expectations-augmented Phillips curve, and in Lucas (1981a), with the monetary-misperceptions version of New Classical economics, the labor market clears, but the labor demand curve shifts as workers are fooled by monetary shocks into misperceiving the real wage. Tobin's first two Keynesian propositions summarized widely shared views (although New Classical economists would be troubled by the very idea of involuntary behavior) and came to textbook Keynesianism from chapter 2 of Keynes (1936), in which Keynes discussed the two classical postulates of the labor market. Keynes accepted the first classical postulate, that the real wage is equal to the marginal product of labor (i.e., the economy is competitive and on the labor demand curve), but rejected the second one, that the utility of the real wage is equal to the marginal disutility of labor (i.e., the economy is on the labor supply curve). Although Keynes's chapter 2 provided an account of why staggered contracts and the concern of workers with relative wages could make nominal wages sticky downward without any money illusion (a precursor of the more formal modeling of Taylor 1980),[4] the textbook version and Tobin's first two Keynesian propositions were consistent with the claim that Keynesian analysis, however practically important, was theoretically trivial: just a classical system with a sticky nominal wage rate. Emphasizing slow adjustment of prices and money wages implied viewing Keynesian unemployment as a disequilibrium situation, a short-run phenomenon of transition periods, rather than accepting Keynes's claim to have shown the possibility of equilibrium with involuntary unemployment (excess supply of labor).

"Writing as J. M. Keynes" for A "Second Edition" of the General Theory, Tobin (1997, p. 7) held that Keynes (1936, chap. 2)

> leaned too far to the classical side, as I learned shortly after the book was published, thanks to the empirical studies of [John] Dunlop and [Lorie] Tarshis. If the first classical postulate were correct, then we would expect real wages—measured in terms of labor's product rather than workers' consumption—to move counter-cyclically. However, Dunlop and Tarshis found that product-wages were, if anything, pro-cyclical. This is not a fatal flaw in the general theory; quite the contrary: my essential propositions remain unscathed. . . . If increases in aggregate demand can raise employment and output without diminishing real wages, so much the better! . . . Nothing is lost by recognizing that imperfect competition and sluggish price adjustment may result in departures from marginal cost pricing, especially in short runs.[5]

Tobin's third central Keynesian proposition was that "Capital formation depends on long run appraisals of profit expectations and risks and on business attitudes toward bearing the risks. These are not simple predictable functions of current and recent economic events. Variations of the marginal efficiency of capital contain, for all practical purposes, important elements of autonomy and exogeneity" (1977, p. 460; see Keynes 1936, chap. 12, "The State of Long-Term Expectation"). This emphasis on autonomous shifts of long-period expectations (Keynes's "animal spirits") rejected the rational expectations hypothesis introduced into macroeconomics in the 1970s by Robert Lucas (1981a), Thomas Sargent, and Neil Wallace, as well as the endogenous, adaptive expectations of Friedman (1968). Tobin's emphasis on fluctuations in long-period expectations of future profits fitted with a view that the Wall Street crash of October 1929 mattered for investment and the Great Depression (the market value of equity, the numerator of Tobin's q, is the present discounted value of expected future after-tax net earnings), in contrast to Friedman and Schwartz (1963), who reinterpreted the Great Depression as a Great Contraction of the money supply resulting from mistaken Federal Reserve policy. Tobin's third central Keynesian proposition also undermined attempts (for instance, by Minsky [1981] and Crotty [1990]) to contrast an allegedly neoclassical Tobin's q, supposedly based on a known probability distribution of underlying fundamental variables, with a more truly Keynesian approach that recognized fundamental uncertainty and exogenous shifts in long-period expectations (see Dimand 2004b).

The fourth central Keynesian proposition in Tobin (1977), following chapter 19 of the General Theory, held that "Even if money wages and prices were responsive to market excess demands and supplies, their flex-ibility would not necessarily stabilize monetary economies subject to demand and supply shocks." This proposition, advanced vigorously by Tobin (1975, 1980, 1992, 1993), placed the Keynesian challenge to what Keynes termed "classical economics" on a level of core theory. Keynes-ianism, as interpreted by Tobin, could not be dismissed as nothing more than the empirical observation (or arbitrary assumption) that money wage rates are sticky downward. Even if prices and money wages responded promptly, the economy might fail to automatically readjust to potential output after a large negative demand shock and might require govern-ment intervention to restore full employment. Making money wages more flexible by eliminating trade unions, minimum wage laws, and the dole might just make things worse. Tobin's fourth Keynesian proposition and the emphasis on chapter 19 as crucial to understanding the message of Keynes's *General Theory* were central to Tobin's Keynesianism: involun-tary unemployment might be a disequilibrium phenomenon, but the sys-tem might not have any mechanism to move it back to the full-employment equilibrium after a sufficiently large negative demand shock. Tobin (1977, p. 460) endorsed "Keynes's challenge to accepted doctrine that market mechanisms are inherently self-correcting and stabilizing." Unlike his first three central Keynesian propositions, Tobin did not claim empirical support for the fourth proposition: since money wages and prices did not in fact respond rapidly to excess demands and supplies, there could not be much direct evidence of what would happen in that counterfactual situation. The case for the fourth proposition had to be made, as in Tobin (1975), at a theoretical level. It was a case that he made explicitly and formally only from the 1970s onward, when Keynesianism was under challenge from natural rate theories, first from the monetar-ism of Friedman (1968) and then from the New Classical economics of Lucas (1981a), which claimed that demand stimulus could increase em-ployment and output only by tricking workers into accepting a lower real wage than they thought they were getting. Unfortunately, Robert Lucas (1981b), in his review article about Tobin (1980), ignored Tobin's first lecture about disequilibrium dynamics, stability, and failure of self-adjustment, concentrating instead on a protest against the description in Tobin's second lecture of Lucas's New Classical approach as "Monetar-ism, Mark II"—that is, just Friedman's natural rate hypothesis and expectations-adjustment Phillips curve with rational expectations in place of adaptive expectations.

"Writing as J. M. Keynes," Tobin (1997, p. 4) stated that "The central questions before economists of our generation are: 'Does our market capitalist economy, left to itself, without government intervention, utilize fully its labor force and other productive resources? Does it systematically return, reasonably swiftly, to a full employment state whenever displaced from it?' The faith of the classical economists assures us 'yes.' The answer of *The General Theory* is 'no.' ... Fortunately, it appears that the remedies lie in government fiscal and monetary policies and leave intact the basic political, economic and social institutions of democracy and capitalism" (contrary to the faith of the young Marxists who, to Keynes's dismay, were prominent among the Cambridge Apostles in the 1930s). Writing as himself, Tobin (1997, p. 27) concluded: "Classical faith that demand-deficient economies will recover on their own failed theoretical and empirical challenge in Keynes's day. It fails now again, more than half a century later."

Microeconomic foundations for the IS/LM

Tobin was present at the creation of Alvin Hansen's one-good version of the IS/LM model of goods market and money market equilibrium that became the mainstay of American Keynesian teaching. Tobin, then a junior member of Harvard's Society of Fellows, and Seymour Harris, as editor of the Economic Handbook Series, were the only people thanked in Hansen's preface (1949, p. vi) for reading and commenting on the manuscript, and Hansen (1949, p. 168n), when citing Tobin (1947/1948), declared, "I have relied heavily upon his analysis." Tobin (1947/1948) had used the IS and LM curves, and the small system of simultaneous equations underlying them, to show that the preference of pioneer monetarist Clark Warburton (1945) for monetary policy rather than fiscal policy rested on an unstated assumption that the demand for money was insensitive to changes in the interest rate.

Post-Keynesians rejected the IS/LM model as underplaying the importance of fundamental, uninsurable uncertainty (as distinct from insurable risk) and because Keynes would never have countenanced representing his theory by a system of simultaneous equations—although it turns out that a four-equation IS/LM model first appeared in a lecture by Keynes in December 1933, attended by David Champernowne and Brian Reddaway, who later published the first models equivalent to the IS/LM (Dimand 2007). Monetarists such as Milton Friedman also shunned the IS/LM diagram as being drawn for a given price level (e.g., see the critiques of the "Yale school" by Brunner [1971] and Meltzer [1989]), except when Friedman used it in Gordon (1974) in an attempt to communicate with his Keynesian critics—an instance later cited by some Post

Keynesians as evidence that mainstream American Keynesian users of the IS/LM were really classical rather than Keynesian. Tobin (1980, lecture 1) responded to this monetarist objection to the IS/LM by using IS/LM diagrams with the interest rate and price level on the axes to analyze situations of full employment, drawing the curves for given output. Tobin continued to find the IS/LM framework useful but devoted his career to extending it and providing richer and deeper microeconomic foundations for its investment, consumption, money demand, and money supply components, particularly with regard to a full range of assets and to stock-flow consistency (Dimand 2004a). Tobin (1980, p. 73) began the third and last of his Yrjö Jahnsson lectures by saying that he would "be particularly concerned with the Keynesian model and the famous IS/LM formalization by Sir John Hicks [1937]. . . . I shall consider critically its possible interpretations, some objections to them raised by others, and some of my own. Yet I want to begin by saying that I do not think the apparatus is discredited. I still believe that, carefully used and taught, it is a powerful instrument for understanding our economies and the impacts of policies upon them." Tobin (1980, p. 94) ended that lecture with "one major general conclusion, namely the robustness of the standard results of Hicksian IS/LM analysis. They survive in these models in which time, flows, and stocks are more precisely and satisfactorily modeled, in which time is allowed for flows to affect the stocks of government liabilities and of other assets too, in which the menu of distinct assets is as large as desired." Many of the extensions that Tobin made to the asset market side of the IS/LM framework pioneered by Hicks (1937) were in the spirit of Hicks (1935a), where Hicks had argued for treating the theory of money as an application of general economic theory to portfolio choice.[6] Tobin (in Gordon 1974, p. 77n) observed that "The synthesis of the last twenty-five years certainly contains many elements not in the *General Theory* [Keynes 1936a]. Perhaps it should be called Hicksian, since it derives not only from his IS-LM article but, more importantly, from his classic paper on money [Hicks 1935a]."

Tobin's doctoral dissertation was on consumption and saving, introducing wealth as well as income as an argument in the consumption function. Tobin's q theory of investment dealt with the other part of the IS (investment/saving) goods market equilibrium condition. Tobin offered microeconomic foundations for both the liquidity preference (money demand) and the money supply components of the LM money market equilibrium condition, making it just one of many asset market clearing conditions. He developed a model of the optimizing commercial banking firm and used it to study how, in a world of many assets that are imperfectly substitutable for each other, the endogenous money supply is affected by changes in the monetary base, a choice variable controlled by the monetary authority (Tobin with Golub 1998), since endogeneity of the money supply does not by itself imply a horizontal LM curve (in contrast to Moore 1988).

Keynes (1936) was the first to write money demand as a function of income and the interest rate, although others had come close before, with Irving Fisher in 1930 stating the marginal opportunity cost of holding real cash balances. Tobin sought to ground such a demand function for noninterest-bearing fiat money in the decisions of rational, optimizing individuals. Tobin (1956), like William Baumol (1952) and Maurice Allais (1947) (see Baumol and Tobin [1989] on Allais's priority), derived the square-root rule for the inventory-theoretic approach to the transactions demand for money from minimization of the total costs of cash management, consisting of the transaction cost incurred whenever interest-bearing assets were converted into means of payment, plus the interest foregone by holding part of one's wealth as money.

Tobin's "Liquidity Preference as Behavior towards Risk" (1958) considered the demand for money as an asset that risk-averse investors held in portfolios even though its expected return of zero was strictly less than the expected return on risky assets, because holding money was riskless in nominal terms. Keynes (1936) had assumed that agents held a fixed expectation of what the interest rate would be in the future, but Tobin, as he told Shiller (1999, p. 885), "wanted to have an explanation for the demand for money that didn't depend on there being a different interest rate from the one which the model produced. That's perfectly good rational expectations methodology. . . . That's what that article was all about. It wasn't about creating the CAPM model or the separation theorem. The separation theorem just came out naturally from the way I was modeling this thing."

Tobin developed a multiasset framework, in which money was an imperfect substitute for other assets, with asset demands linked across markets by the adding-up constraint that asset demands have to sum to wealth, and with flows of saving and investment changing the stocks of assets over time. The adding-up constraint (or, in other models, Walras's Law summing individual budget constraints) makes one asset market-clearing condition redundant, but Brainard and Tobin (1968) warned about the pitfall of implausible implied elasticities for the omitted demand function. Brunner and Meltzer (1993) also developed a multiasset model, but Tobin expressed amazement that "at the same time they have multi-asset substitutable assets and yet, in the end, they come to a monetarist result which seems to be inconsistent with the assumed substitutability among assets, including the substitutability of some assets for money proper" (Colander 1999, p. 124). While incorporating wealth as an adding-up constraint, stock-flow consistency, and optimization in models of specific functions, such as money demand, Tobin refused to think of markets as linked by the budget constraint of an optimizing representative agent (see Geweke 1985; Kirman 1992; and Hartley 1997, on representative agent models). Tobin held that representative agent models were totally unsuited to analyzing the macroeconomic coordination problem posed by Keynes (Dimand 2004a). Tobin objected strongly to claims that overlapping generations (OLG) models, dependent on the very strong assumptions that money is the only asset and that the number of successive generations is infinite, provide rigorous microeconomic foundations for the existence and positive value of fiat money (see his comments in Karekan and Wallace [1980] and in Colander [1999]). While Tobin emphatically did not consider OLG models a satisfactory explanation for the positive value of fiat money, he found them useful for analyzing intertemporal consumption choice. Willem Buiter (2003, F590–F591) observes that "During the 1960s, 1970s, and 1980s, Tobin made a number of key contributions to the theory and empirics of the life-cycle model, putting it in an Allais-Samuelson overlapping generations (OLG) setting. . . . The empirical methodology employed is an early example of simulation using calibration. With only a modicum of hyperbole, one could describe Tobin as the methodological Godfather of the RBC [real business cycle] school and methodology of Kydland and Prescott!"[7]

Tobin's q and the Post-Keynesians

Tobin's relationship with the Post-Keynesians was complicated (see Dimand 2004b). Geoffrey Harcourt saw Tobin as an ally defending Keynesian demand management against monetarist and New Classical challenges and invited Tobin to write the overview chapter of Harcourt and Riach (1997). Tobin (1960) satirized Nicholas Kaldor's theory of distribution, but later Tobin invited Kaldor to give the first series of Arthur Okun lectures at Yale in 1983 and contributed to a journal issue honoring Kaldor (Tobin 1989b). Paul Davidson (1997), advocate of an international currency union under which currencies subject to speculative attack would have only one-way convertibility, nevertheless insists that a "Tobin tax" on currency trades (Tobin 1978) of even a few basis points would disrupt trade and long-term capital flows but would, even if it was just a few percentage points, be insufficient to curb short-term flows of "hot money."

Hyman Minsky (1981, 1986), like Tobin an admirer of Keynes (1936, chap. 19) and of Fisher (1933), and also like Tobin supervised by Joseph Schumpeter and Wassily Leontief as a student at Harvard (both Minsky and Tobin were there from 1946 to 1949), dismissed Tobin as being neoclassical rather than Keynesian at heart. Tobin (1989a, p. 75) protested that Minsky (1986, 5n, pp. 133–138) "accuses the misguided Keynesians of embracing the Pigou-Patinkin real balance effect as a proof that flexibility of wages and prices ensures full employment so that governmental macroeconomic interventions are not needed. This is just not true. I, for example, say the opposite in publications that Minsky knows and actually cites"—such as Tobin (1975, 1980). Tobin (1989a, p. 73), reviewing Minsky (1986), declared that "this 'post-Keynesian' theory is not convincingly linked to the central message of the book, the financial theory of business cycles. Minsky's excellent account of asset pricing and investment decisions is separable from his theory of prices, wages and profit. It sounds like 'q' theory to me."

James Crotty (1990) also contrasted a Keynesian Minsky with a neoclassical Tobin. Tobin and Brainard (1990, pp. 66–67) responded by insisting on their agreement with Keynes's "stress in chapter 12 of the *General Theory* on the inevitable role of non-rational attitudes—optimism and confidence or their opposites—in forming estimates of the marginal efficiency of capital.... Nothing excuses [Crotty's] charge that 'Tobin places Keynes's stamp of approval on the rational expectations, efficient-markets general equilibrium models that are the modern extensions of the classical theory Keynes so vehemently opposed.'" Tobin and Brainard (1990, p. 71) also took umbrage at Crotty's remark about "Tobin's stable and efficient financial markets," protesting that

> We did not use the word "stable." Our word "efficient" referred only to technical market-clearing efficiency. We did not say or mean that stock markets come up continuously with fundamental valuations. In this 1977 article, which Crotty cites, and in others on "q," we followed Keynes in believing that speculation makes prices diverge from fundamental values. Again putting his own word in Tobin's mouth, Crotty says in his footnote 9 that in his 1984 article, "Tobin appears to recant his belief in the valuation efficiency of financial markets." The term "valuation efficiency" does not appear in our 1977 article, and no other writing of ours, individual or joint, asserts such a belief. Tobin had nothing to recant. (See also Tobin and Brainard 1977; Tobin 1984; Shiller 1989)

Tobin (interviewed by Shiller 1999, pp. 887–888) firmly distinguished his and Brainard's q, an observable market variable taken as a datum by agents, from the neoclassical q of Fumio Hayashi (1982), a shadow price that solves an optimization problem.

Is the economic system self-adjusting?

The fourth central Keynesian proposition identified by Tobin (1977) was that even if money wages and prices were flexible, their being flexible would not necessarily ensure stability. According to Keizo Nagatani (1981, p. 117), "The stability question to which Keynes addressed himself in the *General Theory* and that Tobin (1975) discussed is now interpreted as the question whether or not the sequence of temporary equilibria will converge to a short-run equilibrium. This, I believe, is the fundamental problem in macroeconomics. But this is also a very complex problem, to which only a partial answer can be given" (see also De Long and Summers 1986; Driskill and Sheffrin 1986; and Chadha 1989, as examples of the debate ignited by Tobin 1975).

Tobin (1975) presented what he called a Walras-Keynes-Phillips model, in which, even if the model had a unique equilibrium at potential output Y* (which Tobin emphasized was not in fact his opinion), output might continue to diverge further from potential output after a negative demand shock, despite incorporating the Pigou-Haberler real balance effect in the model. The resulting unemployment would be a phenomenon of disequilibrium dynamics, but if there was no convergence to the full-employment equilibrium, it did not matter that the system described by the model lacked an unemployment equilibrium. The stabilizing Pigou-Haberler real balance effect of a *lower* price level (implying a larger real value of outside money, hence higher wealth, hence more consumption) could be swamped by the destabilizing effects of a *falling* price level. Expectations of falling prices reduce the opportunity cost of holding real money balances and hence increase the demand for real money balances, a leftward shift of the LM curve. Tobin (1980, lecture 1), like Minsky (1975), invoked the debt-deflation process described by Irving Fisher (1933): the rising real value of inside debt denominated in nominal terms does not wash out, because the increased risk of bankruptcy raises risk premiums on loans and because the transfer of real wealth from borrowers to lenders depresses spending, since these groups were presumably were sorted into borrowers and lenders by their different propensities to spend. The volume of inside debt far exceeds the quantity of outside money on which the real balance effect acts. Don Patinkin (1965), like A. C. Pigou, had concluded that the real balance effect proved in theory that wage flexibility could restore full employment after a negative demand shock even if the nominal interest rate could not decline (e.g., if it had fallen to zero), even if in practice expansion of aggregate demand would be a faster route to full employment than wage cutting. Tobin (1975) argued that Pigou's case against Keynes was not established even in theory. Clower (1984) and Leijonhufvud (1968, 1981) had also interpreted Keynes as challenging classical economics on theory, not just policy, but on the grounds that Walras's Law did not hold for quantity-constrained demands (i.e., the amount of labor that an unemployed worker cannot sell multiplied by the prevailing wage that the worker is not receiving should not count in the worker's budget constraint), rather than the dynamics of adjustment. Tobin told Colander (1999) that he had nothing against the Clower-Leijonhufvud approach but did not feel that he had been much instructed by it.

Tobin (1997, pp. 12–13) as "Keynes" wrote in the "second edition" of the *General Theory:*

> In chapter 19 I emphasized the negative effects of increasing debt burdens, and Professor Fisher has made a convincing case that debt burdens augmented by deflation exacerbated the Great Depression in the United States. I also agree with Professor Fisher that, whatever may be the effects of lowering the level of money-wages and prices, the process of moving to a lower level is counterproductive. Expectations of deflation are equivalent to an increase in interest rates. For these reasons, I do not regard Professor Pigou's counterthrust as a refutation of the general theory on an abstract theoretical plane, *a fortiori* on the plane of practical policy. Indeed, I remain of the opinion that a fairly stable money-wage will result in less volatility both of output and employment and of prices.

Tobin (1975) stated the crucial necessary condition for stability in his model but did not present the derivation. The necessary and sufficient conditions for stability in Tobin's (1975) Walras-Keynes-Phillips model are derived in Bruno and Dimand (2009), where it is shown that Tobin's model possesses a corridor of stability, such as Leijonhufvud called for in 1973 (reprinted in Leijonhufvud 1981, pp. 103–129). That is, the model is self-adjusting for small shocks but can be pushed outside the corridor of stability by a sufficiently large negative demand shock, so that it then moves even further away from potential output. This feature of the model captures the intuition that great depressions happen only occasionally: most of the time, markets adjust. The reason for the corridor of stability is that one of the stabilizing forces, the so-called Keynes effect by which a lower price level increases the real money supply and so lowers the interest rate, weakens and then vanishes as the nominal interest rate falls toward zero.

Conclusion: "An Old Keynesian counterattacks"

Tobin remained proud to call himself an "Old Keynesian" (see Purvis [1982] and Buiter [2003] on the full range of Tobin's contributions to economics). His disequilibrium dynamic interpretation of Keynes, making chapter 19 central to the *General Theory*, set Tobin apart both from Keynes's opponents and from the defenders of Keynesian unemployment equilibrium. Tobin (1975, 1977, 1980, 1992, 1993, 1997) developed and expounded this disequilibrium dynamic version of Keynesian theory as a counterattack against natural rate theories, showing that even if there was a unique natural rate equilibrium, the system need not be self-adjusting in the absence of governmental stabilization after a sufficiently large negative demand shock. Chapter 19 of Keynes's *General Theory* first appeared as central to Tobin's interpretation of Keynes in 1975 and was joined by the influence of Fisher (1933) in 1980. Too neoclassical for many Post-Keynesians, Tobin grounded asset demand functions (including money demand) and consumption decisions in the optimizing behavior of rational individuals and emphasized adding-up constraints and stock-flow consistency, but he rejected representative agent models with continuous labor market-clearing as useless for understanding the macroeconomic coordination problem. His approach, strongly influenced by Hicks (1935a) and Fisher (1933) as well as by Keynes (1936, chaps. 12 and 19), was recognizably distinct from the rest of the American Keynesian mainstream, which paid less attention to the monetary system, to multiasset modeling, and to disequilibrium dynamics.

Notes

This chapter is based on a paper presented at the conference from participants there and on Keynes at Sophia University, Tokyo, March 2007. I am grateful for helpful comments from Avi Cohen, Omar Hamouda, J. Allan Hynes, David Laidler, Don Moggridge, and Allan Olley at the University of Toronto/York University workshop in the history of economic thought.

1. Because a snowstorm closed airports on the U.S. East Coast during the American Economic Association meetings in San Francisco in January 1996, keeping Tobin in Connecticut, I found myself presenting a paper by Tobin writing as Keynes to the AEA session marking the sixtieth anniversary of the *General Theory*.
2. Tobin was a consulting editor for Fisher (1997) and a contributor to Dimand and Geanakoplos (2005), the latter being the proceedings of a Yale conference on Fisher coorganized by Tobin. His earlier articles on Fisher are also reprinted in the conference volume.
3. Tobin's q is the ratio of the market value of equity to the replacement cost of capital, while, in one of two interpretations given in the *Treatise*, Keynes's Q is the difference between the two (see Dimand 1988).

4. Tobin expressed a high opinion of Taylor's work on staggered contracts and relative wages when Tobin and Taylor jointly taught a graduate course on money and finance while Taylor was a visiting professor at Yale in 1979–1980. Later, Tobin took a sympathetic interest in the research of his Cowles Foundation colleague Truman Bewley (1999), formerly an abstract mathematical economist, who (like Blinder 1991) took the daring methodological step of asking employers why they did not cut wages in recessions: given staggered contracts and that workers care about relative wages, money wage cuts reduce morale and productivity.

5. See articles by Dunlop, Tarshis, Keynes, and Ruggles, reprinted, together with Tobin (1941), in Dimand 2002, vol. 8.

6. Tobin always emphasized his respect for Hicks—for instance, traveling to Glendon College of York University, Toronto, in the summer of 1987, when Hicks, by then elderly and frail, was visiting there.

7. However, when Colander (1999) asked Tobin, "How about real business-cycle theorists?" Tobin replied, "Well, that's just the enemy."

CHAPTER SIX

The New Neoclassical Synthesis and the Wicksell-Keynes Connection

Mauro Boianovsky and Hans-Michael Trautwein

Introduction

Ever since the term "macroeconomics" came into use in the 1930s,[1] the mainstream views on fluctuations of aggregate output, employment, and prices seem to have followed a dialectic pattern of conflict and convergence. As Michael Woodford (1999, p. 2) notes, "[d]iscussions of . . . developments in macroeconomics make frequent references to 'revolutions' and 'counter-revolutions.'" Moreover, the campaigns of conquest have alternated with joint efforts to develop common ground, so that a *Journal of Economic Literature* abstract of the history of macroeconomics could read as follows: "John Maynard Keynes proclaimed his *General Theory* to be the antithesis of Classical economics, but before long the Keynesian Revolution was turned into the Neoclassical Synthesis. This provoked a Monetarist Counter-Revolution and a New Classical Rational Expectations Revolution that culminated in Real Business Cycle theory. The New Keynesian reaction to these challenges has led to the development of the New Neoclassical Synthesis—which is where the (hi)story ends for now."[2]

The "old" Neoclassical Synthesis goes under the name IS/LM. By analogy the new synthesis, or NNS, can be characterized as IS-AS-MP, a three-equations system through which output (gaps), inflation, and interest rates are jointly determined: an intertemporal IS relation is combined with aggregate supply in terms of an expectations-augmented Phillips curve (AS) and a reaction function for monetary policy (MP), typically in the form of a Taylor rule for setting interest rates.

This triad is at the center of Woodford's *Interest and Prices* (2003), an authoritative contribution to the NNS literature that makes an interesting twist in the writing of history. The book is full of references to Knut Wicksell's *Geldzins und Güterpreise* (1898), a landmark in pre-Keynesian monetary theory. Its title echoes the title of the 1936 translation of Wicksell (1898), and the basic IS-AS-MP model that Woodford develops for his extensive analysis of monetary policy is described as a "neo-Wicksellian framework" (2003, chap. 4). It is obvious why Woodford has chosen Wicksell as patron saint for his version of the new synthesis. Setting the focus on the Taylor rule, his concept of a "monetary policy without money" (Woodford 1998, p. 173) has much in common with Wicksell's "pure credit system" and proposal to eliminate inflation by adjusting nominal interest rates to changes in the price level.[3] Moreover, by referring to the Wicksellians of the 1930s, Woodford (2003, p. 5) grounds his advocacy of rule-bound inflation control on the potential nonneutrality of monetary policy: "[I]t is because instability of the general level of prices causes substantial real distortions—leading to inefficient variation both in aggregate employment and output and in the sectoral composition of economic activity—that price stability is important."

Woodford's "attempt to resurrect a view that was influential among monetary economists prior to the Keynesian revolution" (2003, p. 5) is meant to be more than a synthesis of the most recent neoclassical and Keynesian models. It makes, in some respects, a full circle in macroeconomic thinking. As Dennis Robertson famously quipped, "highbrow opinion is like a hunted hare; if you stand in the same place . . . , it can be relied upon to come round to you in a circle" (quoted after Leijonhufvud 2000, p. 12). Sir Dennis, an old-style Wicksellian in his own right,[4] would certainly feel vindicated. However, Woodford also makes a sharp distinction between his neo-Wicksellianism and the original version. He argues that Wicksell and his followers—he mentions Erik Lindahl, Gunnar Myrdal, and Friedrich A. Hayek—"developed their insights without the benefit of either modern general-equilibrium theory or macroeconometric modeling techniques, so that it may be doubted whether Wicksellian theory can provide a basis for the kind of quantitative policy analysis in which a modern central bank must engage" (Woodford 2003, pp. 5–6).

This raises two questions: What are the main parallels and differences between "Wicksellian theory" and Woodford's approach? And to which extent can the latter deal with the issues raised by Wicksell and his early followers? In the following, we examine these two questions—not as an exercise in exegetic exactness but to find out what remains, after Woodford (2003), of original Wicksellian theory that may be of more than purely historical interest. In the second section, we describe Woodford's "neo-Wicksellian framework." In the third section, we identify its similarities with original Wicksellian theory and then examine its differences in the fourth section. We draw special attention to Lindahl's approach because, while being the most similar to Woodford's, it brings out essential contrasts between the old Wicksellians and the new synthesis.[5] Furthermore, these differences are closely related to those between Keynes's approach and the two Neoclassical Syntheses. As Leijonhufvud (1979) has argued, Keynes had a "Wicksell Connection" in the view that failures of the market rate of interest to coordinate investment and saving *ex ante* result in excess demands in goods and labor markets that cannot be cured by price or wage adjustments, unless the interest rate shifts to a level compatible with full employment at stable prices. This perspective is lost in the NNS. The fifth section of this chapter explores the grounds where the Wicksell Connections of Keynes and Woodford diverge. In the final section, we conclude that the new synthesis fails to deal with various issues that were at the heart of the original Wicksellian and Keynesian approaches and that should still be at the center of macroeconomic research.

Woodford's neo-Wicksellian framework

The core of the NNS is a system of three equations that determine the dynamics of output, inflation, and the key interest rate. It comes in various versions for different purposes (see, e.g., Goodfriend and King 1997; Clarida, Galí, and Gertler 1999; Romer 2000; Taylor 2000). In Woodford's version, the system is based on the conditions for intertemporal general equilibrium under rational expectations (2003, pp. 243–47).

The first equation is an IS relation, i.e., a negative relation between output and interest rate variables obtained by log-linearizing the first-order condition of the intertemporal consumption optimum of the representative household:

$$x_t = E_t \, x_{t+1} - \sigma(i_t - E_t \, p_{t+1} - \rho_t), \tag{1}$$

where x denotes the gap between actual output and the "natural rate"; σ, the intertemporal elasticity of substitution; i, nominal interest;[6] p, the inflation rate; and ρ, a disturbance term that represents shocks to the "natural rate of interest." The "natural rate of output" is taken from Real Business Cycle (RBC) theory, representing "a *virtual* equilibrium" in terms of the output "one *would* have if prices and wages were not in fact sticky" (Ibid., p. 9). The natural rate of interest is "just the real rate of interest required to keep aggregate demand equal at all times to the natural rate of output" (Ibid., p. 248). Since Woodford's framework is based on forward-looking behavior, current consumption is determined by expected future consumption; or rather, the actual output gap is a function of the rational expectations of output and inflation (denoted by the operator E) and of the contemporaneous shock and policy variables ρ and i.

The second equation is an AS function in terms of a New Keynesian Phillips curve in which actual inflation equals expected inflation plus the actual output gap:

$$p_t = \beta E_t\, p_{t+1} + \kappa\, x_t, \tag{2}$$

where β is a discount factor and κ is a rigidity parameter. It is assumed that firms act in monopolistic competition and that prices are set in a staggered fashion, by way of a Calvo lottery.[7] In the case of interest rate shocks, a significant fraction of firms will maximize profits by varying their output rather than prices. Price stickiness increases with the degree of strategic complementarity between the price-setting of the suppliers of different goods (affecting κ), such that the output effects of shocks can be large and persistent.

The third equation is a Taylor rule for monetary policy:

$$i_t = i^* + \gamma_p\, (p_t - p^*) + \gamma_x\, (x_t - x^*), \tag{3}$$

where i^* reflects possible variation in the inflation target p^* and disturbances (control errors or mismeasurement). The weight factors γ_p and γ_x describe the intensity of reactions to deviations of actual inflation and the output gap from their target values. The target for the output gap is defined as the steady-state value consistent with the inflation target, $x^* \equiv (1 - \beta)\, p^*/\kappa$. This closes the model by making the Taylor rule internally consistent: the definition of x^* ensures that $I = i^*$ whenever the inflation target p^* is achieved. The reaction function thus permits the determination of the endogenous variables i, p, and x in equations (1)–(3). Woodford argues that the Taylor rule is optimal if the inflation target is set near zero. In this case, the welfare losses that arise from price stickiness and ensuing output gaps will be minimized. The new synthesis thus yields neoclassical results from a model that is labeled (New) Keynesian on the grounds that output adjustments precede, or prevent, price adjustments.[8]

"Ironically, in spite of the fact that Keynesian effects of monetary policy on real activity are powerful in NNS models, monetary policy is best when it eliminates Keynesian effects entirely." (Goodfriend and King 1997, p. 278). Describing his neo-Wicksellian framework, Woodford says essentially the same thing: "In this way it is established that a non-monetarist analysis of the effects of monetary policy does not involve any theoretical inconsistency of departure from neoclassical orthodoxy" (Woodford 2003, p. 238).

Parallels between new and old Wicksellian theories

Woodford's argument that inflation is caused by interest-rate gaps and can be eliminated by a feedback rule clearly refers back to Wicksell's *Interest and Prices* (1898). That book exerted some influence on the evolution of macroeconomics even prior to the NNS. It gave rise to such controversial concepts as the *natural rate* of interest (and unemployment), the *neutrality of money,* and the *cumulative process.* Wicksell's feat was not to coin the phrases,[9] but to combine the underlying ideas in a framework that could serve to analyze the macroeconomic interaction between markets, when nominal rigidities in one market—here, interest-rate stickiness in the relevant financial market—require adjustments of prices and/or quantities in other markets to bring the system back into equilibrium. While the notions of natural rates, neutrality, and cumulative processes were integrated, criticized, and redefined in twentieth-century macroeconomics, Wicksell's key concept of the *pure credit system* received much less attention.[10] In Woodford's version of the new synthesis, that element regained a central place.

The irrelevance of monetary aggregates

The NNS is sometimes presented as "Keynesian macroeconomics without the LM curve" (Romer 2000). It can apparently do without the liquidity preference theory of interest, and it goes straight against the assumption of an exogenous money supply that was part of the old synthesis. Woodford (2003), in particular, stresses that modern monetary policy controls inflation by setting interest rates, not by controlling any monetary aggregate. He tells two stories to support his point.

The first story describes the current practice of central banks that implement monetary policy through a "channel system" of lending and deposit rates within which overnight rates are kept in line with the central bank's interest-rate target (Ibid., pp. 25–31). According to Woodford, this "does not require any quantity adjustments through open-market operations in response to deviations of the market rate from the target rate" (Ibid., p. 28). In his view, the supply of central-bank balances is not essential for inflation control.

The second story is a model of "monetary policy in a purely cashless economy" (Ibid., pp. 64–74) that serves to underpin the neo-Wicksellian framework. Woodford assumes a world of complete and perfectly competitive financial markets in which the representative household optimizes its asset holdings. Even though there are "no monetary frictions whatsoever" (Ibid., p. 31), the system has a central bank that issues a "distinguished financial asset" in terms of its own liabilities. This asset forms "the monetary base" because it defines the unit of account, but in the construction of the model, "changes in the quantity of base money . . . have no consequences for the equilibrium determination of interest or other variables" (Ibid., p. 75). Policy targets are implemented exclusively through adjustment of the interest paid on the central bank's liabilities. Woodford argues that, even in this environment, an interest-rate rule for monetary policy can yield determinate rational-expectations equilibrium paths of prices and interest rates (Ibid., pp. 74–82, 635–637).

Woodford (2003, pp. 31–32) justifies his two stories by indicating that there is a trend toward completely cashless payment systems and by suggesting that the monetary transmission mechanism is better understood if "monetary frictions" are disregarded. In his *Interest and Prices*, Wicksell (1936 [1898], pp. 62–76) used similar arguments to introduce his thought experiment of the "pure credit system," as he intended to restate the quantity theory of money in the general form of an interest-rate mechanism that explains changes in the price level as effects of changes in bank lending. Any positive margin between the "natural rate of interest" (i.e., the expected rate of return to real investment) and the banks' lending rate induces a monetary expansion through the creation of loans and deposits. "For the sake of simplicity," Wicksell presented his analysis of the credit system as a description of a single institution, the Ideal Bank (1936, pp. 70–76). As the Bank sets the loan rate and thereby affects aggregate demand for goods, it can control the price level. The opening and closing of gaps between the Bank rate and the natural rate of interest yielded a general explanation of inflation and deflation without taking recourse to a given supply of base money.

In the same vein, Lindahl (1939 [1930], part II) based his reexamination of Wicksell's *Interest and Prices* on the "simplifying assumption" of a completely centralized banking system. The Bank—which Lindahl interpreted as a public central bank—sets the nominal rate of interest "with a perfectly free hand to carry out its credit policy" (1939, p. 139). As in Wicksell's case, the supply of money (deposits) is endogenously determined by loan demand at the given rate of interest. However, while Wicksell used his concept in support of the quantity theory, Lindahl argued that the latter fails to hold under those assumptions. He used the setting of the pure credit economy to show that price expectations determine both the money supply (deposits) and the price level.[11] Lindahl's approach thus corresponds to Woodford's framework even more closely than Wicksell's version.

Interest rates, inflation, and output gaps

The hallmark of old-style Wicksellian theory is the idea that differences between the loan rate (as shorthand for general credit conditions) and the natural rate of interest cause cumulative changes in the price level and, under certain conditions, changes in the levels and structures of production. The inflationary gaps result either from a rise in the expected profit rate or from a lowering of the loan rate; the converse applies in the case of deflation. The latter case was often used as a simplifying assumption, but the former case was thought to be more relevant and frequent. It was argued that whenever profit expectations of entrepreneurs rise, due to productivity gains from technical change or other factors, it will take time before banks have the information, incentives, and opportunities to adjust the loan rate accordingly. In other words, the market rate of interest tends to be sticky, and a positive shock to the natural rate raises aggregate demand and—sooner or later—the price level. These essentials of Wicksellian theory can be expressed in terms of Woodford's model (equations 1–3): whenever a shock to the natural rate occurs $(\rho > 0)$ and is not swiftly neutralized by the central bank (by raising i), the output gap will increase and produce inflation. The same happens whenever the central bank cuts the target rate (reducing i^*, γ_p, and/or γ_x), thereby lowering the nominal interest rate (i).

In the theories of Wicksell, Lindahl, and Myrdal, the speed and extent of inflation depends crucially on the expectations formed by entrepreneurs and other agents in the system. Woodford (2003, p. 46 n. 40) claims that "Wicksell does not discuss endogenous inflation expectations and so concludes that the price level rather than the inflation rate should rise without bound. Lindahl (1939) was the first to introduce endogenous inflation expectations into the analysis."

This is not quite fair to Wicksell, who, after all, made the famous suggestion that "[t]he upward movement will in some measure 'create its own draught'" (1936, p. 96), because "once the entrepreneurs begin to rely upon [inflation] continuing—as soon, that is to say, as they start reckoning on a future rise in prices—the actual rise will become more and more rapid. In the extreme case in which the expected rise in prices is each time fully discounted, the annual rise in prices will be indefinitely great" (1936, p. 148).[12] Yet, it is correct to say that Lindahl (1939) provided a more systematic discussion of the formation of inflation expectations in the cumulative process.

Lindahl's approach is also closer to Woodford's when it comes to the concept of the natural rate of interest and the development of output gaps. Wicksell (1898) had considered the rate of return to real investment to be independent of the market rate of interest. He identified it with the "natural rate of interest," i.e., with the rate "which would be determined by supply and demand if no use were made of money and all lending were effected in the form of real capital goods" (1936, p. 102). Only if the market rate of interest conforms to this rate, which equals planned investment with planned saving, is it "normal" in the sense of being "neutral in respect to commodity prices." For Wicksell, the natural rate provided not only the equilibrium benchmark but also the attractor for the market rate. He asserted that the loan rate would sooner or later return to its normal level, thus ending the cumulative process (1936, pp. 110, 135). Furthermore, he largely ignored output effects. He certainly noted that a credit expansion creates a "tendency towards an extension of output" (1936, p. 144) and that "the credit institutions, by supporting long-term enterprises, can to some degree force the necessary real capital out of the public" (1936, p. 111), because inflation tends to decrease the consumption of the recipients of sticky wages and fixed nominal incomes. In his *Lectures* (1935, p. 199), Wicksell even conceded that the new investments and corresponding increases in output could counteract inflation, adjusting the yield on real capital to the loan rate, rather than vice versa. However, assuming full employment and slow adjustment of productive capacities, he relegated such nonneutralities of monetary expansion to the rank of secondary effects that do not interfere with cumulative price changes (1936, p. 143). In his view, changes in output were to be explained by alterations of the natural rate of interest alone, not by gaps between the natural rate and the market rate.[13]

Lindahl (1939, pp. 247–249) and Myrdal (1939, pp. 49–53) rejected Wicksell's notion of a natural rate and explored the conditions in which monetary expansion and contraction could lead to temporary or even lasting changes in output. They argued that Wicksell's concept of the natural rate requires complete homogeneity of inputs and outputs or a stationary economy in which relative prices are fixed. Both assumptions are inappropriate for the analysis of a monetary economy in which interest-rate gaps create pressures toward changes in capital stock and output. In a monetary economy, the profit rate *ex ante* is based on expectations about money prices and about the relative price of loans as an opportunity cost. Hence, it is not independent and cannot be an attractor for the market rate of interest. Like Wicksell, though in more general terms, Lindahl defined the equilibrium rate of interest as the rate that matches planned saving with investment and thus makes profit expectations consistent with intertemporal consumer preferences. This implies "such a development of prices as is in accordance with the expectations of the public, so far as this is possible" (Lindahl 1939, p. 252). In this sense, it also accords with Woodford's definition of the natural rate.

Analyzing the transmission of a monetary policy impulse in different scenarios, Lindahl (1939, pp. 161–183) varied his assumptions about initial capacity utilization, the rigidity of investment periods, wage flexibility, and the degree to which expectations are adapted to inflation. If the loan rate is lowered, capacities are fully utilized, and prices are fully flexible, the price level would instantly "soar upwards to an indefinite extent." Under the "more realistic assumption" of an upward "stickiness of wages," consumer prices rise more gradually, but consumption falls nevertheless below planned levels. The firms make "unplanned savings" as they reap windfall profits from the inflation that is caused by the loans financing their expansion of investment. These windfall profits will generate new investments. Total investment will not adjust to planned saving, as in the classical view. It is saving that adjusts to (loan-financed) investment, due to a redistribution of real income. The income mechanism can lead to an increase in output that eventually stops inflation. In that scenario, monetary policy has output effects in the short and the long run. Insofar as these effects are explained by nominal rigidities, Lindahl's approach is clearly similar to the aggregate supply specification in the NNS models of Woodford and others. Moreover, Lindahl demonstrated that monetary policy can change the capital stock and thereby affect the rate of return on real investment. This is a possibility that Woodford, too, discusses in the chapter that follows his presentation of the neo-Wicksellian framework (2003, pp. 352–378).

However, Lindahl did not believe that the central bank could consistently generate output growth by exploiting its power to set interest rates. The price expectations of the public would soon adapt to inflation and accelerate its pace. "The redistribution of incomes in favour of entrepreneurs and to the disadvantage of fixed income receivers and workers" would generate conflicts that could make it "necessary to arrest the movement before the amount of capital appropriate to the lower rate of interest has been accumulated" (Lindahl 1939, pp. 183 and 182). In order to avoid such conflicts, Lindahl pleaded that a clear rule for monetary policy be set.

The management of expectations

One of the main parallels among Wicksell, Lindahl, and Woodford is the conviction that welfare can be improved by the use of an interest-rate feedback rule that minimizes changes in the inflation rate. Wicksell (1936, pp. 1–4) argued that inflation and deflation are a "disturbance to the social mechanism" and that "the ideal position, affording common advantage to the overwhelming majority of the various groups of interests," would be a "perfectly invariable and stable" price level. He thus proposed that "the banks' rate of interest" should follow any movements in the price level. In the case of inflation, it should rise until inflation stops; in the case of deflation, it should fall until deflation comes to an end. The feedback rule could be kept that simple, since the changes in the price level in themselves are sufficient indicators of interest-rate gaps. The policymakers would not even have to ascertain the natural rate of interest, which is hard, if not impossible, to observe (Wicksell 1936, p. 189).

Myrdal (1939, chap. 6) was more skeptical about the signaling qualities of the "general price level." His definition of the relevant price index was quite specific: "business cycle movements should be eliminated as far as possible" by measures that minimize the "movement of a price index weighted with regard to the stickiness of various prices and their significance for profitability and real investment," so as to make new investment equal to "free capital disposal" (Myrdal 1939, p. 199).[14] Unfortunately, Myrdal did not further specify how this "norm" could be made operational as a rule for monetary policy, but his idea to stabilize the stickiest prices earns him an approving reference from Woodford (2003, p. 13 n. 7).

Prior to his famous 1930 study of the effects of interest changes on the price level (English translation in 1939), Lindahl (1929) had published a complementary volume on "the ends of monetary policy," which was dedicated to the discussion of policy rules. Lindahl based his reasoning on two principles for "rational monetary policy" (1929, pp. 4–8). The first principle is to set, publicly announce, and strictly follow a clear norm, in order to inspire trust in the rules of law and exchange. The second principle is to choose a norm that helps to minimize the deviations between intended and actual outcomes of all market transactions. In Lindahl's view, only two norms meet these requirements: (a) the rule of price level stability and (b) the rule that the price level should move in inverse proportion to general productivity. Lindahl (1929, chap. 4) preferred norm b, which had originally been formulated by David Davidson in critique of Wicksell. Lindahl argued that such a norm would lead to efficient risk sharing between entrepreneurs, their creditors, and wage earners. In the case of negative shocks to productivity, a price rise would stabilize the economy by counteracting the negative output effects on profits, and vice versa. When Sweden, after abandoning the gold standard in early 1931, became the first country in the world to introduce price-level targeting, Lindahl was appointed advisor to the Swedish central bank. In this role, which he kept for almost three decades, he became an ardent defender of price-level targeting, without giving up his preference for the Davidson rule. Throughout his career, Lindahl insisted that the main task of monetary policy is to help the public to form consistent expectations, so as to coordinate the individual plans of economic activities. In this respect, Lindahl's approach is quite close to Woodford's description of "central banking as management of expectations" (Woodford 2003, p. 15).

Differences between new and old Wicksellian theories

Despite some similarities, there are essential differences between old-style Wicksellian theory and the NNS. Perhaps the biggest difference is the perspective on the inflation dynamics. In Wicksell's and Lindahl's approaches, inflation is a disequilibrium process, a cumulative price change that results from excess demands in goods and labor markets. If output effects occur, they are due to investment that corresponds to unplanned saving, an unintended freeing of resources from consumption that is accomplished through the market process. In Woodford's version of the NNS, inflation and output variations are results of intertemporal optimization in continuous equilibrium. Woodford claims to have reproduced essential parts of Wicksellian theory without violating "modern standards of conceptual rigor" (2003, p. 6). His model conforms to the standards of DSGE modeling, with forward-looking behavior of the private sector and a minimum of frictions. In our view, however, this sort of progress comes at a cost: the neo-Wicksellian framework has serious deficits when it comes to explaining how the central bank can control inflation in an economy without monetary frictions, and it is not well suited to deal with essential aspects of cumulative processes of inflation and deflation.

Interest-rate control in an economy without monetary frictions

Woodford claims that his model of an economy with "no monetary frictions whatsoever" (2003, pp. 61–74) shows that central banks can control market rates of interest without taking recourse to monetary aggregates. In that model, "markets are perfectly competitive, prices adjust continuously to clear markets, and there exist markets in which state-contingent securities of any kind may be traded" (Ibid., p. 62).

No one would actually hold money in such a world, but Woodford postulates the existence of a monetary base in liabilities of the central bank that define the unit of account and represent nothing but a claim to payment in terms of themselves. As there are no frictions, other riskless nominal assets are perfect substitutes for "base money" (Ibid., p. 63).

Woodford then analyzes the portfolio choice of the representative household and shows that if "base money" is to be held, its rate of interest must equal the rate of return on the potential substitutes. What is more surprising is his conclusion that "the special situation of the central bank, as issuer of liabilities that promise to pay only additional units of its own liabilities, allows the central bank to fix both the nominal interest yield on its liabilities and the quantity of them in existence" (Ibid., p. 63).

This is self-contradictory. If other nominal assets are perfect substitutes for "base money," the central bank is in no special position. It cannot set interest rates independently, since arbitrage processes would shift demand toward the substitutes. And its power to determine the quantity of its own liabilities is irrelevant as long as the issuers of the substitutes can freely vary the quantities of their liabilities. If the central bank is to be in exclusive control of both the price and the quantity of its liabilities, there cannot be perfect substitutes—in other words, there must be monetary frictions that give the central bank a monopolist position.[15]

Apparently, it is difficult to argue that the central bank can control interest rates in a portfolio model where the central bank has no distinct role other than that of providing the unit of account. Wicksell (1898) took a more straightforward way to show what gives the central bank control over interest rates. He presented his pure credit economy as a banking system in which gold has ceased to be the means of payment but remains the standard of value. Wicksell argued that gold should be replaced by a unit that is employed in the accounts of banks both as medium of exchange and as standard of value. Wicksell made this point more explicit when, in his 1919 proposal to reform the Swedish financial system after the suspension of the gold standard, he suggested that the central bank, as a nonprofit institution, should remunerate its deposits at the same rate as the one that it charges for loans.[16] Since commercial banks would need an interest spread to make profits (and thus offer lower deposit and/or higher loan rates), the central bank could dictate the credit conditions. Assuming a cashless economy, Wicksell argued that the central bank could make its discount rate "effective" in the credit market simply by setting the rate paid on the deposits held in the central bank. Private intermediaries would still be able to charge higher interest rates, insofar as they lend money to sectors where the central bank is not willing or able to evaluate and monitor the risks. Some savers may also "risk a portion of their property" and deal directly with "risky and protracted enterprises" through shares and so forth (Wicksell 1936, pp. 74–75). However, none of these assets are perfect substitutes for central bank deposits. In terms of interest-rate control, the presence of other assets does not change the essential features of Wicksell's pure credit system, in which the central bank's deposit rate becomes the basic rate.

Woodford's discussion of the channel system of modern central banking seems to be based on a similar intuition, but it is only introductory rhetoric. There is no role for financial intermediaries in the household-based "rigorous modeling" that leads up to the core model of the neo-Wicksellian framework. Woodford's NNS connection to Wicksell's pure credit economy looks rather loose.

Price stickiness and output effects of monetary policy

Nominal rigidities are the key to explaining output effects of monetary policy in both Woodford's and Lindahl's frameworks. A closer look reveals, however, that Woodford's framework is quite rigid and limited in scope, whereas Lindahl's approach permits the analysis of a wider range of inflation and output dynamics.

In Lindahl's discussion of the cumulative process, nominal rigidities interact with the formation of expectations. As a stylized fact, prices and wages are assumed to be sticky at the beginning, when the loan rate diverges from the expected profit rate. If and when the credit expansion leads to inflation, price expectations will eventually adapt to the pace of inflation. In extreme cases, they will become forward looking and produce an indefinite rise in the price level. The adjustment of expectations to ongoing inflation erodes the (upward) stickiness of prices and wages—a feedback that tends to accelerate inflation. Lindahl thus made expectations, nominal rigidities, and their output effects endogenous to the specific constellations in which disequilibrium develops from interest-rate gaps.

Compare this with Woodford's version of the NNS, where nominal rigidities and the formation of expectations in the private sector are treated as exogenous. Woodford (2003) introduces the assumption of Muth-rational expectations for three reasons: it is considered to be "de rigueur" for macroeconomic dynamics; it is analytically convenient; and with regard to dynamic inconsistency, it helps to make the case for policy rules particularly clear. The problem with the assumption is, however, that it does not permit much interaction between learning and inflation dynamics.[17]

Since the NNS is based on an RBC benchmark, it is quite a challenge to produce substantial and persistent output effects of monetary policy under rational expectations. As pointed out earlier, Woodford achieves this by using a Calvo-style model of staggered pricing in order to derive the New Keynesian Phillips curve (equation 2). However, the timing of price changes in this type of model is independent of inflation—a drawback that is freely admitted by Woodford (2003, pp. 141–142), who nevertheless argues that the method is analytically convenient and empirically plausible. Given the fact that the current mainstream considers the old synthesis and earlier macroeconomics outdated because they had committed the crime of *ad-hocery*, this procedure is certainly unsatisfactory.[18]

A more general line of defense is an *as if* that permeates most of the new synthesis: by analyzing observable inflation and output dynamics *as if* the private sector had rational expectations and *as if* the firms played a Calvo lottery, we can mimic the dynamics that, in the real world, are generated by less forward-looking behavior and endogenous rigidities. This is a strong belief, since Calvo pricing is plausible only, if at all, in an environment of low inflation. Furthermore, as Woodford (2003, p. 243) himself concedes, the log-linear model described above can be used only for "characterizing equilibria involving small fluctuations around a deterministic steady state" with near-zero inflation. But the neo-Wicksellian framework is not just an "approximation" for pedagogical uses; it is now also used for policy analysis. As such, it can be applied only to "fair weather conditions" (Laidler 2006, p. 159), thereby excluding most of the problems of accelerating and high inflation (as well as deflation) that were at the core of old-style Wicksellian theory.

What does the central bank have to know?

Woodford's discussion of rules for monetary policy is highly sophisticated and informative. He examines the differences between Wicksell's original feedback rule with various specifications of the Taylor rule. With regard to equation (3), the obvious differences are the following:

- Wicksell's formula requires reactions to inflation gaps only, not to output gaps;
- Wicksell (and Lindahl) propagated price-level targeting rather than inflation targeting;
- in Wicksell's formula, the central bank would not have to know the natural rate of interest and, hence, not set any interest rate target.

A Wicksell rule would, in principle, not permit any base drift—i.e., monetary policy would have to revert changes in the price level. In view of shocks to aggregate supply, information lags, and other problems, this might have undesired output effects if prices are sticky. This is why Woodford and other advocates of the NNS, including Taylor himself, propose inflation targeting. However, the special charm of the Wicksell rule is that the information requirements are minimal. The central bank needs to react only to perceived changes in the price level. In Woodford's version of the Taylor rule, the bank has to set a basic target rate (the "intercept term" i^*) that (in combination with γ_p, γ_x) yields the natural rate of interest. If the central bank cannot correctly anticipate changes in the natural rate (a plausible assumption), or if it cannot adjust nominal interest immediately and fully to such changes, the Taylor rule of equation (3) may produce undesired inflation and output effects.[19]

The Wicksell-Keynes Connection versus the Wicksell-Woodford Connection

The theoretical connections between Wicksell and Keynes are a large issue that we cannot discuss in detail here. We confine ourselves to pointing out some similarities between the approaches of Keynes and the (other) original Wicksellians, on the one hand, and the Woodfordian NNS, on the other. In this we draw on Leijonhufvud's (1979) reconstruction of Keynes's "Wicksell Connection."

As Keynes noted in his *Treatise on Money* (1930, chap. 13), his analysis of the price-level dynamics that are generated by interest-rate gaps comes close to Wicksell's theory. While Wicksell put the emphasis on "secular" inflation that results from a rise of the natural rate of interest over the market rate, Keynes set the focus on credit cycles and deflation that follows the rise of the market rate over the natural rate. He gave speculators and other agents in financial markets a more prominent role in the cumulative process than they had in the bank-centered theories of Wicksell, Lindahl, Myrdal, and Hayek. However, in all original Wicksellian theories, to which we would add the framework of Keynes's *Treatise*, coordination failures of the interest-rate mechanism were the common theme. The dynamics of the price level (and, for Lindahl, Myrdal, and Hayek, the incipient changes in the levels and structures of production) were seen as results and parts of intertemporal disequilibrium.

In the *General Theory of Employment, Interest and Money* (1936), Keynes had changed his view. He now put the emphasis on changes in effective demand that shift output away from its full-employment equilibrium position, and he discussed these changes in a comparative-static framework. He no longer regarded monetary policy as central, suggesting that interest rates play no role in coordinating investment and saving at all. Interest rates were now determined by liquidity preference, and they would still affect investment by their relation to the marginal efficiency of capital, but saving would adjust *ex post* to investment by way of the income-expenditure mechanism, not by the closing of interest-rate gaps. The *General Theory* does not seem to have a Wicksell Connection,[20] as Keynes (1936, pp. 182 and 243) rejected the concept of a "natural rate of interest" (which he had used in the *Treatise*) even more emphatically than Lindahl and Myrdal had done before.[21]

However, the Keynes of the *General Theory* still belongs to the camp of the old-style Wicksellians, if compared with the old and new neoclassical syntheses in general and to Woodford in particular. After Modigliani (1944), the explanation of underemployment equilibria in the IS/LM-AD/AS framework of the old synthesis had largely boiled down to nominal rigidities in terms of sticky wages and prices. And the consensus view of the new synthesis is characterized by the Blanchard Triangle: all modeling of persistent output gaps is (to be) based on a combination of intertemporal optimization, imperfect competition, and nominal rigidities in goods and labor markets (Blanchard 1997a). While wage and price stickiness is crucial for the New Keynesians and neo-Wicksellians in the NNS camp, it is not essential for Keynes's explanation of underemployment equilibria (1936, chap. 19). In that account, wage and price flexibility could not prevent or cure effective demand failures and involuntary unemployment but, rather, would make things worse. This is also a key aspect of Wicksell's theory of the downward cumulative process, where a reduction in money wages during deflation fails to reduce unemployment unless it has strong indirect effects on the market rate of interest.[22] Furthermore, as Lindahl (1939 [1930]) pointed out, price and wage flexibility is the problem rather than the solution.[23]

In the Wicksell-Keynes Connection, the crucial rigidity is to be found in the financial markets, not in goods or labor markets. Misalignments of the market rate of interest to the rate that would make investment and consumption plans consistent keep the economy out of equilibrium. In the Wicksell-Woodford Connection, this has been ruled out by formulating the relationship between interest and output in terms of a first-order condition of intertemporal equilibrium. If that equilibrium is not optimal, it is a policy failure, not a market failure.

Conclusion

Has the development of the NNS led to a renaissance of Wicksellian macroeconomics? How does it relate to the Wicksell-Keynes Connection of the 1930s? To most economists, these may not be very interesting questions. But when the propagators of synthetic state-of-the-art models use old labels, such as "Neoclassical," "Keynesian," or even "neo-Wicksellian," they apparently wish to indicate that they follow well-established, reputable lines of thinking. So the labels deserve to be taken seriously. This is what we have tried to do here by exploring the similarities and differences between Woodford's neo-Wicksellian NNS and original versions of Wicksellian theory.

Our conclusion is that Woodford's approach has brought back various Wicksellian themes into the current mainstream but that it is a rather limited extension of the Wicksell Connection. It shows that (some) Wicksellian inflation and output dynamics can be reproduced with the rather roundabout techniques of intertemporal general-equilibrium theory (Woodford 2006, pp. 197–198). However, postulating complete financial markets makes it difficult to model Wicksellian interest-rate control. In the aggregate supply block, the inflation and output dynamics result from very restrictive assumptions about the formation of expectations and price-setting behavior; and they rely entirely on nominal rigidities in goods (and labor) markets. Moreover, they are strictly confined to low inflation environments, and they cannot explain the genuinely Keynesian case of output gaps in the presence of price-level stability. So the differences between the old Wicksellians (including Keynes) and the new synthesis help to expose the latter's shortcomings. If Sir Dennis Robertson were still alive, he would probably conclude that the methods for hunting the Wicksellian hare have become very sophisticated. Yet he might also observe that the new instruments are so limited in their scope that they make it hard to see more than a leg or the tail of the hare.

Notes

This chapter was prepared as a paper for the conference on "Keynes' Economics and His Influence on Modern Economics" at Sophia University, Tokyo, in March 2007. An earlier version had been presented at the "The History of Macroeconomics" conference at the Université Catholique de Louvain in 2005. We are grateful to Michel DeVroey, Charles Goodhart, Toshiaki Hirai, and other participants of both conferences for helpful comments.

1. Ragnar Frisch and Erik Lindahl were apparently the first to use the term around 1933; see De Vroey and Hoover (2003, p. 2).
2. For all those claims and labels, see, in due order, Keynes (1936, p. xxi), Klein (1947), Samuelson (1951, p. 336), Johnson (1971), Begg (1982), Miller (1984), and Goodfriend and King (1997).
3. Note the difference between the titles of Woodford (2003) and Patinkin's *Money, Interest and Prices* (1956), a central contribution to the "old" Neoclassical synthesis that (in the Appendix, Note E, pp. 381–397) emphasizes Wicksell's formulation of a real-balance mechanism while downplaying his concept of pure credit.
4. See Leijonhufvud (1979), and Boianovsky and Presley (2009). This is not to say that Robertson subscribed to the idea of a monetary policy without money, but he would have recognized many of the themes in Woodford (2003) as issues discussed in the interwar literature.
5. For a fuller treatment of Lindahl's macroeconomics, see Boianovsky and Trautwein (2006a).
6. Actually, i_t denotes the current value of the nominal interest rate—set by the central bank as in equation (3) below—in relation to its deterministic steady-state value; see Woodford (2003, pp. 77–81).
7. In the Calvo model of staggered pricing, a fraction of goods prices $(0<\alpha<1)$ remains unchanged in the period, whereas the other part $(1-\alpha)$ may adjust flexibly to shocks. Since the "right to change" is drawn in a sort of lottery, the probability of price adjustments is $1-\alpha$ for any good in the model. This is completely unrealistic but analytically convenient; see Woodford (2003, pp. 177–187).
8. Note, however, that the core argument in Keynes (1936) does not hinge on price stickiness. Keynes insisted that even full flexibility of wages and prices would not return the system to full-employment equilibrium.
9. The notion of a natural rate dates back to Smith and Ricardo; see Hayek (1933, p. 110). The phrase of neutral money gained currency only in discussions of Wicksell's concept of the neutral rate of interest; apparently, Bortkiewicz deserves the credit for its coinage; see Hayek (1933, pp. 117–118) and Patinkin and Steiger (1989, p. 135 n. 5). Cumulative processes can be traced back to Thornton and Joplin, but the term itself does not seem to have been used before Myrdal (1939 [1931]).
10. Even the idea of a pure credit system had a forerunner in Mill's discussion of the "influence of credit on prices" (Mill 1871, chap. 12). For discussions of

the concept in the second half of the twentieth century, see Hicks (1989) and the surveys in Trautwein (1997) and Boianovsky (1998).

11. Furthermore, in his review of "Keynes' Economic System," Lindahl (1954, pp. 162–171) argued that the liquidity preference theory of interest has no place in a long-run dynamic theory, where the stock of money is redundant in the determination of equilibrium; see Boianovsky and Trautwein (2006a).

12. In his last comment on the cumulative process, Wicksell (1922, p. xii n. 1) argued that inflation might accelerate even if people adapt their expectations only to past changes in the price level: "As long as the change in prices . . . is believed to be temporary, it will in fact remain permanent; as soon as it is considered to be permanent, it will become progressive, and when it is eventually seen as progressive, it will turn into an avalanche." See also Boianovsky and Trautwein (2001a).

13. Wicksell's theory of the business cycle and his distinctions between cycles, crises, and cumulative processes are discussed in Boianovsky (1995) and Boianovsky and Trautwein (2001b).

14. "Free capital disposal" denotes saving in monetary terms plus "value change, defined as anticipated depreciation minus appreciation" (Myrdal 1939, p. 85).

15. Boianovsky and Trautwein (2006b) discuss these problems with Woodford's model in detail; see also the reaction by Woodford (2006).

16. See Boianovsky (1998, sect. 4). The assumption of identical interest rates for loans and deposits is also made and discussed by Lindahl (1939 [1930], pp. 161–162).

17. Woodford (2003, pp. 252–275) examines some learning dynamics but confines this discussion to the proof that the Taylor principle ($\gamma_p > 1$) ensures convergence to rational expectations equilibria.

18. Goodhart (2004, p. 5) is highly critical of this use of Calvo pricing: "much of the structural foundations, relating to price/wage stickiness in modern macro, rest on a convenient fiction, which has only a distant relationship with reality. Why such procedures are somehow regarded as professionally acceptable, whereas the assumption of adaptive expectations was not (especially when empirical studies generally show that pure backward-looking expectations have a better forecasting record than pure forward-looking ones), is beyond me."

19. Tamborini (2006) demonstrates this with respect to the Taylor principle ($\gamma_p > 1$).

20. It is out of dissatisfaction with Keynes's disregard of the coordinating role of the interest rate that Leijonhufvud (1979) reconstructs the "Z-theory," a loanable-funds theory with output fluctuations that provides the "missing link" between Keynes's *Treatise* and the *General Theory*.

21. The Swedes, on the other hand, did not have much praise for Keynes's *General Theory*; see Ohlin (1937) and Lindahl (1954). They considered comparative-static equilibrium analysis and liquidity preference theory to be retrograde developments, compared with the *Treatise* and their own approaches to dynamic macroeconomics.

22. As Wicksell (1935, p. 26) put it in his discussion of a downward cumulative process, "It is usually incipient unemployment, low wages and decreased consumption, as well as falling prices, which reduce the demand for metallic currency," thereby lowering the market rate of interest toward the "natural rate."

23. See also Boianovsky and Trautwein (2006a) and (2006b).

PART THREE

Rereading and Interpreting Keynes

Dissatisfaction with interpretations of Keynesian theory and Keynesianism, of both old and new vintage, has prompted fresh investigations into Keynes's writings. Scholarship in archival work has flourished, stimulated also by the availability of unpublished papers and an increased awareness of the importance of context in framing ideas and concepts. The essays in this section all share a concern for the language, circumstances, and timing of Keynes' contributions, thus providing new insights into the meaning and relevance of his work.

Roger Backhouse argues that the *General Theory* is molded in the language of mathematics, meaning not the construction of a formal model but the clarification of the different postulates in which classical theory and Keynes's own work rested. Keynes's chosen method was to use mathematical notation to define the problem, with no manipulation of the algebra to derive further results. Mathematics provides the framework for a verbal discussion to which Keynes always gave prominence over formalization, in the belief in the superiority of ordinary language to address economic questions.

Hiroshi Yoshikawa is also concerned with defining the language appropriate to frame Keynes's theoretical achievements, denouncing the inadequacy of past and present attempts to ground the "macro" analysis on "micro" foundations. The point made by Yoshikawa is that the approach based on statistical physics is more adequate to represent the behavior of a large number of microunits since it captures the working of the system as a whole. The core of Keynes's theory is the role of aggregate demand on the level of output and employment, namely, the idea that an increase in aggregate demand mobilizes factors of production from lower to higher productivity sectors. Since rates of utilization of labor and capital in Keynes's *General Theory* are conditioned by the level of demand, unlike in neoclassical theory, the equilibrium (corresponding to underemployment) that is reached is stochastic rather than unique. This gives us the famous Keynesian conclusion that there is no tendency for a capitalist system to come to rest at the point where there would be full employment.

Keynes's principle of effective demand was the end result of a process of thought that took him away from the *Treatise,* in which the monetary analysis was more Wicksellian than Marshallian. Toshiaki Hirai travels the road that ended with the *General Theory,* giving us a detailed map of its turning points, milestones, and detours, thanks to his meticulous study of drafts, tables of contents, and notes held in the Keynes Papers at King's College, Cambridge. The timing of Keynes's new discoveries and concepts was coupled with abandonment of "habitual modes of thought and expression," so that a zigzag, rather than a smooth progression, is a better portrait of the development of his ideas.

In the process of arriving at the full-fledged presentation of his theory, Keynes came up against criticism by his close circle of colleagues and friends. Piero Sraffa was one of them. His name is associated with the Cambridge school of economics as much as Richard Kahn, Joan Robinson, and Nicholas Kaldor are, but Sraffa distanced himself from the others in developing a distinct approach based on the return to classical political economy and an uncompromising opposition to the use of marginal methods in economics. The availability of Sraffa's papers at Trinity College has made it possible to advance our knowledge of this controversial figure who remains a source of inspiration but also of disagreement among those who see in the Cambridge school an alternative to current mainstream economics.

Heinz Kurz carefully examines the explicit and implicit criticism of some of Keynes's concepts made by Sraffa in the latter's scattered notes, short comments, and annotations to his copy of the *General Theory.* Sraffa's disagreement revolved mainly around Keynes's concessions to received economic theory while he was also trying to subvert it. In particular, Sraffa objected to the maintenance of the inverse relationship between investment and the interest rate and, symmetrically, between employment and the wage rate. He was also critical of Keynes's concept of liquidity preference, on the grounds that the concept of liquidity appeared to him vague and ambiguous; Sraffa also took a strong stance against postulating an inverse relationship between the demand for money and the rate of interest, as he found it reminiscent of the marginal utility curve. It was Keynes's use of several marginalist concepts that prevented Sraffa from fully endorsing the Keynesian approach, and even today this remains the dividing line between their followers.

The last chapter of the section, by Gilles Dostaler, draws on the enormous body of work that Keynes left behind, mostly still unpublished, as a basis to assess the man and his achievements. Dostaler's main point is that Keynes's economic theory cannot be uncoupled from his political vision and philosophical conceptions and, above all, from his urge to persuade his fellow countrymen and the world at large of the need and possibility of change in the way economic affairs are conducted. Keynes led a relentless war of words against the dominant views of his time in order for future generations to live in a better world; to persuade others that the change necessary to build that future is possible is perhaps his most enduring legacy.

CHAPTER SEVEN

An Abstruse and Mathematical Argument: The Use of Mathematical Reasoning in the *General Theory*

Roger E. Backhouse

Introduction

The *General Theory* was greeted by many reviewers as a difficult book, written around a technical argument that was developed using mathematics. Thus, the reviewer for the *Times* (quoted in Backhouse 1999, p. 49) wrote that "in substance the book is inevitably difficult, and the semi-mathematical form of some parts of it may alarm the inexpert reader." The *Economist*'s reviewer (E. A. G. R., presumably Austin Robinson, quoted in Backhouse 1999, p. 78) went further, claiming that "even for the ordinary economist the argument, being largely in mathematical form, is difficult." These reviewers were far from alone in their reaction that the book was difficult and mathematical. R. C. K. Ensor (quoted in Backhouse 1999, p. 93), a journalist and author of a volume in the *Oxford History of England*, commented that "The abstruse plunges into close and often mathematical argument," words that paralleled the reaction of the Columbia economist Horace Taylor's remark (quoted in Backhouse 1999, p. 100) that "it is presented in a highly abstruse and mathematical fashion." Keynes's friend, Hubert Henderson, wrote that the *General Theory* was "a very difficult technical book, involving much novel terminology, a considerable use of mathematical symbols" (H. D. Henderson, quoted in Backhouse 1999, p. 125). Across the Atlantic, Alvin Hansen, later to be Keynes's most influential interpreter, in the first of his two reviews of the book, described its argument as "elaborated with the aid of mathematical equations into a closely reasoned and difficult analysis" (quoted in Backhouse 1999, p. 241).

The reviewers quoted above were all writing for a broad audience that needed to be warned that the book contained technical material.[1] However, the claim they were all making went further than that, as the *Economist*'s review indicated: the book was mathematical even by the standards of professional economists at the time. Furthermore, descriptions of the book as "abstruse" by Ensor and, more significantly (because he was an economist), by Taylor implied criticism. They were doing much more than simply warning laypeople that economics was difficult.

This is in marked contrast to the view that rapidly emerged within the profession—that the *General Theory* was not a work of mathematical economics, a view that emerged comparatively quickly as economists began, in the decade after 1936, to translate the book's main ideas into formal simultaneous-equation models, from John Hicks's (1937) simple SI-LL model (later named IS-LM by Hansen) to the fully-fledged general equilibrium model of Don Patinkin's *Money, Interest, and Prices* (1956). By the 1970s, when even this generation of macroeconomic models was being dismissed as having insufficiently rigorous microfoundations, and when Robert Lucas, Thomas Sargent, and others had stepped up the level of mathematics used in macroeconomics by several notches, the *General Theory*'s claims to be considered a work that was to any significant extent mathematical looked even more tenuous.

The main reason for this change of view would appear to be obvious. During this period, economics became more technical and more mathematical for a variety of reasons (see Morgan 2003; Backhouse 2008). The Econometric Society was fostering the growth of more mathematical approaches to economics, exemplified by the Cowles Commission, which became the center of the most advanced mathematical economics in the 1940s. The upheavals in Europe caused the migration of many highly technical economists, and the experiences of British and above all American economists working alongside natural scientists and engineers during the Second World War made them see economics as a more technical discipline. All the while, there was a progressive increase in the level of mathematics that economics students were expected to know, even though it was not until, perhaps, the 1960s that it was possible to assume that an advanced understanding of mathematics was a prerequisite for being an economist.

However, while this may explain why economists began to be impatient with Keynes's style, it is not a complete explanation. It is significant that many of those commenting on the *General Theory*'s mathematics, or rather the lack of it, were interested parties. Paul Samuelson, one of those who propagated the view that Keynes was hostile to the use of mathematics (see O'Donnell 1997, p. 133), did not intend to disparage Keynes—to the contrary, he was a highly influential Keynesian. However, he was arguing, aggressively, for mathematical reasoning to become far more important to economics than Keynes would have allowed (see Mc-Closkey 1986). Most of the macroeconomists who made their reputations after the Second World War did so by creating mathematically more rigorous foundations for the subject. This meant that they had an incentive to play down the mathematics in the *General Theory*, for the less mathematical was the *General Theory*, the more impressive was their own achievement.

On the other side, those who opposed the mainstream view of the *General Theory* also had an interest in playing down the book's mathematical component. Post-Keynesians, as they came to call themselves from the 1970s, wanted to argue that the book offered an economics that was different from what was found in the IS/LM model or models that were mathematically more sophisticated. The arguments of chapter 12 in the *General Theory* or Keynes's article in the *Quarterly Journal of Economics* (1937, reprinted in CWK 14, pp. 109–123), for example, offered arguments about uncertainty that could not be captured either in extant mathematical models or in the equations to be found in the *General Theory*, thereby almost forcing those who emphasized these ideas to play down the importance of the mathematics. Similarly, as regards Keynes's views about the essential features of a monetary economy, it could be argued that mathematical representations, which were largely compatible with theories of general competitive equilibrium in an economy without money, missed the point of what he wanted to say. The result was that Post-Keynesians, like more orthodox Keynesians, also had reason to minimize the extent and importance of mathematical argumentation in the *General Theory*.

The aim of this chapter is to get behind these retrospective views of the *General Theory*, to make the case for seeing it as the work of a trained mathematician, whose background in mathematics shaped the way he constructed the book's argument.[2] Not only does Keynes use a significant amount of algebra; even when he does not use algebra, his verbal reasoning is permeated by a mathematical way of thinking. The structure of the argument and much of the crucial language are those of someone who is thinking as a mathematician. Contemporaries who saw the book as highly mathematical were more perceptive than later commentators, perhaps misled by comparisons with subsequent economic theories, have realized.

This concern differentiates this study from other work on Keynes's use of mathematics. One of these is O'Donnell (1997), who, under the heading of formalism, considers Keynes's attitude toward mathematics, correctly concluding that the widely held view of Keynes as one who opposed the use of mathematics in economics is wrong. This is an argument that draws upon virtually all of the many statements Keynes made about the use of mathematics, including those in the *General Theory*. Thus, although Keynes's attitude toward mathematics needs to be reviewed here,[3] for it provides an essential element in the argument, this study makes a different point. Its concern is not formalism (except insofar as this is relevant to the broader argument) but the relationship between mathematical ways of thinking and the way Keynes constructed his textual arguments.[4]

This chapter develops an argument from Backhouse and Laidler (2004), which in turn built on the interpretation of the *General Theory* offered in *Fabricating the Keynesian Revolution* (Laidler 1999). Laidler's book argued that the *General Theory* and the IS/LM representation of Keynesian theory were the route through which much of the work done in the interwar period entered postwar macroeconomics. Backhouse and Laidler went further in arguing that there was a clear pattern to what economists, after 1936, chose to take from the *General Theory* and what they chose to ignore. Those elements of the theory that could be (and largely were) expressed in formal mathematics were taken up, whereas those that, because of their complexity, could be expressed only verbally were largely neglected, if not ignored altogether. The latter included much that related to time and dynamics, with the result that the theory became more static. The focus on statics began, as Ohlin (1937) correctly pointed out, with the *General Theory* itself, not with Hicks or his followers. This chapter suggests that this focus on statics, even though Keynes himself attached great importance to dynamic arguments, is the result of a style of argument, rooted in Keynes's training as a mathematician, that permeates the *General Theory*.

The motivation for this chapter is to understand Keynes historically— against the context in which he wrote his *General Theory*. My study may, however, be of wider relevance due to the mathematization of economics that has taken place since then. When arguing over how to construct economic theories and over how to use them to inform policymaking, Keynes's authority has been used to support very different positions. Part of the explanation for why economists have been able to use Keynes to support conflicting positions may lie in the previously unexamined question of the argumentative style that Keynes adopted in the *General Theory*. Thus, if renewed interest in Keynes is to go along with deeper historical understanding, the issues discussed in this chapter may be important.

My argument is built up in three stages. The first is to outline Keynes's attitude toward mathematical reasoning. This draws heavily on O'Donnell

(1997), Rymes (1989), and Skidelsky (1992). That is followed, in the subsequent section, by some preliminary remarks on the use of mathematics and mathematical reasoning in the *General Theory*—some basic "linguistic" analysis, if that term can be applied to algebra. In itself, this may not be particularly interesting, but it lays the foundation for the final section, which explores the way Keynes articulates his central claims. Though this covers familiar material—it could hardly be otherwise—it is presented in such a way as to make clear why the early commentators reacted as they did and why, despite Keynes's holding a more nuanced view of the role to be played by mathematics, the *General Theory* can legitimately be seen as far more mathematical in its way of arguing than is suggested by the number of equations on its pages.

Keynes's attitude toward the use of mathematics

Keynes was a disciple of the philosopher G. E. Moore, who attached prime importance to clear thinking and to intuition.[5] Intuition was not only the basis for Keynes's early theory of probability, founded on the notion that probabilities were elementary properties that could be accessed through intuition (CWK 8; see Bateman 1996), but was central to the way he approached economic theorizing (Moggridge 1992, pp. 551–571; Skidelsky 1992, pp. 539–548). The first and fundamental stage in the construction of an argument was intuition or vision—what he called "the grey fuzzy woolly monster" in one's head (Skidelsky 1992, p. 539). A manifestation of this was that Keynes started with a view of the overall structure of the argument he was trying to make and that the details came only later. The second stage was to make precise the concepts and relations involved. The progression was thus from intuition to clear thought. However, rather than progress to a formal mathematical model, Keynes essentially stopped there. He did construct what would now be called models, but they were rarely complete, and any mathematics was always inextricably linked to analysis that was expressed verbally.

Keynes's reason for using mathematics in this way was that he believed that to construct a formal model was to attempt to specify exactly what was and was not to be included in the analysis—to be "perfectly precise."[6] If the world was vague and complex, such an approach would be inappropriate, as Carabelli has argued (see, e.g., 1991, 2003). It was better to stop with the concepts that provided a basis for clear thinking.[7] Thus, although Keynes used mathematics in the *General Theory*, he refused to use a mathematical model to summarize the argument as a whole. His focus was on clarifying the different postulates on which the "classical" theory and his own rested. This comes across clearly even from looking at his chapter headings. He talks of "The Postulates of the Classical Economics" (chapter 2) and "The Principle of Effective Demand" (chapter 3)—the choice of language here of course carries its own message. He then has four chapters in book II, entitled "Definitions and Ideas," which cover choice of units, definitions, and the "meaning" of saving and investment. In books III and IV, the emphasis shifts to building up the theory that underlies the "principle" enunciated in chapter 3. However, although there are, in book IV, three chapters about "theory,"—two on the "general theory" and one on the "classical theory"—these are greatly outnumbered by chapters on concepts: the propensity to consume, the marginal efficiency and capital, and the "incentives to liquidity." Even at this stage of the argument, there is a chapter on "The Essential Properties of Interest and Money" (chapter 17). It is only in book V, on money wages and prices, after the general theory of employment has been "re-stated" (in chapter 18), that Keynes's chapter headings move away from concepts and definitions, though even here one heading, "The Employment Function," suggests the analysis of a specific concept.

An important source for understanding Keynes's use of mathematics in the *General Theory* is found in the lectures he gave in 1932–1933 during the book's preparation. The notes taken by students in 1932 contain the remark, reproduced as a heading in Rymes (1989, p. 77), "Equations are symbolic rather than algebraic." Referring to an equation relating the rate of interest to the quantity of money given the state of liquidity preference, this had, in the previous lecture, been elaborated upon as follows: "One point regarding equations he has used, for example $\rho = A(M)$. This is a symbolic not an algebraic equation. It is only a shorthand method of stating the relations between various complexes. These [symbolic] relations are better because to use algebraic equations we must make assumptions which are too simplified" (Rymes 1989, p. 77).

Referring again to the equation, Keynes explained that in saying that the rate of interest is a function, given liquidity preference, of the quantity of money, "We really mean the complex of rates of interest for different maturities bears [some] relationship with M and A, with A too being a complex relationship" (Rymes 1989, p. 76). This is exactly the way that he had used mathematical notation in the *Treatise on Probability* (1921, CWK 8), in which he had presented mathematical symbols for probability but then gave them meanings that differed from their usual usage. It was as if Keynes wanted a symbol to hold the reader's attention while he talked through what it meant. Though he did not use symbols, he adopted a similar strategy in chapter 12 of the *General Theory*: he talks of "prospective yield" in language reminiscent of expected utility calculations (Irving Fisher's theory had been discussed in the previous chapter), but this was no more than a framework for discussing ideas that could not be analyzed within such a framework.

Keynes took up this theme, of the role of mathematics, in an oft-cited passage late in the *General Theory*:

> It is a great fault of symbolic pseudo-mathematical methods of formalizing a system of economic analysis . . . that they expressly assume strict independence between the factors involved and lose all their cogency and authority if this hypothesis is disallowed: whereas in ordinary discourse, where we are not blindly manipulating but know all the time what we are doing and what the words mean, we can keep "at the back of our heads" the necessary reserves and qualifications and adjustments which we shall have to make later on, in a way in which we cannot keep complicated partial differentials "at the back" of several pages of algebra which assume that they all vanish. Too large a proportion of recent "mathematical" economics are mere concoctions, as imprecise as the initial assumptions they rest on, which allow the author to lose sight of the complexities and interdependencies of the real world in a maze of pretentious and unhelpful symbols. (CWK 7, pp. 297–298)

This emphasizes the point that Keynes attached great significance to the precise meaning of the terms involved and makes sense of the remark, quoted earlier, that equations are symbolic rather than algebraic.[8] Merely to construct a mathematical argument, relying on the conventional meaning of terms, is wholly inadequate.

The *General Theory:* preliminaries

Flick through its pages and the *General Theory* does not appear to be a mathematical book: indeed, given the general absence of diagrams,[9] it probably appears less mathematical that Marshall's *Principles* (1920). Of twenty-four chapters, only half contain mathematical symbols or, in one case, a diagram.[10] Moreover, in many of those chapters, the symbolism appears trivial to the modern reader. Keynes writes down simple functional relations involving functions of one variable, such as his aggregate supply and demand functions, $Z = \varphi(N)$ and $D = f(N)$. He uses derivatives (dC/dY), ratios of changes ($\Delta C/\Delta Y$), and elasticities. He also uses sums and differences as a way to define terms, such as saying user cost is $A_1 + (G' - B') - G$. There is also a formula for the relation between interest rates in different periods, expressing one rate as the ratio of two others. This is all the mathematical knowledge required to understand the argument.

In virtually all these cases, Keynes's method is to use algebraic notation to define the problem, writing down a functional relationship or decomposing a concept into its component parts, before discussing it verbally. The algebra does little more than provide the framework for a verbal discussion, and there is virtually no manipulation of the algebra to derive further results.

There are three exceptions to this generalization. The first is a proof of the relationship between the investment multiplier, k, and the employment multiplier, k', but this is in a footnote (CWK 7, p. 116), and in the text the problem is simplified by assuming them to be equal. The remaining two are in chapters 20 and 21 (CWK 7, pp. 282–285 and 305–306), in which there are some relatively complicated derivations of certain elasticities, though, again, the derivations of formulae discussed in the text are presented in footnotes.[11] However, though this might appear complicated at first, Keynes is doing little more than either deriving elasticities or decomposing elasticities into other elasticities. What Keynes is doing is comparatively mechanical, not analyzing what modern economists would see as behavioral relationships.

This all supports the argument that the *General Theory* should not be seen as a highly mathematical book. However, the same facts about the book can be presented in a different light. The corollary of algebra being used as the framework for a verbal discussion is that the verbal discussion is centered on the algebra. Keynes's method is to specify abstract functional relationships that are then used as the framework around which the discussion is centered. The word "function" is used 109 times in the book, always to denote a mathematical function.[12] To place this in perspective, the term "unemployment" is used only eighty-two times.[13] There is also a curious asymmetry in the way he uses the terms "function" and "curve."

Keynes uses the term "curve" forty-three times.[14] What is significant about this is that it is always used to refer to older theories.[15] It occurs in phrases such as "the demand curve for labor," "the ordinary demand curve," or "the demand curve for capital." These expressions are, in themselves, unremarkable. However, they all occur in discussions of the classical theory. When it comes to expounding his own theory, Keynes talks in terms of "functions." He could have used the same terminology to expound both the classical theory and his own, but he did not. Whether or not Keynes was conscious of this (perhaps he is subconsciously following the language of his predecessors when discussing their ideas and using different language for his own ideas), if one takes the approach that a curve is viewed as sufficiently precise to be drawn on the page, whereas functions denote abstract relationships, the language alone is enough to suggest that his own theory is more general.

Keynes's use of the language here also serves to reinforce his claim that his own theory is more general than the classical. He is arguing that the "curve" of "classical" theory is one possible expression of the relationship depicted in the "function" of his more "general" theory: that it is one of the infinity of possible such curves that one would get from the infinity of possible sets of *ceteris paribus* conditions. This view is supported by the *General Theory*'s one diagram.

This diagram (CWK 7, p. 180), illustrated in Figure 7.1, plots investment and saving vertically and the rate of interest horizontally.

It would be natural to expect symmetry in the treatment of the two curves in the diagram, depicting saving and investment in relation to the rate of interest, but Keynes does not do this. He refers to the "investment demand-schedule," which has a negative slope, and to the "curve" relating

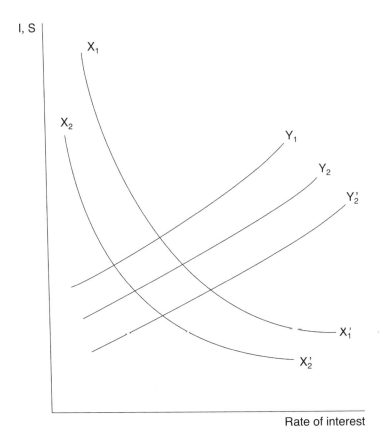

Figure 7.1   The one diagram in the *General Theory*. Source: CWK 7, p. 180, with slight simplification.

saving to the rate of interest, which has a positive slope. The only context in which he treats both curves symmetrically is when referring directly to the diagram, when he talks about the X curve and the Y curve. He considers a shift in the investment demand schedule, pointing out that this will cause a rise in income and hence a shift in the curve relating saving and the rate of interest. The result is that in order to know the outcome of the shift in the investment demand schedule, it is necessary to know the extent to which the saving curve shifts.

There are three points to note about this discussion. First, Keynes's message concerns the failure of the classical theory to allow for changes in the level of income: because income changes, there are three variables to be determined (income, investment = saving, and the rate of interest) but only two equations. The classical theory ignores a dimension of the problem. Second, his objection to the classical analysis involved feedback effects of the nature that one finds in general equilibrium theory (though his discussion is in thoroughly Marshallian terms, not in terms of Walrasian general equilibrium theory). Changes in the rate of interest cause changes elsewhere in the economy that cause the two curves to shift. For Keynes, the "general" theory is one that does not rely on tacit assumptions about independence and homogeneity.[16] Third, Keynes's language is saying that the two curves in the diagram have a very different status. One represents a real relationship, the investment demand schedule; the other, an ephemeral curve that moves whenever there is a change. The subliminal message is that "curves" are unusable. Schedules are legitimate depictions of functional relationships, but curves are not.

This is not the place for a linguistic analysis of the entire *General Theory*, but there are some further points worth noting about the language Keynes uses to denote the components of his theory. The term he uses to describe what subsequent generations of economists have called the consumption function was "the propensity to consume." Similarly, instead of the demand for money, he refers to "liquidity preference," In using such terms, an element of vagueness is built into the terminology, which has been removed in more modern accounts. The exception is the "marginal efficiency of capital," which carries no such association: perhaps this is because it is not a representation of behavior so much as an expectation. With both liquidity preference and the marginal efficiency of capital, Keynes is prepared to speak of a schedule, making it more precise (though he does not refer to schedules as curves). The term "function" is reserved for other types of relations.

The *General Theory:* the central theoretical argument

Even though there are chapters the significance of which is disputed, the *General Theory* has a clear theoretical structure. After exposing the postulates of what he chose to call the classical theory, Keynes outlined "The Principle of Effective Demand" (chapter 3). He made it clear that this lay at the heart of his argument, which was that there is only one point at which aggregate supply and demand are equal—at which effective demand equals the aggregate supply price of output. Classical economics was mistaken in believing that these could be equal at any level of output.[17] The next fourteen chapters (in books III and IV) were concerned with developing the argument in more detail, justifying his claim that the aggregate demand function was different from the aggregate supply function. To do this, he had to explore the determinants of consumption and investment, including the rate of interest. His argument was then "restated" in chapter 18. Throughout, he took the money wage rate as given, which meant that to complete the argument he had to consider the effects of changes in the money wage. He turned to this topic in book V (chapters 19–21), providing reasons why changes in the money wage could not be relied upon to cure unemployment.

This makes it clear that the central theoretical argument is that aggregate demand is not identically equal to aggregate supply.[18] This is the essence of Keynes's difference with classical economics. It is an argument without which his theory would make no sense. It is also pivotal to the reasoning on which his policy conclusions rested. The use of mathematics and mathematical reasoning needs to be viewed in relation to it.

Chapter 3, "The Principle of Effective Demand," is a mathematical argument built around abstract functions of single variables. The entire argument concerns the existence of these functional relations in a comparison of one function with another. They are abstract in that the precise relationship is not specified. As O'Donnell (1997, p. 159) has argued, the discussion of D and Z cries out for a diagram (though, as explained above, to do so might have spoiled the rhetorical contrast between classical curves and his own functions and schedules). The chapter is a justification for thinking about macroeconomic equilibrium in terms of the relationship between two functions. It is, essentially, reducing the economics to an abstract mathematical argument.

Chapter 18, the restatement of the argument that forms the other side of the sandwich, uses no mathematical notation but can be regarded as exploring the same ideas. Moreover, Keynes immediately uses the language of simultaneous equations: "it may be useful to make clear which elements in the economic system we usually take as given, which are the independent variables of our system and which are the dependent variables" (CWK 7, p. 245). "Taking as given" has Marshallian connotations, but dependent and independent variables are the language of simultaneous equations. (It is worth noting that the only other place where Keynes uses this language is when discussing the classical theory of interest in chapter 14.) However, having introduced this language, his list of independent variables is heterogeneous. The rate of interest is in principle a variable, even though it may stand, as in his lectures, for a complex of interest rates. The propensity to consume is a relationship between income and consumption, as is "the schedule of the marginal efficiency of capital" (CWK 7, p. 245). In contrast, the dependent variables are truly variables: the volume of employment and the national income. Keynes therefore uses mathematical language to frame what he is doing but steps back from arguing within the mathematical framework he has introduced.

Other crucial chapters, because they are where Keynes draws out the implications of his theory, are chapter 10, and the three chapters in book V on wages and prices. Chapter 10 is where he expounds the theory of the multiplier, clearly a key component of his theoretical argument and his conclusions concerning policy (see Blaug 1987, chapter 4). Book V is where he establishes the important proposition that changes in money wages cannot be relied upon to restore full employment. In all of these chapters, he relies on algebra: at these crucial points, he is offering a mathematical argument.

This is not to say that the remaining chapters of the *General Theory* are less important. The "filling" in Keynes's theoretical sandwich, chapters 4 to 17, is important in providing the foundations for the theoretical arguments summarized in chapters 3 and 10 and applied in book V. The nonmathematical arguments, therefore, can be seen as supporting a theory that is conceived in terms of abstract functions and can legitimately be argued to be essentially mathematical. The subsequent chapters in book VI, "Short Notes Suggested by the General Theory," which may be fundamental to understanding Keynes's message (see Meltzer 1988), draw conclusions from this mathematical theory.

Though it is not the theme of this chapter, it is worth noting a consequence of Keynes's use of mathematics for the way his theory was developed by his followers.[19] There is a sense in which the skeleton of the *General Theory*'s argument was expressed mathematically (either using algebra or using notions that were readily translatable into algebra). This skeleton was essentially static and even mechanical. The dynamic arguments were not simply absent from the algebra;[20] they were also not expressed in the language of abstract functions in which the central argument is expressed. Thus, when Keynes's followers, from David Champernowne (1936) and Hicks (1937) onward, translated the theory into algebra, the dynamic elements were neglected.

Concluding remarks

In the eyes of modern economists, the *General Theory* is not a work in mathematical economics: much of the argument relies on arguments that are expressed verbally, relying on the reader's intuition and on the perceptiveness of Keynes's observations of the world. If one views the world from a different perspective, his theory appears to rest on shaky foundations. He clearly rejected the formalist mathematics later exemplified by Debreu. Nor did he adopt the method of simultaneous equations. However, as O'Donnell has shown, Keynes did not object to the use of mathematics, merely to what he considered the improper use of mathematics.

However, what makes the book a mathematical book, in a way that Marshall's *Principles* was not, is that Keynes consciously framed the argument in terms of abstract functions. He could have made his central argument about aggregate demand and supply more concrete, by translating abstract functions into curves, but for whatever reason, he chose not to do so. The rest of the book was concerned with laying the foundations for these functions, the language and argument being chosen so as to emphasize the difficulties in reducing the analysis to algebra. However, in presenting the theory as a whole, he adopted intrinsically mathematical language (hinting at simultaneous equations) and also used algebra. If the chapters that relied on explicit analysis of abstract functions and those in which he used significant amounts of algebra (chapters 3, 10, 18, and 19–21) were removed from the book, there would be no General Theory.[21]

Thus, it is perhaps not surprising that some reviewers considered the *General Theory* to be an abstruse and mathematical argument. There was, as most reviewers recognized, much in the book that was nontechnical. However, to understand the central argument, it was necessary to understand an argument that, though far from satisfactory to those looking for mathematical rigor, both was mathematical in nature and relied on abstract mathematical concepts. Even though, as befits someone whose entire career was based on offering policy advice, Keynes's concern was with influencing policy, the *General Theory* was addressed to his fellow economists and was written in a style that required the reader to think as a mathematician.[22] Perhaps that is one of the reasons why the book was so influential for a generation of economists that had mathematical skills that were on average much higher than those of their predecessors.

Notes

I wish to thank Bradley Bateman, Anna Carabelli, and Marco Dardi for detailed comments on a draft of this chapter. None of them bears any responsibility for any errors that remain.

1. The reviews appeared, respectively, in the *Times,* the *Economist,* the *London Mercury,* the *New Republic,* the *Spectator,* and the *Yale Review.*
2. For some purposes, it would be important to go beyond this and to explore in detail the type of mathematics in which Keynes was trained. Clearly, being at Cambridge, where Bertrand Russell and others saw mathematics as a branch of logic, was clearly important for his view of mathematics. However, as explained in the following, this chapter has a more limited aim.
3. Inevitably, given the thoroughness of O'Donnell's account, this chapter discusses material he has already covered. However, the focus is different.
4. A distinction between mathematics and formalism is drawn in Backhouse (1998). The lack of concern with formalism is why work such as Chick (1998) is not discussed here.
5. This section is a much expanded version of one from Backhouse 1997, p. 34. That paper also addresses some other aspects of Keynes's rhetoric.
6. Keynes's attitudes toward vagueness and precision are discussed in detail in Coates (1996, chap. 4), where comparison is drawn with the ideas of Ludwig Wittgenstein, with whom Keynes was in close contact. On the relationship between Keynes and Wittgenstein, see Raffaelli (2006, pp. 173–174).
7. In the *Treatise on Probability* (CWK 8, p. 20 n. 1), Keynes discusses the merits of Bertrand Russell's use of very precise, logical statements with "the English of Hume." Keynes argued that Moore offered "an intermediate style," which exhibited "force and beauty." If one wanted complete precision, then it was appropriate to go with Russell. If one did not, it was appropriate to "understand the substance of what you are saying *all the time*" but without reducing the argument "to the mental status of an x or y."
8. This has been taken as an attack on the formalist mathematics, defined according to Debreu's (1959, p. vii) criterion that the rigor of an argument is tested by its ability to stand independently of its interpretation. O'Donnell (1997, p. 146) persuasively makes the point that Keynes is not attacking the use of mathematics in general.
9. It contains one diagram, discussed below.
10. Numerical computations are, of course, a form of mathematics, but these are ignored as presenting no challenge to readers' understanding, in Keynes's time or ours.
11. The reader also needs to know that φ' and φ'' are the first and second derivatives of the function.

12. This includes seventeen plurals, two uses of "functional relationship," and one of "functional tendency."
13. The most frequently used economic terms are "interest," used 666 times; employment, 586 times; investment, 504 times; and money, 586 times.
14. This includes seven plurals.
15. This observation arose out of a conversation with Yann Giraud and reflects his work on visual representations.
16. The need for such tacit assumptions meant that his critique of the classical theory could be seen as a logical critique: that it was a less general theory than its supporters had believed. I owe this point to Anna Carabelli.
17. This is a statement of Keynes's analysis. It is not being asserted that his characterization of classical economics was justified.
18. Note that this is not making any claim about the "central message" of the *General Theory* in the sense that Patinkin (1982) used the term. This central theoretical argument, as it is called here, could have been used to justify a number of different messages.
19. This paragraph relates the argument of this chapter to that of Backhouse and Laidler 2004.
20. It should be noted that there is the trivial exception of the formula for the rate of interest on CWK 7, p. 169.
21. Chapter 18 is included for the reasons discussed in the previous section. It is a restatement of the argument, and its opening pages are couched in mathematical language, even though Keynes draws back from this. Note that this sentence does not say that if the mathematics were removed, there would be no *General Theory*.
22. This concern with influencing policy by influencing theory is entirely consistent with Keynes's approach to theory and to the level of rigor he chose to employ—his choice of what he called Moore's "intermediate" method, between Russell's formal logic and Hume's English (see note 7).

CHAPTER EIGHT

The *General Theory:* Toward the Concept of Stochastic Macro-Equilibrium

Hiroshi Yoshikawa

he General Theory of Employment, Interest and Money was published in February 1936. It immediately caught wide public attention and provoked numerous reviews and academic articles. Backhouse (1999) compiles a list of those published in 1936: in that year alone, they totaled 123. While some economists hailed the book with great enthusiasm, others were skeptical of Keynes's claim of authoring the "General Theory." Samuelson (1964) described the American scene as follows: "The *General Theory* caught most economists under the age of thirty-five with the unexpected virulence of a disease first attacking and decimating an isolated tribe of south sea islanders. Economists beyond fifty turned out to be quite immune to the ailment. With time, most economists in-between began to run the fever, often without knowing or admitting their condition" (Samuelson 1964, pp. 315–316).

As we know, the *General Theory* initially won a great triumph over neoclassical theory. Macroeconomics became synonymous with the Keynesian economics. However, during the last forty years, the pendulum has swung back to neoclassical macroeconomics, which is now taught (particularly at the graduate level) in leading universities around the world. This chapter briefly surveys the controversies surrounding the *General Theory* or the Keynesian economics. They are nothing but the history of macroeconomics in the last seventy years. In the last section, I explain the little-known concept of "stochastic macro-equilibrium," which I believe is the true microeconomic foundation for Keynes's principle of effective demand.

The early controversies

The *General Theory*, which so intensely criticized the neoclassical theory—Keynes's so-called classical theory—naturally invoked hard counterattacks. Pigou (1936), for example, in his review of the book, was severe: "Einstein actually did for Physics what Mr. Keynes believes himself to have done for Economics" (Pigou 1936, p. 115). Instead, Pigou maintained in the *General Theory*, "we have watched an artist firing arrows at the moon" (Pigou 1936, p. 132). Pigou's frustration is quite understandable. In the *General Theory*, Keynes argued that "from the time of Say and Ricardo the classical economists have taught that supply creates its own demand." Because of this Say's law, "the classical theory is only applicable to the case of full employment" (Keynes 1936a, p. 16). The classical economists allegedly assumed away the problem of economic fluctuations, particularly recessions and depressions. However, Pigou, himself named by Keynes as a representative classical economist of their age, had actually written a book entitled *Industrial Fluctuations* (1929), which has as its frontispiece a diagram nicely showing the ups and downs of British unemployment from 1850 to 1914.

In any case, the early controversies concerned such concepts as saving and investment, Keynes's use of which in the *General Theory* confused his fellow economists. By and large, these controversies were eventually resolved, and what Keynes meant is basically understood today. For this reason, I skip them here and concentrate on a more fundamental issue in the present study.

This fundamental issue is how Keynes's economics in the *General Theory* differs from the orthodox neoclassical theory. This question has inspired economists for generations but still remains unresolved. On publication of the book, both Hicks (1936) and Leontief (1936) compared Keynes's *General Theory* to Walras's theory of general equilibrium. Leontief (1936), for example, argues that the orthodox theory rests on the "homogeneity postulate" by which he means that "all supply and demand functions, with prices taken as independent variables and quantity as a dependent one, are homogenous functions of the zero degree" (Leontief 1936, p. 193). According to this postulate, a change in money supply, M, accompanying proportionate changes in all the prices, keeps quantities demanded and supplied intact—that is, money is neutral. However, once one repudiates this postulate, money is no longer neutral, and all the demand and supply functions now depend on M. Then, within this framework, one can surely seek the level of M that brings about the highest level of employment of labor. The same problem can be actually set up for any product or factor or production. Leontief points out that "the quantity of money which brings about the maximum output of automobiles might be much smaller or much larger than that which would secure the greatest possible employment to some particular kind of labor" (Leontief 1936, p. 194). In this case, given an arbitrary level of money supply, M, unemployment or underemployment ensues. This is Leontief's interpretation of Keynes's *General Theory*. Keynes should have scrutinized this homogeneity postulate and discredited it. However, he did not. Thus, Leontief's verdict is that "Mr. Keynes's assault upon the fundamental assumption of the 'orthodox' economic theory seems to have missed its target" (Leontief 1936, p. 196).

Only a few months after the publication of the *General Theory*, Hicks (1936) also wrote a review article for the *Economic Journal*. He regarded "the method of expectations" as Keynes's most significant analytical innovation in the *General Theory*:[1]

> There thus emerges a peculiar, but very significant, type of analysis. If we assume given, not only the tastes and resources ordinarily assumed given in static theory, but also people's anticipations of the future, it is possible to regard demands and supplies as determined by these tastes, resources and anticipations, and prices as determined by demands and supplies. Once the missing element—anticipations—is added, equilibrium analysis can be used, not only in the remote stationary conditions to which many economists have found themselves driven back, but even in the real world, even in the real world in "disequilibrium." . . .
>
> From the standpoint of pure theory, the use of the method of expectations is perhaps the most revolutionary thing about this book; but Mr. Keynes has other innovations to make, innovations directed towards making the method of anticipations more usable. (Hicks 1936, p. 240)

It is an irony that another new "method of expectations," that is, *rational expectations,* would upset Keynes's economics forty years later. But that is another story.

Within a year, Hicks (1937) had written another paper on the *General Theory*. In this famous paper, entitled "Mr. Keynes and the Classics," Hicks begins with the remark that despite Keynes's sharp attack on the classics, there was actually a lack of "a satisfactory basis of comparison." Hicks's aim was, therefore, to "isolate Mr. Keynes's innovations, and so to discover what are the real issues in dispute" (Hicks 1937, p. 148).

Toward this goal, Hicks presented an aggregate macro model, which subsequently became called the IS/LM model. *Money wages are explicitly assumed to be given; Accordingly, nominal prices are implicitly constant.* The classical system can be represented by the following set of equations:[2]

$$M = kY, I = I(i), S = S(i, Y), I = S. \tag{1}$$

Here, Y, I, and S are nominal income, investment, and saving, respectively. M is nominal money supply, i is the interest rate, and k is a constant called the Marshallian k. In this system, the first money equation determines the level of nominal income, whereas the equality of I and S (or the IS equation) determines the interest rate.

In contrast, Hicks argues, Keynes's model can be represented as follows:

$$M = L(i), I = I(i), S = S(Y), I = S. \tag{2}$$

The money equation now determines the interest rate, which in turn determines the level of investment. Given the level of investment, the IS equation determines the level of income. Hicks regarded the first money equation as crucial for Keynes's theory: "It is the liquidity preference doctrine which is vital. For it is now the rate of interest, not income, which is determined by the quantity of money" (Hicks 1937, p. 152).

Hicks then went on to argue that Keynes's model set up this way was not quite the *general theory:* "We may call it, if we like, Mr. Keynes's *special theory*. The General Theory is something appreciably more orthodox." He maintained that the general theory ought to be as follows:

$$M = L(Y, i), I = I(i), S = S(Y), I = S. \tag{3}$$

In this system, which is nothing but today's IS/LM model, income Y and the interest rate i are simultaneously determined by the IS and the LM equations (or the curves in the textbook diagram). Hicks noted that "with this revision, Mr. Keynes takes a big step back to Marshallian orthodoxy, and his theory becomes hard to distinguish from the revised and qualified Marshallian theories, which, as we have seen, are not new" (Hicks 1937, p. 153). This point can be clearly understood by considering, for example, what would happen when the marginal efficiency of capital rose. Keynes emphatically rejected the idea of its raising the interest rate and insisted that investment increases. Hicks pointed out that "a rise in the marginal-efficiency-of-capital schedule must raise the curve *IS;* and, therefore, although it will raise income and employment, it will also raise the rate of interest" (Hicks 1937, p. 154).

Hicks then argues that the distinction between Keynes's theory and the classical theory does not lie in the middle field of the IS/LM diagram but rather shows up in the limiting extremes. On the one hand, there must be the maximum level of income (at "the full-employment" level, if you like), Y_F. At Y_f, the LM curve becomes vertical, and there the classical theory will be a good approximation in that the IS equation determines the interest rate. On the other hand, if there is the minimum level of the interest rate, then the LM curve becomes flat there. In this case, when the marginal efficiency of capital rises, it increases only investment and thereby employment but does not raise the interest rate at all: "We are completely out of touch with the classical world." Hicks took this case where the interest rate fell to the minimum level as the essence of Keynes's economics. The LM curve would become flat when Y is very low (far away from Y_F), for we know that it becomes vertical when Y approaches Y_F. "So the General Theory of Employment is the Economics of Depression" (Hicks 1937, p. 155). This was the conclusion Hicks drew.

It is important to note that Hicks (1937) assumed that money wages were given even for the classical model. That is why he could say that an increase in the supply of money will necessarily raise total (nominal) income Y, which in turn tends to increase employment. Because of the assumption of constant wages/prices, money is not neutral in his classical model.

Modigliani (1944) explicitly introduced the labor market into a similar macro model and, at the same time, allowed prices and wages to change. In his classical model, both labor demand and supply depend on real wages, and they are adjusted in such a way that demand for labor and supply of labor are equal in equilibrium. Thus, by construction, "full employment" of labor L is achieved in the classical equilibrium. Then, by way of the production function, total output or real GDP is at the full-employment level, Y_F.

Given this full-employment real GDP, the IS equation determines the equilibrium (or "natural") interest rate. Finally, with the full-employment real GDP Y_F and the natural interest rate i^* given, the money equation, which now reads $M/P = L(i^*, Y_F)$, determines the price level. A change in money supply, M, brings about a proportionate change in the price level, P, leaving all the real variables, namely, Y, i, *and* labor employment intact; money is (once again) neutral in Modigliani's classical model.

In the corresponding Keynesian model, Modigliani dropped out the classical assumption that the labor supply depends on real wages and instead assumed that nominal wages are given. This model is basically equivalent to Hicks's IS/LM model. Money is not neutral, of course. In Modigliani's presentation, the crucial assumption underlying Keynes's theory is that nominal wages and, accordingly, prices are inflexible (in the extreme case, constant). This argument appealed to a majority of economists. Indeed, since then, it has become a cliché that the Keynesian economics presumes inflexible wages/prices whereas the classical economics deals with the economy with flexible wages/prices.

Do flexible wages/prices cure the troubled economy? In particular, does a cut of nominal wages/prices save the economy from recession or even depression? Keynes's answer was negative. His argument in the *General Theory* is severalfold. In the first place, nominal wages are inflexible in the real world. One reason, Keynes pointed out, is that workers are concerned with relative wages. They strongly oppose a cut in their own wages, which necessarily worsens relative wages.[3]

Now, even if nominal wages/prices are lowered accompanying an increase in the real quantity of money, the interest rate may not decline when demand for money is very interest elastic. If the interest rate declined, investment may still not respond. And finally, a decline in actual wages/prices may invoke expectations of a further decline in wages/prices, which in turn, would raise the real interest rate. Taken altogether, there is virtually no chance that a decline of nominal wages/prices saves the economy from severe recession or depression.

Pigou (1943) responded to this argument by saying that an increase in the real money supply brought about by a decline in wages/prices would directly raise consumption and thereby aggregate demand.[4] Kalecki (1944) quickly pointed out, however, that a part of "money" is the so-called inside money and that there exist debts in the real economy. He continued: "The adjustment required would increase catastrophically the real value of debts, and would consequently lead to wholesale bankruptcy and a 'confidence crisis.' The 'adjustment' would probably never be carried to the end: if the workers persisted in their game of unrestricted competition, the Government would introduce a wage stop under the pressure of employers" (Kalecki 1944, p. 132).

The same point had been made by Fisher (1933), who advanced the famous debt-deflation theory (see Tobin 1980, chap. 1). Amid the long stagnation of the 1990s, Japan lapsed into deflation. At the time, economists, politicians, and policymakers all argued in unison that deflation had to be stopped. Nonetheless, even today, the idea that if wages/prices are flexible enough, the macroeconomy will be in the neoclassical equilibrium flourishes in the realm of economics.

The Phillips Curve

After the Second World War, it turned out that Keynes's economics had been widely accepted by the economics profession and that macroeconomics had become synonymous with Keynesian economics. This fact is best encapsulated in the bold title of a book written by Klein (1947): *The Keynesian Revolution.*

The established "Keynesian economics" in the textbook is basically the IS/LM model expounded by Hicks (1937). In the standard IS/LM model, price is taken to be constant and is implicitly normalized to be one. This assumption that price is constant was often taken as the Achilles heel of the Keynesian economics, though. In place of deflation, inflation had become an important economic problem in the postwar period. Now, one cannot even hope to explain inflation, let alone provide an effective policy recommendation, by using a theoretical framework that takes price as constant. Precisely at this critical moment, good news arrived. Phillips (1958) had found a kind of negative relationship between the unemployment rate and wage inflation for the British economy during the long period of 1861–1957: wages tend to rise when unemployment is low, and vice versa.

One might wonder why economists made a fuss of this seemingly commonsense observation. The reason is twofold. For one thing, the IS/LM model strengthened by the Phillips curve constitutes a dynamic model in which wages and prices change endogenously. Countless macroeconometric models once fashionable were all some variants of this framework. Second, the Phillips curve showing a trade-off between the unemployment rate and inflation provides policymakers and politicians with a feasible combination of two important policy targets. It was therefore regarded as a useful tool in policymaking. It was against this background that in the early 1960s under the Kennedy administration, distinguished American Keynesians such as Paul A. Samuelson, James Tobin, and Robert M. Solow actively participated in economic policymaking in the United States. The Keynesian economics then practiced was named the New Economics (see Tobin 1974). Arguably, the 1960s was the heyday of Keynesian economics.

Meanwhile, some economists kept asking themselves what was the essence of Keynes's economics or the *General Theory* in light of the neoclassical theory. Clower (1965) pointed out that in the competitive economy where all the agents are price takers, Keynes's consumption function cannot be obtained; consumption must be a function of real wages, and perhaps the interest rate, just as with the labor supply function. This means that Keynes's consumers must make decisions differently than their counterparts in the competitive economy. Clower argued that Keynes's consumer would maximize his/her utility by first taking only prices given. This optimization gives us "notional" demand for goods and services and the supply of labor. These are only notional because they cannot be realized if markets are not in equilibrium. For example, when supply of labor exceeds its demand, a consumer face not only wages in the market but also the quantity of labor he/she can supply as a constraint. In this case, consumption becomes a function not of real wages but of wages times the quantity of labor supplied, namely, income. This is nothing but Keynes's consumption function. Clower made it clear that the *General Theory* or the Keynesian economics presumes that the economy is *quantity constrained* or, more generally, imperfectly competitive.

Actually, prior to Clower, Arrow (1959) had made a point that the assumption of price-taking behavior makes sense only when the economy is in equilibrium, and that in disequilibrium, the market necessarily becomes imperfectly competitive. Specifically, when supply exceeds demand in the market as a whole, each economic agent (or firm) faces a downward-sloping individual (not market) demand curve rather than a perfectly elastic (namely, flat) demand curve. For example, a firm in a competitive market can supposedly sell any amount of goods or services at a given price. This makes sense if the market is in equilibrium. However, when supply exceeds demand in the market as a whole, obviously an individual firm must obey some sort of quantity constraint as well as price.

Clower looked for microeconomic behavior that was consistent with the Keynesian economics. Soon, microeconomic foundations for macroeconomics became an important research topic. A new line of research extended Clower's analysis by introducing many consumers as well as many producers or firms. Primary examples of such general equilibrium analysis of the quantity-constrained economy include Barro and Grossman (1971), Benassy (1975), and Malinvaud (1977). In these analyses, prices are assumed to be constant while quantities change. Negishi (1979) attempted to explore how consistent constant prices are with firm's profit-maximizing behavior by introducing the "kinked" individual demand curve. His analysis is a predecessor of the "New Keynesian Economics" discussed below.

The resurrection of New Classical macroeconomics

Friedman is arguably the author of one of the most influential papers in macroeconomics. In this paper (Friedman 1968), he boldly rejected the existence of a widely accepted downward-sloping Phillips curve in equilibrium (or in the long run). His argument is based on the concept of the natural rate of unemployment. Friedman's definition is as follows: "The 'natural rate of unemployment,' in other words, is the level that would be ground out by the Walrasian system of general equilibrium equations, provided there is imbedded in them the actual structural characteristics of the labor and commodity markets, including market imperfections, stochastic variability in demands and supplies, the cost of gathering information about job vacancies and labor availabilities, the costs of mobility, and so on" (Friedman 1968, p. 8).

It is basically the unemployment rate that would obtain in the neoclassical equilibrium. Obviously, it is akin to what Keynes called "frictional unemployment" in the *General Theory*. Friedman maintained that regardless of the rate of inflation (or, for that matter, deflation), in the long run the actual rate of unemployment must be equal to the natural rate: "To state this conclusion differently, there is always a temporary trade-off between inflation and unemployment; there is no permanent trade-off. The temporary trade-off comes not from inflation per se, but from unanticipated inflation, which generally means, from a rising rate of inflation. The widespread belief that there is a permanent trade-off is a sophisticated version of the confusion between 'high' and 'rising' that we all recognize in simpler forms. A rising rate of inflation may reduce unemployment, a high rate will not" (Friedman 1968, p. 11).

The trade-off only temporarily exists between unexpected inflation and the unemployment rate. Given Friedman's natural rate hypothesis, expectations formation is crucial for understanding the workings of the economy. Phelps (1970), Lucas and Rapping (1969), and others explored the microeconomic foundations of employment and inflation theory. Their works were supposed to be concerned with the Phillips curve, but the dynamics based on expectational errors were actually quite different from the Phillips curve most Keynesians had had in mind. Rees (1970) expressed justifiable bewilderment and made the following observation:

> In a recent issue of this *Journal* Lucas and Rapping (1969) present some original and interesting views on the nature of equilibrium in labor markets. Unfortunately, in the process they seriously misinterpret some of the post-Keynesian literature, leaving the impression that their departure from generally accepted positions is much less substantial than is in fact the case. The issues they raise concerning the voluntary or involuntary nature of measured unemployment have important implications for policy. Although Lucas and Rapping do not explore these implications, they lurk close enough to the surface to make clarification of the issues a matter of importance. . . .
>
> One may also note in passing that the authors sometimes refer to their unemployment rate function as a Phillips curve on the ground that a Phillips curve can be defined as any downward-sloping function relating wages and unemployment. Since the original Phillips relation involves a money wage

rate rather than a real wage rate, and since the direction of causation in Phillips (1958) runs from unemployment to wage changes rather than the reverse, the resemblance is remote. Moreover, Phillips explicitly assumes that labor markets are normally in short-run disequilibrium. (Rees 1970, pp. 306 and 309)

What Rees called the *unemployment rate function* has been subsequently called the *aggregate supply function*. The aggregate supply function produces fluctuations of total output or real GDP around its "natural" or "full-employment" level depending on whether the actual inflation rate exceeds or falls short of the expected rate. This is a New Classical theory. It is no longer a matter of an inflation equation. The whole theoretical framework has changed from the Keynesian economics based on the principle of effective demand to the New Classical macroeconomics based on the aggregate supply function or the natural rate hypothesis.

We would rightly call this drastic change in macroeconomics the Keynesian Counterrevolution; Friedman (1968) opened the door, Phelps (1970) paved the way, and Lucas (1972) completed the counterrevolution. Lucas (1972) introduced rational expectations based on the work of Muth (1961) to macroeconomics. This had an extraordinary impact on the profession, and a great amount of literature on rational expectations has emerged; primary examples include Lucas (1972, 1973) and Sargent and Wallace (1975).

However, for the neoclassical macroeconomic theory resurrected by Friedman (1968) and Lucas (1972), the natural rate hypothesis is arguably more essential than rational expectations; after all, rational expectations are nothing but a particular assumption of expectation formation. In fact, Lucas and Rapping (1969) succeeded in resurrecting the neoclassical equilibrium theory without rational expectations, basing their work on the assumption of adaptive expectations.

The Friedman-Lucas theory based on the natural rate hypothesis is a monetary theory of business cycles. According to this theory, unanticipated changes in money supply produce errors of inflationary expectations, thereby producing fluctuations of employment (or the rate of unemployment) and real output. This theory flourished during the 1970s. However, a majority of the neoclassical economists eventually turned from this monetary theory to real business cycle (RBC) theory.

Kydland and Prescott (1982) advanced RBC theory, which designates technological shocks—to be specific, total factor productivity (TFP)—as the fundamental cause of business cycles. In the Friedman-Lucas monetary theory, business cycles are deviations from the fairly stable "natural" state, which is supposed to be Pareto efficient. Thus, business cycles are an economic problem to be cured. For that purpose, Friedman and Lucas proposed a steady growth of the money supply. In contrast, in the Kydland-Prescott RBC theory, business cycles are nothing but fluctuations of Pareto-efficient equilibrium itself. In this view, recessions and depressions, which were the mother of Keynes's *General Theory,* are no longer an economic problem. The RBC theory is arguably the end of neoclassical theory. The pendulum has swung fully from the postwar Keynesian economics to the neoclassical macroeconomics. Today, it is the neoclassical macroeconomics that is taught in leading universities around the world. The following remark in Lucas (1987) symbolizes the present state of macroeconomics:

> The most interesting recent developments in macroeconomic theory seem to me describable as the reincorporation of aggregative problems such as inflation and the business cycle within the general framework of "microeconomic" theory. If these developments succeed, the term "macroeconomic" will simply disappear from use and the modifier "micro" will become superfluous. We will simply speak, as did Smith, Ricardo, Marshall and Walras, of economic theory. If we are honest, we will have to face the fact that at any given time there will be phenomena that are well-understood from the point of view of the economic theory we have, and other phenomena that are not. We will be tempted, I am sure, to relieve the discomfort induced by discrepancies between theory and facts by saying that the ill-understood facts are the province of some other, different kind of economic theory. Keynesian "macroeconomics" was, I think, a surrender (under great duress) to this temptation. It led to the abandonment, for a class of problems of great importance, of the use of the only "engine for the discovery of truth" that we have in economics. Now we are once again, putting this engine of Marshall's to work on the problems of aggregate dynamics." (Lucas 1987, pp. 107–108)

New Keynesian economics

In the heyday of the neoclassical macroeconomics, the reaction on the part of the "Keynesians" was that the "new" theory was basically old wine in new bottles. Many researchers attempted to "rationalize" inflexible wages/prices for they took inflexible wages/prices as the kernel of Keynesian economics. These research efforts were summarized by Mankiw and Romer (1991) under the heading of "New Keynesian Economics": "New Keynesian economics arose in the 1980s in response to this theoretical crisis of the 1970s. Much research during the past decade was devoted to providing rigorous microeconomic foundations for the central elements of Keynesian economics. Because wage and price rigidities are often viewed as central to Keynesian economics, much effort was aimed at showing how these rigidities arise from the microeconomics of wage and price setting" (Mankiw and Romer 1991, p. 1).

Though New Keynesian economics is not a unified theory, Mankiw and Romer still see a common theme. They explain what they mean by "New Keynesian economics" as follows:

> There are two questions that one may ask about any theory of economic fluctuations.
>
> Does the theory violate the classical dichotomy? Does it posit that fluctuations in nominal variables like the money supply influence fluctuations in real variables like output and employment?
>
> Does the theory assume that real market imperfections in the economy are crucial for understanding economic fluctuations? Are such considerations as imperfect competition, imperfect information, and rigidity in relative prices central to the theory?
>
> New Keynesian economics answers an emphatic yes to both of these questions. The classical dichotomy fails because prices are sticky. Real imperfections are crucial because imperfect competition and rigidity in relative prices are central to understanding why prices are sticky.
>
> Among the prominent approaches to macroeconomics, new Keynesian economics is alone in answering both of these questions in the affirmative. Real-business-cycle theory emphasizes technological disturbances and perfect markets; it therefore answers both questions in the negative. Many older macroeconomic theories rejected the classical dichotomy, but they usually did not emphasize real imperfections as a key part of the story. For example, most of the Keynesian economics of the 1970s imposed wage and price rigidities on otherwise Walrasian economics. Thus the interactions of nominal and real imperfections is a distinguishing feature of new Keynesian economics. (Mankiw and Romer 1991, p. 2)

The key concepts in New Keynesian economics include (a) costly price adjustment, such as "menu costs" (Akerlof and Yellen 1985; Mankiw 1985); (b) the staggering of wages and prices (Taylor 1979); (c) imperfect competition (Hart 1982; Blanchard and Kiyotaki 1987); (d) coordinating failures (Diamond 1982; Cooper and John 1988); (e) efficiency wages (Solow 1979; Yellen 1984); and (f) credit rationing in the credit market (Stiglitz and Weiss 1981).

New Keynesian economics made a strong impact on the profession during the 1980s. However, it is, in my view, fundamentally misguided. First, most works of New Keynesian economics take the aggregate demand as synonymous with nominal money supply—see, e.g., Blanchard and Kiyotaki (1987), Mankiw (1985), and other works collected in Mankiw and Romer (1991). It is not surprising to find Mankiw and

Romer (1991, p. 3) saying that "much of new Keynesian economics could also be called new monetarist economics." In this framework, "demand" or nominal money supply affects real output so long as nominal prices are rigid. Thus, in this approach, the primary agenda is to explain the rigidity or inflexibility of nominal prices/wages in concurrence with the "rationality" of economic agents. This is in accordance with that textbook cliché that Keynesian economics makes sense only when prices are rigid—which again supports the notion that New Keynesian economics is actually old wine.

Effective demand in Keynes (1936a) is, however, real. Here, I emphasize the importance of real demand and cite Tobin:

> The central Keynesian proposition is not nominal price rigidity but the principle of effective demand (Keynes 1936a, chap. 3). In the absence of instantaneous and complete market clearing, output and employment are frequently constrained by aggregate demand. In these excess-supply regimes, agents' demands are limited by their inability to sell as much as they would like at prevailing prices. Any failure of price adjustments to keep markets cleared opens the door for quantities to determine quantities, for example real national income to determine consumption demand, as described in Keynes's multiplier calculus. . . .
>
> In Keynesian business cycle theory, the shocks generating fluctuations are generally shifts in *real* aggregate demand for goods and services, notably in capital investment. Keynes would be appalled to see his cycle model described as one in which "fluctuations in output arise largely from fluctuations in nominal aggregate demand" (Ball, Mankiw, and Romer 1988, p. 2). The difference is important. (Tobin 1993, pp. 46–47)

The second reason why New Keynesian economics is misguided is methodological. In order to provide sound "microeconomic foundations" for macroeconomics, New Keynesian theory analyzes microeconomic behavior of an individual household or firm in great detail. This standard approach is, however, not on the right track. I explain why below.

Stochastic macro-equilibrium

Microeconomic foundations for macroeconomics have been taken to be equivalent to incorporating the analysis of the behavior of an individual economic agent, such as a household or a firm, into a macroeconomic model. Thus, modern "micro-founded" macroeconomics begins with (often dynamic) optimization exercises, which lead to a particular microeconomic behavior of the representative agent. As we have seen in the preceding sections, this methodology applies not only to the neoclassical macroeconomics but also to the New Keynesian economics.

Interestingly, such a methodology is in stark contrast to the standard approach in the natural sciences. When one studies a system consisting of a large number of micro-units—namely, a macrosystem—an approach based on statistical physics is commonly used in physics, chemistry, biology, and ecology. Because there are too many micro-units in the system, it is simply impossible and useless to analyze the behavior of micro-units. The spirit of statistical physics is to give up pursuing the behavior of the micro-unit and instead to capture statistical behavior of macrosystem as a whole. Natural sciences take it for granted that one must take a different approach when studying a macrosystem than when studying the behavior of a micro-unit. Why not in economics? Perhaps surprisingly, this approach based on statistical physics provides the correct microeconomic foundations for Keynesian economics. This section explains why.

Keynes's *General Theory* is a bold challenge to the neoclassical theory. In neoclassical theory, it is postulated that production factors such as labor and capital are fully employed and that the value-marginal products of such a production factor are all equal across sectors, industries, and firms in equilibrium.[5] Factor endowment, together with preferences and technology, determines equilibrium. In the *General Theory*, Keynes pointed out that the factors of production are not fully utilized and, therefore, that factor endowments are not an effective determinant of equilibrium. Keynesian economics has long been debated in relation to unemployment, particularly as regards a very ambiguous notion of "involuntary" unemployment. However, for Keynes's principle of effective demand to make sense, the existence of involuntary unemployment is not necessary; it is enough to assume that there is underemployment in the sense that the marginal products are not uniform at the highest level. In effect, what Keynes said in the *General Theory* is that in demand-constrained equilibrium, productivity of a production factor differs across firms and industries.

Let me clarify this point by using a simple example. Suppose that there are n sectors in the economy and that the amount of labor necessary to produce one unit of product in sector i is a_i. Labor is the only input. Taking the good in the least productive sector, the nth sector, as a numeraire with p_i as the relative price of the ith good, we can arrange sectors in such a way that $p_1/a_1 > p_2/a_2 > \cdots > 1/a_n$. p_i/a_i is the value-marginal product of labor in terms of good n; sector 1 is the most productive sector, sector 2 the secondmost productive sector, and so on. One could interpret sector n as being the lowest productivity sector, such as "household production (housework)," unemployment (job search), and "nonlabor force" status (leisure). Labor in each sector sums up to a given total labor, L. We assume that the demand for the product of the ith sector D_i is given.

In the neoclassical equilibrium, the value-marginal product is equated across sectors: $p_1/a_1 = p_2/a_2 = \cdots = 1/a_n$. Then, it is easy to show that total output in the economy as a whole, or GDP, Y, is given by L/a_n. That is, total output is independent of demand and depends solely on the endowment of the production factor, L, and technology, a_i.

However, when productivity differs across sectors, an increase in D_i raises Y. Even a shift of demand across sectors/industries increases Y. In short, Y depends on demand. In this case, we say that there is underemployment in the economy. It is important to recognize that (involuntary) unemployment is merely a particular form of *underemployment* and that underemployment, defined as differences in the productivity of production factors, is more important than unemployment for the proposition that demand affects total output. There is, in fact, some suggestive evidence for productivity dispersion. Mortensen (2003), for example, documents that wage dispersion has been observed for most economies and concludes that wage dispersion is the consequence of productivity dispersion.

The standard method of statistical physics shows that there must be productivity dispersion in the economy. Not only that, it also shows precisely what functional form distribution of productivity takes and how it depends on the aggregate demand. In my view, this statistical procedure is nothing but the proper microfoundations for macroeconomics (Yoshi-kawa 2003).

Let us consider the economy consisting of S sectors with size n_i, $i = 1, \ldots S$. Here, n_i is the amount of production factor used in sector i. The endowment of production factor in the economy as a whole, N is exogenously given. That is, we have the following resource constraint: $\sum_1^s n_i = N$. The output of sector i, Y_i is $Y_i = c_i n_i (i = 1 \ldots S)$. Here, c_i is sector i's productivity and is given. Productivity differs across sectors. Without loss of generality, we can assume $c_1 < c_2 < \cdots < c_s$. The total output in the economy as a whole, or GDP, Y is then $Y = \sum_{i=1}^s Y_i = \sum_{i=1}^s c_i n_i$. We assume that Y is equal to the *aggregate demand*, $D : Y = D$. D is exogenously given.

We are interested in the distribution of production factor across sectors, namely, $n = (n_1, \ldots, n_s)$. Here comes the fundamental method of statistical physics. It begins with the observation that there are $N!/\prod_{i=1}^s n_i!$ ways or configurations for dividing N into a particular partition $(n_1, \ldots, n_s)$. Because the total number of possible configurations, S^N, is given, assuming equiprobable configurations, we know that the probability of a particular configuration n, $P(n)$ is (inversely) proportional to $\prod_{i=1}^{s} n_i!$.

The fundamental assumption of statistical physics is that the state vector $n = (n_1, \ldots, n_s)$ associated with the highest probability $P(n)$ is actually realized in equilibrium. The idea is similar to the method of maximum likelihood in statistics and econometrics. In our case, we actually maximize $P(n)$ under two constraints. One is that the sum of n_i must be equal to total labor N. Note that because one of the less productive activities can be a job search or unemployment, this constraint does not necessarily mean full employment. The other constraint is that the aggregate output $\sum_{i=1}^{s} c_i n_i$ must be equal to a given level of the aggregate demand, D.

It is important to recognize that this procedure is consistent with the assumptions that economic agents maximize their objective functions and that resources tend to flow out of low-productivity sectors to high-productivity sectors. Prices can also keep changing in a way the standard economic reasoning indicates. However, all these economic "motions" must be taken as stochastic for the purpose of studying the macroeconomy simply because the number of economic agents and also the number of goods and services are so large; the number of households is, for example, of the order of 10^8, and that of firms is of 10^7 in a large economy such as that of the United States. Economic environments surrounding a large number of economic agents and countless goods and services keep changing. Statistical physics strategically gives up pursuing the microbehavior of each agent and instead captures the stochastic behavior of the macrosystem as a whole.

The maximization of probability $P(n)$ associated with $(n_1, \ldots, n_s)$ under two constraints leads us to the exponential distribution. This distribution is called the *Boltzmann-Gibbs distribution* in physics. For analytical details, the interested reader is referred to Aoki and Yoshikawa (2007, chap. 3).

Now, the exponential distribution means that more resources are found in low-productive sectors/industries and less in high-productive sector/industries. The share of labor in a sector/industry declines exponentially as the productivity in the sector rises. More precisely, it depends on exp $-Nc_i/D$. Thus, note that aggregate demand D (to be precise, aggregate demand relative to factor endowment, namely, D/N) corresponds to temperature in physics; high aggregate demand corresponds to high temperature, and vice versa. When the aggregate demand is high, production factors are mobilized to sectors/firms with higher productivity. Okun (1973) makes a similar point, saying that workers climb a "ladder" of productivity in a "high pressure economy." Here, I have provided a rigorous foundation for Okun's verbal argument. I emphasize that the flexibility of prices is of secondary importance in this analysis.

The above analysis provides the proper microfoundations for Keynes's principle of effective demand. Most economists take it for granted both that factor endowments are exogenous because they are physically given and that factor endowments determine the total output. Keynes pointed out that factor endowments, if physically given, are not actually the fundamental determinant of total output because the utilization rates of those production factors are endogenous. The fundamental determinant is the aggregate demand rather than factor endowment.

Dispersions of utilization rates and differences in technology across firms/sectors entail distribution of productivity in equilibrium. The analysis parallel to that in statistical physics suggests that contrary to economists' erroneous belief in the "no arbitrage condition," it is actually impossible to obtain the unique marginal productivity in the economy as a whole. Economists believe that resources must flow to high-productivity sectors. This belief is not necessarily wrong, but what economists must recognize is that flows of resources are not instantaneous and that the mobility of resources is fundamentally conditioned by aggregate demand. As a result, we obtain distribution of productivity in equilibrium. It turns out that the equilibrium distribution of productivity is expected to be the Boltzmann-Gibbs distribution. Just like temperature in physics, the aggregate demand determines the distribution of production factors across sectors with different productivity, thereby determining the level of total output. This is the foundation of Keynes's principle of effective demand.

The concept of equilibrium explained above is basically what Tobin (1972) calls "stochastic macro-equilibrium." He argues that "[it is] stochastic, because random intersectoral shocks keep individual labor markets in diverse states of disequilibrium; macro-equilibrium, because the perpetual flux of particular markets produces fairly definite aggregate outcomes" (Tobin 1972, p. 9).

By way of affecting the transition rates of production factors, aggregate demand conditions "stochastic macro-equilibrium" and consequently determines the level of total output. The important question is then what determines the aggregate demand, D, which is the exponent for the Boltzmann-Gibbs distribution. This is, of course, what Keynes's *General Theory* is all about.

Notes

I would like to thank participants of the Fourth International Conference on Keynes's Influence on Modern Economics, "The Keynesian Revolution Reassessed," held at Sophia University, Tokyo, on March 19, 2008, particularly Maria Cristina Marcuzzo and Toshiaki Hirai for their helpful comments and suggestions. I am also grateful to Brad Bateman for editorial assistance.

1. Hicks (1936) noted that "the method of expectations" was not unique to Keynes but actually had been quite common among Swedish economists such as Lindahl and Myrdal. Hicks himself, in "Wages and Interest: The Dynamic Problem" (1935b), expressed familiarity with such a method. Perhaps that is why he was attracted to what he called "the method of expectations" when he first read the *General Theory*. Hicks's own thought materialized as *Value and Capital* (1939), in which he defined the "elasticity of expectations" and made full use of this concept.
2. The notations are changed into ones with which modern readers feel more comfortable.
3. Note that relative wages are real and, therefore, that workers' concern with relative wages does not invoke irrational "money illusion."
4. Patinkin (1948) emphasizes the theoretical importance of the Pigou effect but is very skeptical about its practical importance, particularly its role during the Great Depression. See also Patinkin (1965).
5. The neoclassical *search theoretical model* leads us to the equilibrium in which unemployment exists, and the value-marginal products of a production factor differ across sector/markets. Lucas and Prescott's (1974) paper entitled "Equilibrium Search and Unemployment" is a primary example. However, in such a model, the "representative" market is tacitly assumed. As a consequence, the value-marginal products are symmetrically distributed around the mean. Though there is a distribution, the value-marginal products in the economy as a whole can be represented by the mean as long as the variance is small. The search-theoretical equilibrium based on the "representative" market is fundamentally different from the Boltzmann-Gibbs distribution explained in this section.

CHAPTER NINE

Keynes's Economics in the Making

Toshiaki Hirai

Introduction

Since the publication of Keynes's *General Theory* (1936) and the advent of the "Keynesian Revolution," many scholars have attempted to interpret Keynes's book and its impact. These Keynesian scholars have put forward their own Keynesian theories or their own versions of Keynes's theories: among the various approaches, the income-expenditure approach, normally taken as the orthodox position; the Post-Keynesian approach, of which there are many versions; and the disequilibrium approach have proven influential. We are, of course, well acquainted with the fierce attacks launched by outsiders, such as the exponents of monetarism and the New Classical macroeconomics, but controversies proving no less fierce also developed within the "Keynes Camp."

Almost all the above interpretations focus solely on the *General Theory*, disregarding Keynes's other economic writings. Since the mid-1970s, however, a new line of research on Keynes's economics has been developed, with studies of Keynes's economics based on the Keynes Papers.[1] The present study belongs to this genre and has two purposes. The first is to clarify a feature of the Cambridge school in the first half of the twentieth century through examination of business cycle theories, identifying in particular two streams—the "Marshallian tradition" and the "Wicksell-type theories."

The second purpose is to clarify Keynes's theoretical development from the *Treatise on Money* to the *General Theory*. Here I will address two tasks, namely, analysis of the theoretical structures of the *Treatise* and the *General Theory* and examination and interpretation of each stage of development based on various manuscripts and correspondence contained in the Keynes Papers.

Two strands within the Cambridge school—with regard to business cycle theories

Within the Cambridge school, two trends can be distinguished in business cycle theories. One trend, represented by Pigou and Lavington, drew its inspiration from Marshall's theory, the "Marshallian tradition," while the other, represented by Robertson, Hawtrey, and Keynes (in the *Treatise*), was—consciously or unconsciously—to take up a Wicksell-type theory and came to contribute greatly to the development of monetary economics, along with Lindahl and Myrdal (the Stockholm school) and Mises and Hayek (the Austrian school).

Marshall and the Marshallian tradition

Marshall's economic system is comprised of three theories: the theory of exchange through supply-demand equilibrium, the (cash balance) quantity theory of money, and the theory of business cycles.[2]

Marshall put forward the theory of exchange, in *Principles of Economics* (1890), as a theory of stable equilibrium of normal supply and demand, which, assuming the constancy of both the marginal utility of money and the general purchasing power of money and confining the object of analysis to one commodity, provides an effective way of working out intertemporal problems.

Marshall presented his version of the quantity theory of money around 1871. He was doubtful of the transaction approach as formulated by Fisher on the grounds that it does not specify the factors that govern the velocity of the circulation of currency. Instead, Marshall stresses the "influence which the credit of a currency exerts on the willingness of the population to hold much of their resources, either directly in the form of cash in hand and at a bank; or indirectly in the form of debentures and other stock exchange securities" (Marshall 1923, p. 47). This idea is the ultimate germ of Keynes's theory of liquidity preference. It should be noted that Marshall also considers that the so-called Marshallian k moves in inverse proportion to an increase in the supply of money, so that an increase in the supply of money would decrease the value of each unit of money more than proportionately. Marshall develops the above argument subject to general credit being normal.

Marshall's theory of business cycles was first expounded in the *Economics of Industry* (Marshall and Marshall 1879). Here he analyzes the case where the general credit structure is shaken. This theory of business cycles is characterized by three points given particular stress. First, there is the role played by the public psychology, and in particular by moods of confidence or diffidence, in causing fluctuations in the level of economic activity. Confidence breeds confidence in the upward phase, while diffidence breeds diffidence in the downward phase.

Second, we have the "multiplier process," invoked in explaining the working of the economy. In both the upward and downward phases, change occurs first in the investment goods sector. This is followed by change in the demand for consumption goods, induced by the increased incomes of those newly employed in the investment goods sector. Third, there is the role played by speculators in causing excessive economic fluctuations.

Essentially, Marshall sees the chief cause of depression as a lack of confidence, which undermines credit. In consequence, the economy fails to adjust means to ends. The solution he comes up with is to ensure that credit is managed within narrower limits. Compared with the theory of exchange developed in *Principles of Economics,* Marshall's theory of business cycles was rather patchy. The work of developing it was left to his disciples, Pigou and Lavington.

Pigou developed his argument in *Industrial Fluctuations* (1927), which is an extended version of part VI, "The Variability of the National Dividend," of *Economics of Welfare* (1920). Pigou takes fluctuations in the level of employment, which is given by the intersection of the supply schedule of labor with the demand schedule for labor, as the main statistical indicator of industrial fluctuations. Starting with this fundamental proposition, Pigou argues that the proximate causes of industrial fluctuations lie in the deviations in the demand schedule from its general trend. He goes on to argue that changes in the demand for labor, in turn, come about either through changes in the expectations of entrepreneurs with regard to the real yield obtainable from investment ("industrial spending") or through changes in the size of real income, and he concludes that the dominant causal factor is the former rather than the latter. Thus, in Pigou's view, the varying expectations of business people are the most important factor contributing to industrial fluctuations (see Pigou 1927, p. 34).

Pigou's theory is based mainly on two analyses: (a) of the factors governing the amplitude of industrial fluctuations and (b) of the factors governing their rhythmic nature.

With regard to analysis(a), Pigou argues that the amplitude of industrial fluctuations depends both on the initial causes and on the environmental conditions in which the initial causes have effect. The initial causes of variations in expectations of the profit to be had from industrial spending include real causes, such as harvest variations, new inventions, industrial disputes, wars, and changes in fashion; psychological causes, particularly errors of optimism or pessimism; and autonomous monetary causes.

The environmental conditions mentioned as influencing the amplitude of industrial fluctuations are monetary and banking arrangements (the principal problem here is forced saving); the policy adopted by industrialists with regard to spoiling the market; and the policy pursued by laborers aiming at making wage rates rigid.

Reacting to the environmental conditions, the initial causes that set industrial fluctuations in motion determine their amplitude. In this argument, Pigou places great emphasis on the multiplier process and the influences that excessive oscillations in the psychology of entrepreneurs have on the economy.

With regard to analysis (b), Pigou identifies two major sets of causes. The first is causes that, though sporadic in nature, start off wave movements once they have come into play: the tendency of human constructions to wear out after a certain interval; the alteration of optimistic and pessimistic errors among entrepreneurs; and processes relating to money. The other causes comprise recurrent factors linked to the periodicity of actual industrial movements.

Pigou's theory of industrial fluctuations is deeply rooted in psychological forces. He stresses that alternation of optimistic and pessimistic errors is the main factor governing both the amplitude and the rhythmic nature of industrial fluctuations. It should be noted, however, that in developing his argument Pigou pays attention to both real and monetary causes, as well as the multiplier process.

Lavington was a Cambridge economist, best known for his book *The English Capital Market* (1921). Lavington first argues that the service that the money market is able to render consists of two activities, namely, the manufacture of money and the transportation of capital. To provide the latter service is to facilitate "the movement of this stream of money, of Command over Capital, whereby the control over a part of the productive resources of society which is available for capital uses is transferred into the hands of those by whom it can most effectively be employed" (Lavington 1921, p. 12). This service is thus related to forced saving. Lavington then proceeds to analyze the money market, both in the normal state (i.e., where the level of credit is normal) and in the abnormal state (i.e., where the confidence to grant credit has been shaken). Lavington's theory of the trade cycle consists in an analysis of the money market in the abnormal state.

Because the treatment in the *English Capital Market* is somewhat dispersed, it is better to follow the more straightforward account in the *Trade Cycle* (Lavington 1922). The key ideas there are drawn from Marshall, Pigou, and Robertson (in *A Study of Industrial Fluctuation*, 1915).

Lavington's basic proposition is two-pronged. On the one hand, he presents the conditions conducive to rhythmic variations in the level of business activity. Modern industrial systems are equipped with features inducing rhythmic patterns and/or cumulative changes—the organization of production by independent entrepreneurs, the decision-making process applied by entrepreneurs based on forecasts rather than facts, and the mutual interdependence of entrepreneurs (Lavington 1922, pp. 52–53).

On the other hand, he exposes the causes that, operating under these conditions, actually induce the rhythmic patterns. The main cause is to be found, he argues, in changes in the level of business confidence. Lavington develops this basic proposition as follows:

First, he assumes that a rise (or fall) in the level of business confidence always induces an increase (or decrease) in business activity.

Second, he emphasizes both the multiplier process and changes in the level of business confidence, taking the effective purchasing power of society into consideration.

Third, he does not consider monetary factors to be important in causing industrial fluctuations. He argues that the principal factors inducing industrial fluctuations have direct relation neither to the price level nor to the monetary or nonmonetary nature of the economy. That said, he accepts that we do actually live in a monetary economy, in which a rise in the level of business confidence causes an increase in purchasing power and thus induces a rise in the price level, which in turn leads to a rise in the level of confidence. This process develops in a cumulative way.

Fourth, and most important, Lavington argues that it is essentially the changes in the level of business confidence that determine the amplitude and periodicity of the trace cycle (Lavington 1922, p. 92).

Pigou's and Lavington's theories of industrial fluctuations represent the Marshallian tradition, in which business confidence, as the psychological factor, and the multiplier process, through which the impact of this confidence is diffused, occupy key positions.

The Wicksell-type theories

In the 1920s and 1930s, immanent criticism of neoclassical economics, as composed of the theory of relative prices and the quantity theory of money, gave rise to an array of monetary economics deeply influenced by Wicksell (1898). Wicksell himself endorsed the theory of relative prices in the form of Walrasian general equilibrium theory-cum-Böhm-Bawerk's capital theory, while he put forward the theory of the cumulative process of capital formation as an alternative to the quantity theory.

Accepting the essential points made by Wicksell, the interwar economists, including Lindahl and Myrdal (the Stockholm school) as well as Mises and Hayek (the Austria school) and Keynes as the author of the *Treatise*, put forward their own brand of monetary economics, going beyond Wicksell (see Hirai 2008, chap. 2). Let us call these interwar economists named above "the Wicksell connection," following Leijonhufvud [1979]. Robertson and Hawtrey might be called the "Wicksell-type theorists" in Cambridge, albeit they are not usually included in the Wicksell connection.

Lines of thinking departing from the Marshallian tradition were initiated in Cambridge by Robertson (1926) under the strong influence of Aftalion and Cassel. In his book, Robertson incorporated the relation between savings, credit creation, and capital accumulation into the non-monetary argument developed in Robertson (1915). Although Robertson was not directly influenced by Wicksell, his theory shares some of the same essential components, and indeed Myrdal and Hayek evaluated Robertson highly on the grounds that he was dealing with similar problems using similar methods. It would not, therefore, be inappropriate to view Robertson's theory as a sort of Wicksell-type theory.

Keynes was greatly influenced by Robertson, and it was very much thanks to this influence that he was able to evolve from his position in *A Tract on Monetary Reform* to that of the *Treatise*. In his case, however, he was aware of his theory's place among the Wicksell connection. (Keynes is dealt with more below.)

It is also appropriate to consider Hawtrey in this context. Hawtrey developed his theory of the trade cycle in *Good and Bad Trade* (1913), which may be regarded as independent of both the Marshallian tradition and the Wicksell connection but closer to the latter than the former.

Robertson

The title "Banking Policy and the Price Level" encapsulates Robertson's main theme in that work: that a policy of credit creation on the part of the

banking system enables entrepreneurs to purchase the real capital necessary to boost production, which in turn induces an increase in money
supply and thus in the price level of consumables. Production increases in
the following period. Although he adopts a variant of the quantity theory
in this argument, Robertson denies, in substance, the classical dichotomy.

Unlike monetary theories such as those found in Hawtrey (1913) and
Keynes (1923), and also unlike psychological theories such as that set
forth in Pigou (1927), Robertson's theory takes the interaction between
real and monetary factors seriously. He divides the fluctuations in output
into "appropriate" and "inappropriate" categorizations. Appropriate fluctuations, which are closely related to the technical and legal structure of
the modern economy, follow a rhythmical pattern to be justified. Inappropriate fluctuations, which are constituted by the excess of actual fluctuations in the volume of output over what would be appropriate ones,
occur due to the use of large and expensive equipment.

Monetary factors are related to the activities of the banking system.
In order to increase the volume of output, real circulating capital is cor-
respondingly required in advance. In order to purchase it, the need arises
to procure the corresponding short lacking (*lacking* is Robertson's somewhat awkward term for savings). When firms cannot arrive at the whole
amount of short lacking required, it is the banking system that provides
the balance. The consumption goods produced in the economy are either
consumed by the public or used by the firms as circulating capital. When
the firms' demand for circulating capital is strong, the public must of necessity be deprived of consumption goods. This is facilitated by the banking system providing credit to the firms.

Robertson develops his theory in two cases: short lacking and short
and long lacking (where investment goods play an important role), but
for the sake of brevity, let us here focus on the latter case.

In this case, the idea of the "demand and supply of short lacking" plays
a central role. In accordance with the phases of the trade cycle, changes
in the level of demand for and supply of short lacking follow different
courses. How the economy deals with this difference depends on the behavior of the banking system. Here let us examine the upward phase.

In order to increase the volume of output, circulating capital needs to
be purchased. For this, procurement of short lacking is indispensable.
The supply of short lacking, however, is made by "hoarding." Hoarding
is a kind of lacking that occurs where money obtained by selling current
output is saved without any guarantee of being applied to the creation of
capital. The supply of short lacking does not increase flexibly enough to
cope with a large and discontinuous increase in the demand for it.

Large excess demand for short lacking is met only with provision of credit by the banking system (see Robertson 1949, pp. 50 and 72). The consequence for the economy as a whole means forced saving.

When short lacking is thus met, the required circulating capital is procured, so that the volume of production increases. The amount of money then increases, and consequently the price level rises. Once this rise occurs, excess demand for short lacking persistently arises due to an increase in consumption or investment by firms, a lengthening of the period of production, a dis-hoarding by consumers, and a direct short lacking by firms. If the banking system goes on supplying money in order to cope with the excess demand, the price level goes on rising cumulatively.

If the banking system provides no credit, firms cannot procure the short lacking required; thus, circulating capital cannot be sufficiently obtained and the volume of production shows no sufficient increase. In this case, the amount of money does not increase, and the price level remains stable.

Thus, stability in the volume of production is placed in a trade-off relation with that in the price level. Such is the feature of the modern capitalistic economy revealed by Robertson's theory.

Hawtrey

Hawtrey's theory of the trade cycle is uniquely monetary in the sense that it sees the main cause of the business cycle in the behavior of banks. The banks attempt to adjust the amount of credit money to a level appropriate to their cash holdings. When they judge the ratio to be inappropriate, they raise (or lower) the rate of interest to decrease (or increase) the amount of credit money. This behavior is argued to induce industrial fluctuations, for it causes the fluctuations in cash (mainly payment to wages) to lag behind those in credit money (which makes up the purchasing power).

Now, let us consider the case in which the banks judge the ratio to be in excess and raise the (short-term) rate of interest to reduce the excess. Hawtrey goes on to explain two major aspects of the fluctuations thus induced. One is that the dealers reduce their orders to the manufacturers due to the increased cost of holding goods. The manufacturers, in turn, cut back their production. Both the dealers and the manufacturers then reduce their borrowings from the banks, which decreases the amount of credit money. The other aspect is that due to the decrease in the amount of credit money, the purchasing power directed toward goods decreases.

Due to the interaction between these two aspects, the economy spirals downward. During this course, wholesale prices, retail prices, and wages go on falling. Between interest rate, wages, and prices, it is the prices that fall most drastically, so that the rate of profits comes to diverge increasingly from the rate of interest. Although wages go on falling as unemployment develops, the fluctuations in wages are not as large as those in prices. Thus, the banks' cash holdings come to be in excess relative to the amount of credit money, and the banks reduce the (short-term) rate of interest to increase the amount of credit money. The process of expansion then begins to develop, reversing the sequence just explained.

The development of Keynes's economics

In the above section, we saw two strands in Cambridge economics concerning business cycle theories. Where does Keynes stand in all this? Finding the answer requires some careful work uncovering the evolution of Keynes's thought between the *Treatise* and the *General Theory*.

Keynes published the *Treatise* in 1930 after seven years' intellectual struggle following *A Tract on Monetary Reform* (1923).[3] The *Treatise* has a Wicksellian influence. Keynes made great efforts to defend the *Treatise* from both internal and the external criticisms up until the end of 1932. He then began to change the line of his argument in a direction that was to lead up to the *General Theory*. This can be characterized as a zigzag process. Finally, I will describe the main features of the *General Theory* and draw comparison between the *Treatise* and the *General Theory*. This will then allow us to see the ultimate outcome of the two influences upon Keynes's own theory of the business cycle.

The Treatise *theory*

The most significant feature of the *Treatise* theory might arguably be considered the coexistence of a Wicksellian theory and "Keynes's own theory" (see Hirai 2008, chap. 5).

On the one hand, the *Treatise* has Wicksellian influences, for Keynes tries to construct his own theory of monetary economics, criticizing both Marshall's quantity theory of money (see Keynes 1930, vol. 1, p. 205) and business cycle theory, which emphasizes the behavior of speculators while embracing Wicksell's view.

The Wicksellian strand of thought in the *Treatise* can be discerned in the following points: the explanation of the fluctuations in price level in terms of a relative relation between the natural rate and money rate of interest, and explanation of the working of the economy based on this relation; the stress on a bank-rate policy for stabilizing the price level; and the acceptance of an equivalence between Wicksell's three conditions for monetary equilibrium.[4]

The principal grounds on which Keynes himself regards his theory as belonging to the Wicksellian stream, however, lie rather in his adoption of the idea that the bank rate influences investment and saving. This idea is used to provide a mechanism to the effect that economic stability (stability of the price level and the volume of output) can be attained by means of interest rate policy.

On the other hand, it should be noted that the *Treatise* has "Keynes's own theory" as well. This theory consists of two parts. The first addresses the determination of variables relating to consumption goods and investment goods in "each period":

(Mechanism 1) The cost of production and the volume of output are determined at the beginning of the current period. Once the expenditure for consumption goods is determined on the basis of earnings, it is automatically realized as the sale of consumption goods proceeds, and the price level as well as the amount of profit are simultaneously determined.

(Mechanism 2) The cost of production and the volume of output are determined at the beginning of the current period. The price level of investment goods is determined either in the stock market or as the demand price of capital goods. Profit is determined as a result.

The second part deals with the determination of variables between one period and the next:

(Mechanism 3) The behavior of entrepreneurs is such that, if they make a profit (loss) in the current period, they expand (contract) output in the next.

I will call this last relation the "TM supply function." Stimulated by the profits (losses) realized in the two sectors, the firms behave in such a way as to expand (or contract) output in the next period. Given output thus determined, Mechanisms 1 and 2 function accordingly. "Keynes's own theory" can thus be expressed as the dynamic process consisting of Mechanisms 1 and 2 working through Mechanism 3.

As a result of this process (which can be called short-period oscillations), the economy may or may not reach long-period equilibrium. Keynes argues that the duty of the monetary authority is to achieve long-period equilibrium by means of bank-rate policy.

In long-period equilibrium, profits are supposed to become zero, investment is supposed to become equal to saving, and the price level is supposed to become stable. Keynes remarks that "every change towards a new equilibrium price level is initiated by a departure of profits from zero" (Keynes 1930, vol. 1, p. 142).

This interpretation sees the *Treatise* as articulating a dynamic process that includes the determination of both the price levels and the volumes of output.

It should be noted that the *Treatise* theory thus interpreted involves three kinds of "dualities," offering alternative and not always compatible analyses. These are the duality of the theory concerning the price level of consumption goods, a theory dependent on either (a) earnings or (b) the rate of interest; the duality of the theory concerning the price level of investment goods, either (c) the bearishness function theory or (d) the idea that prospective yields are discounted by the rate of interest; and finally, the duality of Wicksellian theory and Keynes's own theory.

The third duality rests on the other two. The Wicksellian theory, which is mainly used in the argument of economic policy by means of the bank rate in the second volume of the *Treatise*, adopts b and d, while Keynes's own theory adopts a and c.

The process of development after the Treatise

What characterizes the period up to mid-1932 was that Keynes maintained and improved upon "Keynes's own theory," disregarding the Wicksellian theory.[5] It is important to appreciate how Keynes dealt with the relation between profits and the volume of output. In the *Treatise*, the "TM supply function" was stressed as expressing the dynamic mechanism. Keynes adhered to the function (see his letter to Joan Robinson, CWK 13, p. 380) in the face of considerable criticism. This stance emerges clearly from the manuscript entitled "The Monetary Theory of Production" drafted in mid-1932 (CWK 13, pp. 381–396).

Toward the end of 1932 (see Hirai 2004; 2008, chap. 7), Keynes abandoned the TM supply function, albeit with some hesitation, and put forward a new formula of a system of commodity markets in the manuscript entitled "The Parameters of a Monetary Economy" (CWK 13, pp. 397–405). Here the TM supply function virtually disappeared from the analysis of commodity markets, as a result of which there emerged the model consisting of a system of simultaneous equations based on the equality of investment and saving in which profits do not relate to the determination of prices and output, thereby departing sharply from "Keynes's own theory." This was a turning point toward the *General Theory*.

In the three manuscripts of 1933 (see Hirai 2008, chap. 8), two functions are emphasized—the "pseudo-TM supply function" (see Hirai 2008, pp. 104–105 and 107) and the "pseudo-TM supply function mk2." I use the prefix "pseudo" because the functions, in substance, differ from the (original) TM supply function, although Keynes tends to regard these two functions as continuous with the TM supply function.

The three manuscripts constitute the origins of the *General Theory*'s chapter 3. They conceivably discuss both an equilibrium condition for the level of employment and its stability condition, although no concept corresponding to the *General Theory*'s aggregate supply function appears. In the "First Manuscript" (CWK 13, pp. 62–66), Keynes first put forward a system for determining the level of employment. This was, indeed, a breakthrough.

Keynes's way of formulating the system, however, suffers from certain ambiguities. The central problem in examining the three manuscripts is how consistently one can explain the "Second Manuscript" (CWK 29, pp. 63, 66–73, 87–92, 95–102), which accepts the first postulate of the classical economics, using the concept of the accounting period, and yet succeeds the pseudo-TM supply function mk2. I interpret the pseudo-TM supply function mk2 as describing the stability condition for the equilibrium level of employment. But the argument in terms of the function remains unclear. Moreover, the argument in the "Third Manuscript" (CWK 29, p. 76–101; CWK 13, pp. 421–422), which emphasizes "effective demand,"[6] is somewhat confusing, for it is still developed in terms of the sale proceeds and variable cost. The arguments recognizable in the Second and Third Manuscripts were to disappear thereafter. This has very much to do with the fact that the role played by profit was to change drastically. These ambiguities show how Keynes struggled to work out a new employment theory.

In the "First Undated Manuscript" (CWK 29, pp. 102–111; see Hirai 2008, chap. 9), Keynes appears to have first established the fundamental psychological law and the multiplier theory, while in the "Second Undated Manuscript" (CWK 29, pp. 112–120), he first put forward an investment theory close to that of the *General Theory* (both were written either toward the end of 1933 or in the first half of 1934).

Thus, the end of 1933 saw Keynes making a great advance toward the *General Theory*. Piecing together the arguments made in the fragments concerned, we can confirm that Keynes had by then established the following points: the system of determining the level of employment, the consumption function, the fundamental psychological law, the liquidity preference theory,[7] the marginal efficiency of capital[8] (albeit not yet that of the *General Theory*), and the multiplier theory.

In the manuscript "The General Theory" (CWK 13, pp. 423–456; see Hirai 2008, chap. 10, "The Eve of the *General Theory*") of the spring of 1934, and also in "The Summer Manuscript" (CWK 13, pp. 471–484) of the same year, which comprises the revised versions of chapters 8 and 9 of "The General Theory," Keynes puts forward almost the same theoretical framework as that of the *General Theory* in the area of consumption and investment theories. However, it should be noted that some theoretical ambiguity still remains in the concept of effective demand and the theory of determination of the level of employment. Thus, we might call this period the "Eve of the *General Theory*."

The proofing process of the *General Theory* (see Hirai 2008, chaps. 11–12) continued from the summer of 1934 up to publication. Here I set myself two objectives, namely, to determine (a) how Keynes went through the proofing process and (b) what the main features are.

With regard to objective (a), the following points emerge: Galley1(I) (chaps. 1–19, between early December 1934 and mid-January 1935) represents the most considerably revised work on the topics covered in the table of contents shared by three galleys (see CWK 13, pp. 525–526), while Galley2 (chaps. 1–15, between January and April 1935) and Galley3 (chaps. 2–6, June 1935) represent stylistic revisions of Galley1(I); all the chapters, except for chaps. 4, 5, 12, and 13, were completed in Galley1(I) both in contents and at the stylistic level. (There is also Galley1(II), chaps. 20–25, from March 1935 on.) The largest change after Galley1(III) (chaps. 26–28, June–July 1935) occurred in "The Great Revision" (chaps. 3 and 6–9, in August–October; see Hirai 2008, pp. 159–171). The definitions of some fundamental concepts changed due to alterations both in the definition of "user cost" and in its treatment; in the Michaelmas lectures (November 18), the precautionary motive was argued to be dependent on the rate of interest.

In the case of objective (b), I focused on what kind of changes or difficulties can be detected in the latter half of Keynes's process of development. Here we find two major changes worth noting, one regarding the "employment function," the other concerning fundamental concepts.

In "The General Theory," the Summer Manuscript, and the Pre-first Proof Typescript (summer 1934), the employment function was used as both supply and equilibrium concept. This duality disappears in Galley1(I) up to and including Galley3. In the *General Theory*, however, the duality reappears and overshadows its theoretical structure (see Hirai 2008, pp. 186–191).

Some fundamental concepts in Galley1(I) are related to those in the *General Theory* as follows:

The difference in effective demand, investment, and prime cost in definition depends on whether they include user cost (Galley1(I)) or not (the *General Theory*). From Galley1(I) to Galley III, for example, Keynes argued that income as realized value consistently differed from effective demand as expected value by user cost, emphasizing that effective demand inclusive of user cost matters in determining the level of employment. In the *General Theory*, however, this idea has disappeared.

The definitions of income, profit, and saving are the same.

The equation $U_2 = U_1 - B$ is vital in grasping the relation (where U_2 is the user cost in the *General Theory*; U_1 is user cost in Galley 1(I); and B is cost of the maintenance and improvement of the initial capital equipment).

The main thread runs as follows: In the *Treatise*, the "TM supply function" is stressed as expressing the dynamic mechanism. Keynes adhered to this function after the *Treatise*, in spite of much criticism. Toward the end of 1932, he abandoned it with some hesitation, and from the First Manuscript of 1933 on put forward a new theory of employment, which led to the *General Theory*.

The General Theory

Through the above zigzag process we have seen, in February 1936 Keynes finally published the *General Theory*, destined to spark off the Keynesian Revolution. At this point, we must take a look at the essential points of the *General Theory* (see Hirai 2008, chap. 13).

There are three central themes we can identify as running through the *General Theory*: contrasting potentialities, monetary economics, and underemployment equilibrium.

The *General Theory* sees the market economy as possessing two contrasting sets of potentialities: stability, certainty, and simplicity, on the one hand; and instability, uncertainty, and complexity, on the other.

Keynes argues that the market economy is equipped with several built-in stabilizers and thus has an inherent tendency to converge to equilibrium. It does not, however, reach an optimum (or full-employment) level but, rather, stays at an underemployment level. Based on this "optimistic" vision, he constructs a theoretical model in which the level of employment is determined where the aggregate demand function intersects the aggregate supply function, making use of such concepts as the consumption function, the marginal efficiency of capital, and the liquidity preference theory. The model is constructed in a simple and straightforward way, providing the foundations upon which Keynes presents his economic policy proposals for attaining full employment.

At the same time, however, Keynes repeatedly argues that the stability to which the market economy tends cannot set in unless some conditions are met; failing these, the market economy is doomed to instability. In this respect, we are faced with a structure built on fragile foundations, reflecting the uncertainty and complexity to be observed in the market economy.

Keynes argues that the working of the market economy depends on various psychological factors, such as short-term expectations, long-term expectations (the marginal efficiency of capital and the nature of the stock market), liquidity preference, and user cost.

The other element making the market economy unstable is its vulnerability to large changes in some exogenous variables. Here Keynes's concern is above all about any substantial changes in the quantity of money or in money wages.

Keynes seems confident that the possibility that the market economy will be undermined through the falling away of the above-mentioned conditions is remote and that an economy stuck in underemployment equilibrium could be cured with policies such as public works programs and low interest-rate policies.

Keynes puts forward his theory of underemployment equilibrium as monetary economics, as distinct from the real economics to which "classical economics" belongs. He argues that the monetary economy in which we live can be analyzed only within a framework of monetary economics.

Keynes's fundamental idea is expounded in chapter 21, where he presents two new ways of dividing up economics. One is a division "between the theory of the individual industry or firm and of the rewards and the distribution between different uses of a given quantity of resources on the one hand, and the theory of output and employment as a whole on the other hand" (1936a, p. 293). The other is a division "between the theory of stationary equilibrium and the theory of shifting equilibrium—meaning by the latter the theory of a system in which changing views about the future are capable of influencing the present situation" (ibid.).

In both cases, the criterion of division hinges on money. Indeed, when dealing with the determination of the level of output and employment as a whole in the real world, we must consider the role played by money. This is what Keynes means by monetary economics. Keynes argues that monetary economics in his sense remains "a theory of value and distribution, not a separate 'theory of money'" (1936a, p. 294).

The above considerations show that Keynes's monetary economics aims at analyzing an economy in which money plays an essential role. It is not surprising, then, that Keynes allocates a lot of room to discussion of the rate of interest (chaps. 13, 14, 15, 17, 23, and 24). Apart from his liquidity preference theory, Keynes, in chapter 17, develops a theory of "own-rates of interest," accounting for the way in which the behavior of money becomes an obstacle to full employment.

The central message of the *General Theory* is that left to itself, the market economy will remain in underemployment equilibrium (see 1936a, pp. 249–250). Underemployment equilibrium has four features: involuntary unemployment, equilibrium, stability, and fluctuation.

We may, indeed, go as far as saying that the theoretical structure of the *General Theory* can be characterized as the monetary economics of underemployment equilibrium.

Comparison between the Treatise and the General Theory

The *General Theory* would not have appeared but for the *Treatise,* and yet it is an achievement independent of it. Let us compare the one with the other.

First, in the *Treatise,* the TM supply function plays an essential role in the dynamic movement of the system; the *General Theory* addresses the question of how the level of employment is determined.[9]

Second, the *Treatise* provides no theoretical account of investment and consumption; in the *General Theory,* theories of both investment and consumption are put forward and play important roles in determining the volume of employment.

Third, although we can find some continuity between the concepts of bearishness and liquidity preference (the view that the banking system and the public, with their psychological inclinations, behave interactively; and classification of the motives for holding money), the role assigned to money differs considerably.

Fourth, in the *Treatise,* the rate of interest is a policy variable through which the banking system is supposed to adjust the supply of money to the public's bearishness; in the *General Theory,* the rate of interest is supposed to be adjusted in such a way that the supply of money, which is a policy variable, meets the liquidity preference.

Fifth, the *Treatise* and the *General Theory* nevertheless have the following points in common: both belong to the field of monetary economics and were pitched against neoclassical orthodoxy, prices and output are treated as endogenous variables, and the importance of both monetary and fiscal policies is stressed.

Conclusion

From the late nineteenth century on, economists increasingly concentrated their attention on the phenomenon of exchange in the market. They were concerned with the problem of how resources are exchanged through the price mechanism, assuming full employment and accepting Say's law.

A new approach to economics was initiated by Wicksell at the turn of the century. He put forward the theory of cumulative process as an alternative to the quantity theory. A number of economists of diverse intellectual backgrounds emerged in the interwar period to follow up Wicksell's lead. They were united in their desire to construct a new monetary economics, criticizing the quantity theory, the classical dichotomy, and Say's law. Keynes was one of these economists.

Keynes, however, dispensed with the Wicksellian influence soon after the *Treatise* and ultimately arrived at the *General Theory*. In doing so, he returned to his own roots in Cambridge cycle theory. Here we have a monetary economics that demonstrates underemployment equilibrium. It was an independent achievement, and it generated the Keynesian Revolution.

Having said that, I think that Keynes's methodology, as well as his economics, is of extreme importance at present. It was never as ends in themselves that Keynes constructed his theoretical models but always for the purpose of analyzing and diagnosing the economic problems facing the real economy and proposing polices to deal with them. While observing the real economy, Keynes sought out useful analytical tools or concepts or, when necessary, contrived new tools or concepts applying his own intuition and introspection. These he would then set about elaborating with his powers of speculation.

Reference here to "theoretical models" does not necessarily imply only mathematical models. Keynes perceived the complexity of the economy, which could not be dealt with using only mathematical models. Thus, as argued above, Keynes's theoretical models are built in such a way that the market economy is equipped with two contrasting potentialities. To this end, Keynes took great pains in constructing his models, showing how the level of employment is determined on the one hand, while at the same time giving due weight to the aspect of uncertainty on the other.

The last thirty years have seen the emergence of the "New Classical" school (see Lucas 1975; Kydland and Prescott 1982) as the dominant orthodoxy in macroeconomics. The exponents of this school explicitly and utterly rejected Keynes's economics, his way of thinking, and his social philosophy, arguing the superiority of their models as being constructed rigorously and mathematically from microeconomic foundations. But Keynes would surely have been highly critical of them as being based on the "representative agent," assumed to maximize his/her utility and to be able to form "rational expectations." By assuming this type of *homo oeconomicus,* the New Classical economists construct their models with "pseudo-mathematical methods" (Keynes 1936a, p. 297), which do not go a long way toward analyzing the real economy. I believe that we should welcome the return of Keynes in this sense, rather than blindly following the New Classical school.

Notes

1. Keynes Papers, King's College Archive Centre, Cambridge.
2. This section is based on Hirai (2003, sec. 2 of chap. 2).
3. Marshall's economic system is examined in Hirai (2007a; 2008, chap. 4).
4. Wicksell's three conditions for monetary equilibrium are equality of the natural rate and the money rate of interest, equality of investment and saving, and price level stability.
5. See Hirai (2008, chaps. 6–12). For studies focusing on the same theme, see Asano 1987; Dimand 1987; Amadeo 1989. Rymes (1989) is also an important source of information.
6. It should be noted that the concept of "effective demand" was to undergo several changes before reaching the *General Theory.*
7. Keynes's liquidity preference theory is first developed in "The Monetary Theory of Production."
8. Keynes's theory of the marginal efficiency of capital is first developed in "The Second Undated Manuscript."
9. I also reconstruct the *General Theory* theory in terms of the "heterogeneity-expectations approach," pointing out some flaws in the original. See Hirai (2008, pp. 184–191).

CHAPTER TEN

Keynes, Sraffa, and the Latter's "Secret Skepticism"

Heinz D. Kurz

Introduction

The relationship between Keynes and Sraffa was very close in some respects and quite the converse in other respects. Keynes was deeply impressed by Sraffa's breadth and depth of knowledge, his sharpness and intellectual brilliance, and he found his younger Italian colleague a truly likeable person. There are numerous documents that express vividly their close personal relationship, which grew into friendship (see Ranchetti 2005). Without Keynes's continuous support up until his premature death in 1946, it is difficult to imagine how Sraffa would have fared in an environment like Cambridge, given the peculiarities of his character, his meticulosity, and even his pedantry. Thanks to Keynes, Sraffa could pursue his work without much interference. Keynes, it seems, had full trust in Sraffa's intellectual capabilities and made no serious effort to direct his research. He allowed Sraffa to follow his course and develop his truly novel ideas, which were eventually born into an environment that was not prepared for them and had difficulties absorbing them. Sraffa was and remained a loner amongst the economics profession in Cambridge. Highly respected and even feared by his colleagues, he was hardly ever fully understood (see Marcuzzo 2002; Ranchetti 2002). Sraffa knew how much his critical and constructive work contradicted the received wisdom in Cambridge and elsewhere. Apart from some early attempts at communication, he was reluctant to let his colleagues know what precisely his work was all about, which difficulties he had encountered, which results he had got, and when. Sraffa kept his cards very much to himself and typically disclosed them only in the moment in which he was absolutely sure that what he had to offer was both new and sound. Unlike Keynes, he was horrified by the vision of circulating half-baked ideas and leaving it to others to straighten them out. It is telling that apart from Maurice Dobb, Sraffa discussed his work typically only with mathematicians: in the late 1920s with Frank Ramsey and in the 1940s and 1950s with Abram S. Besicovitch and Alister Watson.[1]

Sraffa was well aware of how much he owed to Keynes's steadfast support and throughout his life was loyal to the man who had brought him to Cambridge and who looked after him so well. However, there is every reason to believe that the two minds hardly ever fully met when it came to economic theory (see Ranchetti 2005). The two scholars had high esteem and respect for one another, but they followed different lines of thought. They were both engaged in a project destined to provide an alternative to contemporary mainstream economics, but they did not directly join forces in this regard. They approached the project from different points of view, and they reached different conclusions as to how to best challenge a doctrine they considered problematic, if not outright wrong.

Since apart from a few instances, on which more below, Sraffa never wrote down in a comprehensive way how he viewed Keynes's achievements as an economic theorist and what he thought in particular of the *General Theory*, we can only indirectly infer from Sraffa's writings, published and unpublished, his assessment of Keynes's work. While Keynes was critical of several of Marshall's views, his thinking was nevertheless to a considerable extent "Marshallian" and remained so. At the same time, he considered Say's law to be the characteristic feature of classical economics and a main obstacle to an understanding of persistent unemployment and depressive tendencies in the economy. Sraffa, in contrast, had convinced himself that the Marshallian symmetrical theory of value and distribution could not be sustained and that the old classical approach to the theory of value was the right starting point of a probing into the laws of production and distribution. The two scholars therefore were at cross-purposes right from the beginning of their encounter and cooperative relationship, despite the fact that both shared a critical orientation toward orthodox economics. We might perhaps say that in Sraffa's view Keynes never managed to free himself fully from the straightjacket of marginalist economics: Keynes's new doctrine of effective demand, while containing some radically new elements, was thwarted by the remnants of the old theory in it (see Garegnani 1978, 1979). This theory sees a tendency toward full employment, brought about by the "forces" of demand

and supply in the various markets, including the "labor market." Because of these remnants of orthodoxy, Keynes's partly revolutionary intellectual message could be tamed and his construction reabsorbed, or so it seemed, into the mainstream, which turned out to be highly elastic with regard to new ideas that at first sight look incompatible with it, namely, the so-called Neoclassical Synthesis.

Sraffa had concluded his rejoinder to D. H. Robertson in the 1930 *Economic Journal* symposium on "Increasing Returns and the Representative Firm" with the following words: "We seem to be agreed that *the* [Marshallian] *theory cannot be interpreted in a way which makes it logically self-consistent and, at the same time, reconciles it with the facts it sets out to explain.* Mr. Robertson's remedy is to discard mathematics, and he suggests that my remedy is to discard the facts; perhaps I ought to have explained that, in the circumstances, I think it is Marshall's theory that should be discarded" (Sraffa 1930, p. 93; emphasis added).

Sraffa's wish did not come true. Keynes and with him most Cambridge economists clung to Marshallian concepts, making use, in particular, of the Marshallian demand-and-supply apparatus. Seen from Sraffa's point of view, this meant that their analyses were flawed. A careful scrutiny would invariably bring the flaws into the open. As regards Keynes's contributions, Sraffa's criticism concerned especially the following:

1. The idea expressed in the *Treatise* that the price level of consumption goods and that of investment goods can be considered as determined independently of one another, and the related idea that the price level of the latter is determined exclusively by the propensity of the public to "hoard" money.
2. The "marginal efficiency of capital" schedule in the *General Theory,* which carried over the concept of a given order of fertility of different qualities of land to the ordering of investment projects.
3. The view that the banking system can control the money supply and that therefore the quantity of money in the system can be considered exogenous.
4. The argument put forward by Keynes to substantiate his view that the liquidity preference of the public prevents the money rate of interest from falling to a level compatible with a volume of investment equal to full employment savings.

While some elements of Sraffa's criticism derived directly from his involvement in discussions of the "Circus," other elements derived from his parallel critical work on the foundations of the received marginalist theory of value and distribution and his endeavor to elaborate an alternative to it.

In this chapter, I deal with the four problems mentioned. In order to better understand Sraffa's objections, we repeatedly have to summarize findings in his parallel work to the extent to which they are pertinent to the issues at hand. It deserves to be mentioned already at this point that while Sraffa was critical of several of Keynes's ideas and concepts, his objections were not meant to undermine Keynes's critical project as such. They were instead destined to knock out elements that could not be sustained and thus eliminate weaknesses of the analysis.

The composition of this chapter is as follows: the second section deals with Sraffa's explicit criticism of Keynes's analysis around his so-called Fundamental Equations in the *Treatise*. While this theme is in itself of little importance, not least because Keynes himself later recanted his respective views, it allows us to introduce some of Sraffa's early theoretical findings, which form the background of his objections also to later ideas of Keynes. The third section turns to Keynes's view that investment projects can be ordered independently of the level of the rate of interest according to their marginal efficiencies of capital. This idea is but another expression of what Sraffa dubbed the "monotonic prejudice" that permeates much of marginalist analysis and which can be sustained only in exceptionally special cases. A truly "general theory," which Keynes aspired to elaborate, had to dispense with this "prejudice." In the fourth section, I turn to Sraffa's critical account of Friedrich August Hayek's monetary overinvestment theory of the business cycle. In it, Sraffa used the concept of "commodity rate of interest," which Keynes then picked up in the *General Theory* in an attempt to counter Hayek's objection that the *Treatise* lacked a proper capital theoretic foundation. The subsequent section addresses Sraffa's criticism of Keynes's liquidity preference theory contained in his annotations in his personal copy of the *General Theory* and two manuscript fragments that Sraffa appears to have composed shortly after the book had been published, but which he apparently had never shown to anybody. The final section then draws some conclusions.

Determination of price levels in the *Treatise*

Using a famous formulation of Keynes, we may say that in the late 1920s and early 1930s both Keynes and Sraffa were involved in a "struggle of escape from habitual modes of thought and expression" (CWK 7, p. xxiii). While Keynes focused on the problem of money and output as a whole, Sraffa focused on the problem of value and distribution.

Sraffa had put forward his criticism of Marshall's partial equilibrium theory in two essays published in the mid-1920s (Sraffa 1925, 1926), which had impressed the scientific community.[2] Yet, as regards an alternative construction, the two papers contain little, except for a few hints in which direction to search. It was in the winter of 1927–1928 that Sraffa experienced a breakthrough in terms of his "systems of equations," which foreshadow his later work (Sraffa 1960, chaps. 1 and 2). Keynes, meanwhile, was working in broadly the same period on "a novel means of approach to the fundamental problems of monetary theory," as he wrote in his preface to the *Treatise* with reference to books III and IV of the work (CWK 5, p. xvii). He was not happy with the outcome and called it "a collection of material rather than a finished work" (CWK 5, p. xviii). The reason was that "The ideas with which I have finished up are widely different from those with which I began. . . . There are many skins which I have sloughed still littering the pages. . . . I feel like someone who has been forcing his way through a confused jungle" (CWK 5, p. xvii).

The original novelty of the *Treatise* was the "Fundamental Equations" for the value of money in book III. They were designed to tackle "The real task of such a [monetary] theory [which] is to treat the problem dynamically, analysing the different elements involved, in such a manner as to exhibit the causal process by which the price level is determined, and the method of transition from one position of equilibrium to another" (CWK 5, p. 120). The quantity theory of money in its various forms, Keynes insisted, was ill adapted for this purpose. He then proposed to break away from the conventional method of starting from a given quantity of money irrespective of the uses to which it is put. Instead he started from the flow of aggregate earnings or money income and "its twofold division (1) into the parts which have been *earned* by the production of consumption goods and of investment goods respectively, and (2) into the parts which are *expended* on consumption goods and on savings respectively" (CWK 5, p. 121; Keynes's emphasis). He maintained that if the two divisions (1) and (2) are in the same proportions, then the price level of consumption goods will equal their respective costs of production. If not, price level and costs will differ from one another, giving rise to (extra, or windfall) profits or losses in the consumption sector.

The price level of consumption goods is said to be "solely determined by the disposition of the public towards 'saving'" and "*entirely independent* of the price level of investment goods" (CWK 5, pp. 129 and 123; emphasis added). The price level of investment goods is said to depend on the public's choice between "bank deposits" and "securities." This is motivated in terms of the observation that the decision to hold the one or the other relates "not only to the current increment to the wealth of individuals, but also to the whole block of their existing capital" (CWK 5,

p. 127). And while in a footnote on the same page Keynes tells the reader that in the present context he uses the term "investing" not in the sense of "the purchase of securities" but in the sense of "the act of the entrepreneur when he makes an addition to the capital of the community," he neverthe-less identifies the price level of newly produced investment goods with the price level of securities. He concludes that the "actual price level of investments is the resultant of the sentiment of the public [i.e., whether it is 'bearish' or 'bullish'] and the behaviour of the banking system," or "by the disposition of the public towards hoarding money" (CWK 5, pp. 128 and 129–130).

In the period from January 1930 to 1932, Sraffa exchanged a couple of notes with Keynes in which he raised objections to which Keynes then answered.[3] Sraffa's objections concerned inter alia the propositions just mentioned,[4] and, at a deeper level, Keynes's view of the determinants of profits. Sraffa disputed Keynes's confounding of securities and fixed capi-tal items "under the ambiguous name of 'new investment goods'" (Sraf-fa's Papers D1/71).[5] This was misleading: in the short run, the (market) prices of new machines depend on the demand of firms that are intent upon expanding (or reducing) their productive capacity, and the prices of securities depend on the demand of investors in financial markets; whereas in the long period, the prices of machines are regulated by their costs of production (inclusive of profits at a normal rate) and those of securities by the rate of interest. It is misleading to identify the price level of newly produced capital goods with that of securities. If in the short run savings exceed investment, then this will have only a small effect on the prices of consumer goods, but it will have a large effect on the price of securities: "in reality the price of [consumer goods] is as sticky as the price of securities is fluid; it would be hard to find two more typical in-stances of an imperfect, and of a perfect, market" (Sraffa's Papers D1/71). Keynes was wrong in assuming that the effect of a fall in consumption demand would be an immediate and proportional fall in price, whereas an increased demand for securities would not appreciably raise their price.[6] Keynes also overlooked the fact that a rise in the price of securi-ties is a source of profits (equal to premiums) that would compensate firms for any losses due to a fall in consumption prices.

Contrary to Keynes's view, the price levels relating to industries pro-ducing investment and consumption goods were not independent of one another. Sraffa's respective objection has at its background the analysis of systems of equations of production he had started to elaborate from November 1927 until 1930 when he had to focus all his energy on pre-paring the edition of David Ricardo's works and correspondence on behalf of the Royal Economic Society.[7] In a system characterized by a circular flow of commodities, Keynes's distinction lacks precision, because one and the same type of commodity may be used both as an investment and as a consumption good. How can the price of such a commodity be determined in two radically different and independent ways?

More important, the two kinds of industries are typically intimately intertwined. In his papers of the 1920s, Sraffa had not taken into account the fact that in modern industrial systems, commodities are produced by means of commodities. He had defended this neglect by pointing out that "the conditions of simultaneous equilibrium in numerous industries" are far too complex and that "the present state of our knowledge . . . does not permit of even much simpler schema being applied to the study of real conditions" (Sraffa 1926, p. 541). "The process of diffusion of profits throughout the various stages of production and of the process of forming a normal level of profits throughout all the industries of a country," he had then surmised, was "beyond the scope of this article" (Sraffa 1926, p. 550). It was precisely this problem that Sraffa began to tackle after he had moved to Cambridge in 1927 (see Kurz and Salvadori 2005; Kurz 2006). By the time he was confronted with Keynes's "Fundamental Equations," which dealt with a closely related problem, he had already established a number of important results.

In a simple numerical example of 1928, there are two industries, the first producing an investment and the second a consumption good. Sraffa tabulated production as follows:

$$17v = (6v + 10)r$$

$$23 = (5v + 4)r$$

Here, 17 (23) units of the first (second) commodity are produced by means of 6 (5) units of the first and 10 (4) units of the second commodity; v is the value of one unit of the capital good in terms of the means of subsistence, and r is the interest factor ($= 1 +$ interest rate). Sraffa calculated $r(\approx 1.582)$ and $v(\approx 2.108)$, represented graphically the relationships between v and r given by the two equations, and identified the solution of the system as the intersection of the two curves (see Fig. 10.1).

Next Sraffa turned to a problem that had bothered economists since the early years of the discipline and that bothered also Keynes: how does the rate of return on capital change consequent upon a change in real wages caused, e.g., by a change in the price of the consumption good, given money wages and given the system of production in use? Answering this question implied disclosing the mathematical properties of a

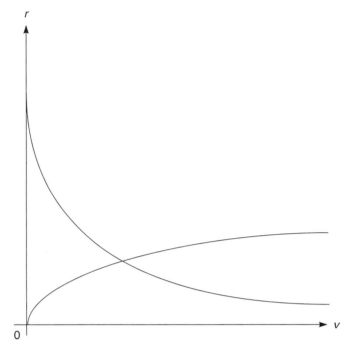

Figure 10.1 Simultaneous determination of interest rate and relative price.

given system of production as regards the distributional alternatives it allows for and the corresponding price vectors supporting these alternatives. Sraffa stressed that it is "as clear as sunlight" that a change in income distribution generally affects the price of the intermediate product relative to the consumption good, and that with a fall in real wages the general rate of return on capital would increase (see, for example, Sraffa's Papers D3/12/7, p. 95). In terms of Figure 10.1, a change in the real wage rate would involve a shift of the two curves and with them a shift of their point of intersection.

Against this background, it should come as no surprise that Sraffa objected to Keynes that "the price of investment goods is determined *in the same way* as that of consumption goods, and a change in the demand for either may give rise (or fail to give rise) to profits or losses" (Sraffa's Papers D1/72/3; emphasis added). Keynes understood that his position could not be sustained and abandoned the idea.

Before we continue, it should be stressed that in terms of his systems of equations, Sraffa had established that the rate of return and relative prices generally depend on two sets of data: (a) the system of production in use, that is, the methods of production actually employed to produce given levels of output, and thus on physical real costs; and (b) the wages share.

We now turn to Keynes's view of the inducement to investment in chapter 11 of the *General Theory*. There Keynes puts forward his concept of the "marginal efficiency of capital." Could this concept be sustained vis-à-vis Sraffa's theoretical findings?

The "marginal efficiency of capital" schedule

Keynes essentially adopted the internal rate of return method when dealing with investment projects from which a manufacturer may choose: "I define the marginal efficiency of capital as being equal to that rate of discount which would make the present value of the series of annuities given by the returns expected from the capital-asset during its life just equal to its supply price" (CWK 7, p. 135). (This method has serious shortcomings, which, however, need not concern us here.) Keynes goes on to argue that the various projects may be ordered according to their marginal efficiencies and then suggests to aggregate them, "so as to provide a schedule relating the rate of aggregate investment to the corresponding marginal efficiency of capital in general which that rate of investment will establish" (CWK 7, p. 136). This he calls the "investment demand schedule," which he confronts with the current rate of interest. He concludes: "the rate of investment will be pushed to the point on the investment demand-schedule where the marginal efficiency of capital in general is equal to the market rate of return" (CWK 7, pp. 136–137).

Keynes rests his argument on the dubious partial equilibrium method: he assumes that the schedule and the money rate of interest are independent of one another. Yet, if one was to depend on the other, or if they were interdependent, the argument in its present form would break down. Several commentators, including Pasinetti (1974), have emphasized that Keynes's argument consists of an adaptation of the classical doctrine of extensive diminishing returns to the theory of investment. This doctrine (see, e.g., Kurz 1978) typically assumes that the different qualities of land can be brought into an *order of fertility*, with the first quality exhibiting the lowest unit costs of production of, say, corn; the second quality, the second lowest unit costs; and so on. In competitive conditions, with a rise in "effectual demand" (Adam Smith), the different qualities of land will be taken into cultivation according to this order. The different qualities of land can also be ranked according to the rent they yield per acre; this ranking is known as the *order of rentability*. It has commonly been assumed that both orders are independent of income distribution and that they coincide.

In the late 1920s, Sraffa showed that this is true only in exceedingly special cases. In general, both orders depend on the rate of interest and do not coincide (see also Kurz and Salvadori 1995, chap. 10). Sraffa established this result in the course of an analysis of the problem of the choice of technique of cost-minimizing (profit-maximizing) producers. He first studied the problem of which qualities of land from a set of alternatives will be cultivated in order to match effectual demand. In around mid-1929, he demonstrated that the order of fertility depends on the rate of interest. Hence, different qualities of land cannot generally be ordered monotonically with respect to that rate: with a change in it, the order will typically change as well.[8] The reason for this is that different methods of production employed in cultivating different qualities of land typically use different capital goods, or the same capital goods in different proportions, relative to labor. Since relative prices of (capital) goods will generally change with a change in the rate of interest, relative costs of production and thus the cheapness of methods will also change. A particular quality of land that at one level of the rate of interest is cost-minimizing at a higher (lower) level may be dominated by another quality of land. It may even "come back" at a still higher (lower) level. A similar result Sraffa then established with respect to a pure capital goods model, focusing attention both on circulating and fixed capital.[9]

Sraffa's findings have a direct bearing on Keynes's investment demand schedule and his closely related view as regards the long-period relationship between the overall capital-labor ratio and the rate of return on capital. Both as regards the short and the long period, Keynes had fallen victim to the "monotonic prejudice" (see Gehrke and Kurz 2006). As regards the former, with a change in the rate of interest it cannot be presumed that the ranking of investment projects will remain the same, because both expected gross revenues and costs will generally be affected by the change. The ranking of investment projects in a descending order of marginal efficiency is thus no less dependent on the rate of interest than the ranking of different qualities of land in terms of "fertility." As regards the long period, there is no presumption that an increase in the capital-labor ratio is invariably accompanied by a decrease in the marginal efficiency of capital in general, as Keynes contended (see, e.g., CWK 7, p. 136).[10]

Sraffa's findings are indisputable. As Mas-Colell (1989) stressed, the relationship between the capital-labor ratio and the rate of return on capital can have almost any shape whatsoever. This implies that the "demand function" for capital in terms of the rate of interest need not be downward sloping in the perhaps only point in which it cuts the given "supply function" of capital (which we may, for simplicity, take to be a straight vertical line). The resulting equilibrium, while unique, would be unstable. We may ask with Marshall, what is the explanatory power of such an equilibrium?

We now turn to Sraffa's assessment of Keynes's liquidity preference theory. In order to get a better grasp of it, we must, for the reasons given earlier, first deal briefly with Sraffa's criticism of Hayek's "Austrian" theory of the business cycle (see Kurz 2000; see also Ranchetti 2002).

Sraffa's criticism of Hayek

In the 1930s, upon the request of Lionel Robbins of the London School of Economics, Friedrich August Hayek assumed the role of a main adversary of Keynes's explanation of unemployment and economic crises in the *Treatise* (Hayek 1931b, 1932b). Hayek advocated instead an explanation of the phenomena that built upon the works of Ludwig von Mises, Eugen von Böhm-Bawerk, and Vilfredo Pareto. When Sraffa was confronted with Hayek's argument, he knew already that its theoretical core—Böhm-Bawerk's theory of capital and interest—was shaky (see Kurz and Gehrke 2006). Therefore, Sraffa must have been amused when, in Hayek's rejoinder to Keynes's reply to his criticism in *Economica*, Hayek maintained that the main weakness of Keynes's argument was its lack of a proper capital theoretic foundation and that Keynes was well advised to adopt Böhm-Bawerk's theory (Hayek 1931a).

Keynes appears to have accepted the criticism but not the proposal, presumably because Sraffa had informed him about the deficiencies of Böhm-Bawerk's capital theory. Was there another option available to make good the lacuna? Keynes appears to have convinced himself that there was indeed such an option and that it revolved around the concept of commodity rate of interest. I am aware of no evidence that Sraffa himself played any role in this. Had he in advance been informed about Keynes's idea, he would in all probability have expressed his reservation. The concept was, of course, already known to Keynes from his work on foreign currency markets and portfolio decisions and his development of the interest rate parity theorem.[11] It had played a role in the *Tract on Monetary Reform* published in 1923 (CWK 4), which Sraffa translated into Italian and published in 1925, and was referred to in the *Treatise*. Last, but not least, it was an indispensable tool in Keynes's, Kahn's, and

Sraffa's dealings on the Stock Exchange.[12] However, in the *General Theory*, the concept of commodity rate of interest assumed an entirely new status, elevated to the role of providing a choice- and capital-theoretic foundation of Keynes's theory of investment behavior, both real and financial. Given its uttermost importance in the central chapter 17 of the *General Theory* and Keynes's explicit wish to relate his analysis to Sraffa's, it appears to be appropriate to deal carefully with how Sraffa defined the concept and put it to work in his criticism of Hayek.

Confronted with Hayek's attack, Keynes found himself in an impasse because he was not familiar with the main building blocks of Hayek's argument. Sraffa, who had studied the contributions of Böhm-Bawerk and Pareto, came to Keynes's defense. First, he took issue with Hayek's claim that the possibility of a difference between own rates of interest and thus a divergence of some rates from the "equilibrium" or "natural" rate is a characteristic of a money economy that is absent in a barter economy (1932, p. 49). With reference to Wicksell's definition (Wicksell 1898, pp. 93ff.) that interest is the surplus in real units of the exchange of physically homogeneous goods across time, Sraffa emphasized that "If money did not exist, and loans were made in terms of all sorts of commodities, there would be a single rate which satisfies the conditions of equilibrium, but there might be at any moment as many 'natural' rates of interest as there are commodities, though they would not be 'equilibrium' rates. The 'arbitrary' action of the banks is by no means a necessary condition for the divergence; if loans were made in wheat and farmers (or for that matter the weather) 'arbitrarily changed' the quantity of wheat produced, the actual rate of interest on loans in terms of wheat would diverge from the rate on other commodities and there would be no single equilibrium rate" (Sraffa 1932, p. 49).

Next Sraffa illustrated his argument in terms of two economies, one with and the other without money. In both economies, loans can be made in terms of all goods for which forward markets exist. Assume that a cotton spinner at time t borrows a sum of money M for θ periods hence in order to buy on the spot market a certain quantity of cotton at price p^t, which he at the same time sells on the forward market θ periods later at a price $p^{t+\theta}$. This means that the cotton spinner in fact borrows cotton for θ periods. Sraffa expounds: "The rate of interest which he pays, per hundred bales of cotton, is the number of bales that can be purchased with the following sum of money: the interest on the money required to buy spot 100 bales, plus the excess (or minus the deficiency) of the spot over the forward prices of the 100 bales" (Sraffa 1932, p. 50).

If we let $i_{t,\theta}$ be the money rate of interest for θ periods, then we have

$$M = (1 + i_{t,\theta})\, p^t - p^{t+\theta}.$$

The commodity rate of interest of cotton between t and $t+\theta$, $\rho_{t,\theta}$, is then given by the amount of cotton that can be purchased by this sum of money at the given forward price, i.e.,

$$\rho_{t\theta} = \frac{M}{p^{t+\theta}} = \frac{(1+i_{t,\theta})\,p^t - p^{t+\theta}}{p^{t+\theta}} = \frac{(1+i_{t,\theta})\,p^t}{p^{t+\theta}} - 1.$$

Sraffa explained: "In equilibrium the spot and forward price coincide, for cotton as for any other commodity; and all the 'natural' or commodity rates are equal to one another, and to the money rate. But if, for any reason, the supply and the demand for a commodity are not in equilibrium (*i.e.* its market price exceeds or falls short of its cost of production), its spot and forward prices diverge, and the 'natural' rate of interest on that commodity diverges from the 'natural' rates on other commodities" (ibid.).

Therefore, out of equilibrium, there is not only one "natural rate," as Hayek had wrongly maintained, but there are many natural rates. Sraffa added that "under free competition, this divergence of rates is as essential to the effecting of the transition [to a new equilibrium] as is the divergence of prices from the costs of production; *it is, in fact, another aspect of the same thing*" (ibid.).

Using classical terminology, what we have here is the well-known problem of the so-called gravitation of "market prices" toward their normal or "natural" levels, where the latter are determined in the way Sraffa had analyzed in his systems of equations (see section 2 above). Sraffa illustrated the basic idea underlying this process of gravitation in the following way: "immediately some [commodities] will rise in price, and others will fall; the market will expect that, after a certain time, the supply of the former will increase, and the supply of the latter fall, and accordingly the forward price, for the date on which equilibrium is expected to be restored, will be below the spot price in the case of the former and above it in the case of the latter; in other words the rate of interest on the former will be higher than on the latter" (ibid.).

In a long-period position of the economy, and setting aside different degrees of risk, etc., all rates will be equal, and their common level depends, as we have seen, on the physical real costs of production and the given rate of interest.[13]

Keynes was very pleased with Sraffa's performance, not only because it had effectively countered the assault on his intellectual project launched by Lionel Robbins and his circle, but also because it had drawn his attention to a concept upon which Keynes thought he could erect his novel edifice. Most important, perhaps, it allowed him, or so he thought, to drive home the main message of the *General Theory,* that it is the downward rigidity of the money rate of interest that is the source of all the trouble.

As we see from his library and his as-yet unpublished papers, Sraffa did not think highly of Keynes's respective argument. I proceed in two steps. First I summarize Sraffa's annotations in chapter 17 of his working copy of the *General Theory.* Then I deal briefly with two short manuscript fragments that were found in his working copy after he had passed away in 1983 (see Kurz 1996; Ranchetti 2002).

Sraffa's criticism of Keynes's liquidity preference theory

Sraffa's annotations in chapter 17

Sraffa scrutinized Keynes's chapter essentially in the same manner he had previously scrutinized Hayek's book, asking whether the concepts used were well defined, whether the argument was developed without contradictions, and whether it mimicked the essential features of the reality it purported to analyze. Since according to Sraffa the theory of liquidity preference "involves *all* the functions considered in the system: it is, in fact, Keynes's system!," the latter stood or fell with it.

Keynes starts the chapter by pointing out "that the *rate of interest on money* plays a peculiar part in setting a limit to the level of employment." Wherein lies "the peculiarity of money as distinct from other assets" (CWK 7, p. 222, emphasis in original)? Keynes defines the money rate of interest à la Wicksell and adds that with regard to all durable goods there is an analogue to the money rate of interest: "Thus for every durable commodity we have a rate of interest in terms of itself, a wheat-rate of interest, a copper-rate of interest, a house-rate of interest" (pp. 222–223). In a footnote he adds: "This relationship was first pointed out by Mr Sraffa, *Economic Journal,* March 1932, p. 50" (p. 223n).

At any given moment of time, these rates will generally not be equal to one another: the ratio between spot and future price will be "notoriously different" between different commodities: "This, we shall find, will lead us to the clue we are seeking. For it may be that it is the *greatest* of the own-rates of interest ... which rules the roost ...; and that there are reasons why it is the money-rate of interest which is often the greatest (because, as we shall find, certain forces, which operate to reduce the own-rates of interest of other assets, do not operate in the case of money)" (pp. 223–224; Keynes's emphasis).[14]

Why is this so? Surprisingly, Keynes approaches the question by defining the own rates of different commodities not in terms of expected changes of prices but in terms of three characteristics that supposedly can all be translated into interest rate equivalents. These are

1. the "yield or output q . . . by assisting some process of production or supplying services to a consumer";
2. the costs of holding the object or "carrying cost c"; and
3. the "liquidity premium" l, expressing the amount, in terms of the object, its proprietor is willing to part company with for the "potential convenience or security" associated with the "power of disposal over an asset during a period" (p. 226).[15]

Keynes concludes: "It follows that the total return expected from the ownership of an asset over a period is equal to its yield minus its carrying cost plus its liquidity-premium, i.e. to $q - c + l$. That is to say, $q - c + l$ is the own-rate of interest of any commodity, where q, c and l are measured in terms of itself as the standard" (p. 226). Sraffa remarks in the margin of this passage: "this contradicts definitions of pp. 222–223."

It is only now that Keynes turns explicitly to the determination of the *expected returns* of different assets. We ought to know, he writes, "what the *changes in relative values* during the year are expected to be" (p. 227; emphasis added). Sraffa comments dryly that this should have been done right at the beginning, when defining the own rates.

Next Keynes assumes that the expected rates of increase (or decrease) of the prices of houses and of wheat, expressed in money, are a_1 and a_2 percent and goes on to say: "It will also be useful to call $a_1 + q_1$, $a_2 + q_2$ and l_3, which stand for the same quantities reduced to money as the standard of value, the house-rate of money interest, the wheat-rate of money interest and the money-rate of money-interest respectively. With this notation it is easy to see that the demand of wealth-owners will be directed to houses, to wheat or to money, according as $a_1 + q_1$, $a_2 + q_2$ or l_3 is greatest" (p. 227).

In the margin of this passage, Sraffa puts a big question mark. Indeed, as he had made clear in his criticism of Hayek, the expected changes in prices fully express differences in the "yield" of different assets, as perceived by the market. How could Keynes's summing up over the a's and q's *not* involve double counting?

Sraffa spots immediately that the usual choice of *money as standard of value* has an important implication: "The point is, that in the case of the rate of the article chosen as standard, *the effect upon it of the expected depreciation is concealed*" (emphasis added). This is a crucial point, which Keynes apparently had lost sight of and which had seriously misled him. For example, if an increase in the amount of money happens to lead to a fall in the value of money, then this would imply an increase in the "money-rate of wheat interest," a fact that, unfortunately, Keynes does not take into account. The same objection reappears in several forms.

Next Keynes brings in the marginal efficiency of capital and compares it with the rate of interest. Sraffa comments: "'Marginal efficiency' and 'the' rate of interest are obscure: the former is not defined in this context and the latter has two definitions on p. 227." It is at any rate misleading what Keynes says, because the rate of interest of an object, whose actual price exceeds cost of production, is according to the definition given on pp. 222–223 (relatively) *high*, not low.

Keynes then expounds his view in terms of the three-assets example. Since in equilibrium the own rates, expressed in the same numeraire, must be equal, one gets the following result: with the own rate of money being constant, "it follows that a_1 and a_2 must be rising. In other words, the present money-price of every commodity other than money tends to fall relatively to its expected future price" (p. 228). Sraffa comments that exactly the opposite follows: "this will *lower*, not raise, their rates of interest." Keynes simply got it wrong.

On the following page, Keynes insists that it is "that asset's rate of interest which declines most slowly as the stocks of assets in general increase, which eventually knocks out the profitable production of each of the others" (p. 229). In the margin, Sraffa asks whether here Keynes should have referred to the concept of marginal efficiency of capital.

In the third section of the chapter, Keynes argues that the elasticity of production of money is zero and its elasticity of substitution close to zero or zero. Sraffa is obviously not convinced by this and spots a few more contradictions. Keynes's view that if wages were not relatively rigid, "the position might be worse rather than better" (p. 232), prompts Sraffa to the sarcastic remark: "as usual, heads I win, tails you lose."

However, Sraffa vividly expresses his agreement with Keynes's proposition that "The conception of what contributes to 'liquidity' is a partly vague one" (p. 240) by underlining the sentence and adding exclamation marks in the margin.

Looking at Sraffa's annotations, one cannot escape the impression that in his judgment the chapter was a mess, confused, and confusing. This impression is confirmed by two manuscript fragments to which we now briefly turn (see Sraffa's Papers I100).

Two manuscript fragments

Sraffa's criticism concerns especially the following elements:

1. The concept of liquidity that Keynes uses is vague and ambiguous.
2. There is no reason to presume that liquidity is always a good thing for each and every agent.
3. Keynes advocates different concepts of commodity rate of interest that are not compatible with one another.
4. Keynes erroneously admits Fisher's effect for all commodities, except money.

With regard to the second element, Sraffa observes that the inverse relationship between holding cash and the rate of interest, i.e., the liquidity preference curve, is reminiscent of the usual *marginal utility curve*: "liquidity is always an advantage, though diminishing." Yet this is not generally true, Sraffa objects. While for some agents it may be the case in a particular situation, for others it may be quite otherwise. Banks, for example, must remain solvent and liquid, but they must also make profits. Since their income consists almost exclusively of interest, they must, with a lower rate of interest, get less liquid in order to keep up their income. Therefore, Sraffa concludes, it is generally impossible to say that there is a definite relationship between the quantity of money and the rate of interest. There is no such thing as *the* liquidity preference curve.

Sraffa insists that advantages associated with carrying an asset have nothing to do with its commodity rate. People who borrow money or any other asset typically do this not in order to carry what is being borrowed until the expiration of the contract but in order to buy with it other things. What is being borrowed is not what is wanted to be kept but the standard in which the debt is fixed. Therefore, it is irrelevant whether a person pays in money or wheat and whether what is borrowed is a durable or a perishable good. Sraffa concludes "that K. has in the back of his mind two wrong notions, which have entirely misled him," namely, (a) that commodities are borrowed to be kept until the end of the loan and (b) that only durables can be borrowed.

There remains, however, the fact that a large quantity of money (cash) and a low rate of interest often go together, which gives the curve a certain plausibility. Yet, Sraffa insists, "causation is the other way round": it is a low rate of interest that is responsible for a large quantity of money, not a large quantity of money that causes a low rate of interest. Attention ought to focus on those who demand loans (investors) and not on those who provide them with liquid funds. Keynes's theory of liquidity preference with its emphasis on the supply of loans, Sraffa concludes, is similar to the old long-period theory of the supply of savings that is elastic with respect to the rate of interest placed into a short-period setting.

The commodity rate of interest, Sraffa insists, depends exclusively on expected price changes and is thus defined with respect to the forward price of a commodity. There are two ways in which the commodity rates of interest can become uniform again: either via changes in prices and/or via changes in production. Surprisingly, Keynes accepts both possibilities for all commodities other than money. This becomes clear when we consider, for example, the case in which agents develop a large propensity to hoard money. Due to the ensuing depressive tendencies in the economy, commodity prices will tend to fall. This implies a rise in the value of money. An expected increase in the value of money implies, however, a lower "own rate of money interest," to use Keynes's peculiar concept. Sraffa emphasizes that "therefore the money rate will be *lower* than other rates and not higher."[16] Sraffa adds that this is "Fisher's effect, which K. admits for all commodities except money." The reference is obviously to Irving Fisher (1892, 1907), who first elaborated the concept of own rates.[17] Sraffa concludes: "Thus in the K. case, the result on rates of int[erest]. is opposite to K.'s conclusion."

In chapter 17, Keynes did not reason correctly and got entangled in a maze of contradictions. Liquidity preference theory, i.e., "Keynes's system," is logically incoherent. Its basic notion is but another expression of the marginal utility of hoarding, which is but a particular aspect of marginal theory. Keynes who with one foot had managed to escape received modes of thought with his other foot was still tightly tied to them.

Concluding remarks

Sraffa approved of Keynes's critical intention but was disenchanted with its execution. It was not only Keynes's occasional sloppiness Sraffa found difficult to cope with. In important respects, he felt that Keynes had granted too much to received economic theory. Keynes's new theory exhibited several loose ends and contradictions and retained in new garb marginalist concepts that Sraffa deemed untenable.

It is ironic to see that the distinguishing feature of what today is known as "Neo-Keynesian" and "New Keynesian" theory is the premise of sticky prices: Keynes is interpreted as an imperfectionist. While there are traces of imperfectionism to be found in his magnum opus, in the central part of it he assumes fully flexible prices. Keynes's analysis therefore cannot be accused of lacking generality because of an alleged assumption of price rigidities. The problem, rather, is whether his explanation of a lower boundary to the money rate of interest (in combination with an inverse investment-interest relation) vis-à-vis flexible prices stands up to close examination. According to Sraffa, it does not. Keynes's argument suffers in particular from neglecting the implications of flexible prices via the value of money for the level of the "own rate of money interest." However, Keynes's failure must not be taken to be orthodox theory's triumph. In Sraffa's view, Keynes failed because in his analysis the orthodox elements overwhelm the truly novel ones.

Sraffa developed his criticism of Keynes from an approach that also considers (long-period) prices as fully flexible. This does not mean, however, that the conventionally invoked "forces of demand and supply" can be expected to generally bring about a full employment equilibrium. The irony is that Sraffa established these findings in terms of an elaboration of the classical approach to the theory of value and distribution. This approach, coherently developed, actually effectively undermines Say's law—the law for which Keynes had thought he could put classical analysis on one side. Keynes, keen to free himself of "habitual modes of thought and expression," was only partly successful.

Notes

This chapter is based on a paper given at the conference "Keynes's Economics and His Influences on Modern Economics," held at Sophia University, Tokyo, March 14–15, 2007. I am grateful to the participants of the conference, especially Richard Arena, Bob Dimand, Cristina Marcuzzo, Nerio Naldi, and Yosh Ono, for valuable comments and suggestions. The view that Sraffa was "secretly skeptical" of Keynes's new ideas was first expressed by Joan Robinson (1978, p. xii).

1. He showed some of his early findings in 1928 to Keynes and Arthur Cecil Pigou.
2. Sraffa's 1925 paper was praised as a masterpiece by leading authorities in economics; see, for example, Oskar Morgenstern's commendation (Morgenstern 1931). Sraffa's assessment of Marshall's analysis contradicted Keynes's opinion, as reported by Harrod (1951, p. 324), that all that one needed in order to be a good economist was a thorough knowledge of Marshall's *Principles* and a careful daily reading of the *Times*.
3. For a detailed account of the correspondence between Keynes and Sraffa, see Ranchetti (2005, pp. 126–130).
4. He was not the only one who had difficulties with Keynes's postulate of the independence of the two price levels. For Richard Kahn and Joan Robinson's difficulties with it, see Marcuzzo (2002, pp. 427–429).
5. References to Sraffa's Papers kept at Wren Library at Trinity College, Cambridge, follow the catalog prepared by Jonathan Smith, archivist.

6. It is interesting to note that this was precisely the approach Keynes had taken in his "banana parable" in the *Treatise*, a thought experiment whose preliminary result had put him on the path toward the *General Theory*.

7. On the close collaboration between Keynes and Sraffa regarding the Ricardo edition, see Gehrke and Kurz (2002).

8. When in 1942 Sraffa resumed his work on his book, he recapitulated his findings of more than a decade before. In a note composed on November 13 entitled "Order of fertility," he asked: "Is it possible in our scheme to arrange a series of lands of different qualities in a descending order of 'fertility' that will be valid for all values of (independently of) r [rate of interest] and w [wage rate]? No, it is not possible" (Sraffa's Papers D3/12/25, p. 1). He illustrated the dependence of the order of fertility, and of the reversal of his order, in terms of a simple example.

9. This involved an investigation of fixed capital goods and the extensive and intensive dimension of their utilization. In this context, Sraffa studied carefully what Keynes in the *Treatise* had to say about the role of "working" and fixed capital in production (see CWK 5, chap. 8). As Sraffa's hitherto unpublished papers show, he was convinced that the growing importance of durable instruments of production had rendered a great elasticity to the modern economic system, which allowed it to increase and decrease considerably the rate of output in response to varying levels of effective demand. This was possible, for example, by switching between a single- and a double-shift system of capital utilization. Keynes's view in the *General Theory* that employment and real wages are of necessity negatively correlated (see the concept of the "employment function"; CWK 7, chap. 20) was difficult to reconcile with this observation, at least when starting from low levels of employment and capital utilization. As is well known, Keynes partly recanted his earlier view on the matter in his discussion with Dunlop and Tarshis.

10. In the 1960s, the possibility that the capital-labor ratio rises (falls) with a rise (fall) in the rate of profits (and a corresponding fall [rise] in the real wage rate) became known as *capital reversing* or *reverse capital deepening;* for a discussion of this phenomenon, see Kurz and Salvadori (1995, chap. 14). The discussion sets aside the problem of "inventions," i.e., the fact that new methods of production become available as time goes by. Here it suffices to point out that Keynes's view is not rendered more credible if inventions are taken into account.

11. See the contributions by Marcello de Cecco and Jan Kregel in this volume. For a criticism of the use Keynes made of the concept of own rates of interest, see also Barens and Caspari (1997).

12. One event is worth telling. In late 1937, Keynes and Sraffa had different views as to the development of the price of lard, one of several pig products, and cotton oil, used to feed pigs. Keynes was convinced that the price of lard could be expected to rise and belittled Sraffa's objections by writing in a letter to Kahn: "If Piero [Sraffa] had ever seen a pig, he would know that the live animal cannot be kept in cold storage waiting till its food stuffs are cheaper" (CWK 12, pp. 22–23). Keynes therefore decided to job from cotton

oil into lard. In a letter to Kahn in October 1937, Sraffa explained his point of view, based on an argument about the fattening of pigs, which culminated in the statement: "The less lard there is in stock, the more (with a multiplier) there is under the skin of pigs" (CWK 12, p. 24). Sraffa therefore expected a fall in the price of lard. Kahn reported Sraffa's argument to Keynes, yet to no avail. As Moggridge writes in his comment on the incident: "Keynes persisted in his view. His losses continued, by the end of 1937 totaling £27,210 on lard. He also lost over £17,000 on cotton oil" (CWK 12, p. 24).

13. According to Sraffa, the banking system can control only the money rate(s) of interest and has to leave the decision about the quantity of money and credit in the system to the public. Money is genuinely an endogenous magnitude.

14. Hayek had argued that crises are caused by too low a money rate of interest; Keynes argued exactly the opposite.

15. In this context it is worth mentioning, as de Cecco (2005) pointed out, that in his lectures on continental banking, which Sraffa gave to third year undergraduates in Cambridge in the springs of 1929 and 1930, he introduced the idea that different assets and commodities may be arranged in order of liquidity. According to de Cecco, Keynes in his theory of liquidity preference was in all probability influenced by Sraffa's respective argument, which can be traced back to Sraffa's studies of "forward exchange rates, around 1919, and provided Keynes with data on the lira's forward rates"; see de Cecco in Kurz, Pasinetti and Salvadori (2008, p. 190).

16. Keynes in one place uses the concept of "own rate of money interest," which, with money taken as standard of value, Sraffa comments, is a "hybrid" concept that "indeed has no other use than to patch up the confusion created," but in fact is only there "to make confusion more confounded."

17. Copies of Irving Fisher's books with annotations in Sraffa's hand are in Sraffa's library.

CHAPTER ELEVEN

Keynes and the War of Words

Gilles Dostaler

LTHOUGH JOHN MAYNARD KEYNES worked out a new economic analysis that eventually served to justify the interventionist policies associated with his name, he defined himself first and foremost not as an economic theorist but rather as a "publicist," in the old sense of the term, as someone who circulates ideas. Declining candidacy for a parliamentary by-election at Cambridge University on November 24, 1939, he wrote to A. B. Ramsay, who had approached him on the matter: "The active political life is not my right and true activity. I am indeed an extremely active publicist. . . . I am on lines along which I can only operate usefully and have my full influence if I am aloof from the day to day life of Westminster" (CWK 22, p. 38). He was concerned with persuading his fellow citizens of the urgent necessity of carrying out the transformations he felt essential to avoid the breakdown of civilization, that "thin and precarious crust erected by the personality and the will of a very few, and only maintained by rules and conventions skillfully put across and guilefully preserved" (1938, CWK 10, p. 447). Keynes proposed a global vision of society, its evils, and the means to overcome them. His influence is connected not only to this economic theories but also to a political vision and a philosophic conception that he skillfully integrated into his numerous activities. He was a man of action, fully engaged in the problems of his time. The economic reforms he advocated were but one element in a process of political and social transformation necessary to save a world threatened by war, revolution, and all forms of extremism.

Keynes left behind an enormous body of work. It is of substantial literary quality and extends across many fields, from philosophy and economics to history and politics. He excelled in all genres: abstract treatises or pamphlets, academic or newspaper articles, official reports or personal correspondences, statistical analyses, and biographical essays. A master of the spoken as well as the written word, his effectiveness as lecturer, conference speaker, member and president of boards of directors, political activist, member of various commissions and committees, and negotiator of private and public, particularly international, affairs was unmatched.

Keynes's life was characterized by combat in diverse battlefields. At the age of twenty, then a student at Cambridge, he presented a fifty-seven-page paper on the medieval philosopher and theologian Peter Abelard before a King's College literary society. In emphasizing Abelard's struggles against the established political and religious powers of his time, Keynes praised Abelard's "dialectical skill" (Keynes Papers UA/16, p. 1)[1] and ability in controversy. But mostly Keynes admired Abelard, who investigated the logic of language and religious discourse and composed numerous hymns, for having been inclined "rather to the war of words than to the war of arms" (ibid., p. 16). Keynes clearly felt kinship with this thinker. As he would do later in describing Marshall, Freud, Darwin, Newton, and others, when he spoke of Abelard, Keynes was also partly describing himself. Keynes mastered early the art of short biography and psychological portrait and practiced the genre until the end of his life.[2] These writings are sprinkled with clues on his own personality and views.

Thus, like Abelard, Keynes rejected violence in spite of the glaring injustices he denounced throughout his life and led a relentless war of words against the dominant views of his time, as much in morality as in politics, economics, art, and other domains. As he once said, we cannot convict our adversaries because of their errors; instead, we must convince them. Keynes gave the title *Essays in Persuasion* to a collection of his articles and extracts of books that he published in 1931, with the following words in the preface: "Here are collected the croakings of twelve years—the croakings of a Cassandra who could never influence the course of events in time. The volume might have been entitled 'Essays in Prophecy and Persuasion', for the *Prophecy*, unfortunately, has been more successful than the *Persuasion*. But it was in a spirit of persuasion that most of these essays were written, in an attempt to influence opinion" (Keynes 1931, p. xvii).

Here Keynes displays his customary false modesty; in fact, he entertained few doubts about his capacity to influence public opinion. In his review of Harrod's biography of Keynes, Hayek wrote of "the supreme confidence [Keynes] had acquired in his power to play on public opinion as a supreme master plays on his instrument" (Hayek 1952, p. 232). In their last meeting, a few weeks before Keynes's death, Hayek asked Keynes if he was not concerned with the use some of his disciples were making of his theories. Hayek tells us that Keynes assured him that "if they should ever become dangerous I could rely upon [Keynes] again quickly to swing round public opinion—and he indicated by a quick movement of his hand how rapidly that would be done" (ibid.).

I will examine in what follows the means used by Keynes to swing public opinion, by spoken and by written words, starting with his apprenticeship in this activity. Concerning Keynes as a speaker, I will rely on contemporaries' testimonies. I will conclude by exploring the links between the language and the message that Keynes and his Bloomsbury friends wanted to transmit to their fellow citizens.[3]

The apprenticeship of the war of words

From an early age, Keynes was aware of his ability to persuade, his mastery of language, his capacity to demolish his contradictors. These talents, which were probably partly innate, were also transmitted to him by his familial milieu. His father, John Neville Keynes, a nonconformist Victorian intellectual, was a lover of language and of rhetoric. He discovered his son's exceptional talents very early and devoted much time to his education, following his career step by step and helping him prepare for examinations, over which the father agonized more than the son. In a certain way, Maynard fulfilled Neville's own disappointed intellectual ambitions. This reminds us of the relations between James Mill and his son John Stuart or of Leopold Mozart and his son Wolfgang Amadeus. The young Maynard could be present at the conversations between his parents and such luminaries as Henry Sidgwick, William Johnson, James Ward, Herbert Foxwell, and Alfred Marshall. He did not have the permission to talk himself but sometimes violated this rule, as recalled by his mother:

> Our children had their own nursery routine but were with us a great deal and loved to be allowed to take their small part in entertaining visitors. Maynard specially enjoyed coming down to lunch and listening to grown-up conversation. Sometimes it was necessary to remind him that he would not be expected to join in the talk himself. He accepted the situation but remarked sadly that it would be "a great drawback." Once when his father pointed out to him that he had not behaved quite so well in company as a

few days previously, he excused himself by pleading that on the earlier occasion he had been preparing himself for it for days and could not always make such an effort. He never failed to be ready with an excuse or an argument in support of his own view. (F. A. Keynes 1950, p. 64)

At ten, Maynard could read the great Latin authors in the original. On February 16, 1896, he wrote in his diary: "I begin to make to-day a list of all the chief books I have read with authors" (Keynes Papers PP/34, p. 8). On April 5 of the same year, he recorded that "the list of books which I have read has now reached 133" (p. 10). Great literary texts dominate the list, although scientific works are numerous. Books interested him by their material appearance as well as by their contents. At the age of nineteen, he started to assemble a collection of rare books and manuscripts that would be, at this death, impressive by its quality as well as by its size. It included, among many other treasures, 150 manuscripts written by Isaac Newton about alchemy, which Keynes bought in 1936. In a radio program broadcast in 1936 titled "On Reading Books," he explained that a reader "should approach [books] with all his senses; he should know their touch and their smell. . . . He should live with more books than he reads, with a penumbra of unread pages, of which he knows the general character and content, fluttering round him" (CWK 28, p. 334).

When he arrived at Eton in 1897, the young Keynes was already a fluent orator and impressively skilful writer. His early papers testify to this, as do others' memories of speeches he then started to make—for example, to support the positions of the Liberal party, which he joined at that time. He very quickly mastered the art of the electoral speech. For the 1911 elections, he spoke easily before twelve hundred listeners. At Eton, he expressed himself vigorously against the war led by Great Britain against the Boers of South Africa and against the protectionism advocated by Joseph Chamberlain and the Conservatives, but also against laissez-faire. Thus, contrary to the current view, Keynes did not evolve from orthodox positions, favorable to laissez-faire, at the beginning of his career, toward an advocacy of state intervention in the 1920s. According to Harrod, John Sheppard, an early friend, observed that Keynes was "violently opposed to laissez-fair" and proposed the following definitions of Conservatives and Liberals in a speech given at a Liberal gathering when he was an undergraduate: "let there be a village whose inhabitants were living in conditions of penury and distress; the typical Conservative, when shown this village, said, 'It is very distressing, but, unfortunately, it cannot be helped'; the Liberal said, 'Something must be done about this.' That was why he was a Liberal" (Harrod 1951, p. 192).

Already very self-confident, Maynard expressed a sense of superiority, even toward his teachers. One of them, Mitchell, wrote in his annual report of 1900 that Maynard "possesses a clear head, an unfailing memory, & first rate ability. Rather a provoking boy in school—reads notes often when he ought to be attending to the lesson, apt to talk to his neighbour unless severely repressed. He gives one the idea of regarding himself as a privileged boy, with perhaps a little intellectual conceit" (quoted in Neville Keynes's *Holiday Diaries,* August 6, 1900, Keynes Papers PP/43).

Spoken words

Keynes was affected by a slight stammer but transformed it into a trump. Contemporaries have testified to the fascination that Keynes's voice exerted over his auditors: "he was a very good speaker. I always said . . . his voice was so bewitching. He had a very musical voice. I can see that people got enchanted by merely listening to his words" (Hayek 1994, p. 92). Lionel Robbins, a friend and colleague of Hayek and also an adversary of Keynes, wrote: "How can one describe for a future age the source of this astonishing ascendancy? . . . What distinguished him rather and made him stand out above all his generation were more general qualities of mind and character: the swiftness of his thought and perceptions; the cadence of his voice and his prose style; his idealism and moral fervour; above all, the life-enhancing quality of his presence. . . . But, all in all, I would certainly regard Maynard Keynes as the most remarkable man I have ever met" (Robbins 1971, p. 193).

The Canadian poet and civil servant Douglas LePan was member of a delegation that met a British delegation led by Keynes in Cambridge, in April 1944. He was dazzled by Keynes, who on this as on many other occasions spoke for hours without notes: "His nature was protean, and his range of expression. He could be magisterial, analytic, scornful, withering, contemptuous, insinuating, persuasive. But as he lifted his head to speak of 'the sweet breath of justice,' I was reminded of the sweetness and youthfulness I had noticed in this expression that first evening in Hall when sitting beside him. There was something cherubic, almost seraphic, about his smile" (LePan 1979, pp. 91–92). There are many other testimonies of this kind coming from the diverse audiences Keynes addressed: students, businessmen, shareholders, civil servants, members of the House of Lords, electors, colleagues, friends. His evidence to the Macmillan Committee, on which he also sat, was a particularly memorable performance. He spoke for five days in February and March 1930, without notes, answering questions about the economic and financial problems of Great Britain, the possible solutions, presenting some of the theses of his *Treatise on Money,* which would be published in October of that year (see CWK 20, pp. 38–270). His speeches as chairman of the

National Mutual Life Assurance Society, from 1921 to 1938, in large part reproduced in the press, constituted an important event in the life of the City.[4]

Accounts attesting to Keynes's skill at verbal jousting abound. Leonard Woolf wrote in his memoirs: "He had the very rare gift of being as brilliant and effective in practice as he was in theory, so that he could outwit a banker, business man, or Prime Minister as quickly and gracefully as he could demolish a philosopher or crush an economist. . . . [H]e might, at any moment and sometimes quite unjustifiably, annihilate some unfortunate with ruthless rudeness" (L. Woolf 1960, pp. 144–145). Bertrand Russell, who was himself very self-confident, wrote: "Keynes's intellect was the sharpest and clearest that I have ever known. When I argued with him, I felt that I took my life in my hands, and I seldom emerged without feeling something of a fool" (Russell 1967, p. 72). For Clive Bell, another early friend, "he has a witty intellect and a verbal knack. In argument he was bewilderingly quick, and unconventional" (Bell 1956, pp. 60–61). Bell, like others, adds, however, that Keynes would express himself with assurance on questions on which he knew little or nothing at all—for example, on shooting methods when he had never handled a gun (pp. 49–50; Bell was an accomplished hunter). Bunny Garnett, latecomer to the Bloomsbury set, records: "He was one of the most brilliant talkers I have known. He would pounce on any remark which interested him, extend it, develop it" (Garnett 1979, p. 147). This did not change as Keynes grew older. Mary Glasgow, who was his assistant when he chaired the Council for the Encouragement of Music and the Arts during the Second World War, said of him: "Supremely intelligent himself, he was impatient of anything less than clear thinking and well-defined aims. He knew what he wanted, and why, and he liked to have his own way. He could be very rude on occasion, and he did antagonise a number of people. Faced with an issue on which he felt deeply—and there were many such—he never hesitated to declare war" (Glasgow 1975, p. 267). For Harry Johnson, who as a student met Keynes shortly before his death, "When he was out of the public eye, he could be extremely kind and charming, and could make somebody feel glad to be alive. On the other hand, when the chips were really down, he could be quite ruthless in the way he dealt with people" (H. Johnson 1974, pp. 133–134).

Keynes appreciated word games, liked to provoke, and enjoyed controversy. He could defend one position one day and then, with equal ease, the opposite position the next. He praised the Hungarian physician that took charge of him from 1939, Janos Plesch—who was also Einstein's physician—because he could put forward a diagnosis with great self-confidence and say the contrary the week after with the same confidence.[5] Moreover, the doctor expounded his ideas in ordinary instead of esoteric and specialized languages. This is what Keynes was trying to do in economics, which is no less an exact science than medicine.

Keynes spent an important part of his life negotiating on all fronts, including neighborhood and domestic rows. During the Second World War, he was the main representative of the British Treasury and made six trips to the United States, some of them lasting many months. This strain on a heart that had had a first attack in 1937 partly explains his death at the age of sixty-two. In numerous letters to his parents, he described the physical effort and unceasing psychological tension linked to countless and endless negotiation meetings and speeches. And the discussions with the Americans were not always the most difficult. During a mission he led to negotiate the reimbursement conditions of the war material supplied by the United States under the Lend-Lease program, and more generally the question of U.S. financial support to Great Britain, he wrote to his mother on November 4, 1943: "my difficulties in bringing London along to a reasonable compromise are not less than those in moving Washington. And our business, taken as a whole, is of enormous complexity."

Appreciation of Keynes's skills as a negotiator was mixed, particularly among his allies. Here is how he himself described this art: "A moment often arrives when substantial victory is yours if by some slight appearance of a concession you can save the face of the opposition or conciliate them by a restatement of your proposal helpful to them and not injurious to anything essential to yourself" (Keynes 1919, p. 27). Those who faced him in debate dreaded the experience, particularly Harry White, who described him to Roosevelt as "an extremely able and tough negotiator with, of course, a thorough understanding of the problems that confronted us" (Harry White Papers, quoted by Skidelsky 2000, p. 324). White sometimes required a replacement, totally exhausted by his one-on-ones with Keynes.

Keynes's friend the economist James Meade was part of a delegation that met nine times in the United States between September 15 and October 9, 1943, to discuss the reform of the international monetary system. Meade gave the following description of Keynes's speech at the first plenary meeting of September 21: "Keynes's speech was absolutely in the first rank of speechifying. I have never heard him better,—more brilliant, more persuasive, more witty or more truly moving in his appeal" (Howson and Moggridge 1990, p. 110). However, with his fatigue intensifying from one meeting to the next, Keynes grew increasingly intransigent and ill-tempered, nearly to the point of breaking off negotiations altogether. The meetings were dominated by verbal jousting between Keynes and White, as described by a British participant: "What absolute Bedlam these discussions are! Keynes and White sit next [to] each other, each flanked by a long row of his own supporters. Without any agenda or any prepared idea of what is going to be discussed they go for each other in a strident duet of discord, which after a crescendo of abuse on either side leads up to a chaotic adjournment of the meeting in time for us to return to the Willard for a delegation meeting" (quoted in CWK 25, p. 364). Meade wrote in his diary: "But it augurs ill for the future unless these negotiations can somehow or another be got out of the hands of two such prima donnas as White and Keynes" (Howson and Moggridge 1990, p. 133). It was obviously the U.S. representatives who had the final word in these discussions. Although they conceded on written formulations, they never made any basic concessions and, being the dominant power, had little motivation to do so. Keynes seemed at times unaware of this fact and believed the mere force of his argumentation could reverse the situation.

As for the Bretton Woods negotiation, we have the testimony of Lionel Robbins, who was a member of the delegation, about one of Keynes's speeches: "Keynes was in his most lucid and persuasive mood; and the effect was irresistible. At such moments, I often find myself thinking that Keynes must be one of the most remarkable men that have ever lived—the quick logic, the birdlike swoop of intuition, the vivid fancy, the wide vision, above all the incomparable sense of the fitness of words, all combine to make something several degrees beyond the limit of ordinary human achievement" (Howson and Moggridge 1990, p. 158).

During the Bretton Woods conference, plenary commissions were not often called, the essential work being done by small committees. Keynes sent his colleagues to these, participating little, but staying in his quarters at the disposition of the British delegates, giving information, advice, or orders. There was much behind-the-scenes settling. The working days were long and often continued into the wee hours. Keynes wrote to his mother on July 25, 1944: "I do not think I have ever worked so continuously hard in my life." Worried about his health and feeling moments of weakness, he avoided late-night discussions and remained under his wife Lydia's constant supervision. On July 19, after dinning with U.S. Treasury Secretary Morgenthau, he suffered a slight heart attack. Throughout the conference, Keynes's personal relations with White and Morgenthau were excellent, but discussions were difficult. Keynes was accused of running his commission at a frantic pace, without taking time to give delegates the necessary explanations, to such a point that Morgenthau was obliged to intervene.

Keynes gave an acceptance speech for the final act of the conference on the evening of July 22, praising White and Morgenthau, even finding a few good words for the lawyers and jurists, whose presence he found annoying. This is how Robbins's diary described the event: "At the end Keynes capped the proceedings by one of his most felicitous speeches, and the delegates paid tribute by rising and applauding again and again. In a way, this is one of the greatest triumphs of his life. Scrupulously obedient to his instructions, battling against fatigue and weakness, he has thoroughly dominated the Conference" (Howson and Moggridge 1990, p. 193). The British Treasury official in Washington, R. H. Brand, wrote to Richard Hopkins, permanent secretary of the treasury: "I hope you will think the Conference was a success. I must tell you that Keynes was without doubt quite the dominant figure. He certainly is an astonishing man" (quoted in CWK 26, p. 113). Keynes's exit received a standing ovation and a chorus of the traditional "For he's a jolly good fellow."

Keynes was also a teacher. Many of his lecture notes have been preserved, some of them reproduced in the *Collected Writings* (CWK 12, pp. 689–783; see also Rymes 1989). They show that Keynes, in the first part of his career, spent much time preparing his lectures, transforming them to fit the evolution of his ideas. After the war, he reduced his teaching load and started to lecture from his book proofs, first *A Treatise on Money* and then the *General Theory*. There is thus a close relationship between the written and spoken words. Keynes's students, as well as the members of the Circus[6] and critics of *A Treatise on Money*, played such a part in the elaboration of the *General Theory* that Joan Robinson has described the book as a collective work (see J. Robinson 1948). According to Harrod, Keynes lacked any kind of author's jealously, integrating suggestions, criticisms, and corrections as easily into his theoretical works as his memorandums: "He was entirely lacking in the kind of obstinacy which so often results from pride of authorship" (Harrod 1951, p. 533). This was part of his strategy of persuasion. Others, finding he expressed their own ideas more clearly and elegantly than they did themselves, would then become close allies.

Austin Robinson described lectures at which other teachers, invited lecturers from abroad, and "spies" from the London School of Economics or other places were often present: "Each year he gave us the development of his ideas to date. And these lectures became something wholly unlike anything else that I have ever known in Cambridge lectures. . . . Gradually year by year the essential features of the *General Theory* emerged" (A. Robinson 1947, p. 40). His political economy club, where Keynes presented one of his last talks, was also a very important place for discussion of his ideas. Here is a vivid description from the then young Harry Johnson of Keynes's attitude during these meetings:

> One of the secrets of his charm was that he would go out of his way to make something flattering out of what a student had said. If the student had made an absolute ass of himself, Keynes would still find something in it which he would transform into a good point. It might well be the very opposite of what the student had said; but the student was so relieved to find that he was not being cut to pieces that he was really impressed by the brilliance of what he was told he *had* said. On the other hand, when a faculty member got up . . . he simply cut their heads off. No matter how ingenious what they said was, he would make nonsense of it. And that, again, flattered the students, because they had been told that they were really incisive and then somebody they knew was really clever was reduced to rubble before their eyes. (H. Johnson 1974, p. 133

Written words

If Keynes had an enormous influence on his contemporaries through his spoken words, it is of course by his writings that his most enduring impact has been exercised. The magnitude and diversity of his production are quite impressive. The thirty volumes of the *Collected Writings of John Maynard Keynes* represent but a fraction of what he wrote in the domain of economics. With the exception of *A Treatise on Probability*, they include none of his important writings in philosophy. Also missing are many papers of a more political nature, as well as memorandums and other official writings. A small part of his correspondence has been published, as have a very few papers of a strictly personal nature. Keynes's archives have been reproduced in 180 microfilm rolls.

The first striking feature of this corpus is the variety of genres between which Keynes moves with equal ease. Letters are not the least important means of persuasion. Keynes corresponded abundantly with his parents, his wife, and his numerous friends but also with a great number of individuals of all milieus, with the humble as well as with the great of the world. With his father and mother, with Lydia Lopokova, with Lytton Strachey, there are thousands of letters, often long and elaborate. He took time and pain to answer rapidly and often in a very detailed way to all those who wrote to him, particularly to those who were writing to criticize him.

Keynes was also a compulsive author of reports and memorandums. From Eton, he wrote to his father on February 9, 1902: "I am finding that, like you, when I am appointed to a committee, I am invariably made to do all the work." This continued until the end of his life. When he was coming out of a meeting, he would often write something, sometimes a long paper in which, under the pretext of summarizing the discussion, he would put forward his own positions. He thus controlled the debates, having fixed the frame. For example, during the Second World War, no one mandated him to write the project of an international clearing union, but his plan for one would become, after numerous versions, the official position of Great Britain and finally constitute one of the pieces of the Bretton Woods conference. Similarly, the reports of the Royal Committee on Indian Currency and Finance, of the Macmillan Commission, and the Liberal "Yellow Book," *Britain's Industrial Future,* are in great part of Keynes's hand, even if he did not sign them.

Keynes was also fond of notes, which his secretary, Mrs. Stephens, would type in many copies on a personal notepaper. He would flood his colleagues with these notes, for example, at the Treasury during both world wars. Many feared that they would find in the morning, in their basket, those notes to which they would need to find the time and energy to answer, sometimes to discover that Keynes had changed his mind by the end of the day.

Newspaper articles were for Keynes another very important means of communication. They even represented an employment, a second source of revenue, after speculation and before teaching. Most of Keynes's main ideas, including the most abstract or technical, were submitted, before or after their final working-out, to the general public in newspaper or popular periodical articles. He carefully controlled the reprinting and translation of his papers in as many media as possible. From 1923, he chaired the board of the politico-literary liberal weekly magazine *Nation and Athaeneum,* where he published many of his own papers and those of his Bloomsbury friends. In 1930, Keynes oversaw the merging of the *Nation* and the Fabian magazine the *New Statesman,* founded by the Webbs in 1913, to become the *New Statesman and Nation.* Still chairman of the board, he closely controlled the periodical's content—witness his abundant correspondence with the editor Kingsley Martin on such matters as the Spanish Civil War, the rise of Nazism, and the Munich Agreement (see CWK 28, pp. 1–222).

Scholarly articles were another means of transmission of ideas, though they did not have the same importance they do today as the nearly exclusive road to the circulation of knowledge in economics. It is by the quantity of scholarly articles published and the quality—however that might be judged—of the journals in which they are published that an academic is now evaluated. If he had been leading his career in an economics department today, Keynes would be accused of dissipating his efforts, publishing too many newspaper and magazine articles, pamphlets, and books, instead of concentrating himself on scholarly articles. He would also be blamed for being at the same time judge and defendant because many of his scientific papers were published in the *Economic Journal,* where he served as editor from the age of twenty-eight until the year before his death. Journals were not at that time managed as they are today. In those days, the editor frequently made the decision to publish a paper alone. Such was the case with Keynes, who rarely consulted others and took much time to read and comment in detail on submissions. This was a way to stay informed of what was going on in theory as well as to have influence on the evolution of ideas.[7]

It is, of course, by his books that Keynes is most renowned by posterity. The *General Theory* is the best known but was not, in Keynes's lifetime, the most read, the most influential, or the best understood. For his books, Keynes adopted a very peculiar arrangement with the publication houses, to ensure the maximum impact. He wrote to be read, to convince his contemporaries. And he took all means necessary, including financial, to succeed in this. Thus, starting with his second book, *The Economic Consequences of the Peace* (which was also his most successful, making him instantly world renowned), Keynes negotiated a lucrative arrangement with Macmillan, the publisher of all his major books.[8] He reversed the usual relation according to which the publisher pays the production and marketing costs of the book and then gives royalties to the author. Keynes financed his books' production himself and took in all the proceeds, paying royalties to the publisher. He could thereby both fix the price of the book and send out as many complimentary copies as he wanted. He was his own press attaché. For example, he sent 380 copies of *How to Pay for the War* to friends and colleagues but also, more important, to decision-makers in all area of public life and to journalists.

Form and content

All of Keynes's books, as well as his other writings, whatever their genre, and whatever the speed with which they were written, are of great literary quality: "Keynes indeed had the lyric gift of making simple words suddenly quicken our senses like the spurt of dust from a bullet; of writing a phrase which, once read, like the last cadence of his essay on Edgeworth, is 'unforgettable, unforgotten.' He would be great as a writer of English, were he great as nothing else" (Phelps Brown 1951, pp. 200–201).

The same is of course true of other Bloomsbury writings, the novels of
E. M. Forster and Virginia Woolf, the biographies of Lytton Strachey, the
art histories and criticisms of Clive Bell and Roger Fry, the political treatises of Leonard Woolf. As witnessed by the Bloomsbury Memoir Club
archives, all these authors also excelled in autobiographical memoir.
Their work shares, moreover, an *air de famille,* a common style. We find
in them analogous visions of the world, similar perceptions of human beings and their states of consciousness. The Bloomsbury friends were in
the habit of reading to each other in loud voice and criticizing their
works in progress. Keynes presented *The Economic Consequences of the
Peace* in this way at about the same time Lytton Strachey did *Eminent
Victorians.* Some have compared Keynes's writing to that of Virginia
Woolf. The great novelist praised Keynes's literary talents in her correspondence with him on December 23, 1937, in which she commented on
his note on her nephew Julian Bell, who had died during the Spanish
Civil War: "I liked the notice on Julian very much. . . . I wish you'd go on
and do a whole portrait gallery, reluctant as I am to recognise your gift in
that line when it seems obvious that nature gave me none to mathematics. Please consider it. Is portrait writing hard work compared with economics?" (V. Woolf 1980, pp. 192–193).[9]

For most economists, and especially economists of our days, Keynes'
writing is bizarre, indigestible if not incomprehensible. *The General Theory* has been described as messy, poorly organized, and repetitive, its
language obscure, opaque, difficult to understand, and especially hard to
formalize. Others have written that it is filled with vague hypotheses and
ambiguous and overly literary argumentations. Shortly after it was published, Keynes was reproached for having renounced mathematical presentation. But this in fact was his clearly expressed intention. Keynes
condemns the "symbolic pseudo-mathematical methods of formalising a
system of economic analysis" (Keynes 1936a, p. 297): "Too large a proportion of recent 'mathematical' economics are merely concoctions, as
imprecise as the initial assumptions they rest on, which allow the author
to lose sight of the complexities and interdependencies of the real world
in a maze of pretentious and unhelpful symbols" (p. 298). The year following the publication of his book, Keynes wrote that he did not want
"the comparatively simple fundamental ideas which underlie my theory . . .
[to] be crystallised at the present stage of the debate" (Keynes 1937,
p. 111). By this time, the crystallization was already afoot, especially with
the birth of the IS/LM model.

Keynes has also been accused of a casual attitude regarding definitions
and terms, sometimes varying their meaning according to the context.

Hayek had already made such a criticism regarding *A Treatise on Money*. Keynes's response to this clarified his vision of language. For him, there is no univocal correspondence between an expression and that to which it refers. In economics, as in other moral sciences, one may use technical language in a less rigorous manner than one would, for example, in mathematics or physics: "A definition can often be *vague* within fairly wide limits and capable of several interpretations differing slightly from one another, and still be perfectly serviceable" (Keynes 1925b, p. 36). Economics is constantly in the process of redefining its terms. Keynes also found an aesthetic advantage to varying words and expressions referring to the same reality. A reader must not be bored or put to sleep. To convince a reader, to lead him or her into understanding, not only must one get rid of the definitional restraints of logical deductive science; one should also shed one's fear of using the tools of rhetoric, especially metaphor. From this point of view, *The General Theory*, like Keynes's other books, is a literary work. To describe economics, its author distances himself from the formalized language of physics and mathematics in order to employ everyday and literary language simultaneously. The world described in works of art and literature, like those dealt with by biographers and psychologists, is a changing, unstable world, one in which the most important decisions are made in uncertainty. It is a world in which individual, subjective experiences are confused and fragmented, in which individuals are not led by rationality. This vision of things applies to both everyday life and artistic creation, to social interactions and economic phenomena. For this reason, traditional scientific language cannot be applied to the material with which those who seek to describe society and the economy are confronted.

Moreover, language and reality, like form and content, do not constitute two separate entities. On this question, the philosopher Ludwig Wittgenstein wrote influential and penetrating analyses that probably influenced Keynes, who was his close friend and protector at Cambridge.[10] Language is one facet of reality, and reality lets itself be seen through language. Behind this there is a conception of the world, of society, of human beings, developed at the turn of the century in England and elsewhere, particularly in Vienna, which is sometimes called "modernism." Art and literature transform the world they describe. The postimpressionist exhibition organized by Roger Fry in London in December 1910, the first important public manifestation of the ethos of the Bloomsbury set, was a symbol of this movement. Virginia Woolf wrote: "On or about December 1910, human nature changed" (see Stansky 1996). Postimpressionism appeared as the form adapted to the new universe, like the narrative style developed by Proust, Joyce, Musil, or Virginia Woolf. It was in this context that Keynes elaborated his own language. It constituted, by its form as much as by its content, an instrument in his struggle to transform social and economic reality.[11]

Even the relation between art and science is not so simple. In *A Treatise on Probability,* Keynes wrote that it was neither through logical process nor statistical inference but rather through intuition that Darwin arrived at his hypothesis that all living species evolved from a few primitive forms into which life was first breathed. Keynes praised the scientific imagination that allowed Freud to put forth a series of innovative ideas, ideas founded on intuition and experience, rather than inductive verification (Keynes 1925a, p. 393). In one of his last writings, Keynes stressed the primordial role of intuition in Newton's work and concluded that the gap so many others see between Newton's alchemical investigations and his serious scientific work does not exist (Keynes 1947).

In a paper prepared for the Apostles Society in 1909,[12] Keynes wrote (Keynes Papers UA/32) that if the talent had been given to him, he would have preferred to have been an artist than a man of science. But there are more similarities than differences between the artistic and the scientific ways of apprehending reality. Recalling Keynes's gift for simple explanation of complicated problems, his friend Clive Bell, who was an art critic, wrote: "In moments such as these I felt sure that Maynard was the cleverest man I had ever met; also, at such moments, I sometimes felt, unreasonably no doubt, that he was an artist" (Bell 1956, p. 61). The formidable influence that Keynes exercised, after his death as well as during his life, is no doubt linked to the way in which he transmitted his ideas as well as to the nature of these ideas. But is not this the case with all great scientists and thinkers, who need also to be artists in order to persuade and convince?

Notes

The Unpublished Writings of J. M. Keynes are © The Provost and Scholars of King's College, Cambridge, 2010. I am grateful for the permission to quote them. I acknowledge a grant from the Social Sciences and Humanities Research Council of Canada. Elie Spiegelman revised my idiosyncratic English. This chapter draws partly on Dostaler (2002, 2007).

1. References are to Keynes Papers, King's College Archive Centre, Cambridge.
2. His portrait of President Wilson in *The Economic Consequences of the Peace* will even inspire Freud and Bullitt's psychological portrait of the U.S. president. On this, see Dostaler and Maris (2009).
3. On the Bloomsbury group, see Dostaler (2007), First Interlude.
4. They are reproduced in CWK 12, pp. 114–239.

5. There are many amusing letters of Keynes to his physician, in which he himself delivers auto-diagnosis with surprising confidence.

6. The Circus is a group of younger friends of Keynes who met in 1931 to discuss the *Treatise on Money*. See CWK 13, pp. 337–343.

7. On Keynes's activities as an editor, see CWK 12, pp. 784–868.

8. Leonard and Virginia Woolf's Hogarth Press would publish most of his pamphlets.

9. On the relations between Keynes and Virginia Woolf, see Bonadei (1994), Wicke (1994), and Goodwin (2007).

10. On the relations between Keynes and Wittgenstein, see Favereau (1985), Davis (1994), and Lavialle (2001).

11. On Keynes and language, see E. Johnson (1978), O'Donnell (2004), and the papers collected in Marzola and Silva (1994). On language and economics, see Henderson, Dudley-Evans, and Backhouse (1993).

12. About this secret Cambridge society, see Dostaler (2007, pp. 27–29).

PART FOUR

Global Crisis: Lessons from Keynes

T HE CHAPTERS IN THIS SECTION make the strong claim that lessons can still be learned from Keynes's sophisticated knowledge of financial markets. What we *should* have learned from him might also be a good title for this final part of the book.

First, as an investor in commodity and currency futures, and then as an analyst of behavior under uncertainty, Keynes was aware of the dangers of leaving the system of payments arising from financial transactions unregulated and argued often for intervention and coordination, both domestically and internationally.

For example, he sketched out a scenario during the Second World War to the effect that when the supply of funds for investment dries up, the stabilizing arbitrage and speculative activities that typically rely on these funds abruptly stop and insolvency rapidly spreads through the global financial system. Asset prices tumble in the absence of the stabilizing anchor, triggering panic selling, which can only be prevented by timely intervention.

This outcome—unfortunately familiar as this volume went to press— was considered by Keynes as another instance of the irrationality of markets in time of distress and the inability of markets to reach equilibrium when agents are not able to close arbitrage margins. Abandoning the law of one price, contemporary behavioral finance has "rediscovered" that mispricing may, indeed, occur in some markets because of the costs and risks agents would incur to correct it.

Marcello De Cecco points out in his essay that Keynes made this point a long time ago, despite the fact that contemporary theorists do not seem to be aware of his work in this area.

The dire consequences of market financial fragility on employment and income were also worked out by Keynes in the *General Theory*, the theoretical insights of which provide a unified body of thought, aiming to demonstrate how the financial system affects output and employment. In the parlance of economic theory, Keynes sought to integrate monetary analysis with an analysis of the real economy.

Since his *Treatise on Money*, Keynes had dealt with the question of how the market eliminates excess inventory and consequently with the question for producers of how much to produce. He argued that measures were needed to reduce excess inventories (which are likely to occur with alarming frequency in the market economy), through buffer stocks schemes or government expenditure, in order to halt the decline in prices and make production profitable again.

Thus, Jan Kregel argues in his essay that the core of Keynes's theory is not captured by the idea of the existence of a stable reaction function of real economic variables to expenditure policy measures. It is the process of adjustment of real and monetary variables to changing expectations about "normal" prices and interest rates that is being worked out in Keynes's theory. In particular, it is explained, by this process, why in the monetary economy investment may not expand enough to produce full employment. Because there is an asset—money—whose rate of return declines more slowly than others' when there is an increase in demand for it, the equalization of returns in all investments though arbitrage are prevented, leaving many unexploited opportunities.

If rational, utility-maximizing agents are not the best model to portray (and understand) economic behavior, and if the market coordination of self-interested individuals may be disrupted as a matter of course, then the different approach adopted by Keynes in dealing with international and domestic malfunctioning of market mechanisms deserves reconsideration.

Anna Carabelli and Mario Cedrini explore the lessons to be drawn from Keynes's approach to the negotiation of the Inter-Allied debts during the Second World War, which follows from a line of thought he had developed in the aftermath of the First World War. They argue that his arguments are still relevant today, in particular when dealing with contemporary global imbalances.

The gap dividing Keynes's method from modern microeconomic models of international finance is very wide: the dividing line lies in Keynes's belief that persistent disequilibria in currency markets could not be resolved by the simple appeal to rational choice theory. This leads to the further difference that Keynes believed that economic interdependence requires policy responses based on the principle of "shared responsibility," rather than on unilateralism.

Today's problems deriving from the twin deficits of the United States (in the federal budget and in the balance of trade) and surpluses in much of the rest of the world resemble the problems of the sterling area countries in the mid-1940s, which Keynes addressed as a representative of the Treasury. Carabelli and Cedrini show that his work on postwar planning during the Second World War points clearly to the nature of different paths of adjustment: the consequences from taking unilateral, bilateral, or multilateral courses of action are still those Keynes outlined during Bretton Woods and the negotiations for a postwar loan from the United States to Britain.

The awareness of the multilateral character of global imbalances implies a need for collective action and well-coordinated responses: for instance, fiscal policies designed to boost the saving rate in the United States while expanding domestic effective demand elsewhere in the world. Through the management of global effective demand and liquidity in the spirit of Keynes, rather than through long-term structural reform along the lines of the Washington Consensus, hope might emerge of recovering from the present global imbalances and the resulting recession.

CHAPTER TWELVE

Keynes and Modern International Finance Theory

Marcello De Cecco

Three are the times, past, present and future; perhaps, however, it would be appropriate to say: three are the times, the present of the past, the present of the present, the present of the future. In fact, these three times are somehow in the soul, nor can I see them having reality anywhere else: the present of the past is memory, the present of the present, direct vision, the present of the future is expectation.

—St. Augustine, *Confessions*, XI, 20, 26

Introduction

One of Keynes's most central theoretical insights, that regarding own rates of interest, was by most analysts of Keynes's thought ignored, overlooked, or belittled. This is a pity, as this aspect of Keynes's theory reveals that much of what was said in the early criticism of his work missed the mark because it disregarded this important part of his work. In particular, people did not realize that his theoretical reasoning was based in a sophisticated understanding of foreign currency markets and portfolio adjustments.

I made this connection quite early in my study of Keynesian economics. When I moved for a year from Cambridge to Chicago in the mid-1960s, I was struck by the disregard of Keynes's writings most of the teachers there (who knew his writings very well) were instilling into their students. This explains why the younger members of the Chicago school built much of their anti-Keynesian apparatus on a simplistic misunderstanding of his work.

As the world economies have become again more intertwined, following the collapse of the Bretton Woods agreements, it appears clearly that Keynes's early work on currency markets and his later work on uncertainty have resurfaced in some of the best and most useful recent work on the cutting edge of economic theory.

Starting at Chicago, 1966

In the autumn of 1965, I was in Cambridge, working on my thesis on Italian monetary policy. Richard Kahn was my supervisor. On a visit to Italy, I was introduced to a leading Italian economist, Federico Caffè. Only a few days after our first meeting, he offered me a scholarship to spend a year as a visiting graduate student at the University of Chicago, with a special connection to Milton Friedman's money workshop. This was, for me, an offer to go and see "the other face of the moon." I accepted immediately and on January 1, 1966, boarded a flight to Chicago.

The place I came to was at the height of its fame as a hub of liberal economics. George Stigler, Milton Friedman, Harry Johnson, Robert Mundell, Henry Schultz, and Al Harberger were there. Friedrich von Hayek had just gone back to Germany. Robert Lucas was not yet there, but I had as fellow students Rudi Dornbusch and Miguel Sidrausky.

The day after my arrival, I visited the rightly famous university library. I looked for Sraffa's *Production of Commodities*. There were two copies. Neither had, in six years, ever been borrowed by anyone.

Following this bad omen, in the next weeks and months I came to realize that nobody read Keynes either. The teachers had, of course, read his theory extensively, but they were bringing up the next generation of economists in complete ignorance of the English school, especially of Keynes. Whenever Keynes was quoted, there was condescension or, worse, a scathing tone that the young graduates absorbed and reproduced unthinkingly. It would come out, in later years, in several papers by Robert Lucas.

I was so irritated by this attitude, having spent many hours reading Keynes on the essence of money and the theory of forward exchange rates, that I decided to write a paper on the subject. I immediately did so but kept it in my drawer until 1979, when I presented it to a conference held in Italy on Keynes and Marshall. It was published that year in the conference proceedings. I doubt anybody except a few Italians ever cast an eye upon it, although it was in English. The location was too remote, the proceedings produced by an obscure local publisher.

I have decided to present it as background to my contribution to this volume. It is very short, and I think it may be of some interest in view of recent publications, like Professor Ono's article dealing with chapter 17 of the *General Theory,* where he proposes using Miguel Sidrausky's famous "money in the utility function" model to obtain a very interesting theoretical result. Miguel's paper was presented the very year I was at Chicago. He was the star pupil of Uzawa Hirofumi, who at the time was

Chicago's leading theoretician and had the best students working with him. Uzawa was not of the same ilk as the other economists in the department and would return to Japan not much later. I was Miguel Sidrausky's good friend and greatly admired his talent, but I thought that the "money in the utility function" solution, although brilliant, was not a necessary complement to the theoretical apparatus offered by Keynes in chapter 17 of the *General Theory*. Readers will judge whether I was, and still am, justified in thinking so.

On chapter 17 of the *General Theory:* a note

In his essay, "The *General Theory* after 25 Years," Professor Harry Johnson states, quite appropriately, that Keynes's book "long ago attained the status of a classic—meaning a book that everyone has heard of and no one has read" (H. G. Johnson 1962, p. 1).

If a survey is made of the economic literature that has followed that book and, in particular, of that part of the literature that has criticized the theory of money contained in it and has affirmed to have departed from it toward new and fruitful directions, it is impossible not to agree with Johnson's statement: one doubts that many of those self-described innovators have really read the whole of Keynes's book. Otherwise, their claims to fame would not rest on the conviction of having discovered something new, as they would know that what they claim for themselves can be easily found in the *General Theory*.

To become aware of this fact, it is true, one has to read chapter 17 of the *General Theory*, where, according to Professor Johnson, Keynes dilates "rather pretentiously on the essential properties of interest and money" (Johnson 1962, p. 3). In my humble opinion, those observations on interest and money have quite a right to pretentiousness, as they not only express the core of the *General Theory* but also aptly formulate the main tenets of the so-called new theory of money.

It is simple and correct to consider chapter 17 as a reformulation of the chapters that precede it as a general theory of asset holding. True, Keynes did not give it that label, but the able economist ought to recognize what wine an unlabeled bottle contains.

"It is natural to enquire," Keynes begins, "wherein the peculiarity of money lies as distinct from other assets, whether it is only money which has a rate of interest, and what would happen in a non-monetary economy. Until we have answered these questions, the full significance of our theory will not be clear." He then proceeds to explain that "the money rate of interest is nothing more than the percentage excess of a sum of money contracted for forward delivery, over what we may call the spot price of the sum thus contracted for forward delivery." He goes on: "It would seem, therefore, that for every kind of capital asset there must be an analogue of the rate of interest on money" (CWK 7, p. 222).

This is the concept of the own rate of interest, which exists on each physical asset in terms of itself: Keynes borrowed the concept, with acknowledgment, from Piero Sraffa, who had expounded on it in his well-known review of Dr. Hayek's *Prices and Production* (Sraffa 1932, p. 50). The idea, however, can be traced further back, to Keynes and Sraffa's joint reflections on the behavior of spot and forward exchange rates, which were given to the public in the article Keynes wrote in 1922 for the *Manchester Guardian Commercial*, in the supplement *Reconstruction in Europe* (Keynes 1922a).

The concept, however, has to be expanded to that of the own rate of money interest, which each asset gives, when calculated in money terms. In Keynes's own words:

> Let us suppose that the spot price of wheat is £100 per 100 quarters and that the price of the future contract for wheat for delivery a year hence is £107 per 100 quarters, and that the money rate of interest is 5 per cent; what is the wheat rate of interest? £100 spot will buy £105 for forward delivery and £105 for forward delivery will buy 105/107 × 100 (=98) quarters for forward delivery. Alternatively, £100 spot will buy 100 quarters of wheat for spot delivery. Thus 100 quarters of wheat for spot delivery will buy 98 quarters for forward delivery. It follows that the wheat rate of interest is *minus* 2 per cent per annum. (CWK 7, p. 223)

From this it follows that "there is no reason why the rate of interest should be the same for different commodities." Having remarked on this, Keynes can safely add that "it may be that it is the greatest of the own rates of interest (as we may call them) that rules the roost (because it is the greatest of these rates that the marginal efficiency of a capital asset must attain if it is to be newly produced); and that there are reasons why it is the money rate of interest which is often the greatest (because, as we shall find, certain forces which operate to reduce the own rates of interest of other assets, do not operate in the case of money)" (ibid.).

Why this is, Keynes will explain soon. From a general standpoint, he asserts, any asset could be taken as a standard of value and, if it was expected to change in value the marginal efficiencies of all assets (i.e., their forward minus spot prices in terms of that asset chosen as a measure of value) would change value in the same proportion, so that the initial ordering of their marginal efficiencies would remain unchanged. If we could build a composite commodity, which would be regarded as representative, according to Keynes the rate of interest on this commodity, and its marginal efficiency, would rule for the economy as a whole.

To obtain this solution, however, the Ricardian problem of the unique standard of value has to be solved, and that—as we know—will be Piero Sraffa's task.

In order to explain the choice of money as a measure of value, Keynes now reviews the distinctive qualities of all assets. Some of them, he notes, by assisting some process of production or by supplying services to consumers, produce a yield or output, measured in terms of themselves. Some assets, if carried over time, suffer wastage and similar costs, which we can call carrying costs. Some assets possess liquidity—i.e., they can be disposed of at little or no loss over their initial cost. By summing algebraically the yield, the carrying cost, and the liquidity premium, we get the total return from the ownership of each asset. This operation, however, has to be considered an intellectual abstraction, as the identification problem we encounter in practice, when trying to quantify the components, is a great one. "To determine the relationship between expected returns on different types of assets, which are consistent with equilibrium, we must also know what the changes in relative values during the year are expected to be" (CWK 7, p. 227).

If we take money as the measure of value, all assets, including money, will have an own rate of money interest. The asset choice, naturally, will favor that asset that will yield the highest own interest, and all assets will be, as a result, produced in those quantities that will equalize the rate of return on them all. This form of asset choice is not naive, nor, as people have said in criticizing Keynes, is it determined by speculative demand. The elements that compound the total yield of each asset are, in fact, a reflection of all sides of asset demand. But, assuming that substitutability exists in a degree high enough to justify the word "choice," all motives will boil down to a unique own interest rate for each asset, strictly comparable with those of all other assets. And in this fashion, there will be no reason for excluding a choice that will be aimed at maximizing this compoundly motivated own rate of return. We are in the presence of a problem of homogenization, similar to those problems we encounter in measuring heterogeneous machines or labor. And all methods of homogenization stand and fall together.

The above quotations ought to have made clear that Keynes's approach to asset choice is a perfectly general one. We can thus legitimately raise our brow at Patinkin's accusation: "Keynes repeatedly emphasizes that the alternative to holding money is to hold bonds, and that any excess supply of the former is diverted to purchasing the latter. There is *never* any indication that it may also be diverted to purchasing commodities" (Patinkin 1965, p. 634). We might also question Friedman's impassioned protestations that monetary theory has to consider the choice between all assets and not only between money and bonds.

We can also legitimately ask, at this juncture, when we are only half way through the reading of Keynes's own treatment of the matter, what is the claim to innovation that Patinkin and Tobin's general equilibrium approach to asset choice can have? They just enlarged on a theme clearly modulated by Keynes and followed one by one the variations he indicated.

But let us continue our analysis of Keynes's own words: "Let us suppose ... that there is some asset (e.g. money) on which the rate of interest is fixed (or declines more slowly, as output increases, than does any other commodity's rate of interest)." How will equilibrium be maintained? What happens is that "the present money price of every commodity other than money tends to fall relatively to an expected future price" (CWK 7, p. 228). And the production of these commodities, accordingly, will shrink, unless it is expected that the cost of production will rise in the future high enough to cover the cost of carrying a stock of those assets produced now to the date of the prospective higher prices.

This will happen in all cases where an asset will exist whose own rate of interest will be reluctant to fall together with the others, as output increases. We are in the presence of a theory of capital accumulation based on a theory of asset choice. Production conditions are known for each asset, and the rate of increase of output and that of capital accumulation will depend on the own rate of return of the asset whose production is not as flexible as that of other assets. Money is just a "rent factor," Keynes says (CWK 7, p. 231), i.e., an indispensable factor of production and asset holding that cannot be produced or substituted for. Asset choice and production thus take place with fixed coefficients. Keynes then explains why he has reasons to believe that such an asset will be money. He assumes that the rate of increase of the money supply will be so small that the ratio of money to other assets will decline, prices will fall, and the rate of accumulation will be low. This is a matter of empirical choice, based on Keynes's own interpretation of the times he lived in and of the economic trends he thought would prevail. But the mechanism is perfectly general. And in this long-period analysis, I do not think that there will be a place for wealth effects, which will have to compete with distribution effects that might occur as prices fall, if the quantity of money rises only slowly. Keynes himself examined the possibility that a

reduction in the wage unit will occur. If, as he assumes, the rate of substitution between money and other assets is zero, then the cash released by
the decrease in the wage unit will be absorbed by asset holders and there
will not be other effects. But, he says (CWK 7, p. 232), "it is not possible
to dispute on purely theoretical grounds that this reaction might be capable of allowing an adequate decline in the money rate of interest";
thus, symmetry is respected and the theory has been expounded in its
general terms.

Keynes believes, however, that there are several reasons why "in an
economy of the type to which we are accustomed it is very probable that
the money rate of interest will often prove reluctant to fall adequately."
The following are the features that distinguish the "liquidity trap":

1. expectations that a fall in money wages will be followed by further
   reductions;
2. stickiness of money wages, which will render improbable the fall
   of the wage unit;
3. inelasticity of the money rate of interest to increases in the quantity of money.

This is Keynes's own sketch of the stylized facts that, in his opinion,
characterized his own time and made the liquidity trap probable. It is evident, however, as reported above, that his theory is completely free from
these restrictions and that it is generally valid. If conditions 1, 2, and 3
apply, we shall have a liquidity trap. Otherwise, the fall in money wages
will induce a fall in the money rate of interest and a proportionate increase in the output of other assets, i.e., an increase in the rate of growth
of the capital stock.

If the conditions of the economy are such

> that this . . . [the money] rate of interest may be somewhat unresponsive to
> a change in the proportion which the quantity of money bears to other
> forms of wealth measured in money, and that money has (or may have) zero
> (or negligible) elasticities both of production and of substitution . . . the
> only relief—apart from changes in the marginal efficiency of capital—can
> come (so long as the propensity towards liquidity is unchanged) from an
> increase in the quantity of money, or—which is formally the same thing—a
> rise in the value of money which enables a given quantity to provide increased
> money services. (CWK 7, p. 234)

In the absence of money, "there is no remedy but to persuade the public
that green cheese is practically the same thing and to have a green cheese
factory (i.e. a central bank) under public control" (CWK 7, p. 235).

He says in conclusion that if one assumes the propensity to consume to be constant,

> no further increase in the rate of investment is possible when the greatest amongst the own-rates of interest of own-interest of all available assets is equal to the greatest amongst the marginal efficiencies of all assets, measured in terms of the asset whose own rate of own interest is greatest. In a position of full employment this condition is necessarily satisfied. But it may also be satisfied before full employment is reached, if there exists some asset, having zero (or relatively small) elasticities of production and substitution, whose rate of interest declines more slowly as output increases, than the marginal efficiencies of capital assets measured in terms of it. (CWK 7, p. 236)

This is the theoretical core of the *General Theory*. But it has been largely overlooked, although it was always there in the middle of the book, in favor of perhaps more colorful but less theoretically profound parts of that patchwork opus.

Moreover, in my opinion, chapter 17 shows better than any later "reconciliation" Keynes's links with neoclassical thought. The chapter develops a general theory of asset holding, and thus of capital accumulation. It is rather easy, in fact, to add to it an exogenously determined rate of growth of the labor force and call it a growth model, where full employment equilibrium growth will be ensured by "neutral interest (which) can be defined as the rate of interest which prevails in equilibrium, when output and employment are such that the elasticity of employment as a whole is zero" (CWK 7, p. 243). Given the saving propensity and the liquidity preference, at any level except the rate of interest that defines the liquidity trap, since movements in the supply of money will affect its relative value vis-à-vis other assets, the rate of increase of the product of the green cheese factory will have to be equal to the rate of growth of the labor force, to produce the "neutral" rate of return that will warrant full employment equilibrium growth.

The return of speculation in foreign exchange and the return of Keynes

When I wrote my short paper on chapter 17 of the *General Theory*, perhaps I ought to have reproduced Keynes's quotation of the passage in Marshall, where Marshall attributes the normal backwardation of most commodity prices, the discount at which forward prices normally are with respect to spot prices, to people's preference for present goods over future goods, their impatience, their refusal to wait.[1] Keynes contrasted his mentor's solution with the alternative one offered in chapter 17, which depends on the zero elasticity of production and low elasticity of substitution, which characterize money: supply conditions of the "modern rent factor," as he defined money, as opposed to the demand conditions of Marshallian monetary theory.

However, liquidity preference, i.e., a phenomenon pertaining to money demand conditions, is one of the theoretical pillars of the *General Theory* and a product of Keynes's joint reflections on probability theory and on the behavior of commodity and financial markets after the First World War.

When I wrote my short paper, international financial arbitrage and speculation had just been resurrected as the Bretton Woods system, which was Keynes and White's joint product, had entered the decade of its final crisis. Short-term capital movements had started to grow again, breaking the segregation that the Keynes-White system had tried to impose on them. With these short-term capital movements, arbitrage and open speculation had begun in earnest. Their return on the scene conflicted with the very essence of the Bretton Woods system, which had been designed as a dirigiste system, in which visible trade was to be freed and encouraged while short-term private capital movements were to be repressed to keep the trade in goods free in the long run and to prevent the foreign currency constraint that had so disturbed national monetary authorities in the interwar years to reappear, making the maintenance of full employment in a single country difficult, even impossible.

In the early 1920s, Keynes had been fascinated, as a private speculator and as an economist, by commodities markets, in which forward contracts had been first developed. There, continental and American operators and even some economists had much greater experience than the British. The reason was a simple. British international trade was conducted in sterling. The problem of how to hedge foreign exchange risk was thus not one a British operator often encountered. Operators using sterling as a foreign currency, on the contrary, had to develop techniques to hedge their contracts. They tended to borrow them from the commodities markets, where the British also dealt in sterling denominated contracts. Even British commodity traders, however, had to deal with the difference between spot and forward prices, which they encountered when they wrote contracts involving the future delivery of a commodity. Backwardation and contango thus were the daily bread of commodity traders even in England.

It was one of Keynes's permanent contributions to economics to have formally connected commodity, money, and foreign exchange markets. He did so by inventing the covered interest parity formula, which can be seen as the basis on which all modern international finance theory and practice rest. He arrived at the formula in a famous article he wrote for the *Manchester Guardian Commercial,* in the supplement *Reconstruction in Europe* in 1922 (Keynes 1922b). He was helped by a discussion he had with the still very young Piero Sraffa, who went to see Keynes in Cambridge, and who impressed the elder economist with his command of the intricacies of commodity markets, and soon after supplied Keynes with a data series on Italian forward exchange rates, which Keynes used in his article, as I mentioned above.

The interest parity theory maintains that forward exchange rate margins, expressed in percentage per annum, tend to be equal to the difference in interest rates in the two countries.

Keynes adapted the articles he had written for the *Guardian*'s supplement, including the one on forward rates, in a book that became famous, *A Tract on Monetary Reform* (1923; CWK 4). There, as he had done in the *Guardian*'s supplement, he proposed official intervention in the forward exchange market, where authorities' actions would not be constrained by actual gold and foreign exchange reserves. A strategy like the one he suggested would soon after, in 1925, be devised and practiced by the Italian finance minister, Giuseppe Volpi di Misurata, who was a well-known financier and speculator. Volpi defended the lira's parity by entering, through the largest Italian bank, the Banca Commerciale Italiana (he kept the Bank of Italy out of it), forward foreign exchange contracts with international finance houses for extremely large sums and managed to hold the lira exchange rate stable while the Italian government was negotiating (from an objective position of weakness) Italian stabilization loans with both the British and U.S. governments. Volpi had to battle against international speculation, which was perhaps encouraged by winks and nods from U.K. and U.S. officialdom, but he was successful. Negotiations were concluded without Italy being pressed into even more disadvantageous conditions by an exchange rate emergency. Then, the Italian authorities stopped renewing forward contracts and allowed them to unwind. The lira began to fall and continued to do so until it was officially stabilized, at what many thought was an overvalued rate, between 1926 and 1927. The secret of Volpi's success was that he knew for sure that his government would not devalue the lira. Once he was certain about that, he could accept any bet by speculators in forward exchange, as they could not know for sure what the government thought the lira rate ought to be. Actual gold and foreign exchange reserves not being involved in bets about forward rates, the minister's defense of his country's currency was not constrained by any limits.

As noted above, after the end of the Second World War, forward markets were muzzled by the Bretton Woods system, which wanted to eradicate short-term private capital movements and managed to do so until external convertibility was restored first to the German mark and soon after to other important European currencies. Concomitantly, the U.S. balance of payments began to deteriorate because of capital exports for rearmament expenditures abroad and U.S. multinational companies' foreign expansion.

As a result, in the 1960s forward contracts began to be fashionable again. There was again reason to hedge. Gold points had been replaced by Bretton Woods fluctuation limits, but when dealing with very large contracts, even those small oscillations could cause, if left uncovered, hefty losses or gains to operators. German and Italian monetary authorities, which wanted to encourage their banks to lend or borrow dollars abroad, revived a forward dollar market exclusively destined for them. They thus fed the budding Eurodollar market. Dealing with the banking system in their own countries, each central bank started a closed market in forward exchange.[2]

After the collapse of Bretton Woods, all these transactions were extended to the free market, so that Keynes's formula became the bread and butter of foreign exchange dealers.

Academic economists started to become interested in foreign exchange again in the late 1950s and early 1960s and much more in the 1970s, when floating rates and pegging attempts gave exchange markets volume and turbulence, especially after foreign trade started growing more rapidly than GDP in many countries. With floating rates, even traders in commodities and manufactured goods had to hedge against losses deriving from movements in foreign exchange. They had to do so in order not to speculate, as Keynes had remarked in the early 1920s.

One would thus imagine that in books and articles dedicated to modern international finance, Keynes would be quoted as the father of the discipline. After all, the forward market is an early and prime example of a derivative market. This was, however, far from the case. His name was forgotten or only fleetingly remembered in a field where his contributions had brought analytical discipline to what had hitherto been mostly practitioners' nostrums and rules of thumb.

This became truly remarkable after the inception of what was called behavioral finance theory. Keynes's writings, especially some chapters in the *General Theory*, contain what can be easily considered the foundations of modern behavioral finance.[3] Chapter 12, "The State of Long Term Expectation," is the first that comes to mind. The beauty contest example is the only thing that some contemporary scholars seem to have taken in, sometimes, although not always, with explicit acknowledgment of the original author. However, the beauty contest example is only one of the possible examples of the markets' irrational behavior. Another equally powerful one is given by Keynes in his study of forward rates. He discovered that deviations from covered interest parity in the interwar period remained unarbitraged until they were as large as fifty or more basis points. In the *Tract,* he wrote:

> To fix our minds, let us suppose that money market conditions exist in which a sale of forward dollars against the purchase of spot dollars, at a discount of 1.½ per cent per annum for the former, yields neither profit nor loss. Now, if in these conditions the purchasers of forward dollars, other than arbitragers, exceed sellers of forward dollars, then this excess of demand for forward dollars can be met by arbitragers, who have cash resources in London, at a discount which falls short of 1.½ per cent per annum by such an amount (say ½ per cent) as will yield the arbitragers sufficient profit for their trouble. If, however, sellers of forward dollars exceed the purchasers, then a sufficient discount has to be accepted by the former to induce arbitrage the other way round—that is to say, by arbitragers who have cash resources in New York—namely, a discount which exceeds 1.½ per cent per annum, by, say, ½ per cent. Thus, the discount on forward dollars will fluctuate between 1 and 2 per cent per annum according as buyers or sellers predominate. (CWK 4, p. 106)

This was the lowest margin speculators would accept to be drawn in. But Keynes noted in the same book that the unarbitraged margin could be much larger.

"Deviations of a lasting nature," Paul Einzig wrote when reiterating Keynes's theory in his well-known book on foreign exchange theory, "were liable to arise, however, among other reasons, because the liquid capital available for arbitrage was not unlimited and at times it was not large enough to bring about readjustment" (Einzig 1962, p. 275).

In any case, wrote Keynes, "So few persons understand even the elements of the theory of the forward exchanges that there was an occasion in 1920, even between London and New York, when a seller of spot dollars could earn at the rate of 6 per cent per annum above the London rate for short money" (CWK 4, pp. 107–108).

In the last thirty years, the pressure of floating exchange rates and technological advances in communications have narrowed unarbitraged margins to only a few basis points, at most. However, the whole modern theory of behavioral finance is meant to disprove analytically Friedman's confident assertion, and superficially convincing proof, that the law of one price will punctually and unfailingly apply to international finance, as arbitrage margins are closed by equilibrating speculation. Little attention is paid to what Keynes wrote on the subject in 1922 and 1923 and then referred to in all his subsequent books.

As far as the interwar period is concerned, very sophisticated econometric analysis recently conducted by Peel and Taylor (2002) on foreign exchange data for that period vindicated Keynes's claim about the fifty basis points being the threshold for arbitrageurs' intervention. The dictum attributed to Keynes, which is perhaps apocryphal, that "markets can stay irrational for longer than you may stay solvent" thus definitely applies to the times when the author allegedly formulated it, presumably after he had his own notoriously bad experiences at playing the market.

A recent "Survey of Behavioral Finance" by Barberis and Thaler (2002),which was published in the *Handbook of the Economics of Finance*, though it does not find it fit to quote Keynes, gives a very apposite critique of Friedman's belief in arbitrageurs' ability to abolish any open margin between two markets or two financial instruments, thus making sure that the law of one price reigns everywhere and at all times. The arbitrage technique most used to realize price convergence, in fact, is so open to mishaps that it caused at least one famous breakdown of the international financial market, in August 1998, with the collapse of the U.S. hedge fund Long-Term Capital Management. This, the authors note, is because arbitrage consists of buying an asset whose price is below what is rationally believed to be its normal level while at the same time shorting a "substitute" asset, that is believed to have similar cash flows to the underpriced one in any future states of the world (Barberis and Thaler 2002, p. 4). Demand for the underpriced asset brings the price back to the right price.

Barberis and Thaler demonstrate that when an asset is mispriced, strategies designed to correct the mispricing can be both risky and costly. So the mispricing can remain unchallenged, because the strategies to correct it, if adopted, would prove to be far from rational, meaning in this case riskless.

It will appear on a moment's reflection that this argument, whose demonstration can be found in Barberis and Thaler's article, is qualitatively almost identical to Keynes's own when he points out that a mispricing of fifty basis points or more is necessary to attract arbitrageurs.

Moreover, as in most treatments of behavioral finance, Barberis and Thaler emphasize that a hidden assumption is made in most arbitrage theories, that supply of funds to invest in arbitrage is limitless and steady. On the contrary, it is neither, and most mishaps in financial markets occur when, after a negative result obtained by the arbitrageur, his investors take fright and reduce their exposures, with obvious vicious circles setting in.

This, of course, is the long version of Keynes's earlier quote and of his famous dictum. Investors' refusal to stay put after a setback leads to the arbitrageurs' insolvency by denying the funds to carry on with the game. If the arbitrageur is self-financed and his pockets are less deep than in the case of investor-financed arbitrage, insolvency may come even earlier, after a shorter spell of market irrationality manages to dry the arbitrageur's funds.

Sometimes, an arbitrage strategy becomes suddenly unfeasible: the operator cannot find any assets to borrow, to develop his or her strategy, at any cost. We have seen this situation recently in other asset markets in the fallout from the subprime lending crisis in the United States. It is a quantity constraint, not a price constraint, that arbitrageurs can run up against were they to use their own funds or to borrow them from other people or institutions.

It was one of the main points of Keynes's theory that each of the parties involved in arbitrage could wear different hats, those of hedging merchant, pure speculator, or pure arbitrageur at different times, but that each could switch from one to any of the other two at any time.

This partial and temporary segmentation of roles was, and still is, the reason for sudden commotions in foreign exchange markets. A trader or pure arbitrageur can become a pure speculator if he or she entertains a firm belief in the future behavior of exchange and/or interest rates or commodity prices. As speculators, they will enter a bet against the market, but at a certain point can suddenly return to playing their initial role, covering their bets. Even more dangerous, as I noted above, is the case where traders, speculators, or arbitrageurs play with borrowed money. The lender can at any time refuse to finance their bets any longer, when a fear arises that borrowers may become insolvent because of the markets turning against them. It does not help that borrowers may know that rationally the market will have to turn again in their favor, after a bout of irrationality. Their rationality may coincide with the lenders' lack of faith in them.

The lenders' sudden bout of absolute liquidity preference, therefore, even if it is only a short one, will be enough to cause the borrowers' ruin, because they cannot carry on with the game and have to close their positions at a loss.

Another much discussed topic of behavioral finance is so-called noise trading. This is a definition invented by DeLong et al. (1989) to describe the activities of uninformed, hence irrational, investors in financial markets, which may derail the operations of informed, hence rational, operators, thus sending markets into irrational and unstable directions. Once again, Keynes, both with his beauty contest example and with his contrast between markets' irrationality and agents' solvency, deals exactly with this sort of argumentation.

The evolution of Keynes's thought, which led him from the belief that rational agents' stabilized markets through arbitrage and speculation to the realization that markets can stay unsettled in spite of the presence of rational agents who exploit the uninformed behavior of irrational agents for their own gain, was, however, a gradual one.[4] In the first article on forward exchange, where he presented the covered interest rate parity, and in the *Tract*, where he reproduced it, Keynes appears firmly convinced of the stabilizing abilities of professional arbitrageurs and speculators and argues in favor of their having a liquid money market at their disposal, to be able to organize their stabilizing response to international traders' uninformed behavior. If there are enough professional arbitrageurs and speculators, and if they are given enough short-term funds to implement their strategies, exchange rates and interest rates will be stabilized. Thus, Keynes, at this stage of his thought, had fully anticipated the theory Barberis and Thaler (2002) attribute to Friedman.

By the time the turbulent decades of the 1920s and 1930s had passed, Keynes had changed his views in favor of what we now call behavioral finance. Rational agents may be present in forces to mount strategies against "noise traders," but their actions may not lead them to make profits and to at the same time stabilize markets.

Keynes, moreover, anticipated, if only discursively and without complete analytical treatment, what Kahneman and Tversky would fully develop in the 1970s and 1980s. Conventions, representation, and framing are concepts that recur all the time in the Keynesian prose, especially so in his most famous book, although the mixture of experimental psychology and probability theory that prevails in Kahneman and Tversky's works is also very similar to that used by Keynes in his *Treatise on Probability*.

In fact, as I have already noted, by reading the *General Theory* and a *Treatise on Probability*, as it were, together, one gets most of the behavioral statements that Kahneman and Tversky would, forty years later, prove by very ingenious experiments, which I am sure Keynes would have loved.

Notes

This chapter was first published in the book *Alfred Marshall e John M. Keynes: rottura o continuità*, edited by Mauro Ridolfi (Perugia: Maggioli Editore, 1980).

1. CWK 7, p. 242. Keynes's quote is in Marshall's *Principles of Economics* (1920, p. 581).

2. Still in Cambridge, between 1964 and 1965 I presented two papers to the Political Economy Club, one on forward exchange rate intervention, the other on the Eurodollar market and central banks' monetary policy. They both remained unpublished.

3. George Ackerlof also makes this point in his December 2007 American Economic Association presidential address. The coincidence was kindly brought to my attention by Bradley Bateman.

4. Bradley Bateman reminded me of a similar process at work in the case of Keynes's adaptation of his theory to the concept of uncertainty. From the *Treatise* through about 1933, Keynes adamantly denied that uncertainty was an important cause of the trade cycle. It took him many years to incorporate his ideas about uncertainty into his economics.

CHAPTER THIRTEEN

Keynes's Influence on Modern Economics: Some Overlooked Contributions of Keynes's Theory of Finance and Economic Policy

Jan A. Kregel

Introduction

It is often argued that Keynes's *General Theory* dealt with macroeconomic aggregates of the real economy in conditions of depression. As a result, many argued that the theory was not general and required the addition of discussions of the economy in "normal conditions" as well as a discussion of the determinants of the nominal price level. In the postwar period, this was achieved through the discussion of the individual or "microeconomic" decisions that produced the economic aggregates in terms of the addition of classical individual optimization theory—what came to be called the "micro" foundations of macroeconomics. The problem of nominal prices was addressed through the addition of the short-run Phillips curve. The result was what came to be called the "Neoclassical Synthesis" and the "monetarist counterrevolution," which paved the way for the rational expectations revolution and the revival of pre-Keynesian classical economics.

Keynes's policy proposals were eviscerated in a similar way, in what has come to be known as "hydraulic" Keynesianism—the use of government tax and expenditure policies to ensure that the level of aggregate expenditure is sufficient to produce full employment. The emergence of stagflation—the simultaneous occurrence of rising unemployment and rising prices—in the 1950s and high levels of inflation in the 1970s created a policy paradox in which fiscal policy could not be simultaneously expansive to support full employment levels of demand and restrictive to reduce excess demand and fight inflation. This brought a return to monetary policy as the instrument seen as most appropriate to fight inflation and produce price stability, supported by supply-side tax incentives as the instrument most appropriate to sustain employment and economic growth. Thus, Keynes's approach to monetary policy by influencing expectations of long-term interest rates was replaced by control of the growth of monetary aggregates, and Keynesian fiscal policy ceased to have a macroeconomic objective but was instead directed toward increasing private incentives through the reduction of the role of government in the economy and the reduction of marginal tax rates to increase investment incentives. The overall level of fiscal stimulus and interest rates thus became residuals, completely reversing Keynes's approach.

The failure of monetarist money growth targeting eventually forced recognition of the endogeneity of money and a return to policy focus on interest rates and expectations. However, this focus was not on expectations of long-term rates but rather on expectations of future inflation rates in the form of "inflation targeting." The failure of supply-side tax reductions and reductions in government activities to provide fiscal balance led to ad hoc budgetary rules to ensure that any new fiscal expenditures were matched with new funding measures.

However, the sharp declines in activity and asset prices during the collapse of the dot-com bubble, the post–September 11 downturn, and the current subprime crisis have created frequent breaches of these principles in favor of a naive type of pre-Keynesian policy in which direct income transfers to support private expenditure and direct liquidity injections to support financial institutions have become the rule rather than the exception. Policymakers appear to have returned to the hydraulic form of Keynesian policy but have lost the theoretical basis that supports it. The reason stems from the initial belief mentioned above, that Keynes's theory was based on the ability to forecast the reaction of economic aggregates expressed in real terms to expenditure policy measures. However, a review of the body of Keynes's work shows that this emphasis on the behavior of real economic aggregates does not represent his contribution to economic theory or policy. This chapter will review the innovative contribution of Keynes's major works and show how they were unified in his *General Theory* (CWK 7) in a policy that is radically different from that normally presented, criticized, and currently employed as Keynesian theory.[1]

The financial building blocks of the *General Theory*

The Tract *and interest rate parity*

The theory that emerges in the *General Theory* contains essential elements of Keynes's contribution to finance theory that were developed in his earlier work, starting with the *Tract on Monetary Reform* (CWK 4). In this book, Keynes addresses the practical problem of what shape monetary policy should take in a world that has abandoned the gold standard. He follows Cassel's proposal that stabilization of the international purchasing power parity of the national monetary unit should replace stabilization of the purchasing power of gold as the principal aim of monetary policy. This was a straightforward attempt to replicate the essential features of the gold standard. Under the gold standard, the free movement of gold would lead profit-maximizing agents to exchange gold for the goods of countries where gold was overvalued due to low domestic prices. This would bring an increase in imports of gold to exchange for commodities in countries where prices were lower than average (and an increase in the export of their products) and a decrease in prices (and an increase in imports) in countries where they were above average. Equilibrium would be achieved when gold and goods stopped moving because the purchasing power of gold was the same in all countries; changes in domestic gold supplies brought gold prices of internationally traded goods into equality, adjusting for transactions costs.

The idea was to design a monetary policy for the domestic currency that would produce the same results. This could be done by linking the domestic creation of money to the relative international purchasing power of money. The link to the quantity of money is obvious, simply representing a shift from controlling the money supply to produce domestic price stability to producing stability in the international purchasing power of money—purchasing power parity. Indeed, Keynes, following Marshall, endorses the general validity of the quantity theory. However, he notes that the expositors of the quantity theory usually have failed to present it in the appropriate form, and he provides a version that moves well beyond the traditional representation. He also provides what are now the traditional provisos concerning the general applicability of purchasing power parity.

More important, he notes a major difference between the new approach and that operating under the gold standard. Under the gold standard, despite large seasonal variations,

the daily balance was adjusted by the movement of bankers' funds. . . . But now it is no longer a purely bankers' business, suitably and sufficiently rewarded by arbitrage profit. If the banker moves credits temporarily from one country to another, he cannot be certain at what rate of exchange he will be able to bring them back again later on. . . . [H]e has learned from experience that unforeseen movements of the exchange may involve him in heavy loss. . . . In fact, the seasonal adjustment of credit requirements has ceased to be arbitrage banking business, and demands the service of speculative finance. Under present conditions, therefore, a large fluctuation of the exchange may be necessary before the daily account can be balanced, even though the annual account is level. (CWK 4, pp. 109–110)

This is because there was implicit protection against exchange rate risk given by the automatic arbitrage within the gold points, and private short-term arbitrage flows had generally ensured that the movement of exchange rates would be well within the gold points precisely because of the limit on fluctuations given by the possibility of physical movements of gold. This assurance would not be present under a managed currency standard since there would be no limit to fluctuations in the event a central bank was not able to operate according to the new operating standard of stabilizing purchasing power parity.

To remedy this deficiency, Keynes recommended the use of forward foreign exchange markets to provide exporters with a means of hedging the increased risk of fluctuating exchange rates on trade flows. In explaining how the operation of the forward market would provide cover against exchange rate risk, Keynes develops the interest rate parity theorem, according to which the forward discount or premium to the spot exchange rate will be determined by the interest rate differential between the currencies.[2]

The method that Keynes uses is similar to the concept of portfolio replication that has been the basis of the advances in financial engineering since the introduction of floating exchange rates in the 1970s. Keynes notes that a commitment to provide foreign currency against domestic currency at a future date at a rate to be determined today can be made with certainty only by borrowing the domestic currency today, converting it into foreign currency at the current spot rate, and investing it at the foreign interest rate until the future date at which it has to be delivered in order to meet the obligation. The cost is thus the spot cost of buying the currency, plus the difference between the interest earned on the deposit of the foreign currency and the interest paid to borrow the domestic currency. Keynes notes that the forward premium derived in this way "indicates a *preference* by the market, on balance, in favour of holding funds" in one market rather than another (CWK 4, p. 123), and that "The difference between the spot and forward rates is, therefore, precisely and exactly the measure of the *preference* of the money and exchange market for holding funds in one international centre rather than another" (ibid., p. 124; emphasis added).

The important point to note here is the formulation of the problem in terms of spot versus forward prices representing the preference for holding one asset rather than another, and the idea that a change in interest rates will create an incentive to take action that brings the relation back into equality. Thus, if a change in the domestic interest rates causes the interest rate differentials to change, it will be profitable to act in the forward market to arbitrage the discrepancy between the forward market and the loan markets in the two countries. If there is a decline in domestic interest rates, the cost of providing forward cover falls, so the existing quote for the forward rate is overvalued, and profit can be made by selling foreign currency in the forward market and by borrowing domestic currency and selling it at the spot rate for foreign currency, investing it at the foreign interest rate, and delivering it forward. Doing so will increase the supply of forward foreign exchange, driving down the forward rate, and increase the demand for spot foreign exchange, pushing up the spot rate. At the same time it increases the demand for domestic borrowing and the supply of foreign loans, increasing the interest rate on the former and decreasing it on the latter. This combination of actions corrects the mispricing of forward foreign currency. If the domestic borrowing rate is fixed, then it is the foreign rate and the spot and forward prices that adjust. In the period in which Keynes was writing, sterling was the global currency, so it could be assumed that the sterling bank rate was fixed by the Bank of England, and the rates of interest on other currencies and their spot rates would be the factors of adjustment.

The Treatise *and the theory of futures prices: normal backwardation*

In the *Treatise on Money,* Keynes (1930) continues his investigation of the relation between spot and forward prices (as well as his concern for the reform of the international financial system). However, he rejects the quantity theory as the basis for the impact of money on prices, instead formulating fundamental price equations for available and nonavailable output, and makes a strong recommendation against returning to the gold standard. In particular, he shifts the focal point of his analysis from the impact of the demand for money on prices to the effective economic decisions in the economy, and in particular on the "effort of producers and the expenditure of consumers" (CWK 5, p. 120).

However, of major interest is Keynes's emphasis on the relation between money and prices. While the fundamental equation for available output looks very much like a cost plus (windfall) profits (normal profits were included in costs) pricing model, with prices given by efficiency wages and the divergence between investment and saving determining windfall profits, of greater interest is the neglected theory of short-period prices outlined in the discussion (in CWK 6, pp. 140ff.) of the behavior of prices in commodity markets.

Here Keynes notes the important influence of how the market eliminates excess stocks on the behavior of prices and on decisions to engage in new production. Again, working from the point of view of today's spot price and a future price, he notes that markets for excess stocks of commodities do not operate in the same way as markets for flow supplies. Instead of falling prices reducing production and increasing demand to restore equilibrium, just the opposite may occur. If the price in the future is expected to be lower than the current spot price, then it will be profitable to sell stocks today to avoid further loss; even if they are needed for production, it would be profitable to sell since it is expected that they can be repurchased at a lower price in the future. This will create additional downward pressure on current market prices, further depressing expected future prices and increasing the incentive to sell existing stocks. The question is thus how the market reverses this declining spiral of prices in order to allow prices to return to normal and provide incentives for new production.

As a solution to this problem, Keynes proposed what he called the "neglected" theory of short period prices expressed in the reduced form equation $pq = xy$.[3] The implication of the equation is as follows: the higher is x, the carrying costs as a share of the normal price, and the higher is y, the time to recovery, the larger the required fall in price to bring the decline in prices to a halt. The implication is that if you want a more rapid return to normal, you reduce carrying costs as much as possible—i.e., you reduce interest rates. The higher is the fall in production or rise in consumption produced by a fall in price, both expressed in q, the lower the required fall in price before recovery. Here the implication is to take measures to reduce the excess stocks as rapidly as possible—by the creation of buffer stock schemes, measures to reduce the increase in production, or other types of government expenditures to decrease the time to recovery and increase the responsiveness of consumption to a fall in price.

Keynes then goes on to "restate the argument in terms of the 'forward market'" (1930, vol. 2, p. 142). Keynes notes that in organized commodity markets there are always two prices, one for current delivery and another for delivery at some future date, and that it is the latter that is of importance to the producer. If the producer can earn his normal profit on his costs of production at this price, "then he can go full steam ahead, selling his product forward and running no risk." However, this relation may be disturbed by the impact of existing stocks on prices for current delivery. If there are no redundant stocks, then "the spot price may exceed the forward price (i.e. in the language of the market there is a 'backwardation')." This means that there is excess demand for current output that can only be met by increasing output. The spot price will then rise until it becomes advantageous to buy for future delivery rather than trying to access the increasingly deficient current supply. This drives up demand for future output, at the same time as it creates an incentive for producers to go full steam ahead and produce output for future sale.

However, Keynes points out that it is not necessary to have abnormal shortages of current stocks for backwardation to exist. He notes that in conditions of balanced supply and demand, there should be no difference between spot and future prices; however, there will normally be an imbalance between producers seeking to sell forward relative to those seeking to hedge against price increases. This will create an excess supply of contracts to deliver the commodity in the future, driving the future price below the spot and creating what has come to be called "normal" backwardation. As long as the price for future delivery remains above existing supply prices, production will continue to take place.

It is in this context that the existence of surplus stocks impedes current production, for it makes backwardation impossible; if backwardation existed along with excess stocks, it would always be profitable to sell today for future delivery, rather than hold the stocks and incur the costs of warehousing, insurance, and so forth. Indeed, Keynes argues, the existence of surplus stocks must cause the forward price to rise above the spot price, i.e., to establish, "in the language of the market, a 'contango'; and this contango must be equal to the cost of the warehouse, depreciation and interest charges of carrying the stocks." That is, the cost of selling spot and buying back for future delivery must be equal to the costs borne by the speculator who buys the stocks and holds them until the future delivery date. As a corollary, the textbook explanation of futures prices emerges as the spot price plus carrying costs for the term of the contract.

However, the important point is the negative impact of redundant stocks on new production and Keynes's observation that "efforts to get rid of surplus stocks aggravate the slump, and the success of those efforts retards the recovery" (CWK 6, p. 145) because of "the additional element of uncertainty introduced by the existence of stocks and the additional supply of risk bearing which they require. . . . In other words, the quoted forward price, though above the present spot price, must fall below the anticipated future spot price by at least the amount of normal backwardation; and the present spot price, since it is lower than the quoted forward price, must be much lower than the anticipated future spot price" (p. 144). Thus, there is no incentive to engage in current production for future sale, and the short-period price analysis gives the conditions required to return to normal production and normal price as given by the fundamental price equation for available goods.[4]

The monetary theory of production

In the interval between the *Treatise* and the *General Theory* (CWK 7), Keynes took a major step toward using these financial concepts to represent the way investment decisions determine the behavior of the economy. Keynes defines the "efforts of producers" as the decision "whether it is expected to pay a firm in possession of capital equipment to spend money on incurring variable costs, i.e. whether the result of spending money on employment and of selling the output is expected to result in a larger net sum of money at the end of the accounting period than if the money have been retained" (CWK 29, p. 66). He also notes with approval Marx's assertion that decisions in a capitalist economy are determined by the relation M-C-M', that is, by spending money today to produce commodities to sell for a larger net sum of money in the future, irrespective of the impact on C, which might be higher or lower. This emphasis on present expenditure compared with future receipts fits quite naturally with the prior analysis of the relation between spot and future prices necessary to ensure profitable production.

Keynes points out to his readers that one of the major changes between the *Treatise* and the *General Theory* is the shift from a theory of a given level of output with well-anchored expectations of normal prices given by the fundamental equations to a theory of changes in the level of output with uncertainty over the level of future prices. Thus, in the *Treatise*, departures from normal positions are represented by unforeseen windfall profits or losses that produce a departure of current prices from the fundamental price equation for available goods. However, windfall profits or losses should bring about changes in normal values, just as the q and c factors in the short-period theory of prices bring about temporary changes in output and consumption. In the *General Theory*, Keynes thus gives up the theory of normal prices with well-anchored expectations of normal values and natural interest rates and investigates how divergence from equilibrium determines adjustment and uncertainty in the system.

He also tells us that splitting up the determination of the rate of interest and the return on investment is an important step in his thinking. However, the form of both these concepts conforms to his prior analysis of relations between spot and forward rates. The differentiation is in terms of the explanation given for liquidity preference and the marginal efficiency of capital. For the former, there is no analysis of the supply-side; for the latter, Keynes introduces the idea of user costs.

References in the *General Theory* to prior financial building blocks

In the *General Theory,* Keynes makes direct and indirect reference to his prior work on financial analysis. This is particularly evident in chapters 16 and 17, where Keynes undertakes his analysis in terms of spot and forward markets. For example, the definition on the first page of chapter 17 of the "[t]he money-rate of interest—we may remind the reader—is nothing more than the percentage excess of a sum of money contracted for forward delivery, e.g. a year hence, over what we may call the 'spot' or cash price of the sum thus contracted for forward delivery" (CWK 7, p. 222). Keynes also notes that every commodity can be expressed in this fashion and that "for every kind of capital-asset there must be an ana-logue of the rate of interest on money" (ibid., pp. 222–223).

Keynes then uses his analysis of different currencies in the *Tract* as a template for the analysis of the different own rates on the individual ef-forts of investors. Indeed, he alerts the reader that he is doing this by point-ing out that "It may be added that, just as there are differing commodity-rates of interest at any time, so also exchange dealers are familiar with the fact that the rate of interest is not even the same in terms of two dif-ferent moneys, e.g. sterling and dollars. For here also the difference be-tween the 'spot' and 'future' contracts for a foreign money in terms of sterling are not, as a rule, the same for different foreign moneys" (ibid., p. 224).

In precisely the same way as he had analyzed interest parity, Keynes notes that just as the forward discount or premium on sterling brings the return on investment in currencies with different national rates of inter-est into equality, there will be an expected appreciation or depreciation in terms of the standard of account that brings the individual own rates of return into equality when evaluated in terms of the standard. This is the a factor that Keynes introduces in chapter 17. In difference from the for-eign currency markets, where the only factor is interest differentials, in the analysis of the whole economy, investors will have a range of invest-ment choices that provide different returns that will be characterized by other factors.

For example, Keynes's analysis of future prices made very clear the important role of carrying costs in determining the relation between spot and forward prices for stocks of commodities. Keynes thus introduces this factor as c in determining the returns of such commodities. Keynes also notes that the investment efforts of entrepreneurs can be represented as the difference between the money spent on producing output and employment and the money return, identified as q, the net return. However, this net return differs from the returns considered in comparing currencies in that there is no single forward or future price but rather a series of future returns. This means that the future stream of returns has to be reduced to a single "price" to preserve the formal relation with interest parity. Keynes does this by proposing to use the net present value of stream of yields, with the expectation of the future yields in each future period representing the impact of the future on the present.

However, he notes that the spot price of an investment must also be corrected for the impact of the future on the present. This Keynes defines as "user cost." Understanding user costs has been difficult for most interpreters of Keynes, and the concept has all but disappeared from macroeconomics. However, it can be quite easily understood with reference to Keynes's work on future prices, described above. Indeed, Keynes again directs his readers to this effect: "The calculation [of user costs] is exhibited in its simplest and most intelligible form . . . in the case of a redundant stock of a raw material such as copper, on the lines which I have worked out in my *Treatise on Money,* vol. II. chap. 29" (1936a, p. 70). However, there is a difference, and Keynes notes that

> In the case of raw materials the necessity of allowing for user cost is obvious;—if a ton of copper is used up to-day it cannot be used to-morrow, and the value which the copper would have for the purposes of to-morrow must clearly be reckoned as a part of the marginal cost. But the fact has been overlooked that copper is only an extreme case of what occurs whenever capital equipment is used to produce. . . . It is an advantage of the concepts of user cost and supplementary cost that they are as applicable to working and liquid capital as to fixed capital. The essential difference between raw materials and fixed capital lies . . . in the fact that the return to liquid capital consists of a single term; whereas in the case of fixed capital, which is durable and used up gradually, the return consists of a series of user costs and profits earned in successive periods. (ibid., p. 73)

Thus, "User cost constitutes one of the links between the present and the future. For in deciding his scale of production an entrepreneur has to exercise a choice between using up his equipment now and preserving it to be used later on. It is the expected sacrifice of future benefit involved in present use which determines the amount of the user cost, and it is the marginal amount of this sacrifice which, together with the marginal factor cost and the expectation of the marginal proceeds, determines his scale of production" (ibid., pp. 68–70).

User cost can thus be "arrived at . . . by calculating the discounted value of the additional prospective yield which would be obtained at some later date if it were not used now" (ibid., pp. 69–70). With user cost built on the analysis of futures prices, the calculation of the net return q, or the marginal efficiency of an investment decision, will require an adjustment to costs that incorporates expectations of the future just as the calculation of the sales proceeds will require expectations of future market conditions. Indeed, Keynes considered the addition of user costs as his only original contribution to the theory of investment. And it comes in the definition of the supply price of capital, rather than the demand price.

Finally, Keynes introduces liquidity preference in the form of a "premium" that attaches to assets as determined by a preference to hold them rather than other similar assets. As noted above, the interest rate that measures the premium for possessing money is already specified in terms of spot and forward prices. Note that Keynes frequently refers to the liquidity premium as the marginal efficiency of money. This is because the analysis of chapter 17 deals with the decisions that bring the own returns of all assets into equality; and because the return on money can also be analyzed in terms of user costs. Here the difference from the analysis of futures prices is not that money has a multiperiod return but rather that it has no carrying costs. However, if money is to be lent, the future price will be above the spot price—i.e., since this contango cannot be explained by the traditional carrying costs of the theory of future prices, which Keynes assumes to be zero on money, it must be determined by some other factor that Keynes defines as its liquidity. Just as Keynes noted that normal backwardation did not require a shortage of stocks, contango in the market need not be caused by an excess supply of money, but it could be caused instead by an imbalance between those seeking to become liquid (to borrow—i.e., to supply forward money) relative to those willing to become illiquid (to lend—i.e., to demand forward money). The difference between selling money today against future receipt of money produced both a price risk, given by the possible change in the capital value of the security received, and the risk of being unable to meet contractual commitments. Alternatively, user cost can be measured as the forgone income that is the result of lending today rather than waiting to lend at high future interest rates.[5]

Thus, Keynes provides a full specification of the returns that will attach in some degree to all investments as given by the difference between spot and forward prices in terms of the three attributes, $q, c,$ and $l,$ all of which are themselves expressions of the impact of the future on the present. The adjustment to equilibrium comes via an analysis of the movement of the a factor. Keynes thus provides a system in which the own rate of own return for every investment possibility, r, is adjusted by a, the discount or premium, and will be determined by the relative importance of q, c, and l. Keynes describes this process as follows:

> To determine the relationships between the expected returns on different types of assets which are consistent with equilibrium, we must also know what the changes in relative values during the year are expected to be. Taking money (which need only be a money of account for this purpose, and we could equally well take wheat) as our standard of measurement, let the expected percentage appreciation (or depreciation) of houses be a_1 and of wheat a_2. . . . [I]n equilibrium the demand-prices of houses and wheat in terms of money will be such that there is nothing to choose in the way of advantage between the alternatives;—i.e. $a_1 + q_1$, $a_2 - c_2$ and l_3 will be equal. The choice of the standard of value will make no difference to this result because a shift from one standard to another will change all the terms equally, i.e. by an amount equal to the expected rate of appreciation (or depreciation) of the new standard in terms of the old. . . .
>
> . . . Now those assets of which the normal supply-price [read "production" price] is less than the demand-price [read "forward" price] will be newly produced; and these will be those assets of which the marginal efficiency would be greater (on the basis of their normal supply-price) than the rate of interest (both being measured in the same standard of value whatever it is). As the stock of the assets, which begin by having a marginal efficiency at least equal to the rate of interest, is increased, their marginal efficiency . . . tends to fall. Thus a point will come at which it no longer pays to produce them, unless the rate of interest falls *pari passu*. When there is no asset of which the marginal efficiency reaches the rate of interest, the further production of capital-assets will come to a standstill.
>
> Let us suppose (as a mere hypothesis at this stage of the argument) that there is some asset (e.g. money) of which the rate of interest is fixed (or declines more slowly as output increases than does any other commodity's rate of interest); how is the position adjusted? Since $a_1 + q_1$, $a_2 - c_2$ and l_3 are necessarily equal, and since l_3 by hypothesis is either fixed or falling more slowly than q_1 or $-c_2$, it follows that a_1 and a_2 must be rising. In other words, the present money-price of every commodity other than money tends to fall relatively to its expected future price. Hence, if q_1 and $-c_2$ continue to fall, a point comes at which it is not profitable to produce any of the commodities, unless the cost of production at some future date is expected to rise above the present cost by an amount which will cover the cost of carrying a stock produced now to the date of the prospective higher price. (1936a, pp. 227–228)

Note here that Keynes is just describing the conditions in which producers can go "full speed ahead" because the spot prices of production are below forward prices, and if producers do so, they will create changes in their forward prices that reduce the gap between production prices and future prices and thus their returns, shifting production and investment to sectors where money returns are higher.

Keynes notes that rather than the money rate of interest setting "a limit to the rate of output, . . . it is that asset's rate of interest which declines most slowly as the stock of assets in general increases . . .]. As output increases, own-rates of interest decline to levels at which one asset after another falls below the standard of profitable production;—until, finally, one or more own-rates of interest remain at a level which is above that of the marginal efficiency of any asset whatever" (ibid., p. 229).

This gives Keynes his formal definition of a monetary economy—i.e., one in which expectations of the future determine present decisions, as one in which there is an asset whose rate of return declines more slowly than all others in the presence of an increase in demand (or, alternatively, the definition of a nonmonetary economy as one in which there is no asset whose liquidity premium is greater than its carrying costs). In such an economy, there is no guarantee that all rates of return will come into equality at a level of investment that produces full employment. Conversely, where this conditions is not met, investment will continue until all resources have been employed—which might require an increase in the employment of labor to produce money. Indeed, Hayek (1943) had argued that this might be the case, and the various composite commodity currency proposals were designed in order to ensure that a demand for money produced an increase in income and employment.

What is money in the monetary production economy?

As Keynes notes, the definition of a monetary economy leaves open the definition of what serves as money—it could be any nonreproducible durable good, but he notes that in modern economies it comes closest to what he defined as "representative" money in the *Treatise* (1930, vol. 1, pp. 9–11). Representative money will have some particular characteristics that cause its return to fall less rapidly or not at all when there is an increase in demand for it. These characteristics he defines in terms of the low or negligible elasticity of production and substitution. Note that this should not be interpreted as an acceptance that money is exogenous—Keynes clearly believed that money was a debt-credit relation and thus was endogenously determined. What was important was that an increase in the demand for money, even if this caused an increase in its supply, would not bring about a decline in its liquidity return or provide a demand for more employment to produce it.

This is a radical departure from the traditional analysis of the value of money that relies on the intrinsic value of the money commodity or the backing that is provided for fiduciary money. It is interesting that the year in which Keynes announced his "Monetary Theory of Production" (Keynes 1933) was also the year that gold ceased to play the role of money and thus no longer performed the role of the real backing for fiduciary money. If money is considered as a debt-credit relation, this raises the question of how debts are going to be settled if there is no ultimate real external asset—or Hy Minsky's question of why he could not get anyone to accept his personal IOUs in the settlement of his debts. The answer to this question is found in recognizing that it is necessary not for there to be an ultimate real asset that will settle all debt relations but rather for there to be some entity that can issue a liability that can be used in settlement of its own debts.

Keynes dealt with the question in his early work on money, and the answer is to be found more explicitly in what is better known as the "state" or "chartalist" theory of money associated with the names of Friedrich Knapp (1924) and Mitchell Innes (1913, 1914). In this approach, money is not a real asset but results from the ability of the state to unilaterally impose a liability on it citizens in the form of a tax that can be liquidated only with the promises to pay that are issued by the state. This meets the contention noted by Innes that the very nature of credit throughout the world lies in the right of the creditor to hand back to the debtor the latter's acknowledgment or obligation.

It thus follows that the creation and destruction of money depends on the goods and services that the state seeks to buy from its citizens, relative to the tax liabilities imposed by the state on them. If the state runs a balanced budget, citizens as a whole can just meet their tax liabilities (although some individuals may not be able to do so). Conversely, if the state spends less than it taxes in an attempt to run a surplus, citizens as a whole will not be able to meet their tax liabilities (although some individuals may be able to do so) unless there are accumulated money balances held over from prior periods in which the state ran a deficit. Here the circuit analysis is important for determining the viability of the system; by tracing the process by which the state employs the national bank or national treasury to create the money that it uses to acquire goods and services from its citizens and, likewise, the way that its citizens employ the money they receive in these transactions to meet their tax obligations. This analysis makes the important point that if the economy is to grow, the state must be running a budget deficit. However, it cannot determine the amount of money that will be held in individuals' money reserve balances. There are a number of reasons why individuals may choose to hold money balances. The risk of a government surplus is one of them, for reserve balances allow the system to meet its tax liabilities. But what is clear is that an increase in the demand for money cannot bring about an increase in its supply unless it brings about an increase in the government budget deficit. This approach thus joins monetary policy and fiscal policy as part of the same policy decision.

It also allows an understanding both of why monetary production economies have unemployment and of the role of liquidity preference and fiscal policy. If the public wants to hold of more money than the state is willing to create through its budget deficits, individuals will cut expenditures and lower effective demand, causing a reduction in private sector activity and creating unemployment. There is a contango on money, and an increase in the demand for money does not bring about an increase in its supply nor does it increase employment. A monetary economy is thus defined as one in which unemployment may be an equilibrium position. Conversely, it also shows that in the absence of money, or if there is only asset money on the wing that is never held, money can never be in contango, and the economy will automatically produce the level of effective demand compatible with full utilization of resources.

Notes

1. To add a personal note similar to that provided by Marcello de Cecco: in January 1966, I had not yet read the *General Theory*, but upon starting graduate school at Rutgers rather than Chicago, Paul Davidson quickly introduced me to the *Treatise* and the *General Theory*. My interest in Keynes's financial contributions started when Davidson challenged his students to explain the four types of speculative markets in chapter 15 of the *Treatise* (1930, vol. 1, pp. 252–253). This led me to the pricing equation in vol. 2 and then to the own-rates discussion in the *General Theory*. I arrived in Cambridge in 1968, eager to employ these tools, only to find that the discussion had moved on to long-period growth and distribution theory. My first attempt to use the tools of chapter 17 was in an endeavor to link Keynes and Sraffa (Kregel 1976), a suggestion that I continued to pursue for some time (e.g., Kregel 1983) without much success. The discussion herein is a summary of a number of papers (e.g., Kregel 1988b, 1993, 1998a, and 1998b) that have tried to show the cohesiveness of Keynes's work through his contributions to financial analysis. I have also tried to show the similarity of the work of Keynes and Fisher (with diametrically opposed results) in this regard (Kregel 1988a, 1999a).
2. The interest rate parity theorem was originally proposed in a 1922 supplement on *European Reconstruction* to the *Manchester Guardian* that Keynes was editing (Keynes 1922a, 1922b).

3. The full derivation is given in Kregel 1993.

4. Indeed, the point Keynes is analyzing is whether an excess of saving over investment could be offset by the decline in the prices of available goods causing an increase in demand to hold them as liquid capital investments.

5. Note that the "carry cost" on money can most easily be thought of as the user cost of money and can be measured by an option premium—e.g., if money is "used" by selling (lending) it today for future delivery, a put option is bought at today's strike price; then if future prices rise, the option can be exercised at the higher price even though a sale has been made for future delivery at a lower price. The option premium would then measure the user cost of money, the cost of being illiquid.

CHAPTER FOURTEEN

Current Global Imbalances: Might Keynes Be of Help?

Anna M. Carabelli and Mario A. Cedrini

Introduction

The 1997 Asian crisis, the failure of the Washington Consensus, the surge of global imbalances, and the global financial crisis with its gloomy implications for world growth prospects are arguably the main reasons lying behind the tendency to rediscover Keynes's work as an international economist. While previous analyses of the faults of the "nonsystem" that replaced the Bretton Woods regime generally reinforced the impression that the Keynesian era was definitively over, the early cracks of the integrationist agenda of the 1990s have contributed to a revival of interest in Keynes's international Weltanschauung. This renewed interest signals both a general criticism of the aggressive globalization of the last decade of the twentieth century and more specific attempts at coping with the current systemic imbalances—themselves in part a legacy of the Consensus epoch. This is the case, for instance, with a "modest proposal" by Greenwald and Stiglitz (2006) to reform the international monetary order in such a (Keynes-inspired) way as to limit the deflationary bias inherent to the global reserve system. In general, as Post-Keynesian economists have argued, the rediscovery of Keynes seems due to the need of a new international monetary system capable of transforming the happy accidents sustaining the spectacular performances of Bretton Woods into permanent features of a more balanced order.

As shown by Vines's review of Skidelsky's (2000) *Fighting for Britain*, revisiting Keynes means approaching a vision "of global capitalism as an *inter*-national system" (Vines 2003, p. 357), deriving from "an extraordinarily clear understanding of how pieces of the global economy interact, driven by the policies of autonomous nations, in an only partly coherent manner" (p. 339). Vines invites us to rethink not only the content of Keynes's international macroeconomics but above all his contributions on "focus and method" (p. 358). In particular, Vines highlights the gap dividing modern microeconomic models of international interaction from the vision advocated by Keynes, who was fully aware of the impossibility of understanding international relations solely by means of rational choice theory. Our contribution is intended to show, in line with these suggestions, that the rediscovery of the "focus and method" of Keynes's thought may disclose some valuable lessons as regards the problem of current global imbalances.

More precisely, we center on Keynes's 1945 memorandum "Overseas Financial Policy in Stage III," (CWK 24, pp. 256–295) which was to became the key document of the negotiations of the American loan to Britain at the end of the Second World War, and suggest using the alternatives he outlined for Britain's transition to the Bretton Woods order as a guide to avoid getting lost in the complicated picture of competing views about the current imbalances. While dealing with the financial difficulties of Britain, overburdened with the costs of financing the Allies' war against Germany, Keynes shaped in the document a model of international adjustment in a context of generalized external indebtedness and an authoritative illustration of how economic interdependence requires "shared responsibility" approaches to solve the situations of impasse it often causes.

As Pressnell (1986) puts it, Keynes attempted to offer a "bold scheme for an international policy of multilateralism in trade and payments that would simultaneously make sterling's problems more manageable and justify Britain in seeking and America in giving financial assistance" (p. 237). The beneficiary of the United States' and Canada's assistance under the Mutual Aid agreements, which nonetheless required London to reciprocate and which were bound to expire at the end of the conflict, Britain had incurred enormous debts with the sterling area countries to finance their common war. The scarcity of reserves and the prospected cease of exchange controls in sterling countries to limit drawings on the dollar pool, which London had centralized for military expenditures, combined with Britain's expected peacetime difficulties in exporting goods and services—commercial exports, invisible earnings, and overseas assets being at their lowest levels—to minimize the chances of balancing the country's external account in the transition period while returning to sterling convertibility. According to Keynes, a lack of American assistance would have compelled Britain to a "Starvation Corner" unilateral policy of austerity and isolationism, in sharp contrast with the declared aims of the new international order. Assistance from abroad was essential to avoid this result, although Britain should resist the "Temptation" to engage in long-term loan agreements with the United States, after collecting the sterling balances into a less manageable huge dollar debt, in exchange for substantial yielding on commercial policy. Above all, Temptation would have prevented the negotiation of an agreement—the essence of a scheme called "Justice"—to redistribute the costs of war according to the role played by the players involved, and among them the sterling area countries. In a world primarily depending on American home trade, the sterling countries—registering surpluses with Britain but an overall deficit with America—were the only nations, together with Latin America, that could act as stimulators for U.S. exports (De Cecco 1979).

Striking similarities appear between the current international situation and that of the immediate postwar age. Keynes's memorandum offered a dramatic portrait of a former superpower confronted with the depletion of its resources and an unsustainable external debt, due also to the country's century-long decline as an exporter. By far the only creditor country in 1945, holding 75 percent of the world's gold reserves and the historical responsibility of helping deficit countries restore trade at a global level, America is today the system's deficit of last resort—the record level of $857 billion, 6.5 percent of GDP, was reached in 2006—whereas the rest of the world (ROW) registers a surplus. Not too different from the position of sterling area countries after the Second World War is the key role currently played in the process by emerging Asian countries. The 1997 Asian crisis has taught developing nations that undervaluation-cum-intervention strategies (Unctad 2006) provide a powerful way out of the new Triffin paradox they were caught in during the 1990s, when foreign borrowing to achieve the desired growth rates exposed developing countries to larger external imbalances, raising the risk of reversals in capital inflows and of consequent financial crisis (Kregel 1999b). Asian countries' accumulation of export surpluses and their foreign lending through exchange reserves have produced "the largest 'foreign aid' programme in world history" (Wolf 2005, p. 25) and, together with increased surpluses in Europe, Japan, oil producers, and other developing countries, allowed the United States, the world locomotive and importer of last resort, to systematically live above its means. But the leading superpower is now compelled by the financial crisis to a severe readjustment, with extremely painful repercussions for both the American economy and global multilateralism. The very words Keynes used in Washington at the press conference for the negotiations of the American loan—"the financial and commercial arrangements of a considerable section of the world have become almost inextricably intertwined with our own financial and economic affairs in London" (CWK 24, p. 462)—might be employed for the current international situation, after replacing London with New York and "a considerable section of the world" with the global economy.

The adoption of different analytical strands to interpret the dynamics of global imbalances and the endogenous character of America's current account balance (Truman 2005) are responsible for the large range of possible future scenarios which have been offered until the burst of the financial crisis in 2008 to speculate about this surprisingly persistent pattern of international economic relations. These scenarios ranged from alarming concern for the risks current imbalances pose for world economic prospects to elegant theoretical justifications for their persistence with uninterrupted global growth; these were but two extremes on the continuum of analyses. The typical reviews of the literature, however, have paid little attention to the type of adjustment, if any—unilateral, bilateral, or multilateral—each suggested scenario is tied to. Here is where the rediscovery of Keynes's legacy might come in as a helpful preliminary guide to reassessing the nature of the problem and possibly providing a scheme of thought for opening new possibilities to overcome the impasse. That Keynes's 1945 memorandum might be used to reformulate the problem of current global imbalances may sound surprising to economists (such as Boughton 2002 and Skidelsky 2000) inclined to consider it as the main weapon of Keynes's fight to save Britain's status as a world power. Nonetheless, as we shall argue, "Overseas Financial Policy in Stage III" was generally concerned with how to restart multilateralism at the global level after the Bretton Woods agreement had left the newly created international institutions with scarce resources to deal with the transition. The "threefold dramatization of choice" (Pressnell 1986, p. 246) for Britain's (and the world's) economic future—Starvation Corner, Temptation, and Justice, discussed in detail below—thus assumes a paradigmatic character and, animated by the same spirit of Keynes's defeated proposals for an International Currency Union (ICU), reveals relevant information about the economist's general effort to reform the international order.

Starvation Corner

The Starvation Corner, "a policy of attempting complete financial independence of the USA" (Pressnell 1986, p. 238), would have implied unilateral adjustment on the part of Britain through austerity and rationing, national planning, and trade controls. Since the sterling area was going to run an overall deficit after the war, London had to resort to foreign borrowing to finance the £3 billion debt it had contracted with its creditors. It was not "a well-chosen moment for a declaration of our financial independence of North America" (CWK 24, p. 271): allowing for the difficulties of borrowing everywhere, the world was a very small place, as the treasury representative in Washington Robert H. Brand told Keynes during the negotiations.

Though strategically relevant, the *Starvation Corner* was a third-best option: "Is not the use of our position as a great consumer, to force our goods out on to the world in return for what the world wishes to sell us, the only new weapon in our armoury and one we cannot do without?" (ibid., p. 274). Nonetheless, if lacking the assistance of the United States, the only alternative left to Britain was to adopt "Schachtian" devices, on the model of the system of bilateral clearing agreements—a barter mechanism—developed by Germany in 1934 to balance trade with its partners at fixed exchange rates. Keynes had previously praised the virtues of the Schachtian alternative, arguing that the system of the future, and his plan for the ICU, was to be "a refinement and improvement of the Schachtian device" (CWK 25, p. 24). Schachtianism may in fact serve against attempts by major creditors to disregard, or act against, as during the interwar period, the "interests of the restoration of international equilibrium" (p. 25). However, as Keynes repeatedly pointed out during the negotiations of the loan, the *Starvation Corner* and its Schachtian consequences would have favored "not merely the acceptance but the advocacy . . . of a system of international economy after the war of a kind to which all sections of opinion, not only in the United States but also in Canada, are bitterly opposed" (CWK 24, pp. 271–272).

Temptation

As an alternative to isolationism, Keynes first envisaged American financial assistance in the form of a loan on easy terms allowing Britain the breathing space to face the transition to the new order and to approach its debt problems with the sterling area. In exchange for the loan, London would have guaranteed free multilateral clearing within the area from the outset and the dismantlement of the empire. Besides expressing concerns for a further, huge, debt in addition to the existing one, Keynes believed it right to reject such an agreement: "the sweet breath of Justice between partners" in the war "would have been sacrificed to some false analogy of 'business'" (CWK 24, p. 279). *Temptation* was clearly reminiscent of the criticisms Keynes had made of the American debt settlement at the end of the First World War, when the false analogy between war debts and private investment had obliged Europe to postpone its recovery program. Moreover, he was well aware that by strengthening Britain's financial dependence on the United States, the loan would compel London to accept the "American conception of the international economic system" (CWK 24, p. 61), which Roosevelt had already established as the price of the Lend-Lease agreement. As the 1947 sterling crisis was to prove, *Temptation* would have inevitably posed serious risks for multilateralism. Keynes himself later asserted, in his correspondence with Robert H. Brand, that to ensure Britain the modicum of confidence it needed to face its postwar problems without the fear of bankruptcy, American credits should have necessarily followed a reapportionment of the legacy of war between the Allies—America itself included. In trying to obtain *Justice,* therefore, Britain should have stood firm against *Temptation* and strategically prepared itself to adopt voluntarily *Starvation Corner* policies in the transition.

Justice

Keynes's own favorite option, *Justice,* required "a general re-consideration of the proper burden of the costs of the war" (CWK 24, p. 280), allowing Britain to be the Americans' partner "in setting up a post-war international economy of the character on which they have set their hearts" (ibid.). According to this approach, the United States should have granted Britain $3 billion as a sort of retrospective Lend-Lease agreement and, in addition, a $5 billion credit line at easy conditions. In exchange, London would have ensured the de facto convertibility of sterling, after approaching its sterling area creditors with a tripartite program of eliminating (£880 million), funding (£1.5 billion), and freeing (£750 million) the £3 billion balances. Not only the late entry of the United States into the war but also the profits realized by the dominions from British war expenditures were among the "number of good reasons" why Britain had to tolerate "a post-war financial burden entirely disproportionate to what is fair" (ibid.). But *Justice* was more than a fair reapportionment of the war burden between the Allies.

At the end of the First World War, after condemning European policymakers for their failure to consider organic interdependence among the variables at work in the affair of Inter-Allied debts and reparations (Carabelli 1995), Keynes had invoked public-spirited statesmanship and "generosity" (CW 2, p. 93) on the part of the United States and Britain, in the form of debt forgiveness, as an indispensable preliminary for Europe to escape from the dilemmas of the settlement. Looking backward to the unsatisfactory settlement of "Europe after the Treaty," he introduced the

ICU plan in 1941 by specifying that the American contribution to the Second World War should coincide with an attempt of setting "the world as a whole on its feet and of laying the foundations of a sounder political economy between all nations" (CWK 25, p. 43). Keynes was aware of the risks a system must tolerate when it depends so critically on the willingness of its most powerful members to respect the rules of the game. His reform schemes in the 1940s were mindful of America's refusal, in the renewed gold standard of the 1920s and 1930s, to take responsibility for the world's destiny by making its gold stock available to debtor countries for the adjustment. Following WWII, the American intervention should have helped to establish a "system of general and collective responsibility, applying to all countries alike" (p. 47).

Justice provided clear continuity with Keynes's earlier plan for an ICU. His request to the United States and the sterling area countries in 1945 that they proactively contribute alongside Britain to creating the postwar world they wished to live in was truly an attempt to revive the spirit of the scheme despite its final rejection at Bretton Woods. In explaining to Robert Brand the "predominant importance" of the "psychological atmosphere of the free gift" proposal, Keynes observed that if "America insists on remaining on a strictly economic basis, that makes it harder for the others [the sterling countries] to depart from it" (CWK 24, p. 340). He was reiterating his 1919 views that the American intervention to reduce the burden of Inter-Allied debts could induce European countries to mitigate their claims on Germany and prepare the way for a "shared responsibilities" scheme destined to ease the rehabilitation of Europe. *Justice* should have generated a sort of spiral mechanism induced by the American gift, pushing the sterling countries to follow the United States in adopting a responsible behavior toward the imbalances. This was the sole possibility for the sterling countries to revitalize their exchanges with America without repudiating the agreements with Britain. Recalling the primary importance of the economic intercourse between the sterling area and the United States for future world trade patterns amounts to a recognition that the ultimate aim of the memorandum was to revive global multilateralism through the defense of Britain's economic destiny. Both the transformation of the American loan into a non-British demand for American goods, which led to the 1947 sterling convertibility crisis, and the economic necessity of the Marshall Plan were to confirm that Keynes's concerns were not misplaced.

Surprisingly enough, if only for the decades elapsed since Keynes prepared this document, these three policy options seem to offer a valuable key to organizing competing interpretations of global imbalances and different related scenarios. "Made in" views of current imbalances, urging unilateral adjustments by the country that is held to be responsible, easily transform into *Starvation Corner* scenarios like that described by Keynes. Though American economists and the U.S. administration have repeatedly called for the appreciation of Asian currencies, this does not seem to be practical policy for the future, unless Asian nations are prepared to tolerate those same risks of overheating and speculation against which they have self protected since the 1997 crisis. "Gloomy views" about current imbalances thus focus primarily on the global austerity program that a U.S. recession as the current one would likely launch. Keynes's *Temptation* option, based on American assistance to Britain of a business character, provides a metaphor for the "imbalances sustainability" views: market mechanisms relying on the strength of the U.S. economy are argued to be enough to ensure the stable scenario of a revived Bretton Woods system, supplemented by a tacit agreement between the main powers. Today's views that reveal awareness of the multilateral character of global imbalances assume that a problem of collective action dooms a coordinated response, as in the case of the "shared responsibility" plan included in Keynes's *Justice* option.

Starvation Corner: "Made in" views about current global imbalances

Keynes's *Starvation Corner* is a model of unilateral adjustment through austerity. The request for one-sided adjustment is quite common in the literature about current global imbalances: some of the most well-known and assertive views center on one or the other of the two main players—the United States and emerging Asian countries—to enforce adjustments of a wholly, or mainly, unilateral character. Chinn's (2005) "twin deficits" theory finds U.S. tax cuts and large government expenditure responsible for increases in the current account deficit. In his view, government borrowing increased the demand for credit and the stock of public debt, thus bidding up interest rates until 2000 and the value of the dollar until 2002 and seriously damaging U.S. competitiveness. Assuming that the gap between the dollar's value and the trade balance derives from slow growth rates in the ROW, except for China, the theory calls for a reduction in the budget deficit and foreign oil imports to moderate America's role as the world consumer of last resort. Although there seems to be little evidence for a true correlation between a budget deficit and a current account deficit, which cannot be explained adequately by specific trade-related factors, Chinn claims that failure to reduce borrowing will "cede to foreign governments increasing influence over the nation's fate" (p. 3).

A mirror image of the "twin deficits" theory is provided by Bernanke's (2005) "global savings glut" hypothesis, which focuses on high rates of saving and depressed levels of capital investment in Asia. Recent reversals in capital flows to emerging countries and undervaluation-cum-intervention strategies would have stimulated savings outside U.S. borders, helped by high oil prices, financial development and growth in emerging markets, and restricted availability of consumer goods in China. Bernanke claims that global desired private savings remained strong even after the 2000 fall in stock-market prices but that low interest rates have progressively become, supported by low mortgage rates and the expansion of U.S. housing wealth, the main reason for the United States' depressed savings. While conventional wisdom states that the United States' external deficits limit investments in the ROW, this view suggests by contrast that excessive savings (or declining investments, with the exception of China) in the ROW are crowding in U.S. deficits. Foreign lending to the United States, which rose continuously in the 1990s, is held to be the key variable for global imbalances in this scenario: the U.S. government being required, after the stock market bubble burst, to run a deficit with a view to sustaining domestic demand (Wolf 2005). The fiscal deficit would thus be the result of the current account deficit; accordingly, the view suggests helping dynamic emerging countries to leave mercantilism and to reassume their "more natural" (Bernanke 2005, p. 10) role as international borrowers through structural and financial reforms.

Starvation Corner: The gloomy views about current global imbalances

Though not without benefits for Asia in terms of a reduced need for export subsidization, sterilization, and reserve accumulation, the "exit strategy" outlined above for surplus developing countries is limited, as remarked, by the practical impossibility of moving toward a floating exchange rate without risks of overheating and speculation. But the assertors of the "twin deficits" theory should not undervalue the global repercussion of an American *Starvation Corner* policy. History provides more than a hint of support to argue that Keynes's dark views about international economic relations were not misplaced: in the absence of the Marshall Plan, that extended his recovery plans for Britain to the whole continent, OECD countries' recovery would have been dramatically slower. *Starvation Corner* scenarios for current global imbalances focus on the unsustainability of U.S. deficits and its net international investment position. In the first half of the current decade, the standard analysis based on capitalizing the U.S. debt flows induced various academics to foreshadow a massive dollar depreciation to shrink the trade deficit to sustainable levels. To be sure, they argued that the United States' current account deficit could not continue indefinitely: after acquiring a large part of the country's capital stock, which would cause negative political reactions in America, foreign investors might fear that their claims on the United States would be expropriated. Alternatively, new information could downsize America's seemingly miraculous level of productivity. Decline in the dollar since February 2002 had been limited to industrial countries and has had small effects on trade balances. A recurrent explanation for that, based on reduced pass-through to import prices and exporters' currency hedging strategies to defend their American market shares, was challenged by arguments relating to the mix of U.S. industrial stagnation—except for high-tech sectors—and strong domestic demand (see Truman 2005), or even to the rapid evolution in the international division of labor after the Asian crisis. It has also been suggested that the American production structure might be so inappropriate for Chinese consumption patterns—or that the United States might be able to export to China only those goods whose production has already been outsourced by American companies—that the impact of the adjustment will occur in a third country (Kregel 2006).

More recent analyses (Krugman 2007) found evidence of investors' myopia, which is the basic condition for a dollar plunge. By raising oil prices and threatening European competitiveness without substantial effects on American import patterns, the dollar's tendency to depreciate adds to the likelihood of foreign investors shifting toward higher-risk assets (IMF 2007) and thus raises the chance of a dollar crisis. Those with gloomy views were predicting that in the case of a dollar plunge, fears of import-price inflation would persuade the Federal Reserve to tighten monetary policy and to sensibly reduce the U.S. standard of living. If the U.S. current account deficit must shrink, demand in the ROW for foreign nontraded goods must necessarily face a positive shock; otherwise the improvement of American net imports would redistribute the recessionary impulse to America's trade partners. That this would come primarily at Japan's and Europe's expense is not surprising, given both their nominal rigidities and the limited corrections possible in developing countries. China, in particular, was expected to improve its competitiveness in the U.S. markets against Europe: a diversification of Asian central banks' portfolios to the advantage of the euro would have pushed the currency's value even higher and increased the risk of a disorderly adjustment. China itself, and emerging countries in general, which have sensibly improved their financial positions, had however been advised not to underestimate the possibility of a gloomy scenario: adjustment through trade would hit countries that highly depend on exports to the United States (Eichengreen and Park 2006).

Temptation: Global imbalances and the strength of a debtor

Recent views about global imbalances showing either natural or structural reasons for their happy persistence may prove to be the victim of their own optimistic assumptions. By relying on the "strength of a debtor" argument, i.e., on U.S. fundamentals and the attractiveness of investing in American assets, these views share with the *Temptation* option as described by Keynes a declared confidence in the possibility of avoiding painful adjustments. As in the case of the American loan proposal, market mechanisms supplemented by intergovernmental agreement—currently in the tacit form of a revived Bretton Woods order, whose systemic outlook, however, exhibits a fundamental similarity with the rationale of *Temptation* as conceived by the American negotiators—are argued to allow a great economic power to tolerate the imbalances almost indefinitely over time. These views draw attention to the fact that the United States' strong deficit may depend on the effects of financial globalization and reflect the flexibility, productivity growth, and investment profitability of the American economy: in sum, its strength, rather than its weakness. Since globalization makes foreign investments less risky, investors should naturally show willingness to operate in foreign countries. Savings have moved beyond national markets and dispersed national current balances; as a consequence, while losing its home bias, the United States has enlarged its capacity to fund deficits. Due to reduced pass-through and valuation effects, i.e., the reduction of American foreign liabilities brought about by a depreciating dollar, the disproportionate growth in the demand for American assets might have ensured a smooth transition (Cooper 2004).

The attractiveness of American financial assets and country-specific factors would induce economies with banking systems poor at allocating capital to invest their excess savings in the United States. Monetary authorities would be acting as financial intermediaries, to the benefit, so to speak, of private savers (ibid.). In a fully globalized world, it is argued, a quarter of global savings would flow to the United States, mirroring the country's share of world economic output, but 15 percent of world saving would be enough to cover American investment abroad plus the trade deficit. As a consequence, both the risk profile of foreign claims on the United States and the historical positive gap between American earnings on foreign investments and payments to foreign investors in America would induce the continuation of a large deficit, provided that American economic growth remains high and the ROW (rather than emerging countries only, as in the past) continues suffering from a financial asset shortage.

However, as shown by Eichengreen (2006a), productivity is growing faster in China than in the United States and capital inflows are directed toward debt rather than equity markets—two reasons to argue that if foreigners are investing in the United States, this is due not to its attractiveness but to its low savings. The rate of return on foreign investments in the United States is probably lower, with respect to returns of American investments abroad, than the theory is compelled to argue (ibid.). Finally, though America is currently earning investment income surpluses even as a net debtor, yield differentials may vanish in the long run, as happened to Britain throughout the first half of the twentieth century, and put an end to the country's privilege (Meissner and Taylor 2006).

Temptation: Bretton Woods revived

Global imbalances appear less troublesome if seen through the lens of the "Bretton Woods II" hypothesis, which argues that the world has never abandoned its most successful monetary system (Dooley, Folkerts-Landau, and Garber 2003). Export-led growth strategies supported by undervalued exchange rates, capital and trade controls, and international reserves accumulation are held to be functional for purposes of Asian countries' desire to cover that same road Europe and Japan traversed in the postwar period to regain a central position in the world economic system. The "trade account" region's desire to export to the United States requires Asian willingness to acquire American securities, whereas the "capital account" region, formed by Europe, Canada, Australia, and Latin America, all currency floaters, is primarily interested in defending its international investment position. That both regions have helped the central country finance its deficit, the former through accumulation of dollar reserves and the latter through its investors pushing up the dollar until 2002, should come as no surprise. Asia is expected to displace Europe in exporting to U.S. markets and to buy out European claims on the United States. Once its path to the center is completed—200 million underemployed workers still wait to be absorbed into the modern sector—the revived Bretton Woods system will engage in reloading other peripheries, like India.

Those supportive of the architectural character of this hypothesis must respond to the legitimate criticism raised by Eichengreen (2004): the analogy between Asia's current performance and that of Europe in the 1950s and 1960s overstates the ability of the heterogeneous, weakly institutionalized group of today's periphery to act in its collective interest. Moreover, the euro provides an attractive alternative to the dollar, and the United States has transformed into a bank with negative net capital. As to Asian countries, sterilization appears a costly operation: policymakers are becoming more and more aware that "the world has changed in ways that diminish the attractions of systematic undervaluation designed to promote export led growth" (ibid., p. 6).

Justice: Shared responsibilities for global imbalances

A number of views about current global imbalances hold patterns of global interdependence responsible for the surge and persistence of these imbalances and include requests for multilateral coordination to ensure their orderly unwinding. The parallel is here with Keynes's *Justice* option, which has its roots in the recognition of shared responsibilities for the imbalances inherited from the war. What is more, *Justice* establishes its quest for a multilateral response to imbalances having a multilateral character on the constraints posed by global interdependence. Examining the ongoing dependence of the ROW on net exports to the United States, the so-called global co-dependency views center on the "out of sync" relationship between the United States and foreign economic cycles (Mann 2005). Low consumption and investment in the ROW in the late 1990s led America to raise its consumption and imports to unprecedented levels, whereas after the 2001 crisis, the U.S. economy was quicker than the ROW in positioning itself on a growth path. Because the ROW uses America as a foreign source of growth, the rising U.S. deficit rests on American imports growing faster when domestic GDP grows as compared with American exports' growth in relation to foreign GDP recovery. Kregel (2006) adds that financial flows accompanying global imbalances are the result of global investment and production decisions that determine the global pattern of trade. Conventional wisdom about global imbalances would mistakenly focus on the willingness of foreign lenders to sustain the U.S. deficit; surplus countries invest in the United States to finance their exports, as in the case of pre–World War I Britain's foreign lending, which promoted exports of capital goods to new countries. Though aiming at different national targets, Europe and Asia—with Latin America rapidly following the same path—adopt the same current account surplus-cum-foreign lending strategy as a substitute for, respectively, the dangerous or unusable device of external and government borrowing. Global imbalances would thus result from national policy choices—reflecting attempts by emerging countries to integrate into international trade and finance and efforts by European firms to acquire American assets and technology.

Recognition of global codependency invites a reevaluation of Europe's and Asia's contributions to the current global imbalances. The 2004 Unctad report generally blamed Europe's sluggish domestic growth on its weak investments and consumption, the result of a mix of restrictive monetary and fiscal policies with a floating exchange rate supporting both the reform of the welfare state and European firms' low-wages strategies. Tightening policies and low labor cost increases during the present decade have turned Germany's current account deficit into a remarkable surplus. Though Germany's and Japan's roles in generating the imbalances are rarely mentioned, they account for a considerable percentage of the combined global surplus (see IMF 2007). On the contrary, the Unctad report underlines China's role as major engine of growth in Asia and its outstanding contribution to increased trade among developing countries. A slowdown of the Asian miracle would likely intensify global price competition on manufactures exported by developing countries and would weaken the expansionary effects of growing demand in the continent. Another reason for the global savings glut lies in the stimulus provided by American growth to raising incomes abroad. "If the surplus regions were to reduce their financing to the United States, they would not be re-allocating their 'savings' elsewhere, but the process of generating these savings would itself be at stake. In other words, the attempt to repatriate funds may have negative consequences not only in the deficit but also in the surplus economies. This poses a dilemma to surplus regions" (Unctad 2005, p. 18).

The mutual consistency of regional policies with persisting imbalances calls for their revision. Kregel (2006) argues that a well-managed system should instead help developing countries fill the gap with developed countries by using export-led growth strategies, but this requires that the latter grow through internal demand rather than by policies such as those adopted by developing countries themselves. The price Europe and Japan have to pay for failure to comply with the rule is that they are the candidates to suffer most from the adjustment. Interestingly, though U.S. policymakers have on various occasions been calling for an acceleration of European growth, only a limited number of academic observers underlined that Europe can be a major part of a multilateral solution. Though those with "gloomy views" suggest that corrections by other surplus countries are at any rate needed to redress the imbalances (Truman 2005), things might have gone differently had Europe played a supportive role.

Justice: Coordination for an orderly unwinding of the imbalances

There is no compelling reason why countries involved in the problem of global imbalances should keep jeopardizing the stability of the world economy and their own growth prospects: multilateral adjustment is in the interest of any key global player. Briefly, a coordinated response to global imbalances would require the United States to boost its saving rate by taking fiscal action and the ROW to counteract the effect of reduced U.S. domestic demand through policies alleviating the burden of global rebalancing. China should keep diversifying its economy and reduce national savings through larger budget deficits and orderly appreciation of the exchange rate. Japan should return to a normalized monetary policy: the strong recovery of investment and consumption should promote the rotation of Asian demand from extraregional exports to the region itself. Emerging Asian countries, except China, should expand government expenditures and encourage household spending through the development of markets for consumers and mortgage credit. Oil-exporting countries should ramp up spending, while Europe needs to sustain its growth through internal demand (Ahearne, Cline, Lee, Park, Pisani-Ferry and Williamson 2007). Market-induced exchange rate changes may then complement these policy initiatives (Eichengreen 2006b).

International consultation with impartial outside mediation such as that provided by the IMF's forum for multilateral consultations and surveillance on global imbalances could help to develop a consensus on common goals. This could reinforce the case for international coordination based on the model of the 1985 Plaza agreement. However, the IMF seems reluctant to abandon the praxis of suggesting the Washington Consensus model of long-term structural reforms (Buira and Abeles 2006) to ensure growth and stability, and participants in the IMF multilateral forum have made little progress in implementing policies according to the agreed general road map. If risks tied to persistently large imbalances are now lower than at the time when the forum was established, this is almost entirely due to the occurrence of the crisis.

Concluding remarks

Due to moderate growth and a weaker dollar, the U.S. deficit began to narrow in 2007. Feldstein (2008), among others, was sure that the dollar could fall further as private investors realized that this is necessarily required for trade imbalances to be reduced, while gradual recovery in saving rates could occur following reduced household wealth and levels of mortgage borrowing (ibid.). However, no specific government intervention was accordingly expected, so that it would have been appropriate to revise upward the risks of disorderly market-induced adjustments. As suggested by Eichengreen (2006b), the lack of consensus on the magnitude and the sign of cross-border spillovers may have led the United States to underestimate the risks of a disorderly correction for its trade partners, with the global rebalancing destined to transform into a global slowdown. Disruptions of credit in the United States in August 2007 and the subsequent subprime crisis of March 2008 with associated losses on bank balance sheets appeared as signs of a crisis of confidence in the U.S. financial markets. Financial turbulence in the United States, coupled with tensions in the housing markets and sluggish consumer spending growth since the end of 2006, were responsible for expectations of a dangerous slowdown in global growth indicators.

True, the crisis economists generally expected was different from the one that occurred in 2008. However, this does not alter the substance of the argument proposed in the present chapter: world economy is suffering from an impressive market-induced adjustment in the form of a major financial collapse seriously endangering economic performances, as predicted by "Starvation Corner" analyses, in both developed and developing countries. More surprisingly, the Bretton Woods II system is *de facto* still there (Dooley, Folkerts-Landau, and Garber 2009), suggesting on the one side that the global imbalances have much to do with the current crisis, and on the other that more structural reasons than those usually advanced to explain them likely favor their persistence. That is why it may be time to revisit Keynes's international macroeconomics and the reform plans he advocated in the 1940s. As we argue in this chapter (the structure of which is recalled in Table 14.1), however, Keynes's way of reasoning about international relations, i.e., the "method" (Carabelli 1988) he worked out to deal with the complexity that characterizes them, may provide valuable insights for today's world despite the fact that times and circumstances have naturally changed; Keynes's proposals may be worth a closer look.

Once "Overseas Financial Policy in Stage III" is seen in continuity with Keynes's attempt in 1919 to provide Europe with a means of escaping from the irreducible dilemmas of reparations and Inter-Allied debts, requiring the "American generosity" as the precondition of a grand scheme for the rehabilitation of Europe, *Justice* appears as a reference model for multilateral international adjustment. The moving from the *Starvation Corner* toward *Justice*, passing through *Temptation*, symbolically represents the progressive enlargement of the spectrum of countries taking part in the adjustment to a more equilibrated world, with the "American Gift"—which Keynes would have called, in the *Economic Consequences of the Peace*, an "act of farseeing statesmanship" (CWK 2, p. 93)—as the starting mechanism of this chain of "generosity."

The United States, Keynes wrote (CWK 24, p. 272) in the memorandum to explain the rationale of his proposal, could "make us an offer, not so much generous as just, using their financial strength not as an instrument to force us to their will, but as a means of making it possible for us to participate in arrangements which we ourselves prefer on their merits if only they can be made practicable for us." *Justice* reflected Keynes's vision of the international order as a complex structure, characterized by organic interdependence among its variables, irreducible dilemmas, and fallacies of composition requiring "public-spirited" interventions by countries only indirectly involved in such conflicts. It was an imaginative solution to let the main trade partners of a highly imbalanced world—which the defense of particular interests against those of the system as a whole would have transformed into a negative-sum game, to the detriment of the general welfare—regain confidence to take part in global multilateralism. Having much in common with Keynes's critique of the

Table 14.1 Current global imbalances

"Overseas Financial Policy in Stage III"	Cause of imbalances	Required adjustment	Scenario
Starvation Corner	"Made in" views	Unilateral adjustment	"Gloomy views"
Temptation	"The strength of a debtor" views	Adjustment through market (bilateral)	Bretton Woods revived
Justice	"Shared responsibilities" views	Multilateral adjustment	Coordination for an orderly unwinding

classical theory in the *General Theory* (Carabelli 1991), "Overseas Financial Policy in Stage III" is a direct attack on the "atomic hypothesis" in international relations. The use of it as a framework for today's views about global imbalances increases the relative importance of "global codependency views" and strengthens the case for a multilateral response to the imbalances. As Keynes observed in his correspondence with Robert H. Brand, the highly criticized proposal of an "American Gift" was conceived as a way of bypassing the apparent impossibility of realizing through intergovernmental agreement the desired "shared responsibilities" plan easing the transition to Bretton Woods (see Cedrini 2008). Although the eruption of the crisis may somewhat paradoxically induce policymakers to focus on purely financial issues rather than on a reform of the system *tout court*, willingness on the part of today's missing third actors, Europe and Japan, to get involved into an orderly correction usually thought of as limited to the United States and Asia—which reduces the chances of its occurrence—might be decisive in this regard. Not only, but all key players should direct their efforts toward the design of a new system preventing, rather than fostering or even simply tolerating, chronic imbalances (see Kregel 2009). The "return of Keynes" might first of all lie in the rediscovery, or the discovery *tout court*, of an unduly neglected method to cope with the complexity of international relations.

Acknowledgments

We acknowledge Bradley Bateman, Sylvie Rivot, Maurizio Franzini, Woosik Moon, Yoshio Watanabe, and Alessandro Lanteri for useful comments on previous versions of this chapter. The responsibility for any errors is, of course, our own.

REFERENCES / CONTRIBUTORS / INDEX

References

Ahearne, A., W. R. Cline, K. T. Lee, Y. C. Park, J. Pisani-Ferry, and J. Williamson. 2007. "Global Imbalances: Time for Action." *Policy Brief in International Economics* 07-4, March, Peterson Institute for International Economics. Available at: www.iie.com/publications/pb/pb07-4.pdf.

Akerlof, G. A., and J. L. Yellen. 1985. "A Near-Rational Model of the Business Cycle, with Wage and Price Inertia." *Quarterly Journal of Economics* 100(5) Supplement: 823–838.

Allais, M. 1947. *Economie et intérêt*. Paris: Imprimerie Nationale.

Allen, F. L. 1931. *Only Yesterday: An Informal History of the 1920's*. New York: Harper & Brothers.

———. 1939. *Since Yesterday*. New York: Harper & Row.

Altig, D. E. 2003. "Introduction: Recent Developments in Monetary Macroeconomics." *Journal of Money, Credit, and Banking* 35(6), part 2: 1039–1043.

Amadeo, E. J. 1989. *Keynes's Principle of Effective Demand*. Aldershot: Edward Elgar.

Andolfatto, D. 1996. "Business Cycles and Labor-Market Search." *American Economic Review* 86(1): 112–132.

Aoki, M., and H. Yoshikawa. 2007. *Reconstructing Macroeconomics: A Perspective from Statistical Physics and Combinatorial Stochastic Processes*. Cambridge: Cambridge University Press.

Arena, R. 1989. "Keynes après Lucas: quelques enseignements récents de la macroéconomie monétaire." *Economies et Sociétés*. Series *Economie Monétaire* 7(April–May): 13–42.

———. 2003. "Beliefs, Knowledge and Equilibrium: A Different Perspective on Hayek." In S. Rizzello, ed., *Cognitive Developments in Economics*, 316–337. London: Routledge.

———. 2004. "On the Relation between Individual and Collective Beliefs: A Comparison between Keynes's and Hayek's Economic Theories." In R. L.

Wray and M. Forstater, eds., *Contemporary Post-Keynesian Analysis,* 249–266. Cheltenham, UK: Edward Elgar.

Arrow, K. 1959. "The Role of Price Adjustment." In M. Abramovitz, ed., *The Allocation of Economic Resources,* 41–51. Stanford, Calif.: Stanford University Press.

Asano, E. 1987. *The Developmental Process Leading to Keynes's General Theory* [in Japanese]. Tokyo: Nihon Hyouronsha.

Backhouse, R. E. 1997. "The Rhetoric and Methodology of Modern Macroeconomics." In B. Snowdon and H. R. Vane, eds., *Reflections on the Development of Modern Macroeconomics,* 31–54. Cheltenham: Edward Elgar.

———. 1998. "If Mathematics Is Informal, Perhaps We Should Accept That Economics Must Be Informal Too." *Economic Journal* 108: 1848–1858.

———, ed. 1999. *Keynes: Contemporary Responses to the General Theory.* Bristol: Thoemmes Press; South Bend, Ind.: St. Augustine's Press.

———. 2008. "Economics in the United States (1945 to the present)." In S. N. Durlauf and L. E. Blume, eds., *New Palgrave Dictionary of Economics.* 2nd ed. London: Palgrave.

Backhouse, R. E., and B. W. Bateman, eds. 2006. *The Cambridge Companion to Keynes.* Cambridge: Cambridge University Press.

Backhouse, R. E., and D. Laidler. 2004. "What Was Lost with IS-LM." *History of Political Economy* 36 (annual supplement: *The IS-LM Model: Its Rise, Fall, and Strange Persistence,* ed. M. De Vroey and K. Hoover): 25–56. Durham, N.C.: Duke University Press.

Ball, L. 1999. "Aggregate Demand and Long-Run Unemployment." *Brookings Papers on Economic Activity* 2: 189–251.

Ball, L., N. G. Mankiw, and D. Romer. 1988. "The New Keynesian Economics and the Output-Inflation Tradeoff." *Brookings Papers on Economic Activity* 1: 1–82.

Barber, W. J. 1990. "Government as a Laboratory for Learning in the Years of the Democratic Roosevelt." In M. O. Furner and B. Supple, eds., *The State and Economic Knowledge: The British and American Experiences,* 103–137. Cambridge: Cambridge University Press.

———. 1996. *Designs within Disorder: Franklin D. Roosevelt, the Economists, and the Shaping of American Economic Policy, 1933–1945.* Cambridge: Cambridge University Press.

Barberis, N. C., and R. H. Thaler. 2002. "A Survey of Behavioral Finance." NBER Working Paper no. 9222. Cambridge, Mass.: National Bureau of Economic Research; reprinted in G. M. Constantinides, M. Harris, and R. M. Stulz, eds. 2003. *Handbook of the Economics of Finance,* vol. 1B: *Financial Markets and Asset Pricing,* 1053–1128. Amsterdam: Elsevier/North Holland.

Barens, I., and V. Caspari. 1997. "Own-Rates of Interest and Their Relevance for the Existence of Underemployment Equilibrium Positions." In G. C. Harcourt and P. A. Riach, eds. *A 'Second' Edition of The General Theory,* vol. 1, 283–303. London and New York: Routledge.

Barro, R. 1974. "Are Government Bonds Net Wealth?" *Journal of Political Economy* 82: 1095–1117.

Barro, R., and D. Gordon. 1983. "A Positive Theory of Monetary Policy in a Natural Rate Model." *Journal of Political Economy* 91: 689–610.

Barro, R., and H. Grossman. 1971. "A General Disequilibrium Model of Income and Employment." *American Economic Review* 61(1): 82–93.

Bateman, B. W. 1996. *Keynes's Uncertain Revolution.* Ann Arbor: University of Michigan Press.

———. 2005. "Scholarship in Deficit: Buchanan and Wagner on John Maynard Keynes." *History of Political Economy* 37(2): 185–190.

———. 2006. "Keynes and Keynesianism." In Backhouse and Bateman, eds., 2006, 271–290.

Baumol, W. J. 1952. "The Transaction Demand for Cash: An Inventory-Theoretic Approach." *Quarterly Journal of Economics* 66(4): 545–556.

Baumol, W. J., and J. Tobin. 1989. "The Optimal Cash Balance Proposition: Maurice Allais's Priority." *Journal of Economic Literature* 27(3): 1160–1162.

Begg, D. 1982. *The Rational Expectations Revolution in Macroeconomics: Theories and Evidence.* Baltimore: Johns Hopkins University Press.

Bell, C. 1956. *Old Friends: Personal Recollections.* London: Chatto & Windus.

Benassy, J. P. 1975. "Neo-Keynesian Disequilibrium Theory in a Monetary Economy." *Review of Economic Studies* 42(4): 503–523.

Bernanke, B. S. 2005. "The Global Saving Glut and the U.S. Current Account Deficit." Remarks at the Sandridge Lecture, Virginia Association of Economics, Richmond, Virginia, March 10. Available at: www.federalreserve.gov/boarddocs/speeches/2005/200503102/default.htm.

Bernstein, M. A. 2001. *A Perilous Progress: Economists and Public Purpose in Twentieth-Century America.* Princeton, N.J.: Princeton University Press.

Bewley, T. F. 1999. *Why Wages Don't Fall during a Recession.* Cambridge, Mass.: Harvard University Press.

Bigg, R. J. 1990. *Cambridge and the Monetary Theory of Production.* London: Macmillan.

Blanchard, O. J. 1997a. "Comment on Goodfried and King." In *NBER Macroeconomics Annual 1997,* 289–293. Chicago: University of Chicago Press.

———. 1997b. "Is There a Core of Usable Macroeconomics?" *American Economic Review, Papers and Proceedings* 87(2): 244–246.

———. 2000. "What Do We Know about Macroeconomics That Fisher and Wicksell Did Not?" *Quarterly Journal of Economics* 115(4): 1375–1409.

———. 2008. "Neo-Classical Synthesis." In S. N. Durlauf and L. E. Blume, eds., *The New Palgrave Dictionary.* London: Macmillan.

Blanchard, O. J., and S. Fischer. 1989. *Lectures on Macroeconomics.* Cambridge, Mass.: MIT Press.

Blanchard, O. J., and N. Kiyotaki. 1987. "Monopolistic Competition and the Effects of Aggregate Demand." *American Economic Review* 77(4): 647–666.

Blaug, M. 1987. *Economic Theories, True or False: Essays in the History and Methodology of Economics.* Aldershot, UK: Edward Elgar.

Blinder, A. S. 1991. "Why Are Prices Sticky? Preliminary Results from an Interview Study." *American Economic Review, Papers and Proceedings* 81(2): 89–96.

———. 1997. "Is There a Core of Practical Macroeconomics That We Should All Believe?" *American Economic Review, Papers and Proceedings* 87(2): 240–243.

Boianovsky, M. 1995. "Wicksell's Business Cycle." *European Journal of the History of Economic Thought* 2(2): 375–411.

———. 1998. "Real Balances, the Price Level and the Unit of Account: From Wicksell to Patinkin and Beyond." *American Journal of Economics and Sociology* 57(4): 579–612.

Boianovsky, M., and J. R. Presley. 2009. "The Robertson connection between the natural rates of interest and unemployment." *Structural Change and Economic Dynamics* 20: 136–150.

Boianovsky, M., and H.-M. Trautwein. 2001a. "An Early Manuscript by Knut Wicksell on the Bank Rate of Interest." *History of Political Economy* 33(3): 485–508.

———. 2001b. "Wicksell's Lecture Notes on Economic Crises (1902/05)." *Structural Change and Economic Dynamics* 12(3): 343–366.

———. 2006a. "Price Expectations, Capital Accumulation and Employment: Lindahl's Macroeconomics from the 1920s to the 1950s." *Cambridge Journal of Economics* 30(6): 881–900.

———. 2006b. "Wicksell after Woodford." *Journal of the History of Economic Thought* 28(2): 171–185.

Boltho, A., and J. Corbett. 2000. "The Assessment: Japan's Stagnation: Can Policy Revive the Economy?" *Oxford Review of Economic Policy* 16(2): 1–17.

Bonadei, R. 1994. "John Maynard Keynes: Contexts and Methods." In A. Marzola and F. Silva, eds., *John Maynard Keynes: Language and Method*, 13–75. Aldershot, UK: Edward Elgar.

Boughton, J. M. 2002. "Why White, Not Keynes? Inventing the Postwar International Monetary System." IMF Working Paper no. 02/52. Washington, D.C.: International Monetary Fund.

Brainard, W. C., and J. Tobin. 1968. "Pitfalls in Financial Model Building." *American Economic Review, Papers and Proceedings* 58(2): 99–122.

Bridel, P. 1987. *Cambridge Monetary Thought*. London: Macmillan.

Brinkley, A. 1996. *The End of Reform: New Deal Liberalism in Recession and War*. New York: Knopf.

Brunner, K. 1971. "'Yale' and Money." *Journal of Finance* 26(1): 165–174.

Brunner, K., and A. H. Meltzer. 1993. *Money and the Economy: Issues in Monetary Analysis*. Cambridge: Cambridge University Press.

Bruno, R., and R. W. Dimand. 2009. "The Corridor of Stability in Tobin's Keynesian Model of Recession and Depression." *International Journal of Applied Economics and Econometrics* 17(1) (January–March): 17–25.

Buchanan, J., and R. Wagner. 1977. *Democracy in Deficit: The Political Legacy of Lord Keynes*. New York: Academic Press.

Buira, A., and M. Abeles. 2006. "The IMF and the Adjustment of Global Imbalances." Paper presented at the G24 Technical Group Meeting, Geneva, March 16–17. Available at: www.g24.org/buab0306.pdf.

Buiter, W. 2003. "James Tobin: An Appreciation of His Contribution to Economics." *Economic Journal* 113(491): F585–F631.

Burnside, C. A., and M. Eichenbaum. 1996. "Factor-Hoarding and the Propagation of Business Cycles Shocks." *American Economic Review* 86(5): 1154–1174.

Burnside, C. A., M. Eichenbaum, and S. Rebelo. 1993. "Labor Hoarding and the Business Cycle." *Journal of Political Economy* 101(2): 245–273.

Calvo, G. A. 1983. "Staggered Prices in a Utility Maximizing Framework." *Journal of Monetary Economics* 12(3): 383–398.

Carabelli, A. 1988. *On Keynes's Method.* London: Macmillan.

———. 1991. "The Methodology of the Critique of the Classical Theory: Keynes on Organic Interdependence." In B. W. Bateman and J. B. Davis, eds., *Keynes and Philosophy: Essays on the Origin of Keynes's Thought,* 104–125. Aldershot, UK: Edward Elgar.

———. 1995. "Uncertainty and Measurement in Keynes: Probability and Organicness." In S. Dow and J. Hillard, eds. *Keynes, Knowledge and Uncertainty,* 137–160. Aldershot, UK: Edward Elgar.

———. 2003. "Keynes: Economics as a Branch of Probable Logic." In J. Runde and S. Mizuhara, eds., *The Philosophy of Keynes's Economics: Probability, Uncertainty and Convention,* 216–226. London: Routledge.

Cedrini, M. 2008. "Consensus versus Freedom or Consensus upon Freedom? From Washington Disorder to the Rediscovery of Keynes." *Journal of Post Keynesian Economics* 30(4): 499–522.

Chadha, B. 1989. "Is Increased Price Inflexibility Stabilizing?" *Journal of Money, Credit, and Banking* 21(4): 481–497.

Champernowne, D. 1936. "Unemployment, Basic and Monetary: The Classical Analysis and the Keynesian." *Review of Economic Studies* 3(3): 201–216.

Chick, V. 1998. "On Knowing One's Place: The Role of Formalism in Economics." *Economic Journal* 108(451): 1859–1869.

Chinn, M. D. 2005. "Getting Serious about the Twin Deficits." Council on Foreign Relations Special Report 10, September. Available at: www.cfr.org/content/publications/attachments/Twin_DeficitsTF.pdf.

Clarida, R., and J. Galì. 1994. "Sources of Real Exchange Rate Fluctuations: How Important Are Nominal Shocks?" CEPR Discussion Papers no. 951. London: Centre for Economic Policy Research.

Clarida, R., J. Galì, and M. Gertler. 1999. "The Science of Monetary Policy: A New Keynesian Perspective." *Journal of Economic Literature* 37(4): 1661–1707.

Clower, R. W. 1965. "The Keynesian Counter-Revolution: A Theoretical Appraisal." In F. H. Hahn and F. P. R. Brechling, eds., *The Theory of Interest Rates,* 103–125. London: Macmillan.

———. 1984. *Money and Markets: Selected Essays of Robert W. Clower.* Ed. D. A. Walker. Cambridge: Cambridge University Press.

Coates, J. M. 1996. *The Claims of Common Sense: Moore, Wittgenstein, Keynes and the Social Sciences.* Cambridge: Cambridge University Press.

Colander, D. C. 1999. "Conversations with James Tobin and Robert Shiller on the 'Yale Tradition' in Macroeconomics." *Macroeconomic Dynamics* 3(1): 116–143.

Colander, D. C., and H. Landreth. 1996. *The Coming of Keynesianism to America: Conversations with the Founders of Keynesian Economics.* Cheltenham, UK: Edward Elgar.

Cooper, R. 2004. "US Deficit: It Is Not Only Sustainable, It Is Logical." *Financial Times,* October 31: A15.

Cooper, R., and A. John. 1988. "Coordinating Coordination Failures in Keynesian Models." *Quarterly Journal of Economics* 103(3): 441–464.

Crotty, J. R. 1990. "Owner-Management Conflict and Financial Theories of Investment Instability: A Critical Assessment of Keynes, Minsky, and Tobin." *Journal of Post Keynesian Economics* 12(4): 519–542.

Davidson, P. 1997. "Are Grains of Sand in the Wheels of International Finance Sufficient to Do the Job When Boulders Are Often Required?" *Economic Journal* 107(442): 671–686.

Davis, J. B. 1994. *Keynes's Philosophical Development.* Cambridge: Cambridge University Press.

Debreu, G. 1959. *The Theory of Value.* London: Wiley.

De Cecco, M. 1979. "Origins of the Post-War Payments System." *Cambridge Journal of Economics* 3(1): 49–61.

———. 2005. "Sraffa's Lectures on Continental Banking: A Preliminary Appraisal." *Review of Political Economy* 17(3). Reprinted in H. D. Kurz, L. L. Pasinetti, and N. Salvadori, eds. 2008. *Piero Sraffa: The Man and the Scholar,* 185–194. London: Routledge.

De Grauwe, P. 2003. *The Economics of European Monetary Union,* 5th ed. Oxford: Oxford University Press.

DeLong, J. B. 2000. "The Triumph of Monetarism." *Journal of Economic Perspectives* 14(1): 83–94.

DeLong, J. B., A. Shleifer, L. H. Summers, and R. J. Waldmann. 1989. "The Size and Incidence of the Losses from Noise Trading." NBER Working Paper no. 2875. Cambridge, Mass.: National Bureau of Economic Research; repr., *Journal of Finance* 44(3): 681–696.

DeLong, J. B., and L. H. Summers. 1986. "Is Increased Price Flexibility Stabilizing?" *American Economic Review* 76(5): 1031–1044.

Deutsche Bundesbank. 2005. "The Changes to the Stability and Growth Pact." In *Monthly Report* April 15–21. Frankfurt: Deutsche Bundesbank.

De Vroey, M., and K. Hoover. 2004. "Introduction: Seven Decades of the IS-LM Model." *History of Political Economy* 36 (Annual Supplement: *The IS-LM Model: Its Rise, Fall, and Strange Persistence,* ed. M. De Vroey and K. Hoover): 1–11. Durham, N.C.: Duke University Press.

De Vroey, M., and P. Malgrange. 2006. "La théorie et la modélisation macroéconomiques d'hier à aujourd'hui." PSE Working Paper no. 2006/33. Paris: Paris-Jourdan Sciences Economiques.

Diamond, P. A. 1982. "Aggregate Demand Management in Search Equilibrium." *Journal of Political Economy* 90(5): 881–894.

Dimand, R. W. 1988. *The Origins of the Keynesian Revolution*. Aldershot, UK: Edward Elgar.

———, ed. 2002. *The Origins of Macroeconomics*, 10 vols. London: Routledge.

———. 2004a. "James Tobin and the Transformation of the IS-LM Model." *History of Political Economy* 36 (Annual Supplement: *The IS-LM Model: Its Rise, Fall, and Strange Persistence*, ed. M. De Vroey and K. Hoover): 165–189. Durham: Duke University Press.

———. 2004b. "Minsky and Tobin on the Instability of a Monetary Economy." In M. Lavoie and M. Seccareccia, eds., *Central Banking in the Modern World: Alternative Perspectives*, 226–243. Cheltenham, UK: Edward Elgar.

———. 2007. "Keynes, IS-LM, and the Marshallian Tradition." *History of Political Economy* 39(1): 81–95.

Dimand, R. W., and J. Geanakoplos, eds. 2005. *Celebrating Irving Fisher: The Legacy of a Great Economist*. Malden, Mass.: Blackwell (also as annual supplement to *American Journal of Economics and Sociology* 64).

Dooley, M. P., D. Folkerts-Landau, and P. Garber. 2003. "An Essay on the Revived Bretton Woods System." NBER Working Paper no. 9971. Cambridge, Mass.: National Bureau of Economic Research.

———. 2009. "Bretton Woods II Still Defines the International Monetary System." NBER Working Paper no. 14731. Cambridge, Mass.: National Bureau of Economic Research.

Dostaler, G. 2002. "Discours et stratégies de persuasion chez Keynes." *Sciences de la société* 55 (February): 123–136.

———. 2007. *Keynes and His Battles*. Cheltenham, UK: Edward Elgar.

Dostaler, G., and B. Maris. 2009. *Argent, Capitalisme et pulsion de mort: Freud et Keynes*. Paris: Albin Michel.

Driskill, R. A., and S. M. Sheffrin. 1986. "Is Price Flexibility Destabilizing?" *American Economic Review* 76(4): 802–807.

ECB (European Central Bank). 2008. "Euro Area Statistics". *Monthly Bulletin*, April: S1–73. Frankfurt: European Central Bank.

ECOFIN. 2005. "Improving the Implementation of the Stability and Growth Pact." Council of the European Union, Report No. 7423/05. Brussels: Council of the European Union.

Eichenbaum, M. 1997. "Some Thoughts on Practical Stabilization Policy." *American Economic Review, Papers and Proceedings* 87(2): 236–239.

Eichengreen, B. J. 1998. *Globalizing Capital: A History of the International Monetary System*. Princeton, N.J.: Princeton University Press.

———. 2004. "Global Imbalances and the Lessons of Bretton Woods." NBER Working Paper no. 10497. Cambridge, Mass.: National Bureau of Economic Research.

———. 2006a. "Global Imbalances: The New Economy, the Dark Matter, the Savvy Investor, and the Standard Analysis." *Journal of Policy Modeling* 28(6): 645–652.

———. 2006b. "Should There Be a Coordinated Response to the Problem of Global Imbalances? Can There Be One?" Paper presented at the United Nations' World Economic Situation and Prospects (WESP), September. Available at: www.un.org/esa/policy/wess/wesp2007files/bp_eichengreen.pdf.

Eichengreen, B. J., and Y. C. Park. 2006. "Global Imbalances and Emerging Markets." In J. J. Teunissen and A. Akkerman, eds., *Global Imbalances and the US Debt Problem. Should Developing Countries Support the US Dollar?*, 14–44. The Hague: Fondad.

Einzig, P. 1962. *The History of Foreign Exchange*. London: Macmillan.

Eisner, R., and R. Strotz. 1963. "Determinants of Business Investment." In Commission on Money and Credit, *Impacts of Monetary Policy*, 59–223. Englewood Cliff, N.J.: Prentice Hall.

Favereau, O. 1985. "L'incertain dans la 'révolution keynésienne': l'hypothèse Wittgenstein." *Économie et sociétés*, série PE (Oeconomia) 3: 29–72.

Feldstein, M. 2008. "Resolving the Global Imbalance: The Dollar and the U.S. Saving Rate." *Journal of Economic Perspectives* 22(3): 113–125.

Fischer, A. M. 1996. "Central Bank Independence and Sacrifice Ratios." *Open Economies Review* 7(1): 5–18.

Fischer, J., L. Jonung, and M. Larch. 2006. "101 Proposals to Reform the Stability and Growth Pact: Why So Many?" DG ECFIN Economic Papers no. 267. Brussels: European Commission.

Fischer, S. 2001. "Interview." In B. Snowdon, H. Vane, and P. Wynarczyk, eds., *A Modern Guide to Microeconomics*, 33–41. Cheltenham, UK: Edward Elgar.

Fisher, I. 1892. *Mathematical Investigations in the Theory of Value and Prices*. New Haven: Transactions of the Connecticut Academy, vol. 9, July.

———. 1907. *The Rate of Interest*. New York: Macmillan.

———. 1933. "The Debt-Deflation Theory of Great Depressions." *Econometrica* 1(4): 337–357; repr., in I. Fisher 1997, vol. 10.

———. 1997. *The Works of Irving Fisher*. 14 vols. Ed. W. J. Barber, assisted by R. W. Dimand and K. Foster, consulting ed. J. Tobin. London: Pickering & Chatto.

Frankel, J., and A. Rose. 1998. "The Endogeneity of the Optimum Currency Area Criteria." *Economic Journal* 108(449): 1009–1025.

Friedman, M. J. 1957. *A Theory of the Consumption Function*. Princeton, N.J.: Princeton University Press.

———. 1968. "The Role of Monetary Policy." *American Economic Review* 58(1): 1–22.

———. 2003. "The Long View: Lunch with the FT." *Financial Times Magazine*, June 3: 12–13.

Friedman, M. J., and A. J. Schwartz. 1963. *A Monetary History of the United States, 1867–1960*. Princeton, N.J.: Princeton University Press for the National Bureau of Economic Research.

Furner, M. O., and B. Supple, eds. 1990. *The State and Economic Knowledge: The British and American Experiences*. Cambridge: Cambridge University Press.

Garegnani, P. 1978. "Notes on Consumption, Investment, and Effective Demand: I." *Cambridge Journal of Economics* 2(4): 325–353.

———. 1979. "Notes on Consumption, Investment, and Effective Demand: II." *Cambridge Journal of Economics* 3(1): 63–82.

Garnett, D. 1979. *Great Friends: Portraits of Seventeen Writers*. London: Macmillan.

Gärtner, M. 1997. "Central Bank Independence and the Sacrifice Ratio: The Dark Side of the Force." *Swiss Journal of Economics and Statistics* 133(3): 513–538.

Gehrke, C., and H. D. Kurz. 2002. "Keynes and Sraffa's 'Difficulties with J. H. Hollander.' A Note on the History of the RES Edition of *The Works and Correspondence of David Ricardo.*" *European Journal of the History of Economic Thought* 9(4): 644–671.

———. 2006. "Sraffa on von Bortkiewicz: Reconstructing the Classical Theory of Value and Distribution." *History of Political Economy* 38(1): 91–149.

Geweke, J. 1985. "Macroeconometric Modeling and the Theory of Representative Agents." *American Economic Review, Papers and Proceedings* 75(2): 206–210.

Glasgow, M. 1975. "The Concept of the Arts Council." In M. Keynes, ed., *Essays on John Maynard Keynes*, 260–271. Cambridge: Cambridge University Press.

Goodfriend, M. 2002. "Monetary Policy in the New Neoclassical Synthesis: A Primer." *International Finance* 5(2): 165–191.

Goodfriend, M., and R. King. 1997. "The New Neoclassical Synthesis and the Role of Monetary Policy." In *NBER Macroeconomics Annual 1997*, 231–283. Cambridge, Mass.: National Bureau of Economic Research.

Goodhart, C. 1994. "Game Theory for Central Bankers: A Report to the Governor of the Bank of England." *Journal of Economic Literature* 32(1): 101–114.

———. 2004. "Monetary and Social Relationships." Paper presented at the European Society for the History of Economic Thought conference, Venice and Treviso, Italy, February 26–29.

Goodwin, C. 1997. "Maynard and Virginia: A Personal and Professional Friendship." *History of Political Economy* 39 (annual supplement: *Economists' Lives: Biography and Autobiography in the History of Economics*, ed. E. R. Weintraub and E. L. Forget): 269–291. Durham, N.C.: Duke University Press.

Gordon, R. J., ed. 1974. *Milton Friedman's Monetary Framework: A Debate with His Critics*. Chicago: University of Chicago Press.

Greenwald, B., and J. E. Stiglitz. 1993. "New and Old Keynesians." *Journal of Economic Perspectives* 7(1): 23–44.

———. 2006. "A Modest Proposal for International Monetary Reform." Columbia University, January 4. Available at: http://www2.gsb.columbia.edu/faculty/jstiglitz/download/2006_Intl_Monetary_Reform.pdf.

Hansen, A. 1949. *Monetary Theory and Fiscal Policy*. New York: McGraw-Hill.

Harcourt, G. C., and P. A. Riach, eds. 1997. *A "Second Edition" of the General Theory*. 2 vols. London: Routledge.

Hall, P. A., ed. 1989. *The Political Power of Economic Ideas: Keynesianism across Nations*. Princeton, N.J.: Princeton University Press.

Harrod, R. F. 1949. *Towards a Dynamic Economics: Some Recent Developments of Economic Theory and Their Application to Policy.* London: Macmillan.

———. 1951. *The Life of John Maynard Keynes.* London: Macmillan.

Hart, O. D. 1982. "A Model of Imperfect Competition with Keynesian Features." *Quarterly Journal of Economics* 97(1): 109–138.

Hartley, J. E. 1997. *The Representative Agent in Macroeconomics.* London: Routledge.

Hauptmeier, S., Heinemann, F., M. Kappler, M. Kraus, A. Schrimpf, H.-M. Trautwein, and Q. Wang, *Projecting Potential Output: Methods and Problems,* 5–56. ZEW Economic Studies. Heidelberg: Physica.

Hawtrey, R. G. 1913. *Good and Bad Trade.* London: Constable.

Hayashi, F. 1982. "Tobin's Marginal and Average q: A Neoclassical Interpretation." *Econometrica* 50(1): 215–224.

Hayashi, F., and E. C. Prescott. 2002. "The 1990s in Japan: A Lost Decade." *Review of Economic Dynamics* 5(1): 206–235.

Hayek, F. A. 1931a. *Prices and Production.* 1st ed. London: Routledge.

———. 1931b. "Reflections on the Pure Theory of Money of Mr. J. M. Keynes," part I. *Economica* 11(33): 270–295.

———. 1932a. "Money and Capital: A Reply." *Economic Journal* 42(166): 237–249.

———. 1932b. "Reflections on the Pure Theory of Money of Mr. J. M. Keynes," part II. *Economica* 12(35): 22–44.

———. 1933 [orig. ed. 1929]. *Monetary Theory and the Trade Cycle.* London: Routledge & Kegan Paul.

———. 1943. "A Commodity Reserve Currency." *Economic Journal* 53 (210–211): 176–184; repr. in F. A. Hayek. 1948. *Individualism and Economic Order,* 209–219. Chicago: University of Chicago Press.

———. 1952. "Review of *The Life of John Maynard Keynes* by R. F. Harrod." *Journal of Modern History* 24(2): 195–198; repr. in B. Caldwell, ed. 1995. *The Collected Works of F. A. Hayek.* Vol. 9: *Contra Keynes and Cambridge: Essays, Correspondence,* 227–236. Chicago: University of Chicago Press.

———. 1994. *Hayek on Hayek: An Autobiographical Dialogue.* London: Routledge.

Hayo, B., and B. Hofmann. 2006. "Comparing Monetary Policy Reaction Functions: ECB versus Bundesbank." *Empirical Economics* 31(3): 645–662.

Henderson, W., T. Dudley-Evans, and R. E. Backhouse, eds. 1993. *Economics and Language.* London: Routledge.

Hicks, J. R. 1935a. "A Suggestion for Simplifying the Theory of Money." *Economica* n.s. 2(1): 1–19.

———. 1935b. "Wages and Interest: The Dynamic Problem." *Economic Journal* 45: 456–468.

———. 1936. "Mr. Keynes's Theory of Employment." *Economic Journal* 46(182): 238–253.

———. 1937. "Mr. Keynes and the Classics: A Suggested Interpretation." *Econometrica* 5(2): 147–159.

———. 1939. *Value and Capital.* Oxford: Clarendon Press.

———. 1989. *A Market Theory of Money.* Oxford: Clarendon Press.

Hirai, T. 1981. *A Reconstruction of Keynes's General Theory.* Tokyo: Hakutoh Shobou (in Japanese).

———. 2003. *Looking at Keynes's Economics from Multiple Points of View.* Tokyo: University of Tokyo Press (in Japanese).

———. 2004. "The Turning Point in Keynes's Theoretical Development." *History of Economic Ideas* 12(2): 29–50.

———. 2007a. "How, and for How Long, Did Keynes Maintain the *Treatise* Theory?" *European Journal of the History of Economic Thought* 29(3): 283–307.

———. 2007b. "How Did Keynes Transform His Theory from the *Tract* into the *Treatise*?" *European Journal of the History of Economic Thought* 14(2): 325–348.

———. 2008. *Keynes's Theoretical Development: From the Tract to the General Theory.* London: Routledge.

Hirshleifer, J. 1958. "On the Theory of Optimal Investment Decisions." *Journal of Political Economy* 66(4): 95–103.

———. 1965. "Investment Decision under Uncertainty: Choice-Theoretic Approaches." *Quarterly Journal of Economics* 79(4): 509–536.

Horii, R., and Y. Ono. 2004. "Learning, Liquidity Preference, and Business Cycle." ISER Discussion Paper no. 601. Osaka: Osaka University—Institute of Social and Economic Research.

Howson, S., and D. E. Moggridge, eds. 1990. *The Wartime Diaries of Lionel Robbins and James Meade, 1943–45.* London: Macmillan.

IMF. 2007. *World Economic Outlook. Globalization and Inequality.* October. Available at: www.imf.org/external/pubs/ft/weo/2007/02/index.htm.

Innes, A. M. 1913. "What Is Money?" *Banking Law Journal* 30(5): 377–408.

———. 1914. "The Credit Theory of Money." *Banking Law Journal* 31(2): 151–168.

Ireland, P. 2004. "Technological Shocks in the New Keynesian Model." *The Review of Economics and Statistics* 86(4): 923–936.

Johnson, C. 1982. *MITI and the Japanese Miracle: The Growth of Industrial Policy, 1925–1975.* Palo Alto, Calif.: Stanford University Press.

Johnson, E. S. 1978. "Keynes as a Literary Craftsman." In E. S. Johnson and H. G. Johnson, eds., *The Shadow of Keynes: Understanding Keynes, Cambridge, and Keynesian Economics,* 30–37. Oxford: Basil Blackwell.

Johnson, H. G. 1962. "The *General Theory* after Twenty-Five Years." *American Economic Review, Papers and Proceedings* 51(2): 1–17.

———. 1971. "The Keynesian Revolution and the Monetarist Counter-Revolution." *American Economic Review* 61(2): 91–106.

———. 1974. "Cambridge in the 1950s." *Encounter,* January, 28–39; repr. in E. S. Johnson and H. G. Johnson, eds. 1978. *The Shadow of Keynes: Understanding Keynes, Cambridge, and Keynesian Economics,* 127–150. Oxford: Basil Blackwell.

Jorgenson, D. W. 1963. "Capital Theory and Investment Behavior." *American Economic Review, Papers and Proceedings* 53(2): 247–259.

Kalecki, M. 1944. "Professor Pigou on 'The Classical Stationary State.' A Comment." *Economic Journal* 54(1): 131–132.

Kareken, J. H., and N. A. Wallace, eds. 1980. *Models of Monetary Economies.* Minneapolis: Federal Reserve Bank of Minneapolis.

Kenen, P. 1969. "The Theory of Optimum Currency Areas: An Eclectic View." In R. Mundell and A. Swoboda, eds., *Monetary Problems of the International Economy,* 41–59. Chicago: University of Chicago Press.

Keynes, F. A. 1950. *Gathering up the Threads: A Study in Family Biography.* Cambridge: W. Heffer & Sons.

Keynes, J. M. 1919. *The Economic Consequences of the Peace.* London: Macmillan; CWK 2.

———. 1921. *A Treatise on Probability.* London: Macmillan; CWK 8.

———. 1922a. "The Forward Market in Foreign Exchanges." *Manchester Guardian Commercial,* Series of Supplements: *Reconstruction in Europe* 1 (April 20): 11–18; repr. with modifications in CWK 4, 94–115.

———. 1922b. "The Theory of the Exchanges and 'Purchasing Power Parity.'" *Manchester Guardian Commercial,* Series of Supplements: *Reconstruction in Europe* 1 (April 20): 6–8; repr. with modifications in CWK 4, 70–80 and 164–169.

———. 1923. *A Tract on Monetary Reform.* London: Macmillan; CWK 4.

———. 1925a. Letter to the Editor [on "Freudian psycho-analysis"]. *Nation and the Athenæum,* August 29; CWK 28, 392–393. [signed "Siela"]

———. 1925b. Notes on fundamental terminology, for a lecture given on April 25; CWK 29, 35–39.

———. 1930. *A Treatise on Money.* Vol. 1: *The Pure Theory of Money;* Vol. 2: *The Applied Theory of Money.* London: Macmillan; CWK 5 and CWK 6.

———. 1931. *Essays in Persuasion.* London: Macmillan; CWK 9.

———. 1933. "A Monetary Theory of Production." In G. Clausing, ed., *Festschrift für Arthur Spiethoff,* 123–125. Munich: Duncker & Humblot.

———. 1936a. *The General Theory of Employment, Interest and Money.* London: Macmillan; CWK 7.

———. 1936b. "On Reading Books." *The Listener,* June 10, in CWK 28, 329–335.

———. 1937. "The General Theory of Employment." *Quarterly Journal of Economics* 51(2): 209–223; CWK 14, 109–123.

———. 1938. "My Early Beliefs," Memoir read to the Bloomsbury Memoir Club on September 9; CWK 10, 433–450.

———. 1947. "Newton, the Man." In *Newton Tercentenary Celebrations, July 15–19, 1946.* Cambridge: Royal Society of London; CWK 10, 363–374.

———. 1971–1989. *The Collected Writings of John Maynard Keynes* (CWK), ed. D. E. Moggridge. 30 vols. London: Macmillan.

CWK 2. *The Economic Consequences of the Peace.*

CWK 4. *A Tract on Monetary Reform.*

CWK 5. *A Treatise on Money.* Vol. 1: *The Pure Theory of Money.*

CWK 6. *A Treatise on Money.* Vol. 2: *The Applied Theory of Money.*

CWK 7. *The General Theory of Employment, Interest and Money,* 1936.

CWK 8. *Treatise on Probability.*

CWK 9. *Essays in Persuasion.*

CWK 10. *Essays in Biography.*

CWK 12. *Economic Articles and Correspondence. Investment and Editorial.*

CWK 13. *The General Theory and After.* Vol. 1: *Preparation.*

CWK 14. *The General Theory and After.* Vol. 2: *Defence and Development.*

CWK 20. *Activities 1929–1931. Rethinking Employment and Unemployment Policies.*

CWK 22. *Activities 1939–1945: Internal War Finance.*

CWK 24. *Activities 1944–1946: The Transition to Peace.*

CWK 25. *Activities 1940–1944. Shaping the Post-War World. The Clearing Union.*

CWK 26. *Activities 1941–1946. Shaping the Post-War World. Bretton Woods and Reparations.*

CWK 28. *Social, Political and Literary Writings.*

CWK 29. *The General Theory and After. A Supplement.*

King, J. E. 2002. *A History of Post Keynesian Economics since 1936.* Cheltenham, UK: Edward Elgar.

Kirman, A. P. 1992. "Whom or What Does the Representative Individual Represent?" *Journal of Economic Perspectives* 6(2): 117–136.

Klein, L. R. 1947. *The Keynesian Revolution.* New York: Macmillan.

Knapp, G. F. 1924. *The State Theory of Money.* Abridged ed. Trans. H. M Lucas and J. Bonar. London: Macmillan.

Kregel, J. A. 1976. "Sraffa et Keynes: le taux d'intérêt et le taux de profit." *Cahiers d'Economie Politique* 3: 135–163.

———. 1983. "Effective Demand: Origins and Development of the Notion." In *Distribution, Effective Demand, and International Economic Relations,* 50–68. London: Macmillan.

———. 1988a. "Irving Fisher, Great-Grandparent of the General Theory." *Cahiers d'Economie Politique* 14–15: 59–68.

———. 1988b. "The Multiplier and Liquidity Preference: Two Sides of the Theory of Effective Demand." In A. Barrère, ed., *The Foundations of Keynesian Analysis,* 231–250. London: Macmillan.

———. 1993. "Keynesian Stabilisation Policy and Post-War Economic Performance." In E. Szirmai, B. van Ark, and D. Pilat, eds., *Explaining Economic Growth,* 429–445. Amsterdam: Elsevier.

———. 1998a. "Aspects of a Post Keynesian Theory of Finance." *Journal of Post Keynesian Economics* 21(1): 113–137.

———. 1998b. "Instability, Volatility and the Process of Capital Accumulation." In G. Gandolfo and F. Marzano, eds., *Economic Theory and Social Justice,* 149–167. London: Macmillan.

———. 1999a. "Capital and Income in the Theory of Investment and Output: Irving Fisher and John Maynard Keynes." In H.-E. Loef and H. G. Monissen, eds., *The Economics of Irving Fisher: Reviewing the Scientific Work of a Great Economist,* 271–283. Cheltenham, UK: Edward Elgar.

———. 1999b. "A New Triffin Paradox for the Global Economy." Remarks Prepared for the Federal Council of Economists and the Regional Council of

Economists of Rio de Janeiro meeting of the 13th Brazilian Congress of Economists and the 7th Congress of the Association of Economists from Latin-America and the Caribbean, September 15. Available at: http://cas.umkc.edu/econ/economics/faculty/Kregel/590b/Winter2002/Readings/Triffin.pdf.

———. 2006. "Understanding Imbalances in a Globalised International Economic System." In J. J. Teunissen and A. Akkerman, eds., *Global Imbalances and the US Debt Problem. Should Developing Countries Support the US Dollar?*, 149–173. The Hague: Fondad.

———. 2009. "Some Simple Observations on the Reform of the International Monetary System." The Levy Economics Institute of Bard College Policy Note 2009/8. Available at: www.levy.org/pubs/pn_09_08.pdf.

Krugman, P. 1995. "What Do We Need to Know about the International Monetary System?" In P. Kenen, ed., *Understanding Interdependence*, 509–529. Princeton, N.J.: Princeton University Press.

———. 1998. "It's Baaack!! Japan's Slump and the Return of the Liquidity Trap." *Brookings Papers on Economic Activity* 2: 137–187.

———. 2007. "Will There Be a Dollar Crisis?" *Economic Policy* 22(51): 435–467.

Kurz, H. D. 1978. "Rent Theory in a Multisectoral Model." *Oxford Economic Papers* 30(1): 16–37.

———. 1996. "Sraffa und die Keynessche Theorie der Liquiditätspräferenz." *Homo oeconomicus* 13(3): 363–391.

———. 2000. "The Hayek-Keynes-Sraffa Controversy Reconsidered." In H. D. Kurz, ed., *Critical Essays on Piero Sraffa's Legacy in Economics*, 257–301. Cambridge: Cambridge University Press.

———. 2006. "The Agents of Production Are the Commodities Themselves. On the Classical Theory of Production, Distribution and Value." *Structural Change and Economic Dynamics* 17(1): 1–26.

Kurz, H. D., and N. Salvadori. 1995. *Theory of Production: A Long-Period Analysis.* Cambridge: Cambridge University Press.

———. 2005. "Representing the Production and Circulation of Commodities in Material Terms: On Sraffa's Objectivism." *Review of Political Economy* 17(3): 413–441; repr. in Kurz, Pasinetti, and Salvadori, eds. 2008.

Kurz, H. D., L. L. Pasinetti, and N. Salvadori, eds. 2008. *Piero Sraffa: The Man and the Scholar.* London: Routledge.

Kydland, F. E., and E. C. Prescott. 1977. "Rules Rather Than Discretion: The Inconsistency of Optimal Plans." *Journal of Political Economy* 85(3): 473–491.

———. 1982. "Time to Build and Aggregate Fluctuations." *Econometrica* 50(6): 1345–1370.

Laidler, D. W. 1999. *Fabricating the Keynesian Revolution: Studies of the Inter-War Literature on Money, the Cycle, and Unemployment.* Cambridge: Cambridge University Press.

———. 2006. "Woodford and Wicksell on 'Interest and Prices.' The Place of the Pure Credit Economy in the Theory of Monetary Policy." *Journal of the History of Economic Thought* 28(2): 151–159.

Lavialle, C. 2001. "L'épistémologie de Keynes et 'l'hypothèse Wittgenstein': la cohérence logique de la *Théorie générale de l'emploi, de l'intérêt et de la monnaie.*" *Cahiers d'économie politique* 38: 25–64.

Lavington, F. 1921. *The English Capital Market*. London: Methuen.

———. 1922. *The Trade Cycle: An Account of the Causes Producing Rhythmical Changes in the Activity of Business*. London: P. S. King & Son.

Leijonhufvud, A. 1968. *On Keynesian Economics and the Economics of Keynes*. New York: Oxford University Press.

———. 1973. "Effective Demand Failures." *Swedish Economic Journal* 75(1): 27–48; repr. in Leijonhufvud 1981, 103–129.

———. 1979. "The Wicksell Connection: Variations on a Theme." UCLA Economics Working Paper no. 165; repr. in Leijonhufvud 1981, 131–202.

———. 1981. *Information and Coordination: Essays in Macroeconomic Theory*. New York: Oxford University Press.

———. 2000. "What Would Keynes Have Thought of Rational Expectations?" In *Macroeconomic Instability and Coordination: Selected Essays of Axel Leijonhuvud*, 3–32. Cheltenham, UK: Edward Elgar.

Leontief, W. W. 1936. "The Fundamental Assumption of Mr. Keynes' Monetary Theory of Unemployment." *Quarterly Journal of Economics* 51(1): 192–197.

LePan, D. 1979. *Bright Glass of Memory*. Toronto: McGraw Hill Ryerson.

Lindahl, E. R. 1929. *Penningpolitikens mål*. Malmö: Förlagsaktiebolaget.

———. 1939 [orig. ed. 1930]. "The Rate of Interest and the Price Level." In *Studies in the Theory of Money and Capital*, 139–268. London: Allen & Unwin.

———. 1954. "On Keynes' Economic System. I and II." *Economic Record* 30: 19–32 and 159–171.

Lucas, R. E., Jr. 1972. "Expectation and the Neutrality of Money." *Journal of Economic Theory* 4(2): 103–124.

———. 1973. "Some International Evidence on Output-Inflation Tradeoffs." *American Economic Review* 63(3): 326–334.

———. 1975. "An Equilibrium Model of the Business Cycle." *Journal of Political Economy* 83(6): 1113–1144.

———. 1981a. *Studies in Business Cycle Theory*. Cambridge, Mass.: MIT Press.

———. 1981b. "Tobin and Monetarism: A Review Article." *Journal of Economic Literature* 19(2): 558–567.

———. 1987. *Models of Business Cycles*. Oxford: Blackwell.

Lucas, R. E., Jr., and E. Prescott. 1974. "Equilibrium Search and Unemployment." *Journal of Economic Theory* 7(2): 188–209.

Lucas, R. E., Jr., and L. A. Rapping. 1969. "Real Wages, Employment, and Inflation." *Journal of Political Economy* 77(5): 721–754.

Malinvaud, E. 1977. *The Theory of Unemployment Reconsidered*. Oxford: Basil Blackwell.

Mankiw, G. N. 1985. "Small Menu Costs and Large Business Cycles: A Macroeconomic Model of Monopoly." *Quarterly Journal of Economics* 100(2): 529–537.

Mankiw, G. N., and R. Reis. 2002. "Sticky Information versus Sticky Prices: A Proposal to Replace the New Keynesian Phillips Curve." *Quarterly Journal of Economics* 117(4): 1295–1328.

Mankiw, G. N., and D. Romer. 1991. *New Keynesian Economics*. 2 vols. Cambridge, Mass.: MIT Press.

Mann, C. L. 2005. "Breaking Up is Hard to Do: Global Co-Dependency, Collective Action, and the Challenges of Global Adjustment." *CESifo Forum* 1: 16–23. Available at: www.iie.com/publications/papers/mann0105b.pdf.

Marcuzzo, M. C. 2002. "The Collaboration between J. M. Keynes and R. F. Kahn from the Treatise to the General Theory." *History of Political Economy* 34(2): 421–448.

———. 2008. "Sraffa and Cambridge Economics, 1928–1931." In T. Cozzi and R. Marchionatti, eds., *Piero Sraffa's Political Economy. A Centenary Estimate,* 81–99. London: Routledge.

Markowitz, H. M. 1952. "Portfolio Selection." *Journal of Finance* 7(1): 77–91.

———. 1959. *Portfolio Selection: Efficient Diversification of Investments.* New York: J. Wiley and Sons.

Marshall, A. 1920 [orig. ed. 1890]. *Principles of Economics.* 8th ed. London: Macmillan.

———. 1923. *Money, Credit and Commerce.* London: Macmillan.

Marshall, A., and M. P. Marshall. 1879. *The Economics of Industry.* London: Macmillan.

Marzola, A., and F. Silva, eds. 1994. *John Maynard Keynes: Language and Method.* Aldershot, UK: Edward Elgar.

Mas-Colell, A. 1989. "Capital Theory Paradoxes: Anything Goes." In R. Feiwel, ed., *Joan Robinson and Modern Economic Theory,* 505–520. London: Macmillan.

Mayer, T. 1978. *The Structure of Monetarism.* New York: W. W. Norton.

McCloskey, D. N. 1986. *The Rhetoric of Economics.* Brighton, UK: Wheatsheaf Books.

Meade, J. 1975. "The Keynesian Revolution." In M. Keynes, ed., *Essays on John Maynard Keynes,* 82–88. Cambridge, Mass.: Cambridge University Press.

Meissner, C. M., and A. M. Taylor. 2006. "Losing Our Marbles in the New Century? The Great Rebalancing in Historical Perspective." NBER Working Paper no. 12580. Cambridge, Mass.: National Bureau of Economic Research.

Meltzer, A. H. 1988. *Keynes's Monetary Theory: A Different Interpretation.* Cambridge: Cambridge University Press.

———. 1989. "Tobin on Macroeconomic Policy: A Review Essay." *Journal of Monetary Economics* 23(1): 159–173.

Milgate, M. 1982. *Capital and Employment.* London: Academic Press.

Mill, J. S. 1871. *Principles of Political Economy, with Some of Their Applications to Social Philosophy.* 7th ed. London: John W. Parker.

Miller, P. 1994. *The Rational Expectations Revolution: Readings from the Frontline.* Cambridge, Mass.: MIT Press.

Minsky, H. P. 1975. *John Maynard Keynes.* New York: Columbia University Press.

———. 1981. "James Tobin's *Asset Accumulation and Economic Activity:* A Review Article." *Eastern Economic Journal* 7(3): 199–209.

———. 1986. *Stabilizing an Unstable Economy.* New Haven, Conn.: Yale University Press for the Twentieth Century Fund.

Modigliani, F. 1944, "Liquidity Preference and the Theory of Interest and Money." *Econometrica* 12(1): 45–88.

———. 1980. *Collected Papers.* Vol. 1: *Essays in Macroeconomics.* Ed. A. Abel. Cambridge, Mass.: MIT Press.

Modigliani, F., and R. Brumberg. 1954. "Utility Analysis and the Consumption Function: An Interpretation of Cross-Section Data." In K. Kurihara, ed., *Post-Keynesian Economics,* 388–436. New Brunswick, N.J.: Rutgers University Press.

Moggridge, D. E. 1992. *Maynard Keynes: An Economist's Biography.* London: Routledge.

Moore, B. 1988. *Horizontalists and Verticalists.* Cambridge: Cambridge University Press.

Morana, C. 2004. "The Japanese Stagnation: An Assessment of the Productivity Slowdown Hypothesis." *Japan and the World Economy* 16(2): 193–211.

Morgan, M. S. 2003. "Economics." In T. M. Porter and D. Ross, eds., *The Cambridge History of Science,* Vol. 7, 275–305. Cambridge: Cambridge University Press.

Morgenstern, O. 1931. "Offene Probleme der Kosten- und Ertragstheorie." *Zeitschrift für Nationalökonomie* 2(4): 481–522.

Morris, R., H. Ongena, and L. Schuknecht. 2006. "The Reform and Implementation of the Stability and Growth Pact." ECB Occasional Paper Series no. 47. Frankfurt: European Central Bank.

Mortensen, D. T. 2003. *Wage Dispersion.* Cambridge, Mass.: MIT Press.

Mundell, R. A. 1961. "A Theory of Optimum Currency Areas." *American Economic Review* 51(4): 657–665.

Muth, J. F. 1961. "Rational Expectations and the Theory of Price Movements." *Econometrica* 29(3): 315–335.

Myrdal, G. 1939 [orig. ed. 1931]. *Monetary Equilibrium.* London: William Hodge.

Nagatani, K. 1981. *Macroeconomic Dynamics.* Cambridge: Cambridge University Press.

Negishi, T. 1979. *Microeconomic Foundations of Keynesian Macroeconomics.* Amsterdam: North-Holland.

O'Donnell, R. M. 1997. "Keynes and Formalism." In Harcourt and Riach, eds., 1997, 131–165.

———. 2004. "Keynes as a Writer: Three Case Studies." In T. Aspromourgos and J. Lodewijks, eds., *History and Political Economy: Essays in Honour of P. D. Groenewegen,* 197–216. London: Routledge.

Ohlin, B. 1937. "Some Notes on the Stockholm Theory of Savings and Investment. I and II." *Economic Journal* 47(185): 53–69 and 221–240.

Okun, A. M. 1973. "Upward Mobility in a High-pressure Economy." *Brookings Papers on Economic Activity* 1: 207–261.

Ono, Y. 1994. *Money, Interest, and Stagnation. Dynamic Theory and Keynes's Economics.* Oxford: Oxford University Press.

———. 2001. "A Reinterpretation of Chapter 17 of Keynes's *General Theory*: Effective Demand Shortage under Dynamic Optimization." *International Economic Review* 42(1): 207–236.

———. 2006. "International Asymmetry in Business Activity and Appreciation of a Stagnant Country's Currency." *Japanese Economic Review* 57(1): 101–120.

———. 2009. "The Keynesian Multiplier Effect Reconsidered." ISER Discussion Paper no. 730. Osaka: Osaka University—Institute of Social and Economic Research.

Ono, Y., K. Ogawa, and A. Yoshida. 2004. "Liquidity Trap and Persistent Unemployment with Dynamic Optimizing Agents: Empirical Evidence." *Japanese Economic Review* 55(4): 355–371.

Padoa-Schioppa, T. 2004. *The Euro and Its Central Bank: Getting United after the Union.* Cambridge, Mass.: MIT Press.

Pasinetti, L. L. 1974. *Growth and Income Distribution: Essays in Economic Theory.* Cambridge: Cambridge University Press.

Patinkin, D. 1948. "Price Flexibility and Full Employment." *American Economic Review* 38(4): 543–564.

———. 1956. *Money, Interest, and Prices: An Integration of Monetary and Value Theory.* Evanston, Ill.: Row Peterson.

———. 1965. *Money, Interest, and Prices. An Integration of Monetary and Value Theory.* 2nd ed. New York: Harper & Row.

———. 1976. *Keynes' Monetary Thought.* Durham, N.C.: Duke University Press.

———. 1982. *Anticipations of the General Theory.* Chicago: Chicago University Press.

Patinkin, D., and O. Steiger. 1989. "In Search of the 'Veil of Money' and the 'Neutrality of Money.' A Note on the Origin of Terms." *Scandinavian Journal of Economics* 91(1): 131–146.

Peel, D. A., and M. P. Taylor. 2002. "Covered Interest Rate Arbitrage in the Interwar Period and the Keynes-Einzig Conjecture." *Journal of Money, Credit, and Banking* 34(1): 51–75.

Phelps Brown, H. E. 1951. "Harrod, Roy F., *The Life of John Maynard Keynes.*" *Economica* 18(70): 199–203.

Phelps, E. S., ed. 1970. *Microeconomic Foundations of Employment and Inflation Theory.* New York: Norton.

Phillips, A. W. 1958. "The Relation between Unemployment and the Rate of Change of Money Wages in the United Kingdom, 1861–1957." *Economica* 25(100): 283–299.

Pigou, A. C. 1920. *The Economics of Welfare.* London: Macmillan.

———. 1927. *Industrial Fluctuations.* London: Macmillan.

———. 1929. *Industrial Fluctuations.* 2nd ed. London: Macmillan.

———. 1936. "Mr. J. M. Keynes's *General Theory of Employment Interest and Money.*" *Economica* n.s. 3(10): 115–132.

———. 1943. "The Classical Stationary State." *Economic Journal* 53(212): 342–352.

Prescott, E. C. 2002. "Prosperity and Depression." *American Economic Review* 92(2): 1–15.

Pressnell, L. S. 1986. *External Economic Policy since the War.* Vol. 1: *The Post-War Financial Settlement.* London: Her Majesty's Stationery Office.

Purvis, D. 1982. "James Tobin's Contributions to Economics." *Scandinavian Journal of Economics* 84(1): 61–88.

Raffaelli, T. 2006. "Keynes and Philosophers." In Backhouse and Bateman, eds., 2006, 160–179.

Ranchetti, F. 2002. "On the Relationship between Sraffa and Keynes." In T. Cozzi and R. Marchionatti, eds., *Piero Sraffa's Political Economy: A Centenary Estimate*, 311–331. London: Routledge.

———. 2005. "Communication and Intellectual Integrity. The Correspondence between Keynes and Sraffa." In M. C. Marcuzzo and A. Rosselli, eds., *Economists in Cambridge: A Study through Their Correspondence, 1907–1946*, 119–137. London: Routledge.

Rees, A. 1970. "On Equilibrium in Labor Markets." *Journal of Political Economy* 78(2): 306–310.

Robbins, L. C. 1971. *Autobiography of an Economist*. London: Macmillan.

Robertson, D. H. 1915. *A Study of Industrial Fluctuation*. London: P. S. King & Son.

———. 1926. *Banking Policy and the Price Level*. London: Staples Press Limited.

Robinson, A. E. 1947. "John Maynard Keynes, 1883–1946." *Economic Journal* 57(225): 1–68.

Robinson, J. V. 1948. "La théorie générale de l'emploi." *Économie Appliquée* 1(1–2): 185–196.

———. 1975. "What Has Become of the Keynesian Revolution?" In M. Keynes, ed., *Essays on John Maynard Keynes*. Cambridge Mass.: Cambridge University Press.

———. 1978. *Contributions to Modern Economics*. Oxford: Blackwell.

Romer, D. 2000. "Keynesian Macroeconomics without the LM curve." *Journal of Economic Perspectives* 14(2): 149–169.

Rosselli, A. 2005. "Sraffa and the Marshallian Tradition." *European Journal of the History of Economic Thought* 12(3): 403–423; repr. in Kurz, Pasinetti, and Salvadori, eds., 2008, 31–50.

Russell, B. 1967. *The Autobiography of Bertrand Russell: 1872–1914*. London: George Allen and Unwin.

Rymes, T. K., ed. (transcribed, edited, and constructed). 1989. *Keynes's Lectures, 1932–35. Notes of a Representative Student*. London: Macmillan.

Samuelson, P. A. 1951. "Economic Theory and Wages." In D. Wright, ed., *The Impact of the Union*, 312–360. New York: Harcourt, Brace.

———. 1955. *Economics, an Introductory Analysis*. New York: McGraw-Hill.

———. 1964. "The General Theory." In R. Lekachman, ed., *Keynes' General Theory: Reports of Three Decades*, 315–347. New York: St. Martin's Press.

Samuelson, P. A., and R. M. Solow. 1960. "Analytical Aspects of Anti-Inflation Policy." *American Economic Review, Papers and Proceedings* 50(2): 177–194.

Sargent, T., and N. Wallace. 1975. "Rational Expectations, the Optimal Monetary Instrument, and the Optimal Money Supply Rule." *Journal of Political Economy* 83(2): 241–254.

Sauer, S., and J.-E. Sturm. 2007. "Using Taylor Rules to Understand European Central Bank Monetary Policy." *German Economic Review* 8(3): 375–398.

Schumpeter, J. 1936. "Review of Keynes's *General Theory*." *Journal of American Statistical Association* 31 (Dec.): 791–795.

———. 1939. *Business Cycles,* New York: McGraw-Hill.

Shiller, R. J. 1989. *Market Volatility.* Cambridge, Mass.: MIT Press.

———. 1999. "The ET Interview: Professor James Tobin." *Econometric Theory* 15(6): 867–900.

Skidelsky, R. 1992. *John Maynard Keynes.* Vol. 2: *The Economist as Saviour, 1920–1937.* London: Macmillan.

———. 2000. *John Maynard Keynes.* Vol. 3: *Fighting for Britain, 1937–1946.* London: Macmillan.

———. 2008. "The Origins of Keynesian Economics and Some Applications to Restructuring and Globalization." In M. Forstater and L. R. Wray, eds., *Keynes for the Twenty-First Century: The Continuing Relevance of The General Theory,* 81–88. London: Palgrave Macmillan.

Solow, R. M. 1979. "Another Possible Source of Wage Stickiness." *Journal of Macroeconomics* 1(1): 79–82.

———. 1997. "Is There a Core of Usable Macroeconomics We Should All Believe in?" *American Economic Review, Papers and Proceedings* 87(2): 230–232.

———. 2000. "Towards a Macroeconomics of the Medium Run." *Journal of Economic Perspectives* 14(1): 151–158.

———. 2003. "Dumb and Dumber in Macroeconomics." Available at: www2 .gsb.columbia.edu/faculty/jstiglitz/festschrift/Papers/Stig-Solow.pdf.

Spahn, H.-P. 2001. *From Gold to Euro: On Monetary Theory and the History of Currency Systems.* Berlin: Springer.

Sraffa, P. 1925. "Sulle relazioni fra costo e quantità prodotta." *Annali di Economia* 2(1): 277–328.

———. 1926. "The Laws of Returns under Competitive Conditions." *Economic Journal* 36(144): 535–550.

———. 1930. "A Criticism" and "Rejoinder." Symposium on "Increasing Returns and the Representative Firm," *Economic Journal* 40(157): 89–93.

———. 1932. "Dr. Hayek on Money and Capital." *Economic Journal* 42(165): 42–53.

———. 1960. *Production of Commodities by Means of Commodities.* Cambridge: Cambridge University Press.

Stansky, P. 1996. *On or about December 1910: Early Bloomsbury and Its Intimate World.* Cambridge, Mass.: Harvard University Press.

Stein, H. 1969. *The Fiscal Revolution in America.* Chicago: University of Chicago Press.

Stiglitz, J. E., and A. Weiss. 1981. "Credit Rationing in Markets with Imperfect Information." *American Economic Review* 72(3): 393–410.

Sturm, J.-E., and T. Wollmershäuser. 2008. "The Stress of Having a Single Monetary Policy in Europe." KOF Working Papers no. 190. Zürich: ETH.

Tamborini, R. 2006. "Back to Wicksell? In Search of the Foundations of Practical Monetary Policy." Dipartimento di Economia Discussion Paper no. 2. Trento, Italy: Università degli Studi di Trento.

Taylor, J. B. 1979. "Estimation and Control of a Macroeconomic Model with Rational Expectations." *Econometrica* 47(5): 1267–1286.

———. 1980. "Aggregate Dynamics and Staggered Contracts." *Journal of Political Economy* 88(1): 1–24.

———. 1997. "A Core of Practical Macroeconomics." *American Economic Review, Papers and Proceedings* 87(2): 233–235.

———. 2000. "Teaching Modern Macroeconomics at the Principles Level." *American Economic Review* 90(2): 90–94.

Tobin, J. 1941. "A Note on the Money Wage Problem." *Quarterly Journal of Economics* 55(3): 508–516.

———. 1947/1948. "Liquidity Preference and Monetary Policy." *Review of Economics and Statistics* 29(2): 124–131; 30(4): 314–317.

———. 1956. "The Interest-Elasticity of Transactions Demand for Cash." *Review of Economics and Statistics* 38: 241–247.

———. 1958. "Liquidity Preference as Behavior towards Risk." *Review of Economic Studies* 25(67): 65–86.

———. 1960. "Toward a General Kaldorian Theory of Distribution: A Note." *Review of Economic Studies* 27(73): 119–120.

———. 1972. "Inflation and Unemployment." *American Economic Review* 62(1): 1–18.

———. 1974. *The New Economics One Decade Older*. Princeton, N.J.: Princeton University Press.

———. 1975. "Keynesian Models of Recession and Depression." *American Economic Review, Papers and Proceedings* 65(2): 195–202.

———. 1977. "How Dead Is Keynes?" *Economic Inquiry* 15(4): 459–468.

———. 1978. "A Proposal for International Monetary Reform." *Eastern Economic Journal* 4(3–4): 153–159; repr. in 2003 in *Eastern Economic Journal* 29(4): 519–526.

———. 1980. *Asset Accumulation and Economic Activity*. Chicago: University of Chicago Press.

———. 1982. "Nobel Lecture: Money and Finance in the Macroeconomic Process." *Journal of Money, Credit and Banking* 14(2): 171–204.

———. 1984. "On the Efficiency of the Financial System." *Lloyds Bank Review* 153 (July): 1–15.

———. 1988. "A Revolution Remembered." *Challenge* 31(4): 35–41; repr. in Tobin 1996a, 661–672.

———. 1989a. "Growth and Distribution: A Neoclassical Kaldor-Robinson Exercise." *Cambridge Journal of Economics* 13(1): 37–45; as corrected and revised in Tobin 1996a, 721–735.

———. 1989b. "Review of *Stabilizing an Unstable Economy*, by Hyman P. Minsky." *Journal of Economic Literature* 27(1): 105–108; repr. in Tobin 1996b, 72–76.

———. 1992. "An Old Keynesian Counterattacks." *Eastern Economic Journal* 18(4): 387–400.

———. 1993. "Price Flexibility and Output Stability: An Old Keynesian View." *Journal of Economic Perspectives* 7(1): 45–65; repr. with additional appendix in W. Semmler, ed. 1994. *Business Cycle Theory and Empirical Methods.* Norwell, Mass.: Kluwer Academic.

———. 1996a. *Essays in Economics.* Vol. 4. Cambridge, Mass.: MIT Press.

———. 1996b. *Full Employment and Growth: Further Keynesian Essays on Policy.* Cheltenham, UK: Edward Elgar.

———. 1997. "An Overview of *The General Theory.*" In Harcourt and Riach, eds., 1997, vol. 2, 3–27.

———. 2001. "Interview." In B. Snowdon, H. Vane, and P. Wynarczyk, eds., *A Modern Guide to Macroeconomics*, 124–136. Cheltenham, U.K.: Edward Elgar.

Tobin, J., and W. C. Brainard. 1977. "Asset Markets and the Cost of Capital." In R. Nelson and B. Balassa, eds., *Economic Progress, Private Values, and Public Policy: Essays in Honor of William Fellner*, 235–262. Amsterdam: North-Holland.

———. 1990. "On Crotty's Critique of q Theory." *Journal of Post Keynesian Economics* 12(4): 543–549; repr. in Tobin 1996b, 66–71.

Tobin, J., with S. S. Golub. 1998. *Money, Credit, and Capital.* Boston: Irwin/McGraw-Hill.

Trautwein, H.-M. 1997. "The Uses of the Pure Credit Economy." In A. Cohen, H. Hagemann, and J. Smithin, eds., *Money, Financial Institutions, and Macroeconomics*, 3–16. Boston: Kluwer.

———. 2000. "The Credit View: Old and New." *Journal of Economic Surveys* 14(2): 155–190.

———. 2009. "The Concept of Potential Output: A History of Origins." In S. Hauptmeier et al., 2009, 5–56.

Truman, E. M. 2005. "Postponing Global Adjustment: An Analysis of the Pending Adjustment of Global Imbalances." Peterson Institute for International Economics Working Paper 05-6, July. Available at: www.iie.com/publications/wp/wp05-6.pdf.

Unctad. 2004. *Trade and Development Report. Policy Coherence, Development Strategies and Integration into the World Economy.* New York and Geneva: Unctad.

———. 2005. *Trade and Development Report. New Features of Global Interdependence.* New York and Geneva: Unctad.

———. 2006. *Trade and Development Report. Global Partnership and National Policies for Development.* New York and Geneva: Unctad.

Vines, D. 2003. "John Maynard Keynes 1937–1946: The Creation of International Macroeconomics. A Review Article of 'John Maynard Keynes 1937–1946: Fighting for Britain' by Robert Skidelsky." *The Economic Journal* 113(488): 338–361.

Vogel, E. F. 1979. *Japan as Number One: Lessons for America.* Cambridge, Mass.: Harvard University Press.

Walsh, C. E. 2003. *Monetary Theory and Policy.* Cambridge, Mass.: MIT Press.

Warburton, C. 1945. "The Monetary Theory of Deficit Spending." *Review of Economics and Statistics* 27(1): 74–84.

Wicke, J. 1994. "'Mrs. Dalloway' Goes to the Market: Woolf, Keynes, and Modern Markets." *Novel: A Forum on Fiction* 28(1): 5–23.

Wicksell, K. 1898 [Engl. trans. 1936]. *Geldzins und Güterpreise. Eine Studie über die den Tauschwert des Geldes bestimmenden Ursachen.* Jena: Gustav Fischer.

———. 1922 [Engl. trans. 1935]. *Vorlesungen über Nationalökonomie.* Vol. 2: *Geld und Kredit.* Jena: Gustav Fischer.

———. 1935 [orig. ed. 1922]. *Lectures on Political Economy.* Vol. 2: *Money.* London: Routledge & Kegan Paul.

———. 1936 [orig. ed. 1898]. *Interest and Prices. A Study of the Causes Regulating the Value of Money.* London: Macmillan.

Wolf, M. 2005. "Will Asian Mercantilism Meet Its Waterloo?" Richard Snape Lecture, Melbourne, November 14. Available at: www.pc.gov.au/lectures/snape/wolf/wolf.pdf.

Woodford, M. 1998. "Doing without Money: Controlling Inflation in a Post-Monetary World." *Review of Economic Dynamics* 1(1): 173–219.

———. 1999. "Revolution and Evolution in Twentieth-Century Macroeconomics." Paper presented at the conference on "Frontiers of the Mind in the Twenty-First Century," Library of Congress, Washington, June 14–18; forthcoming in P. Gifford, ed., *Frontiers of the Mind in the Twenty-First Century.* Cambridge, Mass: Harvard University Press.

———. 2003. *Interest and Prices: Foundations of a Theory of Monetary Policy.* Princeton, N.J.: Princeton University Press.

———. 2006. "Comments on the Symposium on *Interest and Prices.*" *Journal of the History of Economic Thought* 28(2): 186–198.

Wooley, J. T. 1984. *Monetary Politics: The Federal Reserve and the Politics of Monetary Policy.* Cambridge: Cambridge University Press.

Woolf, L. 1960. *Sowing: An Autobiography of the Years 1890 to 1904.* London: Hogarth Press.

Woolf, V. 1980. *The Letters of Virginia Woolf.* Vol. 6: *1936–41.* London: Hogarth Press.

Yellen, J. L. 1984. "Efficiency Wage Models of Unemployment." *American Economic Review* 74(2): 200–205.

Yoshikawa, H. 2003. "The Role of Demand in Macroeconomics." *Japanese Economic Review* 54(1): 1–27.

Zouache, A. 2004. "Towards a 'New Neo-Classical Synthesis'? An Analysis of the Methodological Convergence between New Keynesian Economics and Real Business Cycle Theory." *History of Economic Ideas* 12(1): 95–117.

Contributors

RICHARD ARENA (GREDEG, University of Nice-Sophia Antipolis, and CNRS)

ROGER E. BACKHOUSE (University of Birmingham)

BRADLEY W. BATEMAN (Denison University, Granville, Ohio)

MAURO BOIANOVSKY (University of Brasilia)

ANNA M. CARABELLI (Università del Piemonte Orientale, Italy)

MARIO A. CEDRINI (Università del Piemonte Orientale, Italy)

MARCELLO DE CECCO (Scuola Normale Superiore di Pisa, Italy)

ROBERT W. DIMAND (Brock University, St. Catherines, Ontario, Canada)

GILLES DOSTALER (University of Quebec, Montreal)

TOSHIAKI HIRAI (Faculty of Economics, Sophia University, Tokyo)

JAN A. KREGEL (Levy Economics Institute of Bard College; Center for Full Employment and Price Stability, Kansas City)

HEINZ D. KURZ (Departments of Economics and The Graz Schumpeter Centre, University of Graz, Austria)

MARIA CRISTINA MARCUZZO (Università di Roma, La Sapienza)

YOSHIYASU ONO (Institute of Social and Economic Research, Osaka University)

HANS-MICHAEL TRAUTWEIN (University of Oldenburg, Germany)

HIROSHI YOSHIKAWA (Faculty of Economics, University of Tokyo)

Index